DOGMA

LIVING AND WORKING

THE MIT PRESS
CAMBRIDGE, MASSACHUSETTS
LONDON, ENGLAND

PREFACE

Living and Working focuses on research we have conducted in the last decade on the architecture of domestic space, and was developed simultaneously through studies of the history of domesticity and a wide range of design projects. There is no cause and effect between these two parts, but a continuous tension between critical inquiry and attempts to reform what is the most familiar and yet difficult kind of architecture: the house.

"Living and working"[1] commonly refers to a housing accommodation where it is possible to live and work in the same place. More specifically, live/work accommodation emerged in the United States between the 1960s and 1970s. Initially live/work was a grassroots transformation of former industrial structures into houses that combined residence and workspace—as in the case of the loft—but soon it was appropriated by real estate and transformed into a commercially successful (and controversial) housing type.

This book expands the idea of living and working beyond its literal interpretation as live/work, questioning the relationship between house and work that has been at the core of the historical evolution of domestic space for millennia. Since its "invention," domestic space has always been a place of work, as it is the place where we reproduce ourselves. Yet this space is also defined as private, which means that reproduction is considered a natural duty of the family and especially of women. The seclusion of the family household was reinforced with the modern separation between home and workplace, and by making the house a form of private property.

This condition naturalizes reproduction, projecting an idea of the home as safe haven, away from the promiscuity of nonfamily social relationships. It proposes to move beyond this idea of the home, by questioning not only the privatization of reproduction but also—and especially—the idea of the home as a form of property. The main argument of this research is that *home* should be considered a cooperative structure in which it is possible to live and work and where domestic labor can be socialized beyond the family.

The projects presented in this book were developed in different contexts. Some have been developed as contributions to exhibitions, some as competition entries, and others as commissions. As such, these projects were conditioned by specific briefs that often took for granted the idea of domestic space as a private realm. Each project was thus an attempt to rethink its brief, putting forward the idea of a more cooperative form of living that would question at the same time the typological setup as well as the ownership regime. These proposals are unavoidably approximations of this ambition, but together they can be seen as an attempt to move beyond the given parameters within which architecture conventionally conceives of housing.

Problems of domestic space—such as its commodification and its gendering—cannot be reduced to mere architectural questions, and yet the architectural project can be a place of reflection and offer opportunities to uncover the relationships between housing policies and their spatialization. While working on these projects we have always kept in mind that their implementation would require a much wider shift in conceiving the house no longer as a commodity, whose form is determined by its exchange value, but rather as an infrastructure defined by its use value. Such a shift is not just a matter of architecture but a broader social reform that would challenge the current economic and political regime.

Living and Working continues a tradition that we can call "typological design," which consists in reforming existing housing types toward alternative forms of habitation. The question of typology has a long history within our discipline. The word type comes from the Latin *typus* which means figure, symbol, emblem. The Latin term has roots in the Greek *tùpos*, which means mark, and the Sanskrit *tùpto*, which means to beat, strike, leave a mark. These etymologies of the term make clear that type has to do with marking an object or body so that it can belong to a class or a group of things. Discourses on type in architecture emerged in the nineteenth century as a way to classify buildings not so much in terms of their style or image, but in terms of their spatial and structural organization. As is well known, the earliest definition of type in architecture was formulated by Antoine Chrysostome Quatremère de Quincy in his *Dictionnaire historique d'architecture* (1825). For Quatremère, type represents not an image or a model to be copied, but an idea that can serve as a rule for the model. In spite of this idealist understanding, type as a design tool was prompted by the industrialization of the building process, and the consequent standardization of design and construction which found in mass housing one of its most important manifestations. It was with the rise of mass housing between the late nineteenth and early twentieth centuries that typological design became a method whose goal was not only standardization, but also the subtle imposition of class and gender roles through specific norms and spatial layouts. In the 1960s, interest in typology—that is to say, in the discourse on type—reemerged in the writings and studies of architects such as Saverio Muratori and Aldo Rossi.[2] This "third revival" of typology (after its theorization at the beginning of the nineteenth century and its instrumentalization by the modern movement) had a historicist flavor since it was seen as a way to anchor architectural design to the history of the city at large.[3] Rossi's interpretation of typology was influenced by the historian and theorist Giulio Carlo Argan for whom architectural form is inevitably rooted in historical precedents.[4] Even though Rossi emphasized the link between type and economic factors such as property, what many discourses on type seem to have missed is that types are informed not only by ideas, mass production, or historical lineage, but also—and especially—by the way political institutions, social relationships, and market forces define ways to occupy space. This is especially true in the case of housing, whose typological resolution has always been the product of class and gender politics.

Housing types are thus not innocent vessels of "everyday life" but apparatuses that translate politics and economy into spatial conditions. There is no doubt that the most important typological aspect of modern housing was the separation between workspace and home and the individuation of the heteronormative nuclear family.[5] In light of this interpretation of type, typological design is here understood not as acritical reproduction and variation of existing established types, but as a process both of revision and of critique of the way domestic life has been translated into residential architecture. In some projects, such revision and critique are more radical than in others, depending on the context within which they have been developed. When it comes to housing, architects know that it is difficult to modify typological constraints because these are linked to a wider spectrum of issues such as law, economy, and social relationships whose complete grasp goes far beyond a mere disciplinary understanding of architecture.

A type is not a model to be copied, but rather the deep structure of buildings; as such, the relevance of the projects presented in this book lies in the way they attempt to rethink the architecture of domestic space not in terms of its image but in terms of its spatial relationships.

The introductory essay is thus a conceptual and critical background that situates the projects within the long history of domesticity as one of the most crucial and controversial political projects, focusing specifically on the Western construction of the domestic as a private realm—a model eventually exported worldwide through colonialism. The essay interprets the house from the vantage point of work understood as the combination of both productive and reproductive activities. The text should therefore be read as the result of a long-term inquiry into the history of domestic space, parts of which were previously published in three separate books—*Like a Rolling Stone* (2016), *The Room of One's Own* (2017), and *Loveless: The Minimum Dwelling and Its Discontents* (2019)—and a few other essays.[6] The making of these books and the writing of the essays was parallel to the making of the projects presented in this book, and as such both projects and writings should be read as a unitary attempt to reclaim the design of housing as the most important task for architecture.

Like all our work, this book is the result of a collective effort. For this reason, we would like to thank our past and present collaborators at Dogma, without whose labor the content of this book would not have been possible. Many thanks to Thomas Weaver whose intellectual support and friendship through the years have been a major contribution to our work, and to Matthew Abbate for his exacting editing. We are grateful to Celeste Tellarini for patiently helping us in managing, editing, and improving the material presented in the book, and to Lilian Pala for putting together the initial draft version. We are very much indebted to Nene Tsuboi who has worked on the graphic design of this and our previous publications; our collaboration has been a defining aspect of Dogma's work. Thank you to Maria Shéhérazade Giudici for advising us through the making of this book and for supporting us by publishing our previous studies on domestic space, *The Room of One's Own* and *Loveless*. The following people and institutions have been fundamental in supporting the research and projects presented in this book: Nikolaus Hirsch, Gabriele Mastrigli, Elia Zenghelis, Liesl Vanautgaerden, Tuomas Toivonen, Leonard Ma and New Academy, Jennifer Sigler, Beth Hughes, Francisco Sanin, Tatiana Bilbao, Fernando Márquez Cecilia, Christophe van Gerrewey, Neeraj Bhatia, and Adrian Lahoud. This book is dedicated to the memory of Lorenz Alarik Adriaens.

1 Frances Hollis, *Beyond Live-Work: The Architecture of Home-based Work* (New York: Routledge, 2015).

2 Aldo Rossi, *The Architecture of the City*, translated by Diane Ghirardo (Cambridge, MA: MIT Press, 1982).

3 Anthony Vidler, "The Third Typology," *Oppositions* 7 (Winter 1976): 1–4.

4 Giulio Carlo Argan, "On the Typology of Architecture," *Architectural Design*, no. 33 (December 1963): 564–565.

5 Maria Shéhérazade Giudici, "Counter-planning from the Kitchen: For a Feminist Critique of Type," *Journal of Architecture* 23, no. 7–8 (2018): 1203–1229.

6 In this book's introductory essay, we have integrated passages from the following essays: Pier Vittorio Aureli, Leonard Ma, Mariapaola Michelotto, Martino Tattara, and Tuomas Toivonen, "Promised Land: Housing from Commodification to Cooperation," *E-flux Architecture* (Fall 2019), https://www.e-flux.com/architecture/collectivity/304772/promised-land-housing-from-commodification-to-cooperation/; Pier Vittorio Aureli, Martino Tattara and Marson Korbi, "Loveless: A Short History of Minimum Dwelling," in *Home Futures: Living in Yesterday's Tomorrow*, ed. Eszter Steierhoffer and Justin McGuirk (London: Design Museum, 2018); Pier Vittorio Aureli and Martino Tattara, "The Home at Work: A Genealogy of Housing for the Laboring Classes," *Harvard Design Magazine*, no. 46 (Fall/Winter 2018); Dogma, "The Forest and the Cell: Notes on Mosej Ginzburg's Green City," *Harvard Design Magazine*, no. 45 (Spring/Summer 2018); Dogma, "A Short History of the Private Room," in *The Room of One's Own* (Milan: Black Square, 2018), 4–33; Pier Vittorio Aureli and Martino Tattara, "Production/Reproduction: Housing beyond the Family," *Harvard Design Magazine*, no. 41 (Fall/Winter 2015): 132–138.

LIVING AND WORKING: TOWARD A CRITICAL HISTORY OF DOMESTIC SPACE

Today more than ever, production transcends the boundaries that, since the onset of modernity, have separated domestic space from the workplace. New forms of production imply an overlap between work and life to the point that they become indistinguishable. When work is no longer confined within the nine-to-five schedule, it seems difficult to maintain the illusion that the domestic sphere is a refuge from the reality of production. With the rise of freelance work, for example, domestic space has become a new kind of integrated workspace: the kitchen and the living room, even the bedroom, besides being traditional sites of domestic work, become an improvised office or studio. Yet today, despite radical technological changes, social instability, and new forms of living and working, domesticity in its most traditional format of the family home is still the prevalent idea of habitation. Domesticity, perceived as a "retreat" from the world, is still imagined as the place where it is possible to reconstruct authentic social relationships. This idea of the home was precisely the purpose of the modern domestic interior, which, since its invention in the eighteenth century, was seen to exist in compensatory opposition to the work sphere. Commenting on the emergence of the domestic interior, Walter Benjamin wrote that, "for the private individual, the place of dwelling is for the first time opposed to the place of work. The former constitutes itself as interior. Its complement is the office. The private individual, who in the office has to deal with reality, needs the domestic interior to sustain him in his illusions."[1]

For millennia, the organization of the household gave form to an intimate relationship between domestic and working activities. Not only were productive activities from food processing to craftsmanship performed by all members of the household, women and children included, but they were often performed side by side with domestic chores such as cooking, cleaning, and childrearing. This condition dramatically changed with the rise of the modern capitalist city, which has been historically planned and built by establishing spatial and juridical dichotomies such as public/private and production/reproduction. Many scholars and social movements, the feminist one in particular, have challenged the ideological distinction of production from reproduction.[2] Production refers to remunerated working activity performed in exchange for a wage, reproduction refers to the reproduction of ourselves, an activity that to this day is largely unpaid because it was and still is considered the natural labor of the family. The artificial separation of production and reproduction was the outcome of social initiatives promoted by reformers first in England and then in other European countries and soon embraced by both private philanthropists and states, both to control the working class and to educate workers in the values of the bourgeois family. Such initiatives were predicated on a set of binaries—male/female, husband/wife, breadwinner/housewife, private/public—whose logic defined the very purpose of the house as a private space in which relationships among household members were considered natural, not political. While the husband was expected to work outside the home, the wife was expected to take care of the household as her duty toward the family. It is within the dichotomous logic of the home as a space that separates the inside from the outside, the private from the public, and society from family, that reproduction as nonwork was distinguished from production as work. Although traditional gender roles have been radically contested in the last fifty years, and neoliberal austerity has undermined the possibility of forming a family for many people, the architecture of the house still perpetuates them in its spatial organization.

Within the history of Western domestic space, the house represents the private domain of the family as opposed to the public domain of the city. The purpose of such a public/private distinction was precisely the division of labor between productive and reproductive work. As Maria Mies wrote, "in this process, the sphere where labor power was reproduced, the house and the family, was defined into nature, but domesticated nature, while the workplace became the place for public, social ('human') production."[3] Even though this condition became the norm with the rise of industrial capitalism and has been exported worldwide through colonialism since the nineteenth century, its ideological roots are located deep within the history of Western domesticity as the latter emerged in antiquity and was rediscovered at the beginning of modernity. In the following notes, we would like to trace an archaeology of Western domestic space and its modern reinvention through the architecture of housing. Our main argument is that it is impossible to understand the logic of the home without considering the relationship between reproductive and productive work, between *living and working*.

ENCLOSURES

We might believe that the permanent home has always existed as a form of habitation. Yet looking back at *Homo sapiens*' 300,000-year history we realize that the permanent home only emerged about 18,000 years ago. Far from a linear process, the rise of the permanent home was a gradual back-and-forth between nonsedentary, semisedentary, and sedentary forms of life. It is a mistake to think of the presedentary life of hunter-gatherers as devoid of any sense of permanence and territoriality. Hunter-gatherers had a strong sense of association with territories which was organized not by possession of land but by the focus on landmarks such as paths, tracks, sacred sites, haunts, water holes, and mountains.[4] These landmarks signposted the relative position of kin groups in a way that is different from the tracing of boundaries. The permanent home was not the first "architecture" built by *Homo sapiens*: already during the Upper Paleolithic, hunter-gatherers built ancestors' tombs, such as those found at Sungir, and communal storage spaces such as the monumental mammoth bone house found on the Russian plains.[5] They even built imposing

(1) Plan of a Pitjantjatjara camp at Konapandi in the Musgrave Ranges, Australia, June 1933 (adapted from Paul Memmott)

monuments such as the 11,000-year-old temples found at Göbekli Tepe, which were used by nonsedentary groups to gather and engage in complex rituals, feasting, and trading.[6] In spite of not living in permanent homes, hunter-gatherers had a strong sense of commitment to places without projecting on them any sense of property. Indeed the term hunter-gatherers can be often misleading, because it is used to comprehend a wide spectrum of forms of life that included fully migratory bands, and seminomadic and even semisedentary communities whose members shifted from one to another fixed settlement or occupied permanently a single settlement from which a part of the population seasonally departed to occupy shifting camps. As argued by archaeologist Lewis Binford, many hunter-gatherer societies were foragers who regularly stored products and were consequently less mobile.[7] Moreover, contrary to widespread common sense that associates farming with sedentary life, many hunter-gatherers interacted with their land in a cultivation-like manner. And yet these forms of cultivation, which should be considered more like forms of horticulture than full-fledged agriculture, would not give rise to an accumulation of surplus.

Because of their homes' lack of permanence, most of hunter-gatherers' life would happen under the eyes of their peers. As argued by anthropologist Peter J. Wilson, this condition of life in full visibility endowed hunter-gatherers with a strong sense of focus and attention.[8] Without the need of walls or any form of visual obstruction, hunter-gatherers knew where to go or not go, where to look or not look. It was precisely this enhanced attention that gave hunter-gatherers a strong sense of reciprocity and a spatial order which was reflected in the careful way they would temporarily settle. This is visible for example in the plan of an Aboriginal Pitjantjatjara campsite recorded in 1933 in the Musgrave Ranges in Australia (figure 1). The windbreaks that shelter people are not simply scattered across the site; they compose units disposed according to precise kinship rules.[9] Hunter-gatherers were building shelters which reflected communities' adaptation to the conditions of specific environments. Whether fully mobile or semisedentary, hunter-gatherers possessed skills in placemaking far more sophisticated than those of sedentary people. Above all, the main characteristic of their way of life was a strong sense of sharing, which was reflected in many cases by the way in which shelters would only be places for rest while most activities would take place in the open.

This situation gradually changed with the rise of the permanent home, a process that was triggered in certain parts of the world by many factors including climate change (the end of the Ice Age) and the need to increase security and permanence. Building permanent homes increased people's attachment to their place and household, and the fixed house became not just a shelter but the embodiment of the sense of property in the form of land, the home, and what the home contains. In fact, asymmetrical forms of power did not emerge with the rise of the first large-scale farming communities, but with the consolidation of households as permanent structures whose appearance predates the beginnings of agriculture. While there are examples of large-scale egalitarian communities, the household is seldom egalitarian. As anthropologist David Graeber and archaeologist David Wengrow argue, "the most painful loss of human freedoms began at the small scale—the level of gender relations, age groups, and domestic servitude—the kind of relationships that contain at once the greatest intimacy and the deepest forms of structural violence."[10] The architecture of the house, with its fixed system of partitions, did not create gender or kinship roles, but greatly reinforced them by allocating people a rigidly defined and enclosed space.

To visualize the shift from a hunter-gatherer way of life to sedentism it may be useful to compare the hunter-gatherer settlement found at Ohalo II, dated 23,000 BP, with the semisedentary Natufian settlement found at Nahal Oren and dated 11,500–10,000 BP, both in Israel. Ohalo II consisted of six brush shelters and a burial site built on the shore of the Sea of Galilee (figure 2).[11] There is evidence that the hunter-gatherers that settled at Ohalo II were not only living there for long periods but also engaged in some form of cereal cultivation. Although there are traces of grinding inside the huts, the hearths were built in between them. Because of this, people would be outside of their shelters for most of the time, and many domestic activities such as cooking would be shared among the small community. By contrast, Nahal Oren is a typical Natufian settlement of circular dwellings whose walls were made of stone (figure 3).[12] The presence of the hearths inside the shelters reveals how these were "privatized" within each house. In the Natufian dwelling the house seems to individuate a household whose main reproductive activities are now internalized within the enclosure of the house's walls. This represents an emerging principle that will be fundamental for the sedentary way of dwelling in many parts of the world, namely the transformation of home into an enclosure that clearly defines an inside and an outside, a private and a public space.

Wilson argues that the building of homes as permanent architecture is an "event" in human history whose magnitude is comparable to both the rise of language and the use of fire.[13] By enclosing themselves within permanent boundaries, early sedentary communities gave to their social relationships an increasingly precise spatial definition that was both visual and physical and thus more explicit than the ephemeral shelters built by hunter-gatherers.

With the rise of more intense forms of domestication of animals and plants, laboring activities increased and as a consequence households and houses became bigger, to make space both for the rising labor force and for storing production surplus. The houses found at Çayönü Tepesi in south Anatolia, which incorporate rectangular structures made of stones joined by clay and mortar, are a clear embodiment of this process (figures 4–6).[14] Most probably these stone structures were sturdy foundations on top of which the dwellers of Çayönü built their houses in mud brick or other light building materials. The foundations not only kept the houses dry but also functioned as storage, as in the case of the so-called "cell-building" whose plan is made up of twelve small storage rooms. As archaeologists Kent Flannery and Joyce Marcus argue, 8,700 years ago the community living at Çayönü underwent a radical economic transformation which brought cereal cultivation and the herding of sheep and goats.[15] This economy prompted the building of private storage spaces

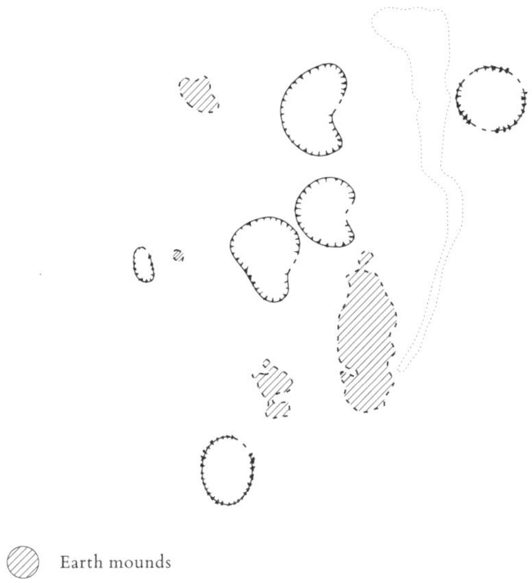

(2) Hunter-gatherer settlement at Ohalo II, Israel, 23,000 BP (adapted from Dani Nadel, Ehud Weiss, D. R. Piperno, 2012)

(3) Natufian settlement at Nahal Oren, Israel, 11,500–10,000 BP (adapted from Nigel Goring-Morris, Anna Belfer-Cohen, 2013)

(4) "Cell" building, Çayönü Tepesi, Turkey, 7500 BCE (adapted from Aslı Erim Özdoğan, Mehmet Özdoğan, 1999)

(5) "Pebble-paved" building, Çayönü Tepesi, Turkey, 7500 BCE (adapted from Aslı Erim Özdoğan, Mehmet Özdoğan, 1999)

(6) "Cell" building, Çayönü Tepesi, Turkey, 7500 BCE (adapted from Aslı Erim Özdoğan, Mehmet Özdoğan, 1999)

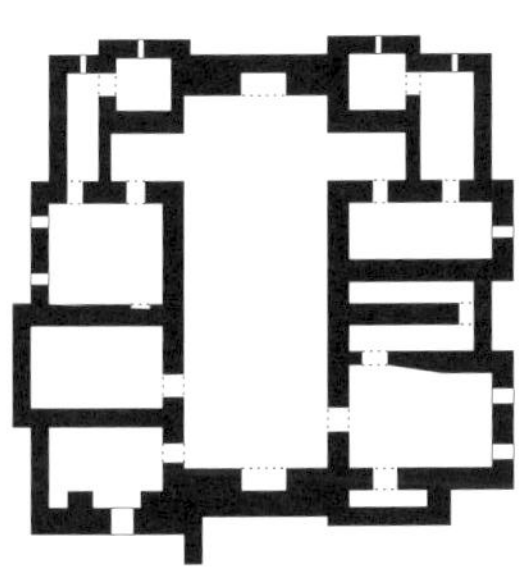

(7) Ubaid tripartite house, Tell Madhur, Iraq, 4500 BCE (adapted from Michael Roaf, 1988)

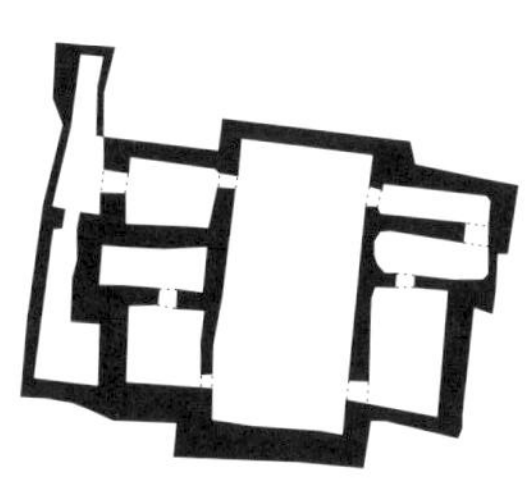

(8) Building I, Değirmentepe, Turkey, 4470 BCE (adapted from Bekir Gurdil, 2004)

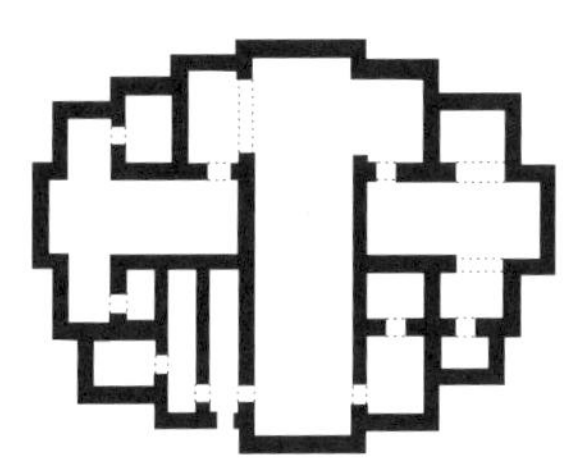

(9) T-shaped house, Kheit Qasim, Iraq, 4500 BCE (adapted from Jean-Daniel Forest, 1980)

2 m

which extended families placed in the basement of their houses in order to hide them from the rest of the community. What is interesting to note in the plan of the "cell-building" is how the subdivision of the home into rooms presupposed a shift from the circular undivided home, prevalent in the Epipaleolithic period, to the rectangular plan which became increasingly widespread with both the rise of sedentism and the beginning of more intense forms of cultivation.[16] The rectangular plan became dominant at the moment the house became not simply a shelter for humans, but also—and especially—a storage for goods.

The evolution of Neolithic homes from one-room to multiroom structures was related not just to storage but also—and especially—to the sexual division of labor between men and women. For example, in the typical tripartite house of the Ubaid period (figure 7), the representational space of the house devoted to ritual and hospitality occupies the central room and defines two separate poles of domestic space: the female space for food processing, weaving, and nurturing infants and the male space for storing goods and administering the house.[17] This tripartite model is an archetypal form in which multiroom aggregation both divides and unites the different functions and gender roles within a clear hierarchical logic (figures 8–9). As such, the tripartite house foreshadows the representational role of the house as a place of mastery and hospitality while hiding and diminishing its reproductive functions.

SPECIALIZATION AND SUBDIVISION

The duality between the representational and the reproductive role of the house becomes even stronger in one of the most important examples of Western domesticity: the ancient Greek household. Archaeologists have noted that in many Greek settlements starting in the seventh century BCE, house form changed from the megaron type (the one-room house, figures 10–13), to the oikos type (multiroom, figures 15–16).[18] In many cases the oikos type emerged from the retrofitting of the megaron type, as in the case of the ancient houses found at the archaeological site of Zagora (figure 14). According to archaeologist Alexandra Coucouzeli, the segmentation of the one-room into a multiroom type may be understood as a response to the economic pressure of growing settlements and consequent necessity to organize laboring activities more carefully in order to increase the productive capacity of the household.[19] For Coucouzeli this tendency would lead to the traditional fifth-century Greek domestic space in which separation of both functions and gender roles became a fundamental purpose for the house as oikos.[20]

The term oikos addresses the organization of the house as a household, namely a group of people sharing a common residence. By virtue of their life in common, the household becomes a clearly discernible social-economic unit whose role in the organization of the city is fundamental. Despite its exclusion from the political life of the city, the latter would not exist without the functioning of the oikos, a fact acknowledged by Aristotle who regarded the household as the basic unit of the polis.[21] Here, hidden in plain sight, lies the fundamental hypocrisy of rendering domestic space as a private sphere to be separated from the public sphere, since the existence of the latter depends on the well-functioning of the former.

Taking as a model the life of the Greek polis, Hannah Arendt in her book *The Human Condition* made the well-known distinction between labor, work, and *vita activa*, i.e., politics. According to Arendt, work in the sense of *opus* is the production of lasting material objects such as a chair, a pot, or a poem.[22] The value of these objects is their enduring legacy: they may even last longer than the persons who created them. In ancient times, the value of work was commensurate with its legacy. Contrary to work, labor is the sheer unending business of the reproduction of our species: eating, sleeping, and washing, giving birth to and raising children, taking care of the elderly and of the maintenance of the house, activities that within the Greek oikos were performed by women and slaves. For this reason, following Aristotle, Arendt located the sphere of labor in the house as a space clearly distinguished from the *vita activa* of the polis which was accessible only to the adult male population. Greek and Roman culture emphasized a contempt for laboring activities involving toil and routine; for their male elites, the virtuous life was one freed from domestic chores and other laboring activities. Yet both cultures were aware that the solid ground upon which the life of the city rested was the labor of domestic life; although deemed outside politics, labor was unavoidably the source of life and thus of political life as well. The historian Ruth Westgate has argued that the rise of the Greek oikos as a domestic space clearly separated from public space and organized by the secluding logic of the internal courtyard is linked to the ideology of citizenship.[23] Not only did the internal courtyard enhance surveillance and thus the chastity of women, since in many poleis citizenship was strictly linked to legitimate parentage; according to Westgate the sealed Greek house centered on the courtyard reflected the male owner's independence as an active citizen whose participation in the political life of the polis could only be ensured by an obedient, secluded, and self-sufficient household.[24] It is for this reason that the architectural organization of the oikos as a private space became increasingly a matter of public concern, since housing layouts in many poleis were increasingly standardized, also because of the adoption of the gridiron as city layout. With the increasing specialization of gender roles within the household, the centripetal architecture of the oikos, with its rooms aggregated around a courtyard, orchestrated different activities.[25] Even though the use of rooms in the Greek house was flexible, there was a distinction between the front and the back of the house. This separation is visible in houses found at Olynthus (figure 15). Close to the entrance of these dwellings we find the *andron*, the only decorated room of the house, where the homeowner would entertain his (male) friends; in the back of the house, often buffered from the courtyard by a small portico, we find the hearth room or *oecus*, the space normally occupied by women. Although women's mobility within the house was not restricted, when a male guest visited the house women withdrew to the back rooms. As archaeologist Lisa C. Nevett argues, the emergence of the andron is part of a tendency in the ancient Greek oikos toward the physical separation of different individuals and activities within the household.[26]

(10) Megaron house, Nichoria, 1100 BCE (adapted from Mazarakis Ainian, 1997)

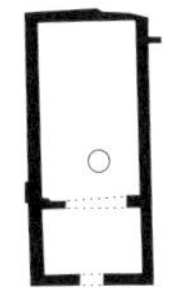

(11) House A, Eutresis, 2000–1600 BCE (adapted from Hetty Goldman, 1931)

(12) House F, Korakou, 2000 BCE (adapted from Karl W. Blegen, 2018)

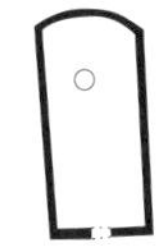

(13) House Q, Rakhmani, 1700–1000 BCE (adapted from Alan J. B. Wace and Maurice S. Thompson, 2011)

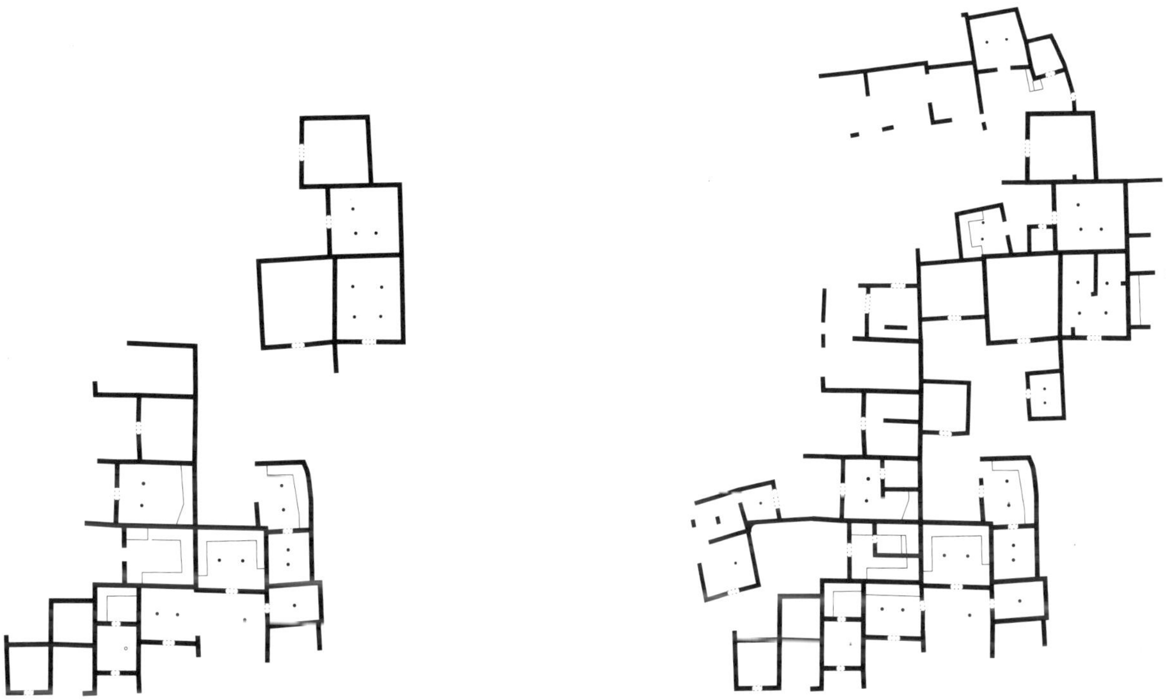

(14) Transformation of one-room houses into multiroom houses, Zagora, Greece, 760 to 700 BCE (adapted from Alexandra Coucouzeli, 2007)

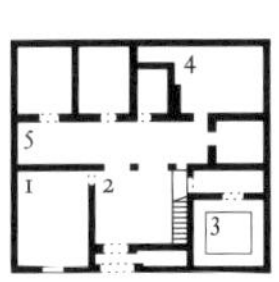

(15) House, Olynthus, fifth century BCE (adapted from Lisa Nevett, 2001)

(1) shop, (2) court, (3) andron, (4) oecus, (5) porch

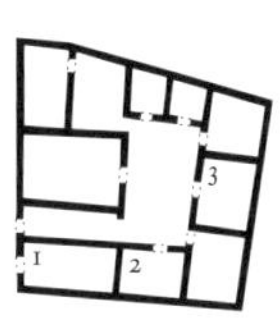

(16) House C, Athens, fifth century BCE (adapted from Lisa Nevett, 2001)

(1) shop, (2) andron, (3) oecus

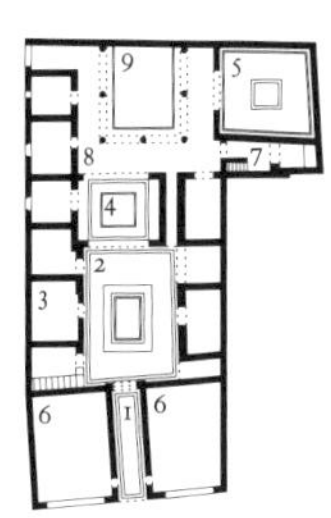

(17) House of the Tragic Poet, Pompeii, second century BCE (adapted from Shelley Hales, 2003)

(1) vestibulum, (2) atrium, (3) cubiculum, (4) tablinum, (5) triclinium, (6) taberna, (7) culina, (8) peristyle, (9) fishpond

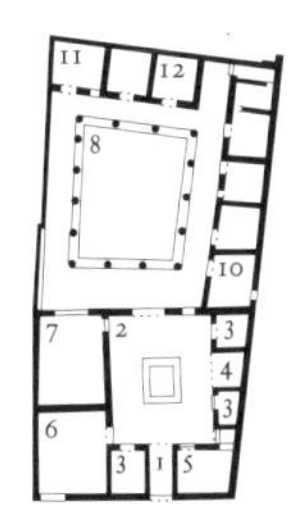

(18) House of the Lovers, Pompeii, first century BCE (adapted from Shelley Hales, 2003)

(1) fauces, (2) atrium, (3) cubiculum, (4) ala, (5) service room, (6) shop, (7) triclinium, (8) peristyle, (9) oecus, (10) service area, (11) cubiculum, (12) room

5 m

By assigning rooms to specific activities, architecture naturalizes social relationships, giving them their proper location within the house. In this way the form of the house becomes the most tangible manifestation of economy as the practice of *oikonomia*, household management. The framing of spaces with walls is dictated not only by a spatial symbolism, the aim of which is to sustain and reinforce the natural relationships within the family, but also by the goal of making the sequence of spaces as frictionless as possible. Unlike the city, where there is the possibility of confrontation, the house must create the conditions of perfect harmony for frictionless cohabitation, which in Xenophon's *Oeconomicus* is compared to a dance governed by a carefully orchestrated choreography.[27] And it was precisely the image of the house as a space of frictionless cohabitation that became a powerful metaphor of governance at large.

In his analysis of different types of power, Aristotle repeatedly compared the authority of the head of household to that of the head of state.[28] This patriarchal understanding of political power resonates with many ancient cultures in which the power of the senior male of the house is understood as that of the king over his subjects. Perhaps none more than the ancient Romans made a strong link between state power and household power, celebrating the latter as the absolute ideological core of Roman patriarchy.[29] The symbol of the centrality of household power is the word that gave form to our modern understanding of home: the domus (figures 17–18). Domus addressed the house of wealthy Romans as both household and physical structure. The Greek root of this Latin word is *demo*, which means to build. Yet the declension of *domus* into words such as *dominus* and *dominium* makes clear that *domus* addressed a domain organized around a vector of command represented by the power of the paterfamilias over his household. It is not by chance that the Latin term *familia*, indicating an institution that was meant to be headed by the *pater*, comes from a proto-Italic word *famn-lo*, which means servile. The domus was thus the stronghold of the Roman proprietor, whose role was acknowledged by the ruling authorities as the very foundation of Roman society.[30] Especially with the rise of the Empire, in the first century CE, the subordination of the household to the paterfamilias was believed to mirror the way in which society was subordinated to the paternal and yet severe power of the emperor.[31] It is possible to argue that the Roman domus was conceived of as a place whose main architectural purpose was to theatricalize the power of the paterfamilias and make it visible to both those inside and those outside the family.

While the Greek oikos was secluded from the outside, the Roman domus was open toward the street through a monumental entrance which allowed passersby to peer through the house. In this way the private domain of the house as the symbol of the homeowner's power over his family was made public by being visible from the street. Additionally, as archaeologist Andrew Wallace-Hadrill has remarked, the Roman domus was articulated in order to accommodate guests.[32] All spaces of the house were arranged along the central axis which was the guests' line of sight when entering the domus from the *fauces*, the small passage that connected the street to the atrium. From there guests could move through the main spaces of the house starting from the atrium, a veritable public space where the paterfamilias would welcome guests and perform the ritual of *salutatio*, the morning greeting of his cohort of friends and allies, the tablinum, a room generally located on a side of the atrium opposite to the entrance and used as the homeowner's study and house archive, and the peristyle, a garden often surrounded by a portico. This visual approach, framed by columns or focal objects, foregrounded the most monumental and public spaces of the house while hiding utilitarian spaces such as the kitchen, which was relegated away from the entrance in order to prevent the smell of food from compromising the solemnity of the image offered to visitors. In contrast with the secluded courtyard of the Greek oikos, the Roman atrium was guarded but accessible to passersby, and as such it was conceived as a celebratory space analogous to a public forum. The use of columns in both atrium and peristyle and the architectural motives for the frescoed decorations were meant to increase the sense of publicness and monumentality of the wealthy private domain. Romans were conscious that by displaying marble statues and panel paintings in their domus they were privatizing features that the ancient Greeks used to signify public space.[33] The self-aggrandizing logic of the domus was often pumped by the addition of explicitly public facilities such as baths, libraries, and even basilicas. The publicness of the domus was thus instrumental in establishing and reinforcing the political status of the homeowner, who used his own house to conduct business by receiving and entertaining his vast network of supporters. Many free citizens derived their income from their ownership of properties in both city and countryside. In the mind of these homeowners, property revenue was understood as the only viable economy to support their public career. As such the domus with its plethora of "public" spaces such as atrium, tablinum, triclinium, and gardens was a place of work understood not as manual labor, but as intense social networking. Wallace-Hadrill argues that what characterized the Roman domus was its lack of privacy, since wealthy Romans did not make any distinction between the house as a place of work and the house as a place of leisure. Differentiating between *negotium* (work) and *otium* (leisure) was more a matter of time than space.[34]

And yet it was precisely the intensely public character of the domus that sometimes necessitated its opposite: privacy, something that in the domus could only be found in the intimacy of the cubiculum. The cubiculum was a small room often used as a bedroom, but also as a space for small and informal reception. Although the use of the cubiculum was highly flexible, its small dimensions evoked an intimate use that radically contrasted with the publicness of the rest of the domus. As such, cubicula were not only places for work, sex, informal chat, and receptions, but also places for concentration, studying, silence, and above all contemplation. This is the reason why the cubiculum would become the privileged place for early Christian worship when their faith was not yet officially and peacefully recognized.[35] The very option of locking oneself in a cubiculum, out of sight, became the root for a new idea of the self and individuality, which eventually triumphed with the advent of Christianity. Within a society that made politics into relentless social networking, retreating from public life became the prerogative of those who could afford the luxury of being alone. Leisure thus was not just not-work, but rather being protected from too much public interaction. It is in this way that *otium* as a possibility of being away from public interaction became the root of one of the most influential ascetic practices of the Western world: monasticism. As paradoxical as it may seem, it was precisely the permissive space of the cubiculum that was the very archetype of the ascetic hermit cell.

TOGETHER AND APART

The individual living cell is one of the most important archetypes of modern domesticity. This archetype has multiple origins, but one of the earliest known contexts in which it flourished as a form of dwelling may have been within the practice of monasticism. The word monk comes from the Greek *monos*, which means alone: the monk is he or she who chooses to renounce property, living a life of solitude away from both family and community. This form of life has existed for millennia, and the earliest known organized monastic tradition surviving to this day is the one initiated by Gautama Buddha between the fifth and fourth centuries BCE. In the Buddhist tradition, monastic life was inspired by the wandering ascetics who rejected possessions and lived a life of solitude and meditation. This way of life implies that any working activity is meant just to support subsistence and the possibility of living away from society. These wandering ascetics utilized caves, mountain peaks, and boulders as retreats during the rainy season. Buddha himself recognized that this way of life was harsh, and in the fifth century he established the *sangha* (meaning assembly, association, or company) in order to allow ascetics to mutually support each other. It was this form of monastic organization that gradually evolved into a spatially defined typology of habitation known as the *vihara*. The Gautamiputra Vihara (second century CE, figure 19), which is part of the Nasik Caves in India, can be interpreted as an exemplary form of Buddhist monastic life and of monasticism in general. This vihara is comprised of small cells for one person of equal size surrounding one large space for rituals and communal activities. The plan of the Gautamiputra Vihara can be understood as a diagram that makes explicit the process of individuation through which individual existence is constantly negotiated within a community. Here lies the fundamental tension between individual and collective ways of life which is the most important spatial theme of monastic architecture, and which in the Western tradition is exemplified by the opposite poles of hermitic (solitary) and coenobitic (communal) life.

The history of monasticism can be interpreted as a constant dialectic between opposites such as individual and collective life, contemplation and work, freedom and discipline. This is very much the case with Christian monasticism, whose architecture can be seen as a fundamental contribution to the formation of major themes of Western domestic architecture. Christian monasticism arose between Egypt and Syria in the fourth century CE as a hermitic life pursued by individuals to escape both the pressure of social life and especially the institutionalization of Christian cults. Yet the origins of Christian monasticism are also linked to the issue of work, which, as the historian Peter Brown has argued, was debated for millennia in the Near East.[36] Work looms large in many myths and legends of this region, such as the opening passages of Genesis where Adam and Eve are evicted from the wealth of the Garden of Eden and condemned by God to a life in which subsistence can only be achieved by hard work. Hermitic life was an attempt to live a mendicant existence devoid not only of possessions and household but also of what these inevitably implied, i.e., the social obligation to work. It is not by chance that early monks inhabited small lodgings often located in deserted places that nevertheless were not too far from villages, so that their solitary life could be sustained by the alms of local communities. These structures well represent a fundamental paradox of monastic life: the hermit's freedom from social obligations was often made possible only by the support of working people. It was precisely the difficulty of hermitic life and its dependence on lay support that prompted early hermits to form loose communities know as *laura* (figure 20) which preserved solitary life while ensuring mutual support. This form of monastic life was conceptualized by Roland Barthes in his book *How to Live Together* as an ideal, commonly shared environment.[37] As Barthes remarked, the loose aggregation of individual cells allowed the monks to live both together and apart. In this way monks could preserve their own "idiorrhythmy" (from the Greek *idios*, meaning particular, and *rhythmos*, meaning rhythm, rule).[38] Yet the popularity of monasticism in Egypt gave rise to more formalized communities which evolved in the dominant form of Western monasticism: the *coenobium* (from the Greek *koinos*, common, and *bios*, life). Unlike the *laura*, the *coenobium* required some form of planning which resulted in more compact and introverted settlements, often enclosed by a wall (figure 21). The purpose of these walls was not defense, but rather the representation of the monks' sense of community and secession from the outer world.[39] Yet this secession was always more ideological than real. Even though monastic communities were self-sufficient places of living and working, their subsistence was provided by estates which sometimes were cultivated or supervised by laypeople.

While the early monasteries were often appropriations of existing structures such as temples and houses, the development of the *coenobium* prompted monks to carefully plan their monastic premises. Such emphasis on planning was motivated by the important fact that coenobitic monasticism required a shared conduct of life, a rule which prescribed the monks' daily activities. Such regularity of life was totalizing because it was meant not only to reinforce a communal ethos, but also to transform mundane activity into a form of continuous worship. As Giorgio Agamben has noted, the goal of monasticism was not to impose a rule of conduct to life, but to erase any difference between life and rule so that life itself could acquire a discernable form.[40] It is for this reason that monks attempted to translate every daily practice into the architecture of the monastery by assigning to each space a specific function.[41] Moreover, the increasing number of monks joining coenobitic communities required a more systematic approach to housing, as is visible in the reconstruction of early monasteries such as those founded on the abandoned village of Tabennisi by Pachomius (figure 22), the author of the first known Christian monastic rule and effectively the founder of coenobitic monasticism.[42] Because coenobitic monasticism

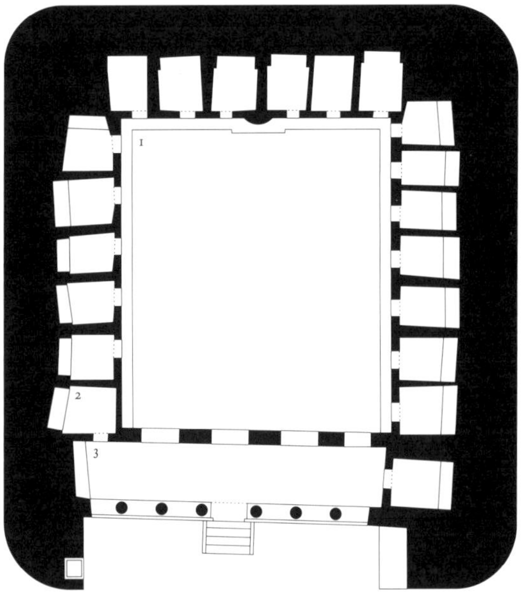

(19) Gautamiputra Vihara,
Nasik, India, second century CE
(adapted from James Ferguson, 1880)

(1) hall, (2) cell, (3) veranda

5 m

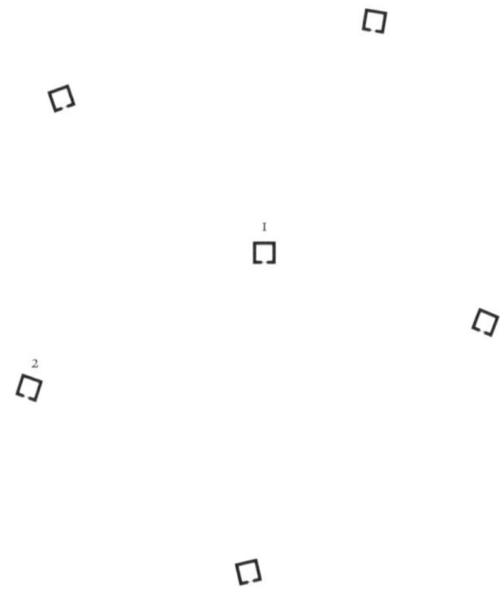

(20) Diagrammatic plan of a *laura* during
the lifetime of its founder-hermit,
fourth century CE
(adapted from Ossa Raymond Sowers, 1952)

(1) cell of the founder-hermit, (2) cell

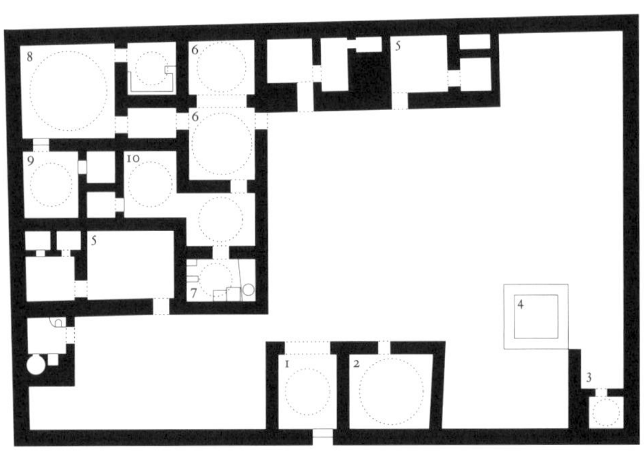

(21) Pachomian fold or house,
Taban Kellia hermitage, Nitria, Egypt, c. 600 CE
(adapted from Darlene Brooks Hedstrom, 2011)

(1) vestibule, (2) storage, (3) latrine, (4) well,
(5) apartments for anchorites, (6) guest reception,
(7) kitchen, (8) elder's oratory, (9) elder's bedroom,
(10) disciple's bedroom

5 m

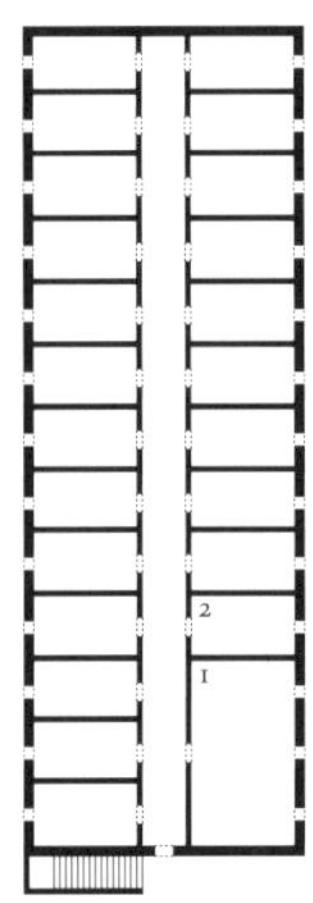

(22) Pachomian fold or house,
Tabennisi, Egypt, fourth century CE
(adapted from Ossa Raymond Sowers, 1952)

(1) common room, (2) individual cell

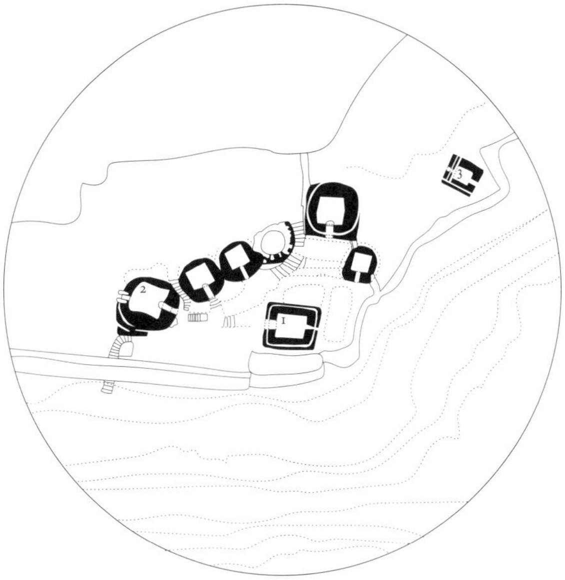

(23) Monastery at Skellig Michael,
Ireland, ninth century CE
(adapted from Walter Horn and Carl Bertil Lund, 1973)

(1) church, (2) cell, (3) oratory

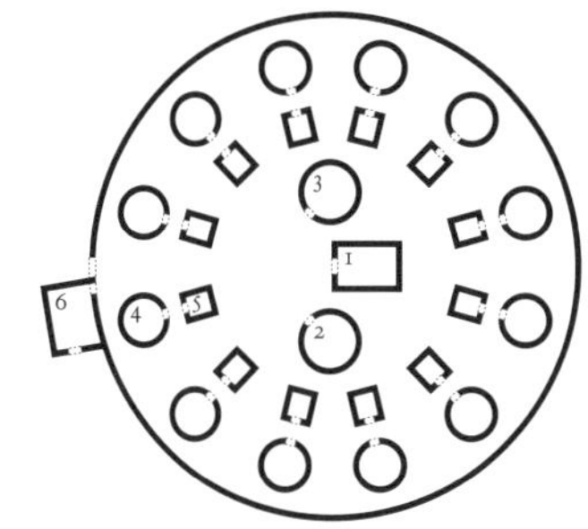

(24) Abingdon Abbey,
Oxfordshire, England, founded 675 CE,
schematic plan after description in the *Abingdon Chronicle*
(adapted from Walter Horn and Carl Bertil Lund, 1973)

(1) church, (2) refectory, (3) abbot, (4) dwellings,
(5) oratories, (6) parlor

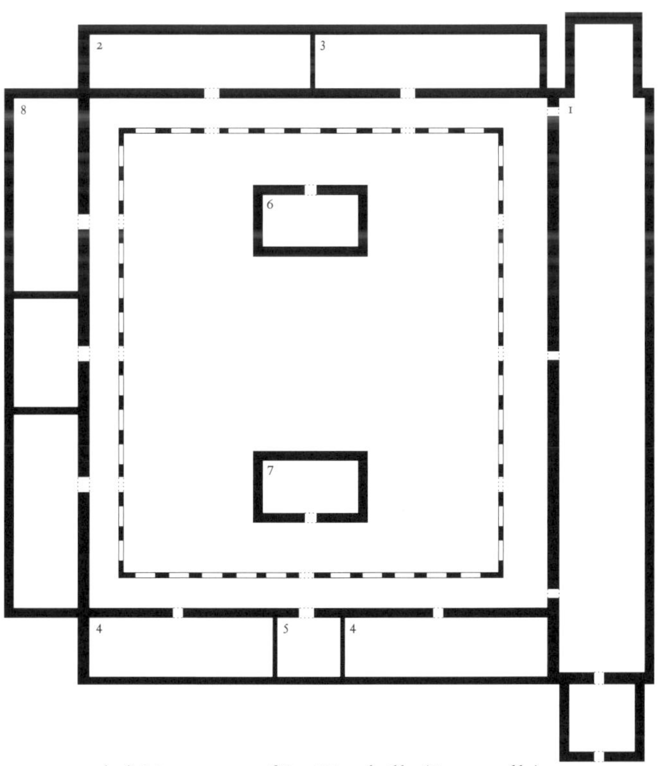

(25) Monastery of St. Wandrille (Fontanella),
Seine-Maritime, France, founded 649 CE,
reconstruction by Walter Horn
(adapted from Walter Horn and Carl Bertil Lund, 1973)

(1) church of St. Peter, (2) cellar, (3) refectory,
(4) dormitory, (5) solarium, (6) library,
(7) archive, (8) abbott's chamber

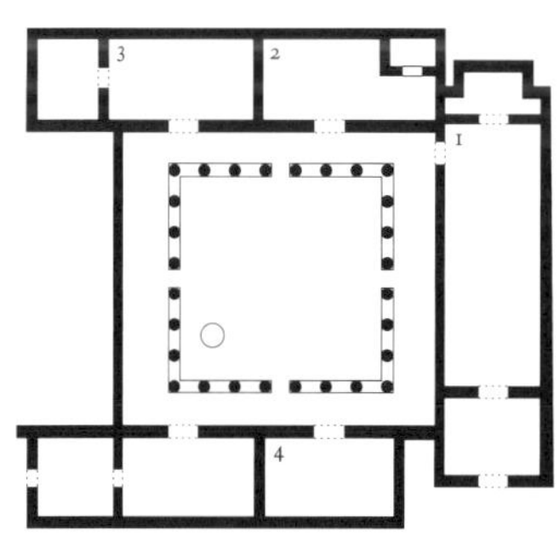

(26) Monastery of Abbot Gundeland,
Lorsch, Germany, 765–775 CE
(adapted from Friedrich Behn, 1964)

(1) church, (2) refectory, (3) dormitory, (4) cellar

5 m

(27) Camaldolese hermitage,
Camaldoli, Italy, founded 1012

(1) monk's cell, (2) garden, (3) main church, (4) chapel

10 m

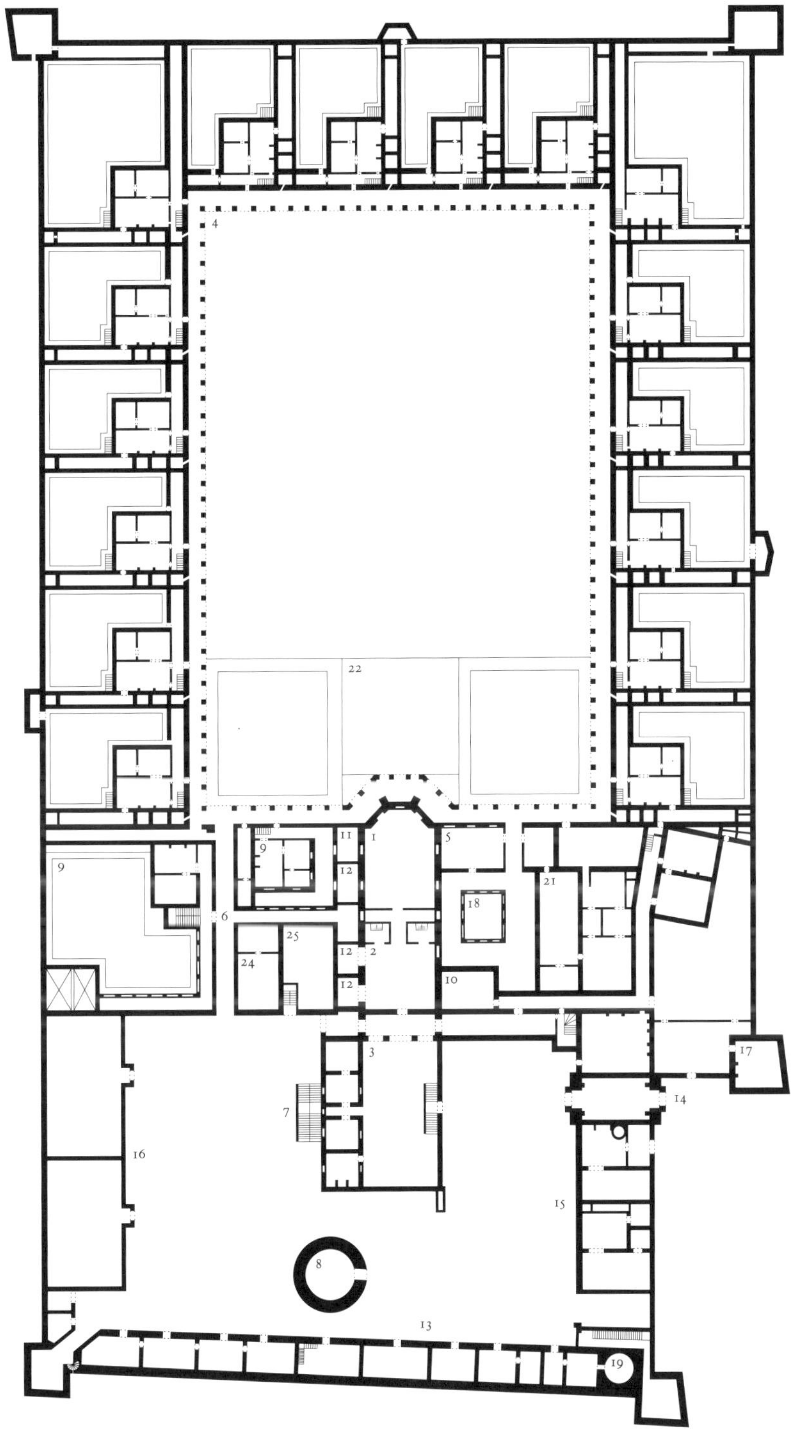

(28) The Charterhouse,
Clermont-Ferrand, early thirteenth century
(adapted from the reconstruction by Eugène-Emmanuel Viollet-le-Duc)

(1) monk's choir, (2) lay brothers' choir, (3) prior's forecourt, (4) great cloister, (5) chapterhouse, (6) passage to the great cloister, (7) prior's house, (8) dovecote, (9) individual cells with garden, (10) chapel of Pontgibaut, (11) sacristy, (12) chapels, (13) stables and rooms of the lay brothers, (14) gate, (15) guesthouse, (16) barns, (17) watchtower, (18) small cloister, (19) bakehouse, (20) kitchen, (21) refectory, (22) cemetery, (23) prison, (24) subprior's house, (25) subprior's garden

10 m

required a shared way of life, early monastic dormitories were probably conceived as rows of equally sized rooms located on either side of an alley and complemented by a common room.[43] Possibly inspired by the regular form of workers' settlements in ancient Egypt, Pachomian dwellings functioned not just as places of retreat but also as productive hubs, since manual laboring activities were a way for monks to avoid idleness and give a more regular rhythm to their daily life. Such inclination toward labor as the main rhythm of life contributed to the idea of the monastery as an autonomous community, even if complete self-sufficiency was often difficult to achieve.

With the diffusion of monasticism in Western Europe, both hermitic and coenobitic models gave rise to a multitude of hybrid forms that combined the looseness of the self-standing cell and the unitary logic of the monastic compound. Examples of this hybrid form were Celtic and Irish monasteries such as Abingdon Abbey (figure 24) and the still surviving Augustinian monastery of Skellig Michael in Ireland, founded in the ninth century (figure 23).[44] This model of monastic life based on self-discipline and loose communal aggregation was countered by the rise of the Benedictine rule, drafted by Benedict of Nursia in the sixth century. The Benedictine rule prescribed a monastic community strictly collectivized as one household and headed by a paterfamilias—the abbot. This tendency of monastic life was reflected in a more rigidly planned compound composed around a yard surrounded by galleried porches, the cloister. Besides representing the detachment of the monastic community from the outside world, the purpose of the cloister was to lay down a clear, legible path that united the places of all the monk's daily activities, such as church, dormitories, refectory, chapter, and the library, as is visible in the reconstruction of the Abbey of Fontanella built in the ninth century (figure 25). Although the Benedictine rule puts emphasis on work as a fundamental activity of monastic life, in many Benedictine abbeys monks performed mostly intellectual and worship activities, delegating manual work to laypeople. In this respect the cloister proved efficient in segregating the monks' circulation from all other working activities that were part of the monastic complex (figure 26). The best illustration of this condition is the so-called Plan of St. Gall (ca. 820–830), which is not the plan of a specific complex but the illustration of an ideal plan of a Benedictine monastery drafted in the scriptorium of the monastery of Reichenau during the two reform synods held in Aachen in 816 CE. This plan should be interpreted as an attempt to codify the planning principles of the "ideal" Benedictine abbey at a time when coenobitic monasticism was backed by Carolingian emperors to consolidate their political control.

The St. Gall plan shows how, besides the monks' premises accessible from the cloister, the monastic compound included a plethora of working spaces such as stables, kitchens, workshops, a brewery, an infirmary, storage, and even a special house for bloodletting, each housed in a specific building in orderly fashion. The monastery therefore became a precise orchestration of living and working activities which were integrated within the same complex yet kept strictly separated. It is precisely this aspect that made monasteries the harbingers of modern domestic space, whose main logic is unity through separation. An important feature of the Benedictine monastery was the dissolution of the hermitic cell into the collective dorm. It was precisely the pressure of such constant togetherness (and the economic success of monasteries) that prompted the return in the twelfth century to traditions that combined both coenobitic and hermitic forms of life, as in the case of Carthusian and Camaldolese monks. In the latter, the monks inhabited single-person lodgings tightly aggregated within enclosed compounds (figure 27). Within both these monastic movements, the monks emerged from their cells only for mass and a few other communal activities, spending the rest of their time in solitude. In both Camaldolese and Carthusian communities, hermitic life was possible thanks to other monks who could not pursue such a secluded life. In the case of the Carthusians, the community was divided into "fathers" and "brothers": fathers pursued living and working in solitude, while brothers partook of various forms of labor necessary to support the life of the community, and as such they slept in dormitories rather than isolated cells (figure 28). Often the division between "fathers" and "brothers" (like the division between monks and laypeople) reflected the class composition of monastic communities, since contemplative life was reserved to those coming from wealthy families. Both Camaldolese and Carthusian lodgings were carefully designed houses made of rooms each assigned to a specific activity that defined the ritualized existence of its inhabitant, such as meditating and studying, attending to manual work, praying, and sleeping. Each lodging included a garden in order to allow outdoor life without the need to exit the house. The Carthusian lodging was exceptionally big: it included a cellar and garden on the ground floor, a dining/study room, a sleeping alcove, a small oratory, and a corridor for meditation on the first floor, while the second floor, the attic, would be reserved for manual labor. This arrangement was typified into a template replicated in different monasteries. In this way monastic architecture anticipates the typological uniformity of mass housing, whose design and production were only made possible by the extensive standardization of both domestic habits and spatial templates. Yet monasteries anticipate also the problems associated with collective lodging, such as the management of life in all its aspects, the separation of activities, the exploitation of servants, and the disciplinary control of inhabitants. From being places of rejection of established social norms, Western monasteries ended up (re)producing powerful models of domestication and management. Yet the complex history of monasticism, made of myriad attempts at finding ways to live together, became also a laboratory of ways of life whose influence would be decisive in the elaboration of alternative models of domestic space.

LIVING AND STUDYING

An important offspring of the monastic compound was the collegium, the habitation of the students of a medieval university. The term collegium does not refer to a specific building, but to an associative form that was born in England and became widespread in Europe from the thirteenth century.[45] The collegium as specific architectural type of habitation organized around a cloister arose for the first time in England when, under the pressure of the Hundred Years' War between England and France,

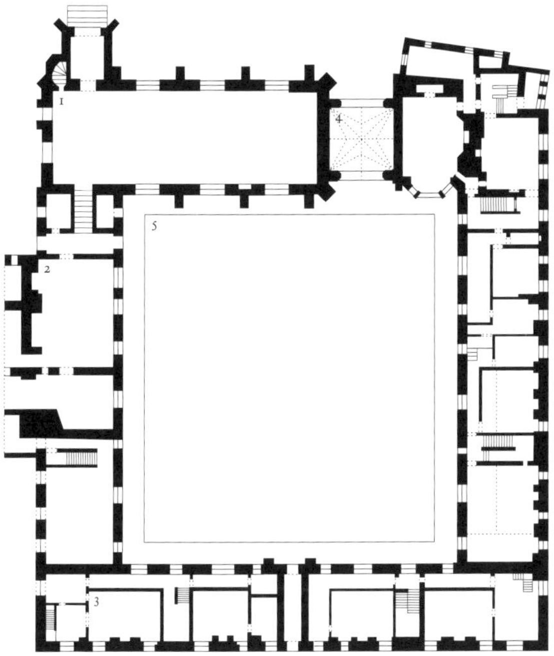

(29) Merton College,
Oxford, founded 1264, detail
(adapted from Marson Korbi, 2019)

(1) hall, (2) kitchen, (3) rooms, (4) gatehouse,
(5) fellows' quadrangle (fifteenth–seventeenth centuries)

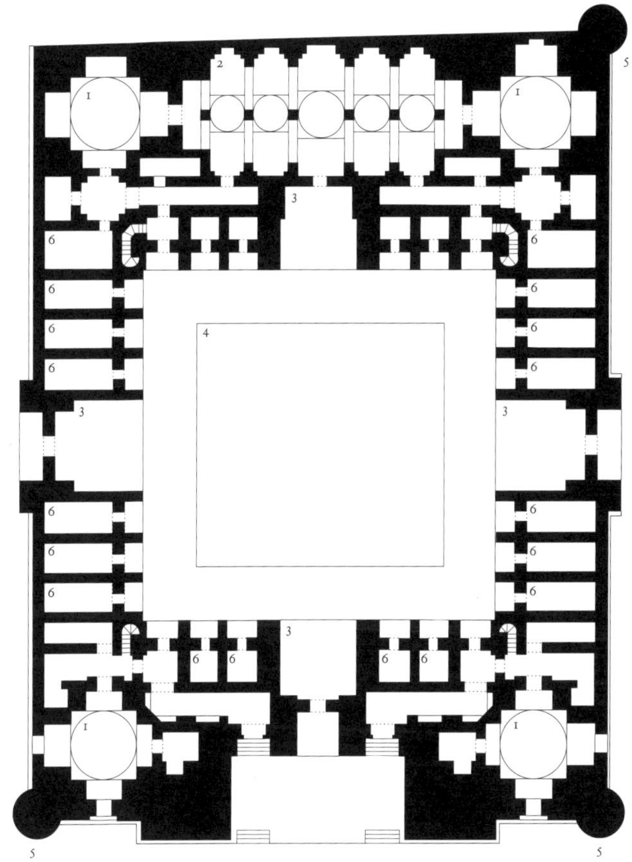

(30) Ulugh Beg Madrasa,
Samarkand, Uzbekistan
(adapted from Timothy M. Ciccone, 2019)

(1) lecture halls, (2) mosque, (3) inward-facing iwans, (4) courtyard,
(5) corner towers (guldastas), (6) dormitories (hujras)

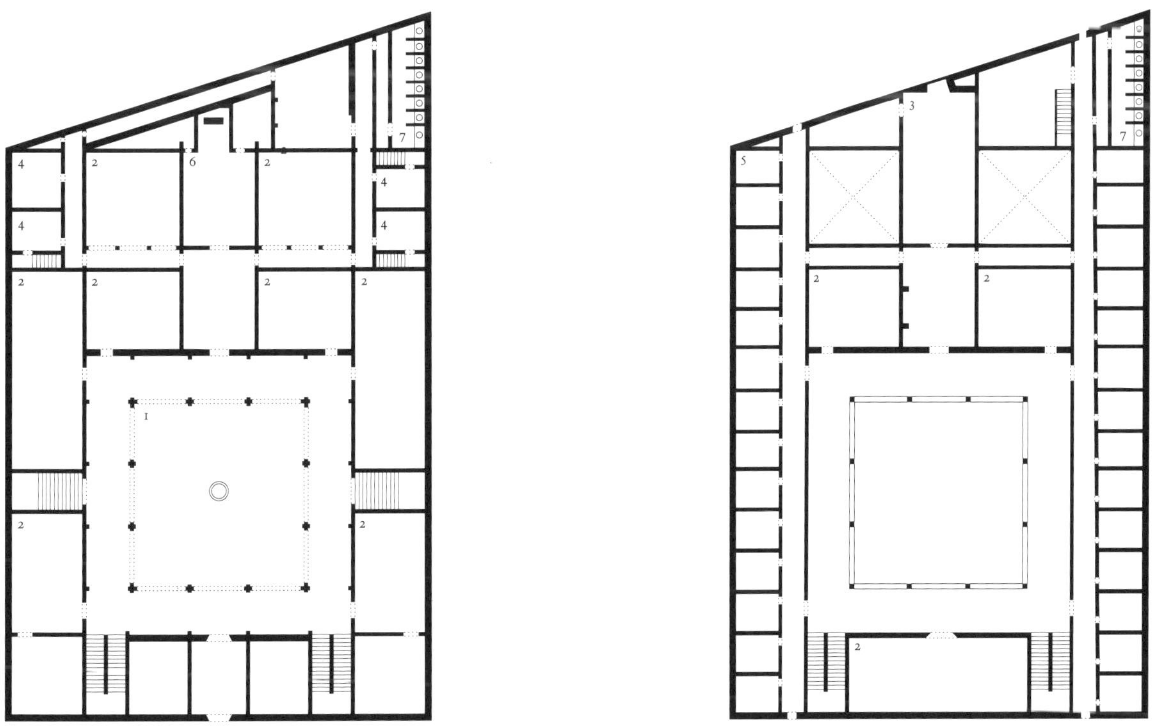

(31) The "Sapienza,"
Siena, 1492, plan
architect: Giuliano da Sangallo
(adapted from Giuliano da Sangallo, c. 1490s–1516)

5 m

(1) cloister, (2) classroom, (3) library, (4) teachers' rooms, (5) students' rooms, (6) chapel, (7) latrines

the English crown decided to create a scholarly hub in Oxford that would compete with Paris and other major university centers in Europe. The programmatic core of the college was on the one hand the *aula*, or hall where teachers imparted their lessons, and on the other hand the accommodation for students. While at the beginning the halls were often improvised in churches, and students rented accommodations from private citizens, soon the college was formalized as a distinct type organized around a central cloister, as visible in Merton College, whose earliest premises were built in the thirteenth century (figure 29). The appropriation of the claustral form responded to both pragmatic and symbolic purposes. The cloister ensured the possibility of opening up space within a dense urban fabric, but it also provided the best spatial organization to a community that followed a strictly ritualized life similar to that of monks but centered on studying rather than praying. Because the collegium represents the earliest form of collective living focused exclusively on intellectual labor, the cloister also symbolized an idea of concentration and focus as opposed to the hectic ethos of medieval urban life. As such, the college as cloistered institution contributed to the ideology of cultural production as seemingly autonomous and self-sufficient pursuit.[46]

Besides the monastery, the Islamic *madrasa* with its introverted organization centered on the courtyard can also be considered a model for the collegium (figure 30). This type of spatial organization made legible in spatial terms the institution's will to form a unitary figure, distinct from everything existing around it. Unlike monasteries, whose premises were often built in rural areas, both madrasa and collegium were built within cities, and their claustral form was crucial to the preservation of their spatial autonomy.

An innovative feature of the medieval collegium was the student lodgings, which were organized in rooms for groups of students, often equipped with small studios for reading and writing. Even more than the monastery, the collegium gave rise to a typology of collective living within which the management of circulation became a paramount design issue. In this regard, an interesting example of the architecture of the college is Giuliano da Sangallo's plan for the Sapienza in Siena (figure 31). The term *sapienza* was used in Italy from the fourteenth century to address an institution like the English college. In 1481, the municipality of Siena asked two architects—Sangallo and Francesco di Giorgio—to provide plans for the extension of the existing college by designing a coherent architecture that included both spaces for teaching and accommodation for students.[47] Of the two projects, the one by Sangallo presents innovative solutions such as the introduction of two long, narrow corridors that served the students' rooms. Through these corridors, Sangallo separated—in an unprecedented manner—the access to the rooms from the gallery surrounding the courtyard, increasing spatial efficiency and privacy. This is most likely one of the earliest examples of domestic plans characterized by a fully developed application of the corridor as a means of distribution. In this plan, the student's private room becomes a terminal space, separated from the rest of the building and served by the corridor (which, unlike loggias, is intended only for circulation). Sangallo's plan for the Sapienza can be interpreted as the moment in which the organizational legacy of monastic architecture gave rise to the typological formation of modern institutions such as the school and the prison. If initially the distributive logic of the monastery served the monk's longing for a ritualized existence, its legacy ended up giving form to a kind of managerial architecture whose goal was both the management and the control of subjects.

THE SPLINTERING LOGIC OF DOMESTIC SPACE

While monastic architecture anticipated the managerial logic of modern domesticity by obsessively mapping space through specific functions and activities, medieval homes were far less defined and often consisted of rectangular enclosures with a minimum of internal subdivision (figures 33–36). Like many examples of premodern domestic space in different parts of the world, houses in medieval Europe were places for both living and working. Division between these activities was minimal or nonexistent, especially in houses of peasants and lower-income households. This means that the sexual division of labor within households was present but offset by the fact that different activities such as working or attending to domestic chores were often happening in close proximity. This condition is visible in medieval rural houses such as those that once existed in the village of Wharram Percy in Yorkshire between the eleventh and fifteenth centuries (figure 33). In these houses most residents inhabited unobstructed narrow and long dwellings whose form and orientation derived from the parcel of cultivable land known as a croft.[48] The core of the houses was the hearth, often located close to the entrance on the long side of the house. Both entrance and hearth provided a sense of orientation for the residents, whose indoor life would unfold around the hearth's light and heat. As suggested by archaeologist Jane Grenville, the central area marked by entrance and hearth was the "houseplace," a multipurpose functional area that established a social syntax of authority in which distance from the entrance meant higher status.[49]

With an increase of agricultural production and the consequent possession of more goods and animals, peasant households could expand and develop some form of partitioning that subdivided the longhouse type into two or three rooms in order to separate the spaces reserved for people from those reserved for animals. As observed in previous examples of domestic spaces, subdivision of the home into multiple rooms was needed to improve the productive and reproductive capacity of the household by creating more specialized areas for living and working. Both in villages and cities, whose economic and demographic growth skyrocketed after the eleventh century, internal subdivision of homes emerged again as a way to better organize the life of the household.

Medieval domestic space in the form of the multistory townhouse is inextricably linked to the rise of a specific class of people, which in medieval England were known as *burgeis*, a term that derives from the Latin *burgensis*, used in medieval Europe to refer to residents of a borough who contributed customary payments to the town's authorities. The term *burgeis* conflated civic status, self-importance, and above all property ownership. In

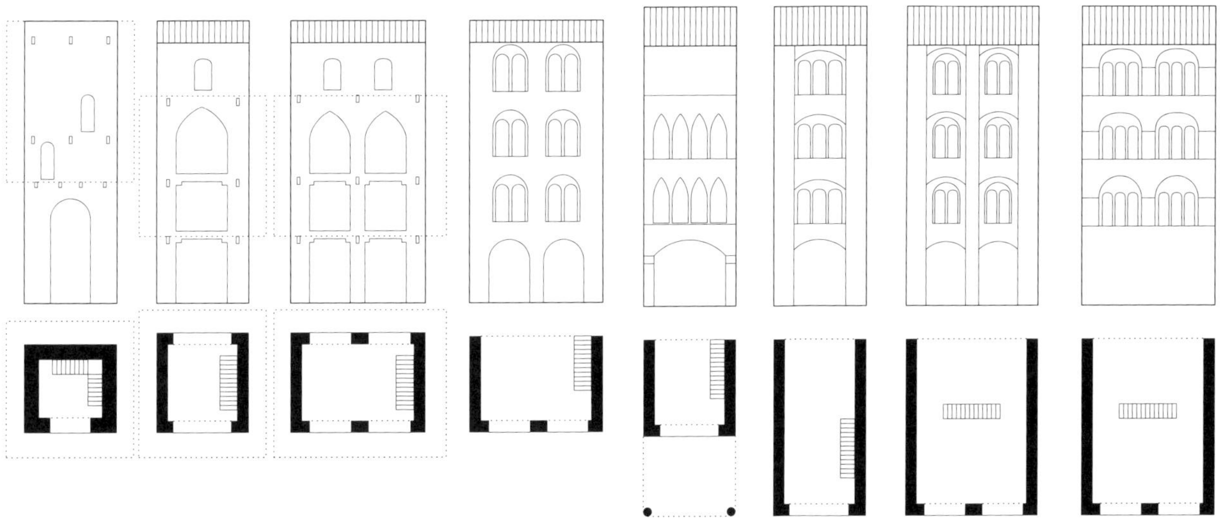

(32) Townhouses,
Pisa, thirteenth century, reconstruction by Giovanni Fanelli
(adapted from Giovanni Fanelli, 1982)

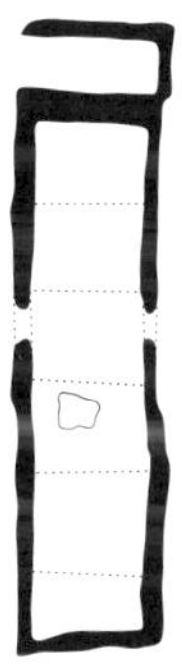

(33) Peasant's house,
Wharram Percy, England,
thirteenth century
(adapted from
Susan Wrathmell, 1996)

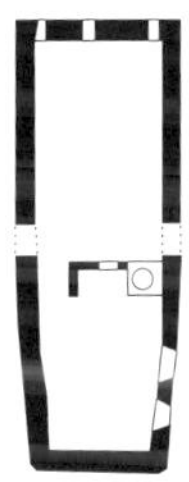

(34) Higher Uppacott farmhouse,
Widecombe, England,
thirteenth century
(adapted from Elizabeth
Gawne, Jenny Sanders, 1998)

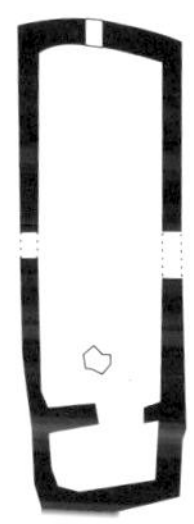

(35) Hound Tor farmhouse,
Widecombe, England,
thirteenth century
(adapted from Elizabeth
Gawne, Jenny Sanders, 1998)

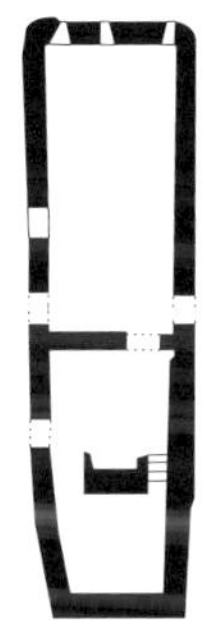

(36) Higher Tor farmhouse,
Widecombe, England,
thirteenth century
(adapted from Elizabeth
Gawne, Jenny Sanders, 1998)

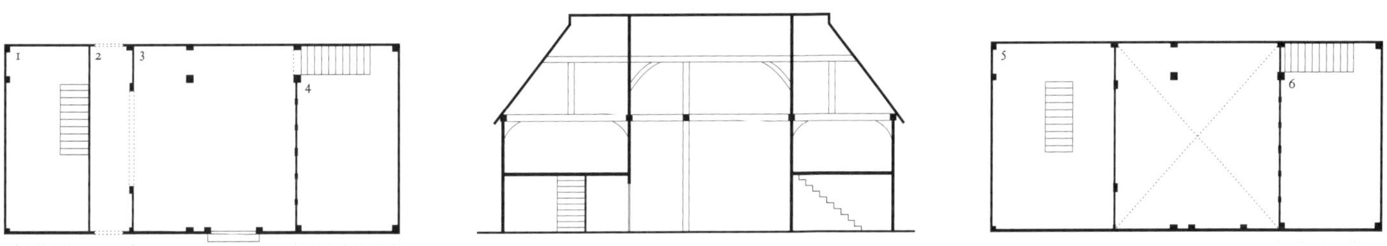

(37) Bridge Cottage,
Uckfield, England, fifteenth century
(adapted from Bridge Cottage Heritage Centre)

(1) services, (2) cross passage, (3) hall, (4) parlor, (5) ancillary chamber, (6) solar

5 m

many medieval cities of Europe, citizenship in the form of participation in the political life of the town was strictly bound to the ownership of property in the form of a house and workplace and the exercise of a profession represented by a guild or franchise. Domestic space, organized in orderly fashion, was thus not just the necessary space for living and working but also an asset, the ostensible symbol of the citizen's social and political status. It was this condition that gave form to one of the most enduring types of modern Western architecture: the townhouse, the quintessential house of the bourgeoisie (figure 32). Unlike the habitations of the urban feudal clan, which were modest homes clustered around the chief's tower or small fortress, the bourgeois townhouse was an independent structure, directly accessible from the street. Its form was based on the extrusion of small land parcels. With massive increase of population, the authorities of many prosperous European cities such as Siena or Bruges subdivided land along streets into long and narrow plots in order to provide as many residents as possible the opportunity of building their home.[50]

The most important feature of this housing type was its relationship with the street, mediated by the façade, whose architecture—its openings, balconies, or loggias—defined the public status of the private space within the city. The ground floor was occupied by the workplace which opened onto the street with porticos or large doors.[51] Because of the narrow proportions of urban plots, room subdivision was organized vertically, but within each floor further subdivision could be easily obtained by means of wooden partitions.[52] This allowed homeowners to quickly subdivide the house if commercial premises needed expanding or extra space was required to accommodate more storage or sleeping accommodations for apprentices. Because the medieval townhouse mixed living and working, its domestic life was promiscuous. Not only did productive and reproductive activities happen side by side, but apprentices were effective members of the household, fed, accommodated, and disciplined exactly as the children of the householder.[53] Moreover, women's lives were often less restricted at that time compared with what they would become with the rise of modern domestic space: wives were expected to attend to domestic chores such as cooking and childcare, but they were also involved in the husband's business and often took the lead in productive activities when the husband was incapacitated or deceased. Yet it was such social promiscuity that prompted bourgeois households to aspire to a more rigid compartmentalization of activities through a clearer internal subdivision.

Tension between promiscuity and subdivision is at stake in one of the earliest sophisticated forms of bourgeois houses: the English timber-frame houses built since the thirteenth century by well-to-do merchants and craftsmen (figure 37). In studying this type of house, the historian Felicity Riddy has argued that its careful spatial organization forces us to rethink the well-established assumption that modern domesticity as the locus of middle-class privacy and comfort emerged only in the seventeenth century.[54] Unlike most medieval houses, which often consisted of one-room habitations, English timber-frame houses were built as compounds subdivided into specialized rooms such as the shop—often located at the ground floor—the *aula* devoted to eating and socializing, and the camera for sleeping.[55] Moreover, these spaces were often complemented by service rooms such as pantry and kitchen, while larger houses included a wine cellar and a chapel. The use of timber rather than masonry construction eased expansion and further subdivision and thus made this building technology optimal for a class of residents whose ethos had been shaped by economic growth and social mobility.[56] The multiroom house was also ideologically distinct from the one-room housing of the poor, because in the former residents could eat, sleep, and work in different spaces while in the latter they could not. Separation of activities ensured spatial order, a choreographing of hospitality, and the efficiency of routines which became an essential trait of the bourgeois household. Domestic order was also a consequence of the strict surveillance exercised by guilds over the activity of merchants and artisans. Not just the quality of products but also the training and accommodation of apprentices who lived in the master's domestic premises were constantly under scrutiny, and this prompted a more careful separation of activities.[57] Thus, in the English timber-frame house reemerged the splintering logic of the home as the orchestration of activities whose orderly unfolding is the best guarantee of both social order and the homeowner's sense of possession.

THE RETURN OF THE OIKOS

The splintering logic of the house is best epitomized in the most important invention of modern domestic space: the apartment. The word apartment filtered into English through the French *appartement*, which is in turn the adaptation of the Italian *appartamento* or Spanish *apartamiento*, meaning—from the Latin *ad partem*—something separated. Apartments are independent groups of rooms within a larger structure, often coinciding with the abode of a specific household. Since the nineteenth century the apartment has been the most important format of city dwelling for middle and lower classes in continental Europe, serving as the basic unit of housing blocks. Yet the origin of the apartment can be traced back to the architecture of the Italian Renaissance palazzo, the large palace of wealthy families and their cohorts of servants. The Italian Renaissance palazzo is arguably an important source of many tropes of modern Western domesticity, as it embodied the ambition to turn the home into a representation of social status. To a certain extent, palazzi were enlargements of townhouses, and their appearance was a symptom of the growing political and economic power of families whose wealth derived from emerging lucrative activities such as banking and trade. For wealthy owners, building a palazzo was instrumental to legitimizing their wealth through *magnificentia*, a concept derived from ancient sources such as Aristotle and Cicero[58] and which consisted in using expenditure for private buildings as an ostensible way to contribute to the public image of cities.[59] Magnificence required the palazzo to be not only a large house but also, and especially, a coherent block within which internal distribution and façade had to be governed by impeccable symmetry, something that was difficult—if not impossible—to implement within the extremely intricate topography of medieval cities.

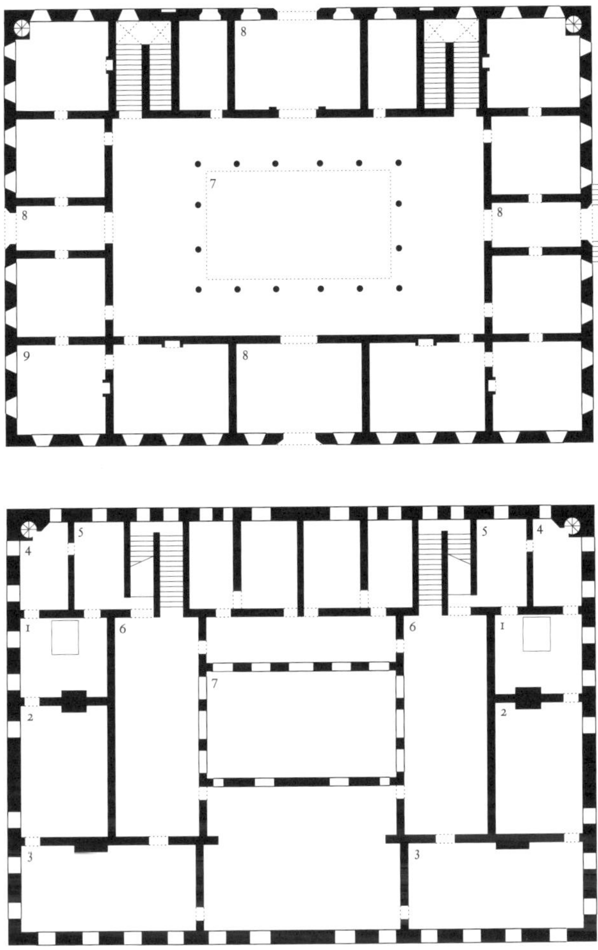

(38) Palazzo Strozzi,
Florence, 1489, ground floor and piano nobile
architects: Benedetto da Maiano, Giuliano da Sangallo
(adapted from Peter Thornton, 1991)

(1) bedroom, (2) antechamber, (3) sala, (4) wardrobe, (5) closet, (6) open loggia, (7) courtyard, (8) passageway, (9) shop

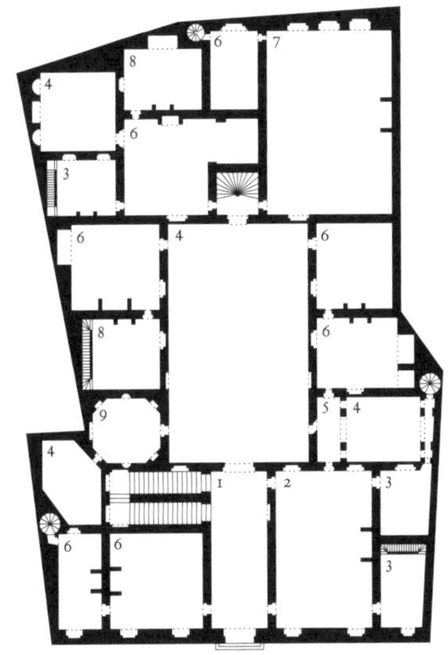

(39) House on an off-square site,
from Serlio, *Book VII: On Accidents*
(adapted from Sebastiano Serlio, 1575)

(1) passageway, (2) saletta, (3) ancillary room, (4) courtyard, (5) small loggia, (6) bedroom, (7) sala, (8) chamber, (9) chapel

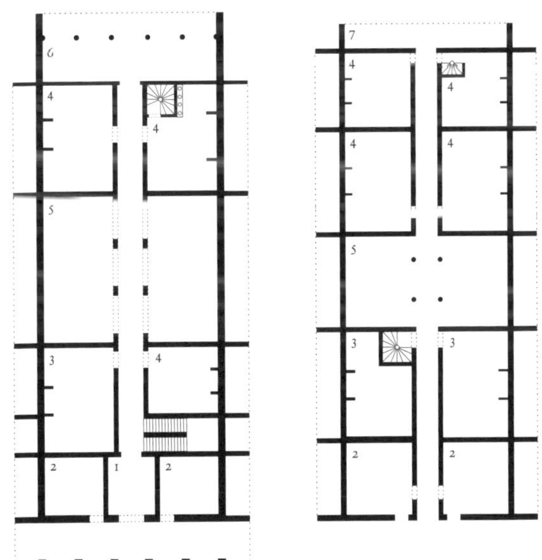

(40) Houses for Merchants,
from Serlio, *Book VI: On Habitations*
(adapted from Sebastiano Serlio, c. 1549)

(1) vestibule, (2) shop, (3) saletta, (4) bedroom, (5) courtyard, (6) loggia, (7) garden

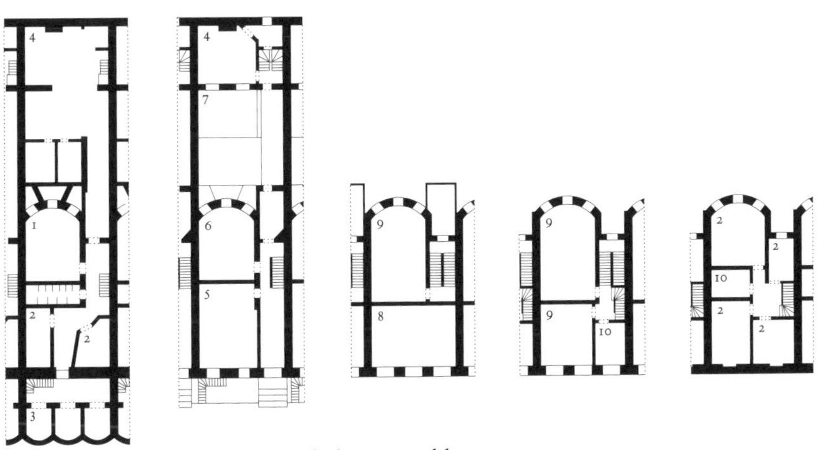

(41) Terraced house,
Bedford Square, London, 1775–1780
(adapted from Stefan Muthesius, 1982)

(1) kitchen, (2) servants' room, (3) cellar, (4) stable, (5) sitting room, (6) dining room, (7) backyard, (8) drawing room, (9) bedroom, (10) bathroom

5 m

It is interesting to note that the emergence of the architect as a recognizable "author" of buildings coincides with the rise and diffusion of the palazzo within Italian cities between the fourteenth and fifteenth centuries. Even if their building could take several decades, palazzi were planned as unitary complexes, and it was precisely the necessity of planning that required a "professional" architect to provide a plan and supervise construction. From Leon Battista Alberti's recommendations on the design of domestic space in his treatise *De re aedificatoria* (ca. 1450) to Francesco di Giorgio's diagrammatic plans of palazzi in his *Trattato di architettura* (ca. 1481), the main problem of designing this type was not so much the external appearance of buildings, but rather their spatial distribution. Because they housed so many people within a strictly hierarchical logic headed by the homeowner, palazzi were complex compositions of asymmetrical social and gender roles kept together by elaborate household rituals. The design of palazzi inaugurates one of the most enduring design techniques that will be crucial for the development of modern domestic space: the art of distribution. Francesco di Giorgio was among the earliest architects to use the term *stribuzioni di stanze* (the distribution of rooms), and in his plans he labeled the different rooms and tried to establish a coherent nomenclature in order to define them.[60] Within distribution, the architect conceives buildings by compartmentalizing space in rooms marked by a specific assigned use. As such the architecture of the palazzo—and its rural alter ego, the villa—resurrected the logic of *oikonomia* of ancient Greek households, applying an even more rigid taxonomy of room types than its predecessor.

The starting point of this taxonomy is the owner's bedchamber, the camera, which represented his prerogative to privacy, the possibility of disconnecting himself from the rest of the house in order to rest and work. All the other rooms were arranged according to the position of the bedchamber in a progression from the most private to the most public spaces of the house, from the camera to the sala (hall) through the anticamera.[61] Thus, the house became a telescopic gradient from private to public with implications for the social status of the guest, whose importance was made evident by how much access he was given to the most private rooms of the house.

One of the clearest examples of this logic is Palazzo Strozzi in Florence designed by Benedetto da Maiano and Giuliano da Sangallo, where the piano nobile is divided into two apartments each of which consists of an enfilade of rooms that goes from the loggia to the closet (figure 38). Besides managing social roles, palazzi had to accommodate many activities and many people, including a large cohort of servants and workers whose lodgings were located in the mezzanine, a "service floor" positioned either below or above the owner's apartments. In this way, palazzi became apparatuses of individuation and separation of both functions and subjects. Despite its compartmentalizing logic, however, within the palazzo domestic and working activities still existed side by side. For example, not only were bedchambers places for both rest and work, but the ground floor usually contained spaces for business and sometimes even craft activities.

It was precisely this coexistence of many activities and many residents of different rank that prompted architects and patrons to carefully plan the palazzo as a composition of strictly defined spaces. This emerging concern for the planning of domestic space is reflected in Sebastiano Serlio's *Sixth Book on Architecture: On Habitations in and outside the Cities* (ca. 1540s), which represents the first-ever attempt to illustrate a complete range of domestic architectural models, each addressed to a different social class (figure 40).[62] Serlio's unprecedented inclusion of all classes in his treatise denotes his realist acceptance of an increasingly unequal society, but is also an echo of the attempt of public authorities to regulate housing standards within overcrowded cities. Moreover, as argued by Myra Nan Rosenfeld, Serlio here developed a rational system of domestic planning which reflected changes in the structure of the middle- and upper-class family, whose form was gradually moving from the extended clan bound by kin relationships to a more individualized "nuclear" family.[63] The emergence of this new kind of family unit required a more compartmentalized space with increased privacy compared to what was customary in the medieval townhouse. This tendency is reflected in Serlio's plans for the houses of merchants, artisans, and what he called in Venetian jargon "citizens," a distinct class made of doctors, lawyers, and civil servants. Houses for these subjects were conceived by Serlio as sequences of function-specific rooms whose linear composition was adapted to the long and narrow form of the medieval land parcel. These plans reveal a great effort to optimize the difficult relationship between property subdivision and domestic decorum understood as the possibility of segregating as much as possible the different activities of the house.

What is striking about Serlio's house models, such as those for well-off artisans and citizens, is their diagrammatic logic, as if houses were no longer experienced as lived spaces but rather conceived as abstract frames whose goal is the correct spatial management of the residents' lives. From a typological point of view, Serlio did not invent much vis-à-vis the average middle- and upper-class townhouse in cities like Lyon or Venice; he simply rationalized and systematized this type of housing by mediating between the opposing conditions of classicist symmetry and site constraints. Site adaptation of complex residential patterns was presented in his *Seventh Book on Architecture*, on "situations," where among other things Serlio illustrates how to insert and subdivide houses to be built on irregular sites (figure 39).[64] One striking example presented in this book concerns a small palazzo subdivided into several units.[65] Here Serlio demonstrates how to subdivide not just the building into different apartments, but each apartment into a defined set of rooms. In doing so he copes with multiple issues such as correct sequencing of rooms from the most public to the most private spaces, providing sufficient light and ventilation to each room by inserting small open shafts, while fitting the whole complex into what he defines as a "bizarre" site in which only one side can have openings. Such an example encapsulates what will become the drama of middle-class apartments during the next four centuries, namely the mediation between the correct distribution of rooms in order to ensure privacy and comfort and the frequent irregularity of sites to be found in cities characterized by high density and high cost of land.

It is precisely by dealing with these quintessential problems of modern housing that Serlio's domestic architecture inaugurates a kind of design tool that in the nineteenth century will be addressed as a "type." According to the canonical definition by the French theorist Quatremère de Quincy, a type is not a model to be copied, but the deep formal structure of buildings.[66] As such, type does not address so much how a building looks as its internal organization. Although such a definition of type can apply to any kind of building, it was with the emergence of housing and the search for appropriate systems of distribution that typological design became the most important vantage point through which architecture is understood and produced. As a design approach, typology is not a mere outcome of the architect's invention, but rather the translation into built form of given social conditions such as class, gender roles, and property. Serlio's typological design seems to anticipate an attitude that would become dominant in the era, as architecture became the process of standardizing and normalizing power relationships within the very fine grain of domestic life. In spite of the fact that the *Sixth Book on Architecture* was his only book to remain unpublished, a few architects' knowledge of it was enough to contribute to the emergence of a speculative way to build houses in series.[67] Yet, in contrast to Serlio's models, in many examples of seventeenth- and eighteenth-century townhouses built around Parisian and London squares, working activities, especially those involving manual labor, were increasingly ejected from the home in order to reinforce the latter's status and privacy vis-à-vis the hectic life of mercantilist cities.

Until the eighteenth century, the merging of work and residence within the same building was very common in the townhouses of many European cities. However, from the seventeenth century onward, wealthy classes started to cultivate the idea of domestic space and family life as a refuge from the promiscuity of working relationships. This ideology was at first an attribute of social status, but strong European states such as France also promoted it in the effort to separate as much as possible the private space of reproduction from the public sphere of production. Indeed, Renaissance theorists like Alberti had already made a case for houses being the domain of women, while men though enjoying privacy at home were expected to spend most of their time outside it.[68] Only in the eighteenth century did elites succeed in eliminating working spaces from their houses, turning them into proper residential spaces.

One of the most important examples of an exclusively residential form of domestic space was the English terraced house (figure 41). An offspring of the medieval townhouse, the terraced house can be considered a dwelling reduced to its most generic form: two parallel party walls that frame floors divided into front and rear rooms. The party walls function as loadbearing structure, service spine, and above all as property lines that neatly separate one house from another. The strict rectangular form of the terraced house was meant to be consistent with the principle of property subdivision following which cities were divided into blocks, blocks into houses, and houses into rooms. Terraced houses were often developed within estates whose landowners prohibited the creation of any kind of working space in order to guarantee the high-end status and thus the value of their property.[69] Indeed zoning, that is to say the planning technique of segregating functions—especially housing and workplace—finds its origins in the bylaws imposed by London landowners on their residential estates.[70] The separation of housing from workplace was also triggered by the kind of family favored by wealthy classes and later imposed on the working class: the domesticated nuclear family in which relationships are based (supposedly) on disinterested affection. It was precisely this disinterested affection that made the nuclear family the fertile ground for the naturalization of female reproductive labor when the family values of the upper bourgeoisie were transmitted to the lower classes.

The rise of this kind of domesticity based on the self-sufficient nuclear family and the separation between dwelling and workspace should be understood within the larger social tendency of what Maria Mies has called "housewification."[71] This term addresses the political process through which domestic labor was enclosed and privatized within the house and naturalized as a duty of the woman. This process took myriad forms, from direct violence against unmarried women to stripping females of their right to work outside the home.[72] Domestic space both reflected and enabled this process by segregating reproductive activities like cooking or childcare from the more public spaces of the house such as the hall, which would thus become the modern living room. Eventually, this process resulted in the individuation of the nuclear family as a strictly private entity separated from the public life of the city. In this sense the ejection of working activities from the house was prompted not only by developers in order to increase the value of their estate but also—and especially—by the bourgeois mentality according to which the house is a safe haven, a refuge from the promiscuous world of working relationships. If this ideology first arose among middle and upper classes, from the nineteenth century it was imposed on the lower classes to "educate" them to the virtues of bourgeois life and prevent social unrest.

HOUSING THE LABORING CLASSES

With the rise of capitalism, the increasing compartmentalization of domestic labor at the scale of the nuclear family countered practices of communality and sharing which were dominant among the lower classes.[73] This tendency is visible in one of the earliest Western examples of housing for the laboring class, the Fuggerei of Augsburg (Germany), built at the beginning of the sixteenth century and financed by the banker Jakob Fugger, one of the richest men in Europe at that time (figure 42).[74] The Fuggerei is a compound made up of 52 houses arranged in rows. The complex was developed as a variant of the poorhouses which spread in fourteenth-century Europe to provide social relief.[75] As such, the poorhouses can be understood as an offspring of the medieval hospital, an extremely important institution which catered not only to the ill but also the poor. The novelty of the Fuggerei was that it housed the so-called *Hausarmen*, pious residents willing to work and in need of economic relief.[76] Therefore, unlike the medieval hospital and the poorhouse, the complex discriminated between the poor person as worker and the poor person as beggar. In the Fuggerei, only productive poor people willing to work and support their families were welcomed. Indeed, the houses were rented for one Rhenish florin per year, the equivalent of the monthly income of a day laborer.[77] Residents could work in their houses, but the complex was meant to house laborers who would seek employment outside of their domestic spaces.[78] As in many subsequent housing projects, the uniformity of types and the standardization of both plan and façade implied the overall class homogeneity of the residents. Yet the austerity of the architecture was not only motivated by economic conditions but also had ideological implications, as it was meant to inspire in the residents a sense of abnegation informing a life dedicated exclusively to labor, both inside and outside the home. Domesticity was reduced to a minimum and subordinated to the goal of reproducing a disciplined workforce; in the Fuggerei, there were no significant public spaces, and even the chapel was a later addition. This project is an early example of how the ascetic devotion to work became a fundamental ideological aspect of housing for the laboring classes.

Max Weber famously distinguished the outer-worldly asceticism of monastic communities from the inner-worldly one of early capitalist mentality, in which work is no longer a means to live but becomes an end in itself.[79] Such self-abnegation required a domestic life that was both strictly separated from the workplace and perfectly ancillary to it. From a capitalist point of view, the welfare of workers—including their access to decent lodging—is a crucial precondition for efficient production. It is precisely with these ideas in mind that the English neoclassicist architect John Wood the Younger published in 1781 his seminal treatise on the "habitations of the laborers" (figure 43).[80] This publication is unprecedented because it was the first architectural book to be devoted exclusively to the housing of low-income workers. Wood presented a series of housing plans and elevations based on a cottage type of his own design and marked by a conscious rejection of ornament and rather sophisticated functional layouts. In the cottages, rooms are given precise functions related to the most essential aspects of domestic reproduction: cooking, sleeping, and cleaning. Unlike vernacular houses, whose spaces were indifferently used for both domestic labor and working activities, Wood's cottages excluded remunerated work. With this project, Wood was reacting to the housing crisis affecting the English countryside after the common fields were privatized by the parliamentary enclosures, resulting in the eviction of masses of peasants who found themselves in dire economic conditions. As noted by Daniel Maudin, Wood's neoclassical cottages were designed to fit this newly privatized landscape in which the rapid rise of urban inhabitants and the consequent demand for increasing food production required the rural population to become a docile workforce.[81] Like the simple architecture of the Fuggerei, Wood's housing projects evoked an austere way of life in which workers were made productive by receiving just the minimum amount of welfare in the form of a basic dwelling. Yet it was precisely its ascetic character that made Wood's project unsustainable. Rather than austerity, the cultivation of a sense of homeownership and petit bourgeois pride became essential to the project of housing for the laboring classes. Only in this way could devoting one's own life to work both outside and inside the home be considered a worthy sacrifice.

With the advent of industrialization, traditional family values were deeply challenged, as many people from rural territories were forced to move into big cities where they could find only sordid forms of lodging such as the infamous rookeries in London.[82] It took some time before capitalists realized that an unruly domestic life would endanger the productivity of workers. One of the earliest systematic efforts to approach the problem of housing for the laboring classes from the vantage point of the ruling class was architect Henry Roberts's influential 1850 pamphlet *The Dwellings of the Labouring Classes*, which can be interpreted as both a continuation and a critique of Wood's pioneering treatise.[83] While the problem of housing in nineteenth-century London was not seen as something that needed to be solved by public intervention, toward the second half of the century various (private) societies were formed to tackle the issues surrounding workers' living conditions. Among these, the Society for Improving the Conditions of the Labouring Classes distinguished itself by formulating new typologies for dwellings, which were created in collaboration with Roberts. While his pamphlet contains a few models of lodging houses for unmarried workmen and laborers, or for widows or women, most of his attention was directed to the development of family units that were based, much like Wood's project, on the reinterpretation of the countryside cottage. To promote the ideology of ownership and avoid the inherently morally dangerous conditions of larger collective lodging houses, Roberts's houses were generally characterized by an internal layout which reinforced the privacy of the dwellers and, within each family, the authority of the parents (figure 45). Inside each unit, the children's rooms were accessed from the main living room while the parents' room could be reached only from the scullery, thereby preserving its seclusion and giving the adults control over the rest of the unit. Access to the house itself was treated with great carefulness. While larger and earlier housing models were based on open galleries as in the case of Roberts' Model Houses for Families in Streatham Street, built in 1851, in later types staircases were first placed in a recess in the front elevation so as to serve the flats directly from the landing.

What emerges in Roberts's model is not just an ambition to separate activities and gender roles within domestic space, but also the attempt to seal the household into a flat that becomes an enclosed microcosm. This project reveals how, from the very beginning of its modern history, housing for the laboring classes was meant to educate its residents to the bourgeois values of the middle class. Among these values, the most important was that of the "nuclear family," which strengthened the link between co-residence and kinship. Maria Mies has noted that this idea of the family seldom existed before the nineteenth century, especially among the poor and peasants, and that it was promoted in countries like France and England as a way of giving moral and economic order to the domestic life of the lower classes.[84] As Mies writes, with the help of state legislation, capitalism expanded family values from the propertied bourgeoisie to the working class, encouraging women to stay at home in order to breed the next generation of workers.[85] It was precisely this tendency to individuate the nuclear family as the fulcrum of industrial work that prompted social

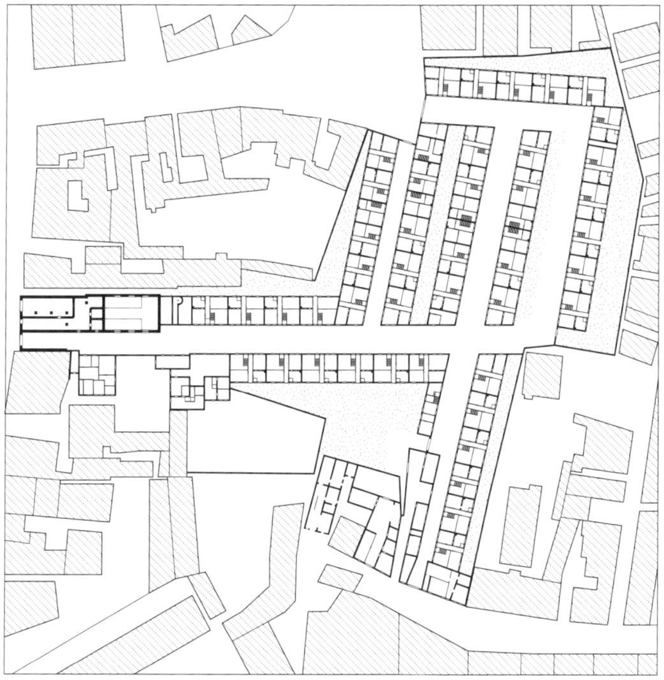

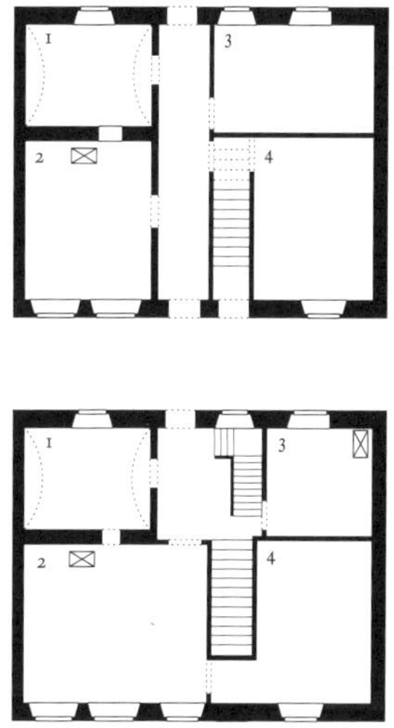

(42) Fuggerei housing complex,
Augsburg, founded 1521,
general plan (left), ground floor and first floor
(adapted from Hüsniye Bayankulu, 2014)

(1) room, (2) stube, (3) kitchen, (4) bedroom

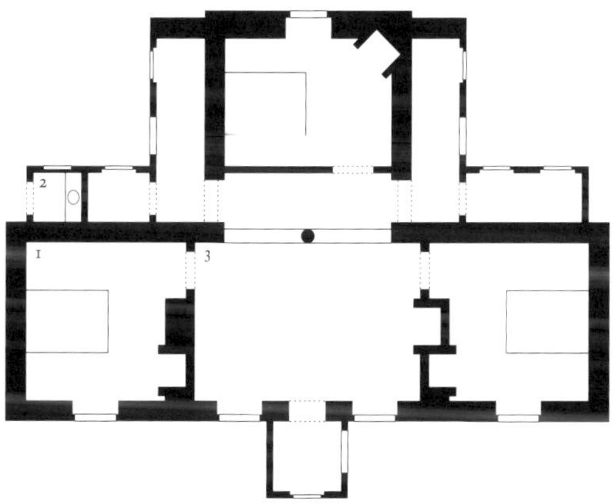

(43) Cottage with three rooms
architect: John Wood the Younger
(adapted from John Wood the Younger, 1781)

(1) bedroom, (2) toilet, (3) hall

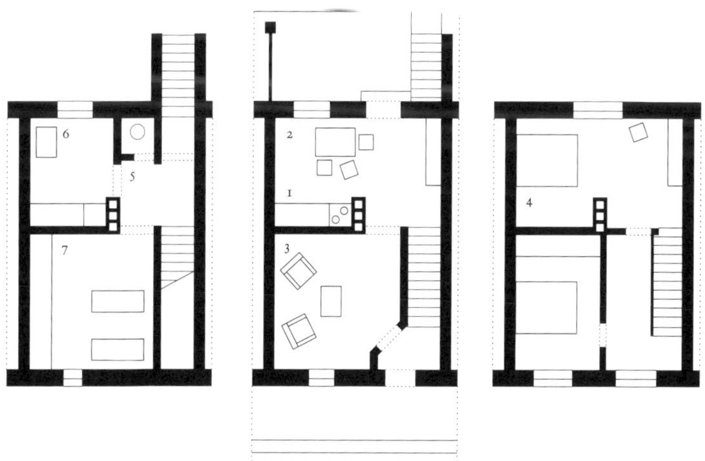

(44) Row housing,
Hellerau, 1910–1911, ground floor
architect: Heinrich Tessenow
(adapted from Marco De Michelis, 1991)

(1) kitchen, (2) dining room, (3) living room, (4) bedroom, (5) toilet

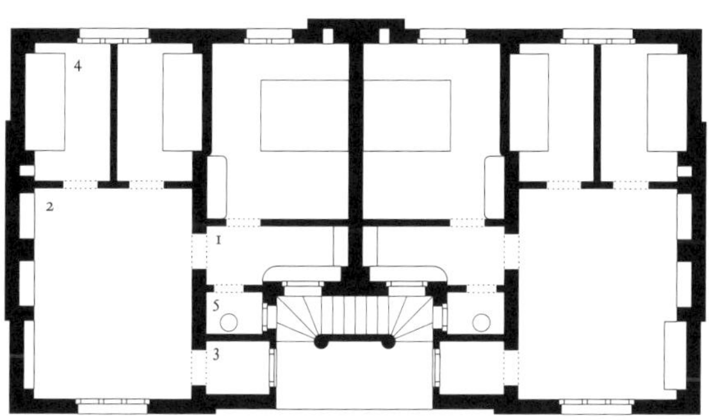

(45) Double house with four distinct tenements on two floors
architect: Henry Roberts
(adapted from Henry Roberts, 1850)

(1) kitchen, (2) living room, (3) hallway, (4) bedroom, (5) toilet

reformers to conceive of the home not just as lodging but as an idealized microcosm.

In the early twentieth century this understanding of the home was embraced throughout Europe by entrepreneurs who saw the small cottage as the best model for building residential and service centers as appendixes of places of production. One of the most interesting models of houses for the laboring classes developed as company towns may be the garden city of Hellerau, near Dresden.[86] This pioneering project was undertaken by carpenter and entrepreneur Karl Schmidt as part of a larger housing reform project initiated by the German state in 1890 and supported by the vast majority of the German bourgeoisie. The master plan, conceived by Richard Riemerschmid, determined that all of the dwellings in Hellerau were to be constructed as single-family houses with attached gardens, which served as the site for the domestication of working men's leisure on the one hand and of women's productive labor on the other. By being able to cultivate a small private garden, women would finally be defined as proper housewives, who could now contribute in a "gender-appropriate capacity" to the financial well-being of the family.[87]

Crucial to the Hellerau plan was the subtle class distinction embodied in the different housing types. Hermann Muthesius designed the villa quarter of Hellerau, which was meant to be occupied by middle-class inhabitants with a smaller portion for lower-income workers, while Heinrich Tessenow designed a series of simple and modestly sized housing units (figure 44). What is remarkable about Tessenow's houses is their lack of decorative elements and the reduction of livable space to those functions that were considered essential for the immediate survival of the family.[88] Tessenow's houses thus anticipated the "minimum dwelling," a crucial concept in housing that was debated at the second International Congress of Modern Architecture (CIAM) held in Frankfurt in 1929, in which the bourgeois home would be reduced to a minimum so that it would be affordable to workers. While Muthesius's houses still projected traditional middle-class values onto the laboring classes, Tessenow's austere architecture maintained the typology of the house with a garden but reduced this model to its most basic form. In Hellerau, domestic architecture seemed to be suspended between the petit bourgeois character of the garden city and the ascetic self-abnegation typical of working-class lodgings. The garden itself embodied the conflict between these two ideals, since it was meant to be both a pastoral microcosm and a place of labor to support the family's welfare.

AGAINST THE DOMESTIC

Parallel to the rise of domestic space as temple of family values exists a tradition of anti-domesticity embodied in the many attempts to accommodate alternative kinds of households. A seminal example of anti-domestic space was the Phalanx, a community of approximately 1,600 inhabitants theorized by Charles Fourier in his social treatise *Théorie des quatre mouvements et destinées générales* (1808).[89] The Phalanx (from the Greek term indicating a compact body of troops) was to be a group of peers living in a communal palace known as the Phalanstery and surrounded by agricultural and industrial facilities. As in a monastery, the life of the Phalanx was obsessively scheduled by working and leisure activities, yet the goal of such organization was not just self-discipline but rather the socialization of all aspects of life from production to reproduction. The Phalanstery was made of wings of apartments enclosing communal gardens and served by generous indoor galleries. Both gardens and galleries were imagined by Fourier as a way to encourage social relationships among the inhabitants. The Phalanstery's main goal was to centralize housekeeping in order to free the residents—and especially women—from the burden of domestic labor. It was precisely the emancipatory ambition of Fourier's Phalanstery that made the latter an influential model for communitarian living in the nineteenth and twentieth centuries.

As Dolores Hayden has argued, the popularity of communitarian visions such as the one proposed by Fourier spread for the first time in the United States in the nineteenth century, starting with the foundation of the Fourierist organization of the North American Phalanx in 1849.[90] Following decades of agitation about labor rights, equitable land redistribution, and women's emancipation, the United States became a fertile ground for experiments in new forms of communitarian living. Both religious and secular communitarian movements shared a critical view of the emerging type of habitation for middle-class American families—the suburban isolated cottage—as lonely, wasteful, and oppressive. In the United States, from its very beginning, political reformers and state authorities put a lot of effort into encouraging the middle class to embrace the values of both family living and private property.[91] Against these values, Fourierist groups as well as religious communes advocated a collective way of life in which domestic activities would be socialized, freeing inhabitants from the burdens of property and repetitive daily labor.[92] A radical example of collectivist experiment was the Perfectionist movement founded by John Humphrey Noyes in 1848, whose principles included the abolition of private property and family living.[93] Their mansion house in Oneida was made of wings of single-person rooms equipped with a small storage space and connected through galleries to a multitude of communal services, a spatial organization that proved to be influential in the proliferation of typologies for communal living in the nineteenth and twentieth centuries (figure 46). Yet the influence of these radical models went far beyond utopian religious communities and inspired more secular initiatives whose main priority was the emancipation of women from domestic life, as in the case of what Hayden in her seminal book *The Grand Domestic Revolution* addressed as material feminists. Within this movement one of the most important figures was Marie Stevens Case Howland, a feminist and fierce critic of the traditional single-family home and its social values.[94] Howland's experience of living at the Familistère—a housing complex inspired by Fourierist principles and built in 1845 in Guise (France) by Jean-Baptiste André Godin for his foundry's workers and their families—led Howland to determine that the cooperative logic of the Phalanstery was a fundamental contribution to her project to socialize domestic labor at the scale of the city. In 1884, in collaboration with Albert Kimsey Owen and John J. Deery, Howland expanded Fourierist principles by founding the ultimately unrealized socialist colony of Topolobampo (Sinaloa, Mexico, figure 47). Planned as a grid of blocks cut by diagonal streets, the colony included three types of dwellings: residential hotels, communal patio houses, and detached cottages that shared collective kitchens. This trio of typologies was intended to articulate a gradient of collective life, with traditional ways of living represented by the cottages and more radical forms of living represented by the hotels. Yet all dwellings were to be supported by centralizing housekeeping and other forms of cooperative infrastructure such as child and elderly care, promoting the total socialization of domestic labor across the community.

Besides these radical initiatives, alternatives to family life were also advanced in a more commercial way, as in the case of hotels.[95] This form of lodging became widespread especially in the United States, where social mobility and the uprootedness of workers became a hallmark of American society. An early and popular form of hotel living took place inside private homes in the form of boarding rooms. These rooms were offered by private residents to men and women at a price that included both meals and housekeeping.[96] Boardinghouses commercialized reproductive activities and were often run by women, thus professionalizing domestic labor and challenging the common view of women's work as a labor of love for her family. For this reason, public commentators and city authorities attacked boarding as a deviant form of housing and encouraged entrepreneurs to build a dedicated type of accommodation that became known as the residential hotel (figure 48). The most outstanding examples of this typology, which proliferated in the second half of the nineteenth century, were the "palace hotels" built as sumptuous palazzi, as in the case of the Palace Hotel in San Francisco (1875) which comprised rooms for single occupancy, apartments for families, and a plethora of collective amenities such as lobbies, halls, saloon, and restaurants. In these hotels, housekeeping was centralized and efficiently managed, making them profitable for their owners and attractive for those who wanted to avoid the burden of domestic chores. Hotel life became so popular among the upper and middle classes that this typology influenced even forms of long-term accommodation such as the kitchenless apartment, a typology of housing that became ubiquitous in large cities like New York.[97] An early declension of the kitchenless apartment complex was the home club initiated by the architect Philip Gengembre Hubert in New York in 1881—a project that is also interesting as it represented the first occurrence of cooperative housing in the United States. Home clubs offered a variety of housing units for both singles and families supported by centralized housekeeping and collective spaces such as dining room, library, and lounges; the Chelsea Hotel remains perhaps the most notorious example of this type of dwelling (figure 49).[98] The home club became an influential model for cooperative housing in countries like England, Switzerland, Denmark, Germany, and Sweden in the early twentieth century.[99] Ebenezer Howard's cooperative "quadrangles," which he proposed as part of his reformist project for new "garden cities" to be built around London, can also be considered an offspring of the home club concept.[100] Implemented at Homesgarth in Letchworth, the quadrangle was designed by Harold Clapham Lander as a communal house that combined the full privacy of the individual home and the benefits of centralized housekeeping (figure 50). The plan of the quadrangle reflected the private and collective aspects of the house by aggregating individual houses around a portico in the manner of a monastic cloister. Communal facilities like a large dining hall and a childcare center were directly accessible from the portico. Yet this model was not further implemented in Barry Parker's and Raymond Unwin's planning for the garden city of Letchworth, which was instead made of single-family cottages, anticipating the typological rationale of the first social housing act in England in 1919. What is interesting about these early cases of cooperative housing is that they tried to introduce hotel life within more stable forms of habitation by translating the collective ethos of communal living into attempts at collective ownership.

In its early phases, hotel living was a middle-class phenomenon. Yet, with the massive migration of workers to cities, entrepreneurs started to develop affordable lodging in the form of "mid-price hotels" and rooming houses. Hotel living became so diffused in North American cities that entire districts such as South of Market in San Francisco, Skid Row in Los Angeles, and the Main Stem in Chicago were inhabited almost exclusively by single dwellers. Affordable residential hotels represented the zero degree of domestic architecture: sequences of equal-size rooms served by long corridors as visible in the notorious National and Delta hotels in San Francisco (1907, 1910; figure 51). Even if cheap residential hotels offered the user just a sparsely furnished room, their downtown location gave access to a rich offering of amenities such as bars, diners, and clubs. As such the residential hotel became the hotbed of a radical anti-domestic way of life that was often chosen by its residents and not just embraced by necessity. There was nothing utopian in residential hotels: they were built for profit and their range of offerings—from palace to rooming house—was strategically geared to users of a specific class and race. Yet their massive proliferation in cities like San Francisco, New York, and Los Angeles made them affordable to larger numbers of people, thus disrupting the totalizing ideology of family living. Residential hotels were not just homes for transient people, but also a sort of communal houses that fostered solidarity among residents beyond the scale of the family. Thus, hotels became an important form of accommodation for elderly and disabled dwellers who could count on networks of mutual aid self-organized by hotel residents.

The most politically radical reinterpretation of the legacy of the American residential hotel as a critique of bourgeois domestic space was put forward by critic and poet Karel Teige in his book *The Minimum Dwelling* of 1932.[101] Teige wrote his text as a polemical response to the concept of *Existenzminimum* proposed in 1929 by CIAM architects during their congress in Frankfurt. For these architects, the minimum dwelling as an *Existenzminimum* was largely based on the reduction of the bourgeois apartment to its smallest dimensions. Against this concept Teige proposed a model of housing in which every person would be granted a private room while all other domestic functions including bathroom, kitchen, and child care would be socialized beyond the family. With this idea of minimum dwelling, Teige proposed to dismantle the traditional domestic space and its subject—the nuclear family—by limiting the private space to the personal room.

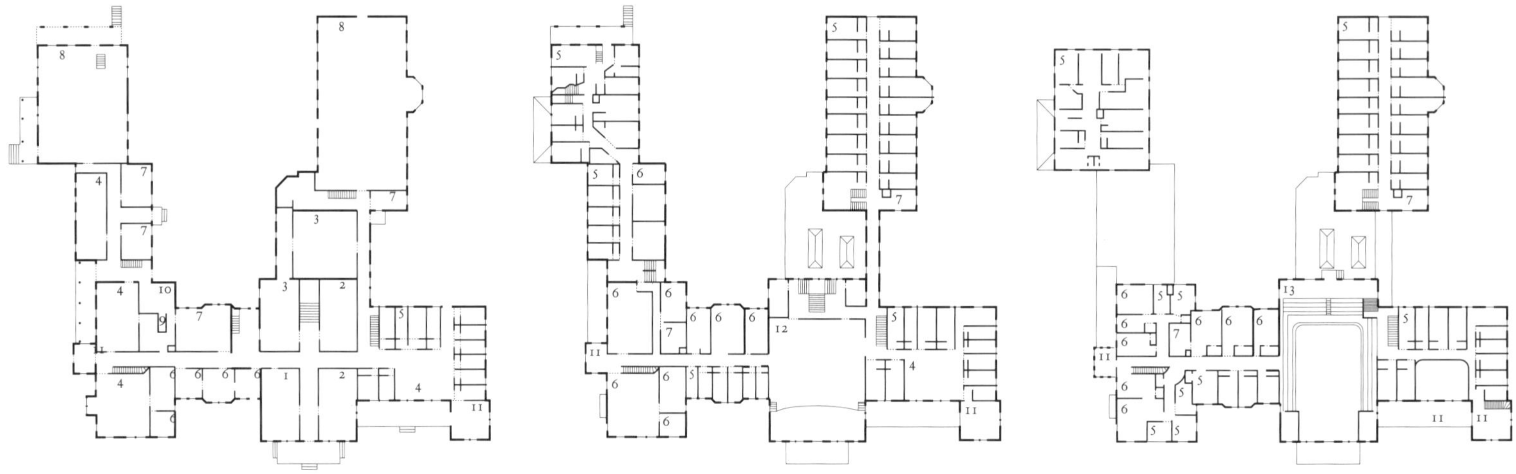

(46) Second Mansion House,
Oneida, 1861–1878, ground floor, first floor, and second floor (adapted from Dolores Hayden, 1976)

(1) office/cloakroom, (2) reception room, (3) library, (4) sitting room/parlor, (5) single bedroom, (6) shared bedroom, (7) bathroom, (8) lounge/workshop, (9) nursery, (10) nursery kitchen, (11) tower, (12) hall, (13) balcony of hall

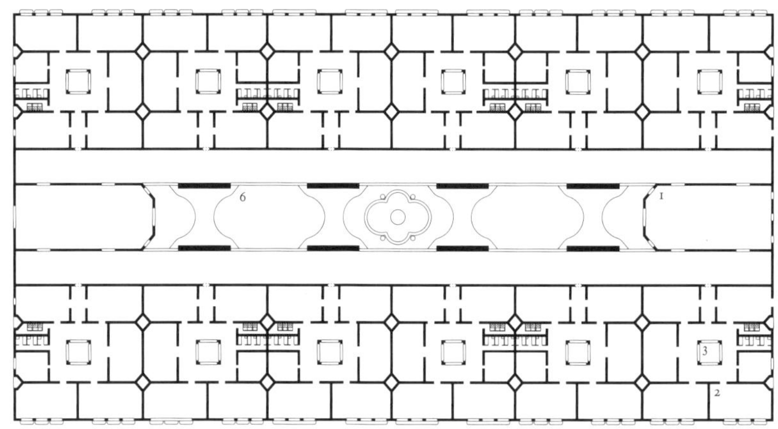

(47) Communal patio houses,
Topolobampo, Mexico, 1885, general plan
Marie S. Howland and Albert Kimsey Owen with architect John Deery (adapted from Albert Kimsey Owen, 1885)

(1) kitchen, (2) room, (3) patio, (4) bathing area, (5) toilets, (6) garden

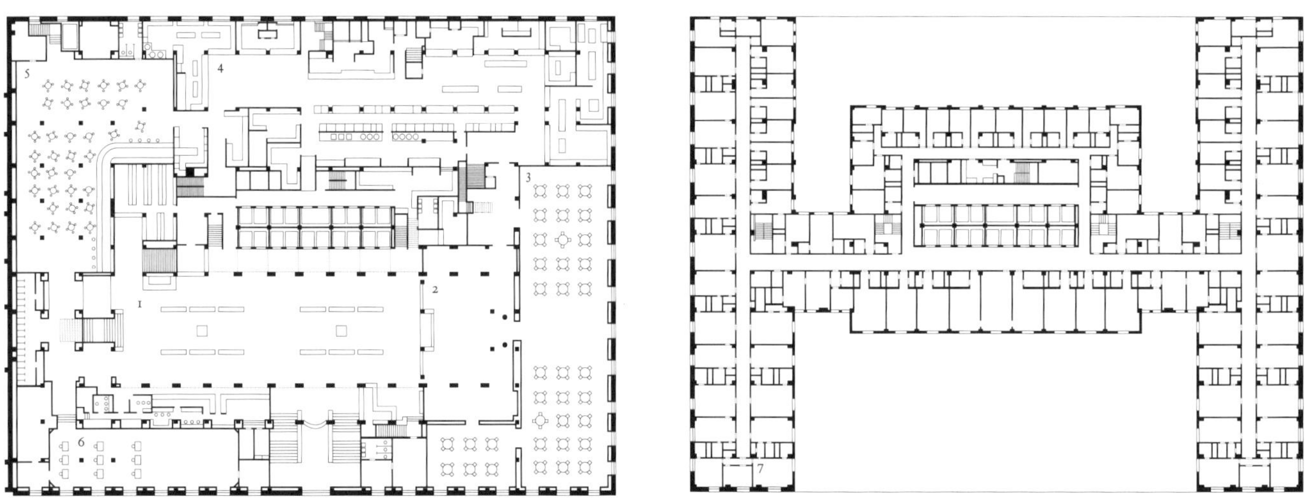

(48) Commodore Hotel,
New York, 1919, ground floor and typical floor
architects: Warren and Wetmore (adapted from Marson Korbi, 2020)

(1) lobby, (2) palm room, (3) restaurant, (4) kitchen, (5) men's bar, (6) men's writing room, (7) room

10 m

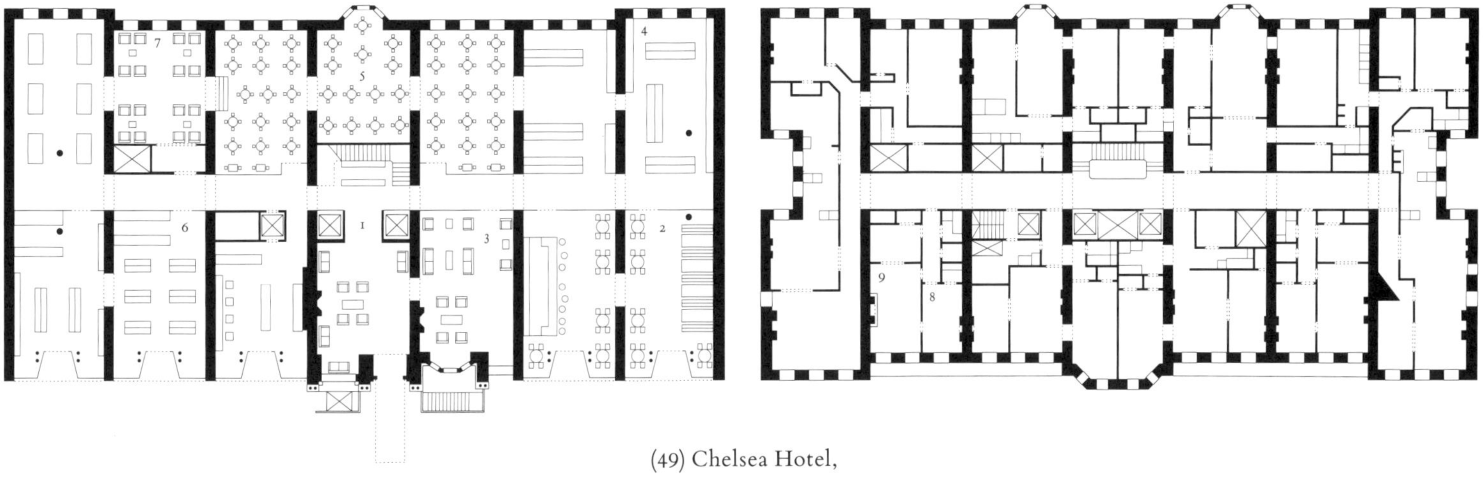

(49) Chelsea Hotel,
New York, 1883, ground floor and typical floor
architect: Philip G. Hubert (adapted from Philip G. Hubert, 1884)

(1) lobby, (2) cafe, (3) ladies' living room, (4) kitchen, (5) dining room, (6) shop, (7) restrooms, (8) chamber, (9) parlor

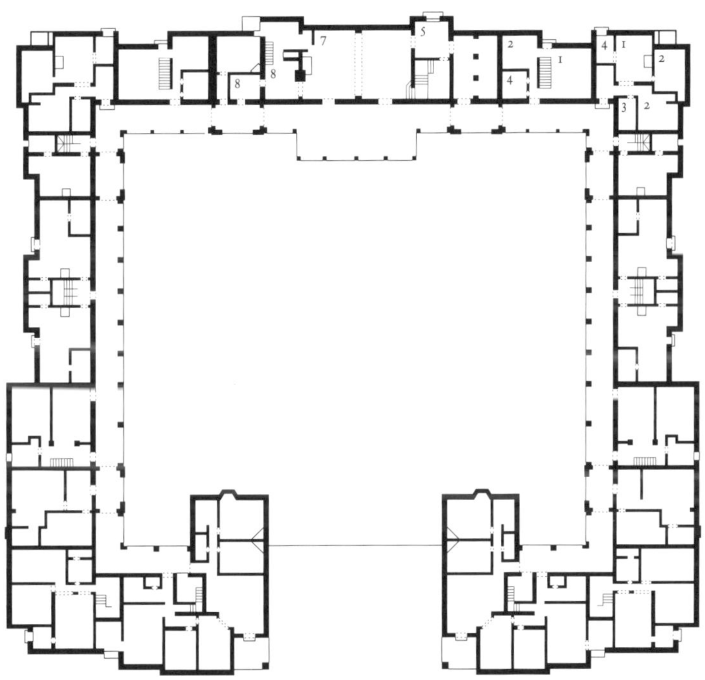

(50) Homesgarth Cooperative Quadrangle,
Letchworth, England, 1909
architect: Andrew Clapham Lander (adapted from Karen A. Franck, Sherry Ahrentzen, 1991)

(1) living room, (2) bedroom, (3) bathroom, (4) pantry, (5) hallway,
(6) lobby, (7) dining hall, (8) service room

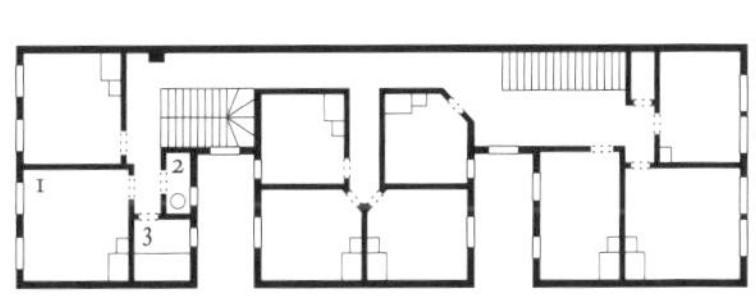

(51) Delta Hotel,
San Francisco, United States (adapted from Paul Groth, 1994)

(1) bedroom, (2) toilet, (3) bathroom

5 m

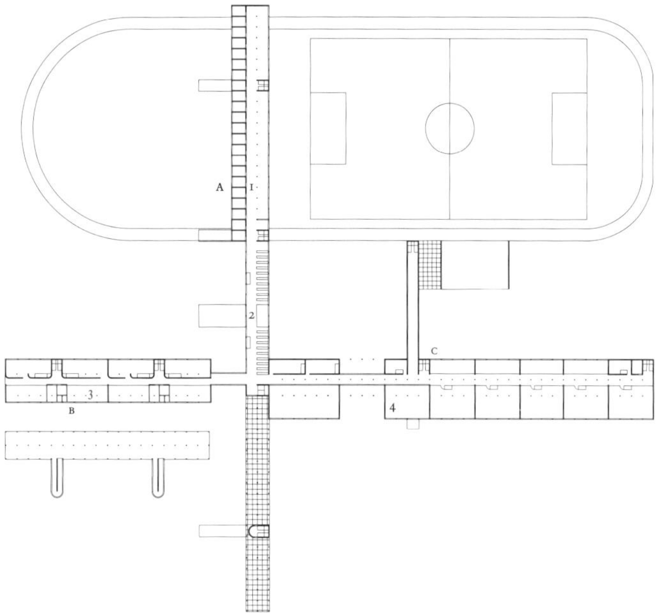

(A) adults' building, (1) reading, working, and resting room, (2) entrance hall with private lockers; (B) preschool children's building, (3) canteen; (C) children's building, (4) canteen for precooked food

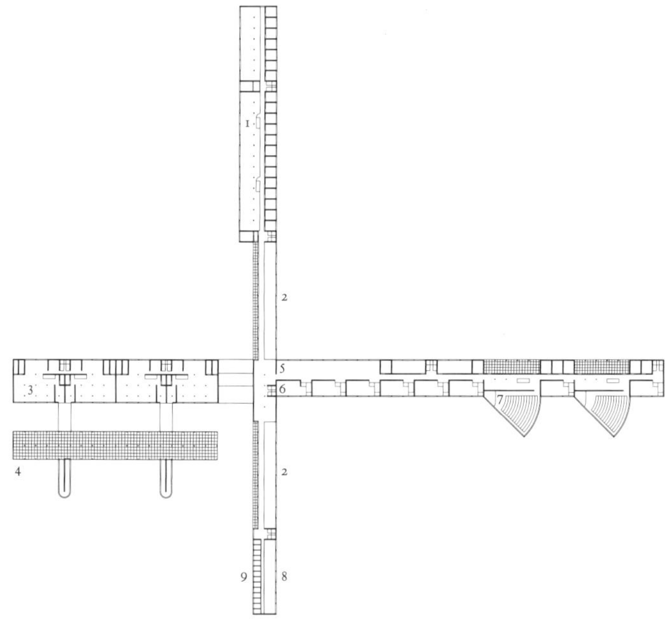

(1) reading, working, and resting room, (2) opening to the collective canteen, (3) kindergarten (<3 years old), (4) kindergarten (5–8 years old), (5) resting rooms, (6) bedrooms for children, (7) auditorium, (8) opening to the library, (9) individual reading rooms

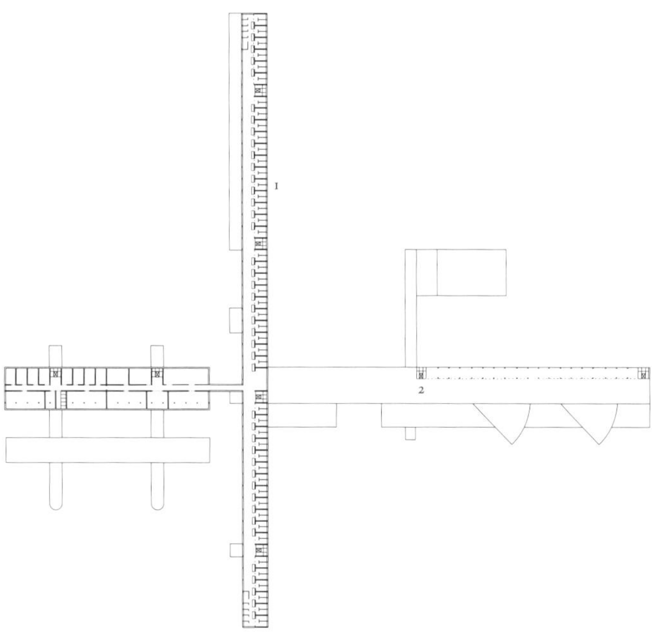

(1) single-person lodgings, (2) collective roof

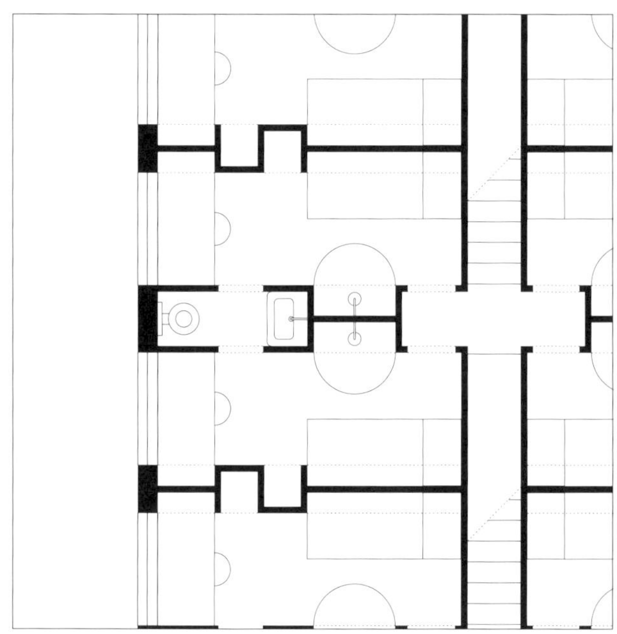

1 m

(52) Model for Dom-Kommuna,
1928–1930
architects: Mikhail Barshch, Vyacheslav Vladimirov
ground floor, fourth floor, and typical floor with single person's lodgings
(adapted from Moisei Ginzburg, 1934)

10 m

20 m

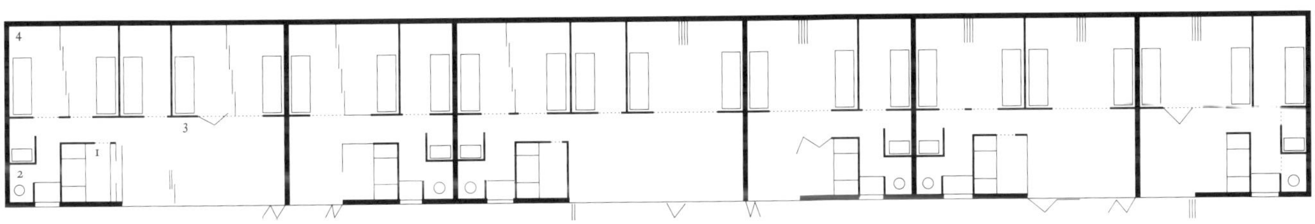

(1) kitchen, (2) toilet, (3) living room, (4) bedroom

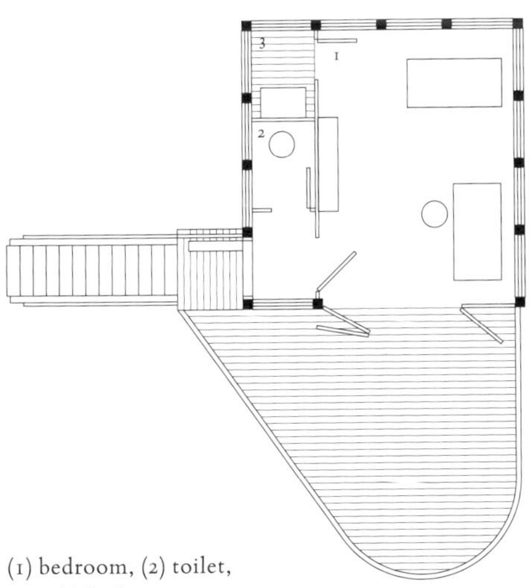

(1) bedroom, (2) toilet,
(3) bathroom

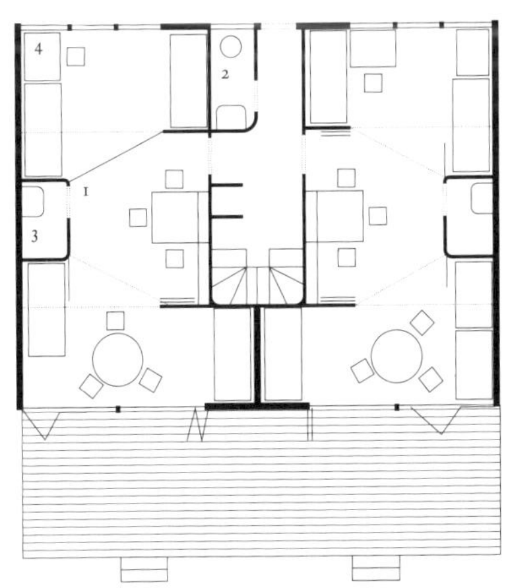

(1) common room, (2) toilet,
(3) bathroom, (4) room

(53) House for the State Planning Committee (GOSPLAN),
1929
architects: Moisei Ginzburg, OSA
general plan, block of family apartments, one-room unit, and hostel for married people
(adapted from Moisei Ginzburg, 1934)

2 m

In addition to the American residential hotel, another source of inspiration for Teige's interpretation of the minimum dwelling was the experiments in communal housing developed by Soviet architects in the 1920s.[102] Among these experiments, the most rigorous in elaborating a new model of collective housing based on the sharing of domestic facilities were the studies developed by the members of the OSA group led by architect Moisei Ginzburg. The work of this group, an account of which can be found in the pages of the journal *Sovremennaya Arkhitektura*, was the response to a more general concern with how to reorganize life in Soviet Russia in the aftermath of the Bolshevik revolution.[103] An important and unprecedented reform that took place in the early days of Soviet power was the 1918 Code on Marriage, the Family and Guardianship, which established absolute parity between men and women and introduced the possibility of divorce. Moreover, the militancy of feminist movements such as Zhenotdel, the section of the Russian Communist Party devoted to women's affairs, and Lev Trotsky's influential writings on everyday life were an important inspiration for Soviet architects who tried to reinvent domestic space by challenging the traditional notion of the household.[104] Above all, the abolition of private property and women's access to the workforce prompted many architects to think of the house no longer as an isolated compound, but as a system of communal facilities for the socialization and professionalization of domestic labor.

At first the OSA architects devoted themselves to the possibility of "supercollectivization," whose logic was based on granting everyone a small cell for rest while collectivizing everything else. An example of this tendency was the model for a Dom-Kommuna (communal house) proposed by OSA members Mikhail Barshch and Vyacheslav Vladimirov in 1928, in which an entire housing unit was organized as the crossing of two linear structures: one in the form of a high-rise slab containing the individual lodgings, and the other as a sequence of low-rise public services like libraries, auditoriums, workspaces, dining rooms, kitchens, and other facilities (figure 52). In this model, small cells of six square meters were arranged in such a way that two of them could easily be joined together to create larger bedrooms for couples. The housing complex was organized into different sectors, each of which was dedicated to a specific age group, so that single adults were separated from preschool and school-age children in an attempt to minimize the role of the family. This model of "supercollectivization" was strongly debated among OSA members since it raised questions about the stressful aspects of living together in large and concentrated "social condensers." In response to this concern, OSA members, especially under the influence of sociologist Mikhail Okhitovich, shifted their focus from compact to more dispersed housing arrangements such as in Ginzburg's proposal for a Green City (1930), a scheme that he proposed in several variations including a study for the GOSPLAN (State Planning Committee, figure 53). Green City offered Ginzburg the possibility of reducing the logic of "supercollectivization" to a more gradual condition that would allow residents to constantly negotiate their way of living together. The most important design move was to break down the logic of the Dom-Kommuna into one-person kitchenless units. Built in timber, these units were meant to be easily dismountable and moved according to the inhabitant's needs and desires, giving dwellers the choice to live either in relative isolation or within clusters. Because of the lack of kitchens, the one-person houses were not meant to be independent units. A system of communal facilities distributed at regular intervals along the infrastructure would serve the dispersed homes without the need to create dense settlements. Ginzburg's Green City represents one the most radical reinventions of domestic space ever attempted. It removed housing from both property and family, reducing it to its most generic condition, a personal and universal room served by collective amenities. Yet OSA's research on new housing models ended at the beginning of the 1930s because, in the words of Politburo member Lazar Kaganovich, "a communist city had existed since 1917 when the Bolsheviks took power," making clear that only the building of large quantities of housing units—and not the radical reform of domestic space—was the answer to the Russian housing question.[105] This approach to housing effectively ended any forms of typological experimentation, reducing the production of housing to a technical problem.

Criticism and rejection of nondomestic typologies became widespread also in the capitalist West. In the United States, authorities, state officials, and real estate entrepreneurs became hostile to the proliferation of nondomestic forms of living such as the residential hotel.[106] Its ubiquity and affordability could potentially diminish the appeal of family life and its architectural counterpart: the single-family house. Already at the beginning of the twentieth century, social reformers of the Progressive Era associated the proliferation of residential hotels with urban blight.[107] They assumed that a stable workforce and social peace could only be achieved by ensuring that both middle and working classes were rooted in their domestic abodes. In particular, the scholars affiliated with the influential department of sociology of the University of Chicago viewed single-room occupancy as a subversion of the distinction between private and public life and thus as a dissolution of the family for which the home—preferably the suburban home—was the only, inevitable template.[108] Often located downtown, residential hotels offered workers the possibility of living in close proximity to the workplace. This opportunity to mix living and working in the same district clashed with the rising imperative of zoning laws, whose main goal was to separate as much as possible home from work in order to reinforce the image of the home as a pastoral haven.[109] Above all, it was the modern state's obsession with private property and the conviction that anyone should own their own house that eradicated any alternative form of living.

THE RISE OF SOCIAL HOUSING

To understand the perpetual tension between paternalist control and a struggle toward emancipation, one can simply try to dissect the meaning of the term *social housing*. Anna Granath Hansson and Björn Lundgren argue that social housing is a "floating signifier," or in other words "a term with no agreed-upon meaning."[110] For them, it is precisely the vagueness of the term that leads to misunderstanding rather than a constructive dialogue about the advantages (or disadvantages) of such a system. While the Cambridge dictionary describes it as "homes provided by the government for people with low incomes to rent cheaply," a more recent definition provided by the European Federation of Public, Cooperative, and Social Housing describes it as "homes for rent or accession to ownership for which there are defined rules governing access to households with difficulties in finding housing."[111] The difference between these two definitions emphasizes how, in the course of the twentieth century, the meaning of social housing has shifted from state-funded homes to the broader category of affordable housing, in which the house is meant to be sold and bought on the market and thus privately owned. Moreover, the very meaning of affordable housing has proven to be elastic. If according to its original definition affordable meant that rent was commensurate to income, today affordability is measured in terms of market parameters, which means that affordable housing is actually expensive in cities marked by intense real estate speculation. The lack of definition of social housing reflects the very complex history of this kind of housing and the conceptual opaqueness of the term *social*. "The social" is a quintessentially modern category that addresses institutions concerned with the management, government, and reproduction of society and therefore positioned between the dimension of the public and that of the individual. According to Gilles Deleuze, "the social" can be considered a domain where desires, freedom, and forms of empowerment can be achieved, and yet at the same time a sphere where continuous control and enforcement is exerted by authorities.[112]

It is therefore clear why the sphere of "the social" emerged with the advent of industrialization and the rise of capitalism, when the problem of governing the population and its reproductive power became strictly interwoven with that of production and capital accumulation. In this historical context, housing became one of the fundamental institutions for governing the social. Dwelling was not only the space necessary to guarantee those acceptable living conditions needed for social reproduction, but also a perfect *dispositif* capable of taming its inhabitants by stimulating the aspiration toward respectable middle-class values. And yet in spite of many attempts by private parties to initiate projects of affordable homes for workers, the state was reluctant to directly intervene and build housing, in order to avoid upsetting the cornerstone of capitalist society which is property in the form of home (and especially land). Exemplary in this case is the predicament of England in the second half of the nineteenth century. In 1866, Parliament introduced the Sanitary Act, whose goal was to tame the overcrowding of workers' lodgings, as well as the Labouring Classes Dwelling Act, which allowed municipalities to borrow funds at preferential rate from the Public Works Loan Commissioner, thus establishing the first form of public "subsidy" for workers' housing.[113] The beneficiaries of these acts were the various private "model dwellings companies"—such as the Society for Improving the Conditions of the Labouring Classes for whom Henry Roberts provided his influential housing models—whose main goal was to build homes for workers for a rate of return. For this reason these companies were known as "Five per cent philanthropy," as they mixed social engagement with the possibility of profit. Among them, the Peabody Trust represents an interesting case. The Trust, a philanthropic venture founded in 1862 with its goal to "ameliorate the condition of the poor and needy of this great metropolis, and to promote their comfort and happiness," developed from the 1860s onward a series of housing blocks with small family apartments to be rented to respectable workers.[114] Between 1863 and 1885 the buildings of the Trust (which still functions today) were designed by Henry Astley Darbishire, whose austere approach would prove seminal in establishing a specific aesthetic for social housing. A remarkable aspect of Darbishire's Peabody housing projects is that they introduced for the first time in the history of social housing the archetype of the "estate," a coherently planned compound in which the blocks of houses are placed around semipublic open spaces. An example of this arrangement is the Peabody Housing Estate in Islington, completed in 1865, in which the housing blocks frame an introverted garden/courtyard. Irina Davidovici has argued that the building of social housing in the form of "estates" had both pragmatic and ideological motivations.[115] Because building large quantities of houses required considerable capital investment, grouping them into larger complexes and standardizing their features, from floor plans to façades, lowered construction costs and thus increased returns on the investment. Moreover the "compound form" of the estate was instrumental to a project of social control whose main goal was the strict separation between public and private space, which within the estate informed not only the privatization of the housing unit but also the separation between the open spaces of the estate and the public street. In terms of apartment layouts, Darbishire's Peabody housing units were far more rudimentary than the fully choreographed floor plans proposed by Henry Roberts. Unlike Roberts's Model House for Four Families, Darbishire's houses had both shared bathrooms and sculleries at each floor. And yet, if we compare the several estates designed by Darbishire, we can notice an effort to optimize the individuation of each housing unit by replacing long corridors—such as those of Islington Estate—with a more compact core of vertical circulation and communal services proposed at Blackfriars Road. Such design choices were motivated by the Trust's ambition to not simply shelter workers, but also educate them to the appreciation of privacy. This goal was reflected by the selective criteria of eligibility applied to those who who lived in these estates. The Trust stipulated that, in order to have access to a Peabody unit, workers had to be married and have a steady income, thus limiting the offer to the "respectable poor," which, unsurprisingly, had always represented the ideal subject of charitable housing.[116]

In the history of social housing, the "invention" of the nuclear family looms large. The idea of the family, which as a legal concept seldom existed before the nineteenth century, especially among the poor and peasants, was promoted by European nation-states like France and England as a way of giving moral and economic order to the domestic life of the low-income classes.[117] With the help of state legislation, capitalism spread family values from the bourgeoisie to the working class, encouraging women to stay at home in order to breed the next generation of workers.[118] It was precisely this tendency to individuate the nuclear family that prompted social reformers to conceive of the home as a pedagogical device aimed at "civilizing" the habits of the workers and their families.

Such a goal appeared extremely urgent to the French bourgeoisie in the aftermath of the Paris Commune of 1871, an event that made clear the need to tackle the question of housing for the working class. Some conservative politicians and entrepreneurs introduced, for example, the model of the *Cité Ouvrière*, whose initial form as proto-garden suburb was inspired by the workers' housing built in 1853 in Mulhouse by industrialist Jules Dollfus. A remarkable example of this model of social housing was the workers' houses built in Passy-Auteuil in Paris (1880) based on small villas of four rooms that had to be paid for over a period of twenty years (figure 54). The payment for the house over a long period of time was also instrumental in enforcing strategies of control and confirming established power relations, given that an unruly lifestyle could easily lead to the tenants' eviction.[119] Yet, as in England, these early forms of social housing proved impractical because their speculative character made them unaffordable to the majority of workers.[120]

It was in light of this problem that social reformers such as those gathered in the powerful think tank Musée Sociale promoted the law on *habitations à bon marché*, promulgated in 1894.[121] The main goal of this law was to make credit available to construction societies in order to favor low-cost housing with tax exemptions. In the intentions of its promoters, the law on affordable housing would ultimately favor property over tenancy, since homeownership was identified as a barrier against the threat of collectivist ideals, as well as a cure for the workers' "immoral" behaviors. Jules Sigfried, a key member of the Musée Sociale and promoter of the *habitations à bon marché* law, rhetorically asked: "Do you want to create, at the same time, contented men who are true conservatives; do you want simultaneously to combat misery and socialist errors; do you want to increase the guarantees of order, of morality, of political and social moderation? Then let us create workers' housing!"[122]

Both the English "model dwellings" and the French *habitations à bon marché* were based on a mix of speculation and social utility whose goal was to accommodate workers without disrupting the housing market. Yet this model proved insufficient to confront the "slumification" of large industrial cities, because it was detached from any overreaching planning strategy; in particular, the model did not tackle land use, which proved to be the major obstacle in cities where speculation was rampant. It was precisely the impossibility of advancing any large-scale housing reform that finally convinced the more advanced sectors of the liberal bourgeoisie—such as the Fabian Society in England or the Musée Sociale in France—that the provision of housing for workers could only be advanced through comprehensive planning policies. This was the motivation behind the Local Government Act promulgated in 1888 by the English Parliament, which established county councils in England and Wales. Among them was the London County Council, which represented the first metropolitan-wide municipal authority in matters of planning and housing. The first housing estate built by the LCC was the Boundary Estate in East London, planned by the architect Owen Fleming and completed in 1900; with its orderly urban form anchored to a central monumental circus, the Estate shows what scale and level of coordination could be achieved if housing was no longer left to philanthropic enterprises but rather promoted by the planning authority of municipalities that had power to acquire large portions of land.

In this approach to housing, planning played an important role. Such an attitude was especially evident in the Netherlands, one of the earliest countries in Europe to directly engage with the problem of housing. In 1901 the *Woningwet* housing act was approved by the Liberal government, under the pressure of the Social Democratic Party. The act introduced for the first time in history the concept of *sociale woningbouw* (social housing), and it aimed at providing financial support to housing associations whose purpose was exclusively to build homes for workers.[123] The *Woningwet* was a comprehensive policy that addressed the project of housing by focusing on all aspects of its production, from land acquisition to construction. It forced municipalities to establish regulations for newly built houses; city extensions would thus be governed by precise regulatory frameworks. It is in this context that Hendrik Petrus Berlage was able to plan the extension of Amsterdam Zuid in 1914 as a comprehensive urban scheme in which social housing is the protagonist. Defined by Berlage as *stedebouw* (city building), this approach combined architecture and planning as one project that translated building regulations into a legible morphology made of coherently planned blocks and generous green spaces. The most significant result of this planning effort was De Dageraad housing complex designed by Michel De Klerk and Piet Kramer and completed in 1922, which, with its orderly composition of blocks of different shape and size, represents one of the finest examples of social housing ever built. In examples like these we see the attempt to conceive social housing no longer as an enclave strictly separated from the city as in the case of the Peabody housing estates, or as individual housing blocks as in the case of affordable housing built under the *habitations à bon marché* law. The comprehensive legislation of the *Woningwet* made social housing the main fabric of the city.

Beside planning and construction, the *Woningwet* also empowered the state to provide strict guidelines in terms of housing typologies through the Dutch Housing Institute (figure 55).[124] Against the rather loose types of speculative tenement houses within which the use of rooms was flexible, the Institute promoted residential typologies bespoke to the nuclear family and carefully subdivided into rooms devoted to specific functions and gender roles. In the intentions of the Institute, the plans were meant not only to individuate the nuclear family, but also to encourage petit bourgeois habits such as a sense of ownership of the house in spite of the renting status of the flats.

This approach to housing became a generalized tendency, because the tacit goal of twentieth-century liberal democracies was to build a society of homeowners, and social housing was conceived as an introduction to homeownership. The implicitly conservative character of social housing was especially evident in the way many modern architects accepted the gendered organization of the family home. It is therefore not surprising that in a sketch of the Immeuble Wanner in Geneva (1928–1929), an application of the concept of the Immeubles-Villas of 1923–1925, Le Corbusier portrays a man "dressed in trunks and tank

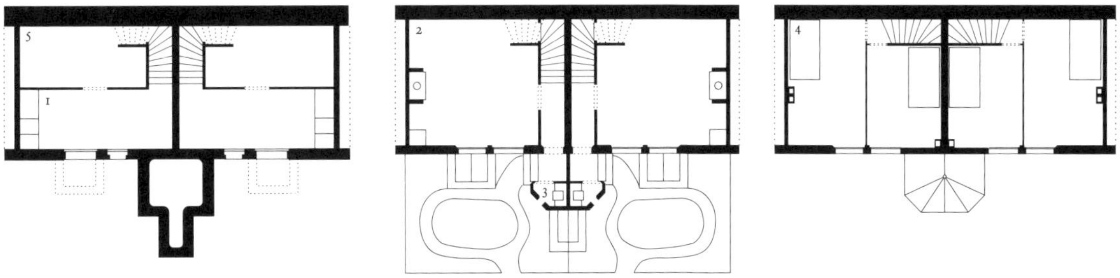

(54) House for a family,
Passy-Auteuil, Paris, 1880, plan
architect: E. Cacheux
(adapted from Roger H. Guerrand, 1967)

(1) kitchen, (2) common room, (3) toilet, (4) bedroom, (5) storage

(55) Examples of preferred dwelling types in Amsterdam:
H. P. Berlage, Algemeene Woningbouw Vereeniging, Tolstraat, 1912; Michel de Klerk, Eigen Haard, Zaanstraat, 1918; J. C. van Epen, Algemeene Woningbouw Vereeniging, 1915
(adapted from Nancy Stieber, 1998)

(1) kitchen, (2) toilet, (3) bedroom, (4) living room

(56) Basic small house plan,
United States
(adapted from National Housing Agency, 1946)

(1) kitchen, (2) bathroom, (3) bedroom, (4) living room

(57) Skivhus housing block,
Miljonprogrammet, Sweden, 1965–1974, typical plan
(adapted from Olle Stigenäs and Fredrik Gilck, 2011)

(1) kitchen, (2) living room, (3) toilet, (4) bedroom, (5) storage

2 m

top pounding a punching bag placed in a *jardin-suspendu*" and a woman watching on a balcony with her hands resting on a railing on which a blanket hangs—"as much a symbol for her as the punching bag for him"[125]—thus revealing how gender roles were traditionally understood and how the social agenda of domestic space was geared toward the avoidance of political and gender conflict.

After the Second World War, under the pressure of a strong working-class movement on the verge of uprising, Western states decided to embark on large public housing programs that were influenced by the ideas developed in the first half of the twentieth century. It is for this reason that the national housing systems that emerged after the Second World War had a partially decommodified character. Housing was established as a right for workers, yet the right to housing was granted by the state to ensure a tight relationship between production and reproduction, effectively privatizing reproduction as the housewife's duty. Additionally, the deployment of a very limited number of types, all variations of the family apartment, became the instrument to promote the idea and the culture of a privately owned domestic space. A clear example of this is the Miljonprogrammet, an ambitious public housing program implemented in Sweden between 1965 and 1974 by the Social Democratic government, aiming at building one million units in ten years. Despite the overall quantitative ambition, architecturally this project was dominated by a few types, among them the three-room apartment—an updated version of the Henry Roberts model, still informed by the same gender and social connotations (figure 57).

It was precisely the rendering of the housewife's work as a "labor of love" that was radically contested in Europe and the United States during the 1970s by a group of feminists who demanded wages for housework.[126] In doing so, these activists wanted to make explicit how domestic labor was an essential element in capital's extraction of surplus value. For thinkers such as Selma James and Mariarosa Dalla Costa, the institution of the family is the main link between capitalistic production and work at home, since it brings together waged workers with unwaged workers such as the unemployed, the old, the children, the ill, and housewives. In this way, the home functions as a distributive mechanism through which wages extend from the wage earner to all those who are underwaged, not yet waged, or no longer waged. As Kathi Weeks has observed, the house thus functions as a "privatizing machine of social reproduction"[127] that allows workers outside of the home to endure longer hours of work for lower wages.

When social housing began to be privatized by the state as home property in the 1980s, the privatizing ethos of the house was already encoded in these enclosed households built as social housing. The privatizing logic of housing was thus the premise—and not just the consequence—of the commodification of housing that happened with the crisis of the welfare state.

HYPERCOMMODIFICATION

The core of postwar welfare programs was the building of large quantities of public housing. As mentioned earlier, the production of housing has to be understood as the product not of a benevolent state, but of the struggle between workers and capital which reached its peak of intensity in both Europe and the United States during the "glorious thirty" (1945–1975). Following war mobilization and subsequent reconstruction, the demands of a mature and well-organized workers' movement prompted states to invest in public housing as a way to maintain and control a reliable workforce. Yet while the working class's bargaining for social rights was thriving, liberal democratic states in the West were already planning to counter this tendency by gradually privatizing housing through easy access to credit and the consequent "democratization" of private ownership. Even before British Prime Minister Margaret Thatcher's "right to buy" policy was introduced in 1979, many European governments began to wonder if renting a home for life was a desirable prospect for working-class dwellers. With the growth of workers' purchasing power, state policymakers understood that the real estate market could provide a more convenient way to produce housing for the majority of the population. This approach was already anticipated by the federal government of the United States in the aftermath of the Great Depression. As the purchasing power of working- and middle-class consumers had collapsed, the government boosted demand for housing by introducing the standardized mortgage. In this way the state encouraged widespread homeownership by easing credit to (white) workers' families. It is in this context that the suburban home became the most desirable form of housing.

An interesting example of how the federal state backed market-driven construction of suburban homes is the typical plan for a small suburban cottage drafted by the National Housing Agency in 1946 (figure 56). Given to private developers as a design guideline, the plan encapsulates all the tropes of suburban dwelling such as the increasing number of bedrooms, abundance of closets, storage, and a large kitchen. The standardized mortgage was designed by policymakers as a way to allow workers to aspire to better homes while forcing them to take on debt, and thus forcing their reliance on a steady job. This predicament reveals the original "ascetic" purpose of the mortgage as the making of the indebted worker, who has no choice but to work in order to repay their debt and sustain their family's consumerist lifestyle. This is why the spreading of consumer culture, partly encouraged by the welfare state, has to be understood within the logic of mortgage and debt. Only by making workers aspire to more—such as a larger house—would their dependence on steady work be enforced. It was for this reason that, from the 1970s onward, liberal democratic states empowered the real estate market to take control of the production of housing, by initiating a gradual process of hypercommodification in which homes were produced not just for dwelling but also—and especially—as commodities to be sold and bought. In a context of hypercommodification, the use value of the house, its capacity to support a decent and desired form of dwelling, is replaced by the house's exchange value, its capacity to appeal to investors and developers as a financial asset. The role of the house as commodity was solidified by new forms of loan in which batches of individual mortgages were sold to investors as a mortgage-backed security, as in the Federal Home Loan Mortgage Corporation launched in the United States in

(58) Wohnsiedlung Rautistrasse,
Zurich, 2005, typical plan
architect: Frei Gubler Architekten

(1) kitchen, (2) dining room, (3) living room, (4) toilet, (5) bathroom, (6) bedroom, (7) storage

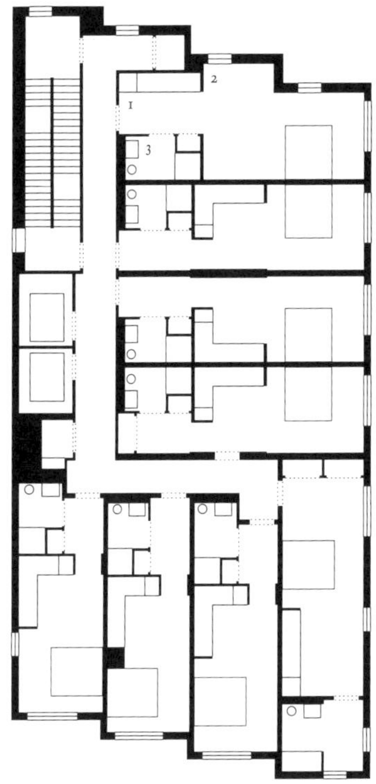

(59) Carmel Place,
New York City, 2013–2016, typical plan
architect: nArchitects

(1) kitchen, (2) studio, (3) bathroom

5 m

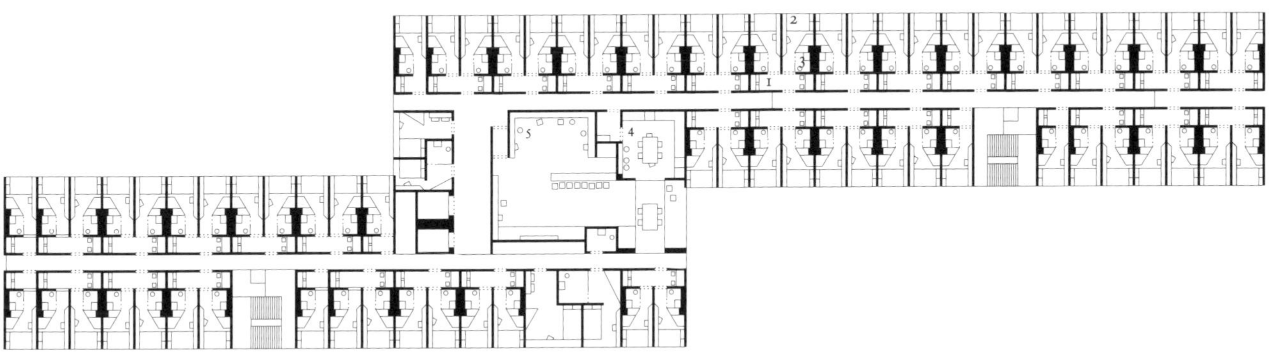

(60) Old Oak building,
The Collective, London, 2016, typical plan
architect: Whittam Cox Architects

(1) kitchenette, (2) studio, (3) bathroom, (4) kitchen, (5) common room

10 m

1970. Once under such condition of financialization, the home's most profitable value was its location, determined by proximity to social and symbolic capital. To this day, land is considered by banks as the best collateral for credit, and, on average, 70 percent of the cost of a house is the price of land. On top of this, in the last decades many states have sold their public land to private companies and investors, thus drastically reducing their ability to build housing at a low price.

The commodification of housing also had repercussions on the form of the house. For example, to sustain their aspirational role as commodity, housing units must appear as diverse as possible. Rooms with odd shapes, façades with uneven fenestrations and distribution of balconies have become frequent formal tropes of contemporary housing. This tendency is very visible in the *Grundrissfibel*, an influential handbook of housing plans produced in Switzerland between 1999 and 2012.[128] Most of the housing plans illustrated in the handbook belong to private or subsidized homes. The handbook offers an indicative snapshot of housing typologies during neoliberal times. Despite the overwhelming formal diversity of homes presented, all housing units refer to self-contained family households (figure 58). Some are larger, some are smaller, yet they are all diligently subdivided into different rooms which clearly spell out their functions: living room, bedroom, etc. Housing today comes as a vast assortment of formal variations, but typological aspects such as the number of rooms and the possibility of sharing services like extra bedrooms for assisted living or kitchens are rarely challenged. This situation responds to the commodity status of the home in which aspiration to own a *proper* house plays a fundamental role in forcing dwellers to commit to a mortgage. The commodity status of the home became extreme with the rise of luxury housing typologies, from the megavilla to the pencil tower. Here, the primacy of the house's exchange value over its use value is manifested by the fact that these are most often used as secondary homes and/or financial assets for investors' portfolios. Their formal qualities, sumptuous materials, and commanding views over the city are meant to be consumed as an image, since very little or no dwelling happens in them.

Another significant symptom of the hypercommodification of housing is the emergence of nonfamily housing typologies such as co-living. In recent years, in cities like London, New York, and San Francisco, where land and housing prices are very high, home property based on mortgage is no longer affordable for the middle class and rent is again the most profitable form of housing speculation. This condition especially affects the younger generations, whose budget and increasingly precarious existence do not allow them to afford mortgages. This new wave of housing for rent has dramatically reduced unit size to the bare minimum. Private companies specialized in renting rooms, such as WeLive and The Collective, offer accommodations that essentially replicate those of the old commercial residential hotels, but, unlike the latter, are pumped with an overdose of rhetoric about living collectively. One of the first built co-living developments is Old Oak, created by The Collective (figure 60). Located in London's zone 3, in a site characterized by warehouses and low-rise housing, the ten-story building is organized in two parallel slabs of small rooms on top of shared facilities. Typologically, each two adjacent rooms share a small kitchenette located in a windowless room between the circulation space and the room. As calculated by Federico Coricelli, the rental cost of such units is over 50 percent of the average income, far above the traditional 30 percent generally considered to be an affordable rent.[129] Given the high prices, it is clear that companies such as The Collective target young professionals, the much celebrated (and much exploited) "millennials," while they exclude people in most urgent need of these types of dwellings, such as elderly people and people with disabilities.

In recent years, austerity policies and increasing precarity of life are challenging the family's role as cornerstone of society. As Melinda Cooper emphasizes, the family was central to neoliberal arguments against public investment and education, and key to their proposal for a new economic order powered by private investment and household debt.[130] Yet the recent wave of austerity measures introduced by governments since the 2007–2008 recession has seriously endangered the formation of families among new generations. This situation has convinced developers and city authorities in many North American and European cities to drastically reduce the size of apartments to accommodate singles, couples, or couples with one child. An extreme example of this type of housing in which small apartment size is the direct result of land costs is the microflats housing at Carmel Place in New York, designed by nArchitects in 2013 (figure 59). The architects responded to the need for affordable housing by devising small, completely self-sufficient dwelling units, each containing bathroom, kitchen, and a murphy bed which neatly converts the living room into a bedroom. The architects even conceived custom built-in furniture to minimize the apartment footprint while providing the inhabitant(s) with a fully equipped flat. Despite its modest size, the microflat presents itself as a compressed version of the single-family house, containing the same conventional set of spaces—bedroom, living room, kitchen, bathroom. Even within the extreme conditions of a microflat, the legacy of the family household is still very strong, and it informs the conviction that each housing unit, no matter how small, has to remain self-sufficient and thus still a private home.

LIVE/WORK

The history of commodification of housing is perfectly embodied by one of the most controversial types of housing to emerge in the last fifty years: the so-called "live/work." This type refers to an accommodation that combines living and working spaces within the same unit. Its historical trajectory from cheap lodgings for artisans and artists to luxury apartments to speculative studio-flats is a cautionary tale of the way even the most precarious form of habitation can be turned into expensive commodity.

The diffusion of the live/work type is directly linked to the emergence of freelance work and small-scale companies whose spatial premises do not fit into traditional workspaces such as the factory and the office. By combining living and working into superimposed floors, or in the same space, the live/work type seems to echo the medieval townhouse in which production and reproduction unfolded side by side. Until the eighteenth century, the textile industry in England was still a cottage industry, as many workers from this sector—both in cities and the countryside—worked from home. In her important study on "work-home," Frances Hollis described the district of Spitalfields in London, a major global center of the textile industry which was populated by large and complex work-homes.[131] Built by rich master weavers, these work-homes included an extensively glazed loom-shop on the top of the master's houses, which were initially built as dwellings with a shop on the ground-floor; most probably, apprentices slept in the loom-shop and ate with the servants of the house. As Hollis argues, however, the noise and dirt of the productive space made these work-homes increasingly impractical. And yet work-homes survived also after the Industrial Revolution as hybrids between home-based and factory-based work, as in the case of a Coventry terrace, where a single shaft from a common steam engine ran through the attic workshops belonging to different households. As noted by Hollis, this arrangement proved very convenient for the workers' families as it gave them both autonomy in combining paid work, domestic work and child care, as well as a sense of solidarity and community across households.[132] With the intensification of mass production and zoning laws that separated residential and industrial districts, home-work became either the privilege of highly skilled craftsmen like watchmakers, or a form of family-run business such as the Italian *capannone*, a small manufacturing shed attached to a single or multifamily detached home.[133]

But the direct progenitor of the contemporary live/work type is the "studio," a purpose-built space for artists who lived and worked within the same premises. As argued by Elena Palacios Carral, the artist studio space addresses a type of living and working space that is distinctively different from the traditional artist or artisan workshop (the Italian *bottega* or the French *atelier*), because from the beginning it addressed the artist no longer as employer of collaborators or apprentices, but as individual worker.[134] The artist studio is thus linked to the rise of freelance work in which self-employed individuals often work in their home. Between the eighteenth and nineteenth centuries, first in Europe and later in the rest of the world, the traditional master artist was replaced by the freelance artist, disenfranchised from any form of guild structure, and when this type of artist became widespread in cities like Paris, London, and Berlin, developers started to build studio spaces targeted to this specific subject. A remarkable example of this type of habitation is the St. Paul Studios on Talgarth Road in London, which were designed by Frederick Wheeler in 1890. Each unit included a large double-height space lit by a generous window and placed on top of two floors of living space, which included a reception room where the artist could receive customers as well as a basement for the kitchen and the housekeeper's room. A more economical example of studio space for artists was those built on the north side of Pembroke Garden in London by speculator Charles Frederick Kearley around 1890 (figure 62). Compared to the St. Paul studios, the Pembroke studios were conceived for moderate- or low-income artists. This status is reflected in their modest scale and in the fact that living space is reduced to the mezzanine and a small bedroom, so that the workspace becomes the main program of the house. Moreover, they were conceived for a bachelor artist, thus reinforcing the bohemian stereotype of the artist detached not only from any form of professional association, but also from any form of family relationship. The artist studio as live/work accommodation inaugurated a precarious and radically individualized form of living and working that would become widespread with the rise of the post-Fordist mode of production of more recent times.

In some cases, purpose-built artists' studios were created as cooperative premises in which artists could share domestic equipment like kitchen, bathrooms, storage, and exhibition space. An interesting New York example is Tenth Street Studio Building, commissioned in 1857 by merchant John Johnston and designed by Richard Morris Hunt (figure 61). Tenth Street Studio Building can be considered the earliest living and working space designed exclusively for the needs of fine art artists. This cooperative studio space—which helped to establish Greenwich Village's reputation as an art district—was designed in order to balance a generous space for each artist and a spacious gallery. When the building was at risk of being taken over by the market, a group of artists pooled their resources to purchase it and make it a cooperative in which residents could rent their accommodation at moderate price. And yet purpose-built artist studios, especially when built by commercial developers, proved to be expensive even when they were meant to cater to low- or moderate-income tenants. A major obstacle for affordable live/work spaces is real estate's commodification of housing, which has made generous living and working space impossible in many cities. However, perhaps an even bigger issue is restrictive zoning laws, which, in the course of the twentieth century, have made the coexistence of residence and workplace all but impossible. In this regard, a very interesting type of live/work space, which in its initial declensions offered cheap accommodation to artists and challenged the separation of home and workspace, was the loft. This type of live/work consists of one large industrial space with minimal partitioning, and although it is a distinctively New York invention it has quickly become a model for live/work worldwide.[135] Ironically, the origins of the loft are rooted in the effort by the authorities of New York City to ban homework in the garment industry, a condition which was widespread in nineteenth-century Lower Manhattan. The so-called "sweatshops," in which entire families were involved in working activities related to garment manufacture, were hosted in overcrowded tenement houses. When this arrangement became not only unsanitary but also negative for profit, city administration pushed entrepreneurs to separate home from work, and it was for this reason that they built small manufacturing spaces which were bigger than houses but smaller than factories. Conceived as stacks of unobstructed spaces, lofts were truly "vertical factories" served by the first electric-powered elevators. Starting in the 1930s, under the pressure of more restrictive zoning laws productive activities migrated to the suburbs, leaving an abundant quantity of loft spaces vacant. From the 1950s, many artists began to rent lofts, and soon these stacked "shoeboxes" proved to be cheap and suitable not only for

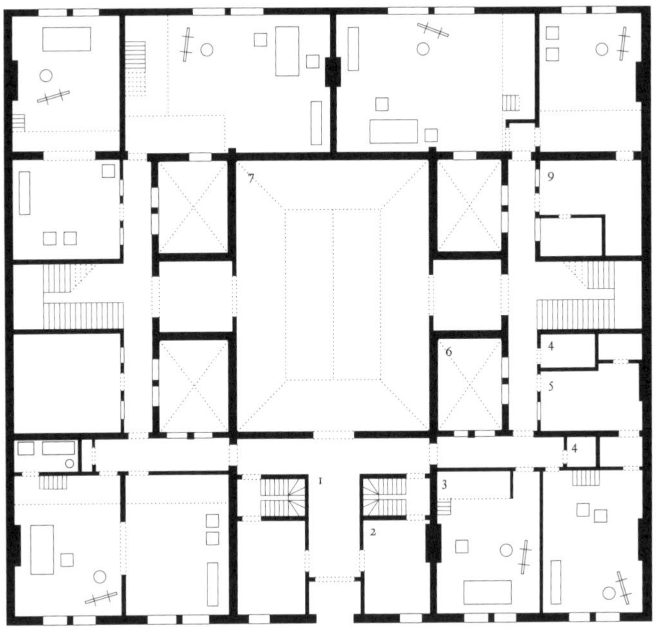

(61) Tenth Street Studio Building,
New York, 1857, plan
(adapted from Annette Blaugrund, 1997)

(1) hallway, (2) small duplex apartment, (3) studio, (4) toilet, (5) bathroom, (6) court, (7) exhibition hall, (8) concierge, (9) foyer

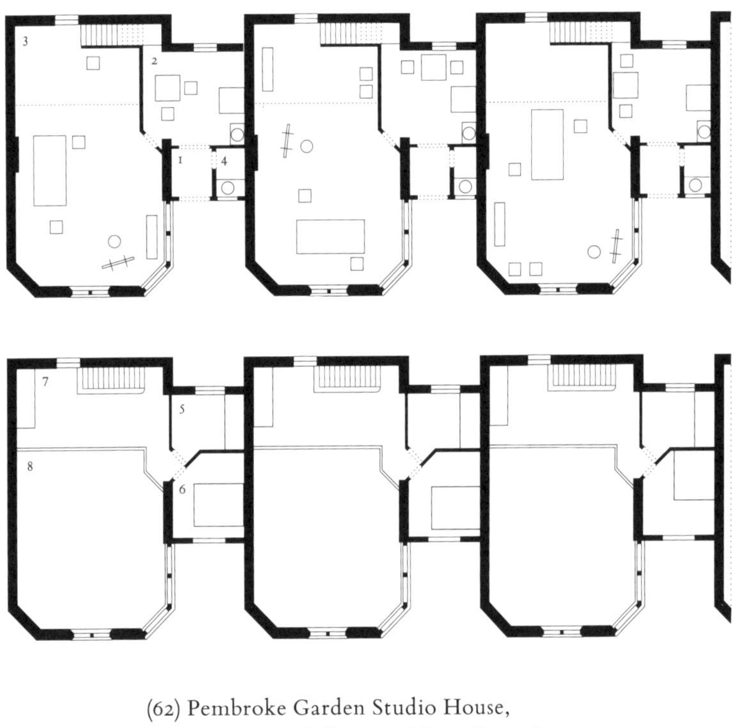

(62) Pembroke Garden Studio House,
London, 1890s, ground-floor and first-floor plans
builder: C. F. Kearley
(adapted from Hermione Hobhouse, 1986)

(1) hallway, (2) kitchen, (3) workspace, (4) toilet, (5) bathroom, (6) single bedroom, (7) balcony, (8) double height

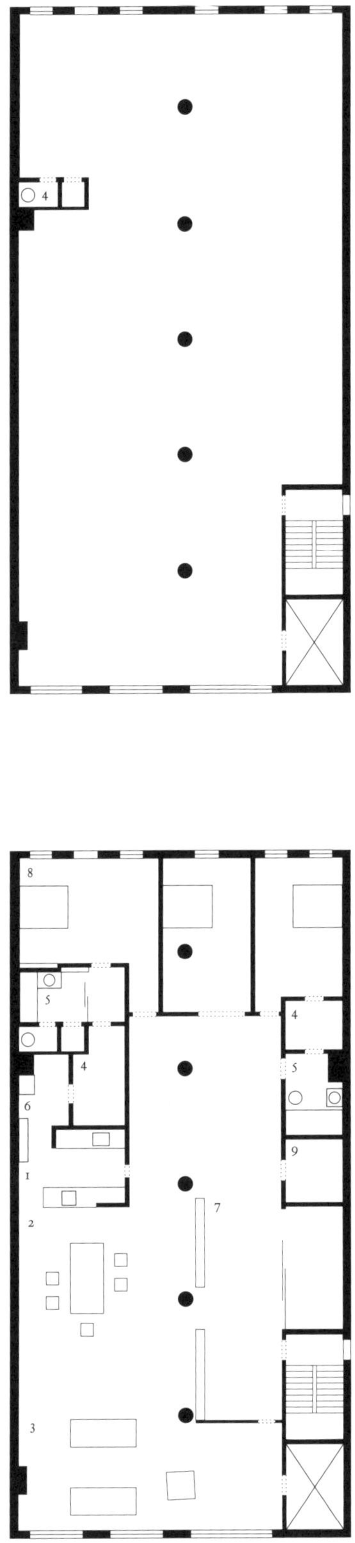

(63) 481 Greenwich Street Apartment 3B,
New York, early 1900s,
original floor plan (above) and
transformation into a luxury apartment, 1980s

(1) kitchen, (2) dining room, (3) living room, (4) toilet, (5) bathroom, (6) laundry, (7) library, (8) bedroom, (9) storage

2 m

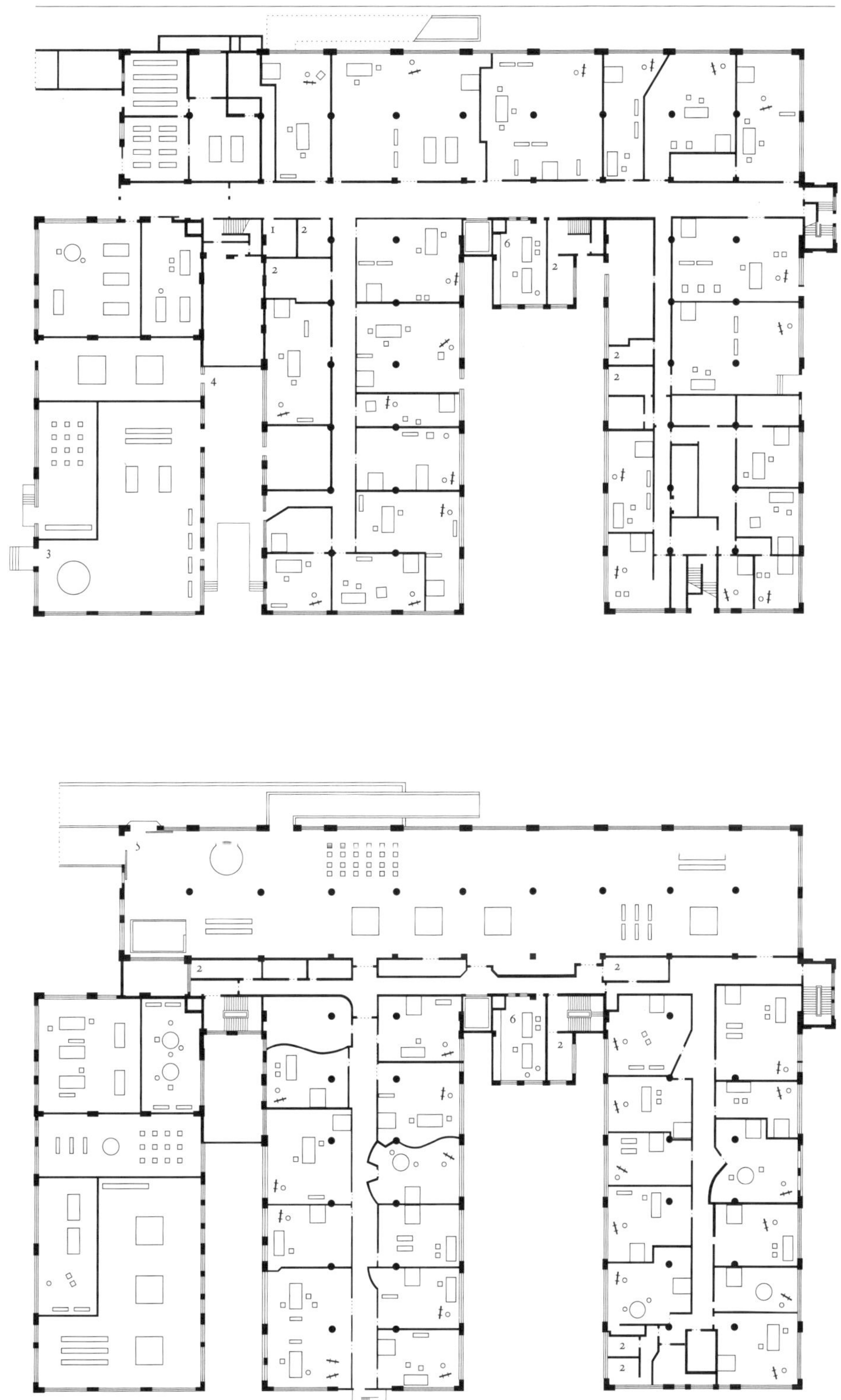

(64) Project Artaud,
San Francisco, 1971, ground-floor and first-floor plan
architects: Berline & Associates

(1) tool room, (2) toilet, (3) gallery, (4) open courtyard, (5) performance space, (6) kitchen

5 m

working but also for living. The artists' appropriation of the loft as space for both living and working can be considered the first reuse of an industrial structure, pioneering what would become a dominant trope of postindustrial metropolises.

The empty and generous floor plan offered an unscripted space: artists' appropriation of lofts coincided with the rise of new forms of art that transcended the customary differences between painting, sculpture, and performance, and the loft became the ideal space for unbound experimentation. The lack of partitioning made the loft a space in which life and work, production and reproduction, work and "no-work" blended completely, as is evident in the iconic images of 1960s lofts such as those of Robert Rauschenberg and Frank Stella. Yet to live in a loft was against the law until 1964 when an artist-led initiative pleaded with the city to legalize loft living. The approval of this initiative by city authorities backfired, ultimately harming the artists' condition by opening the doors to market speculation. While the legalization process proved lengthy and complicated for artists, it became a fast track for real estate speculators who made loft living a new form of luxury accommodation, turning it into a successful model for high-end residential renovation. It is interesting to note that, once appropriated as luxury living, the spatial arrangement of lofts changed to adapt to more traditional domestic space. This is visible in a loft space on Greenwich Street which was transformed into a high-end residence in the 1980s, at the time of the golden age of real estate conquest of Soho (figure 63). Here the unobstructed space of the loft was subdivided into a three-bedroom apartment with a large living space whose function was to represent the idea of loft living, even though the space was no longer used as art workspace. In this and similar cases, live/work became just a legal loophole that allowed developers to convert industrial buildings into expensive homes. The same story of grassroots appropriation which inadvertently opens up market speculation happened in other cities like San Francisco, where the legalization of live/work spaces was advocated by artists; once achieved in 1988, it became a notorious trick for developers to buy and transform cheap industrial buildings into residential development, as in the case of the Clocktower condos, a former industrial building turned into expensive live/work loft apartments. This type of conversion became especially lucrative with the dot-com boom of the 1990s, when "loft living" became appealing to a wider high-end market: between 1997 and 2000 there were more than 1,400 conversions in the city.[136] At this point it became fully evident that live/work spaces were no longer built or inhabited by artists, but by anyone who could afford these spaces. Due to the lack of clarity on the extent to which the inhabitant of the live/work must engage with the "arts," and on what is work in the live/work space, the San Francisco Planning Department arrived at the conclusion that enforcing these definitions was not possible. This lack of clarity led not only to the appropriation of the live/work typology by the speculative market, but also to the overproduction of spaces whose residential character was ambiguous. For this reason, in the last twenty years many live/works in San Francisco have been transformed into office spaces. These shortcomings pushed the San Francisco Board of Supervisors to adopt a temporary moratorium on construction of live/work space in 2001.

It is interesting to note that, in San Francisco, the legalization of live/work spaces was the result of artists' advocacy, and specifically of one successful grassroots initiative which was the transformation of a 1920s tooling factory for the American Can Company into an artists' live/work communal house.[137] Known as Project Artaud (figure 64), it was initiated by artist John Krysiak, who rented the factory and soon involved a group of colleagues in the renovation process. The artists formed a cooperative and, with a loan from the city, they bought the building and used space-holders' membership fees to repay the debt. In order to secure the nonprofit character of the project, they wrote articles of incorporation which stipulated from the beginning the nonspeculative nature of the space, de facto withdrawing it from the market. A fundamental spatial asset of Project Artaud was the flexibility of its industrial structure, which allowed artists to subdivide it into large live/work studios and a plethora of communal spaces, including a large performance space. Residents learned how to build partitions and maintain the building, and they even held classes about self-building. Yet the crucial aspect of Project Artaud was its ownership model, in which, from the beginning, residents established a lifetime space-holder lease which prevented anyone from profiting from their share of property. Project Artaud thus represents an interesting model in which a live/work space preserved its original purpose against market appropriation thanks to the strategic vision of its residents. And yet, in the landscape of postindustrial reconversion, this kind of initiative remains an exception, especially because city authorities tend to believe that urban transformations cannot happen without the involvement of private capital. It is for this reason that in the last decades attempts at decommodifying housing have started mainly from private initiatives, mostly from cooperatives, with little help (and sometimes with great hostility) from the city authorities.

AGAINST PRIVATE PROPERTY

In the absence of any form of public investment in housing, initiatives such as housing cooperatives present an alternative to private homeownership by placing limitations on the speculative value of housing, particularly in forms like the limited equity housing co-op (LEHC), where residents do not own their dwellings directly but rather own a share of the corporation that owns the housing complex they inhabit. LEHCs differ from other cooperative arrangements because the price of the ownership shares is determined beforehand by the members of the associations themselves, and is therefore not influenced by the fluctuations of the real estate market. For example, in a zero-equity housing cooperative, if residents leave, they are allowed to receive back the entire sum they initially paid. LEHCs were already present in America during the 1920s as the already-mentioned luxury home clubs, but their scope evolved through time to become more politically and socially progressive.[138] In order to ensure the stability of bylaws, and to prevent them from being changed for the gain of some residents over others, LEHCs usually collaborate with government agencies or land trusts to receive funding and to stabilize contract conditions.

Another example is the German Mietshäuser Syndikat or Syndicate of Tenements; founded in 1992, its aim is to appropriate and reprogram existing capitalist forms of ownership, implementing a collective property of commons.[139] The ownership scheme of each Syndicate project is divided into two main shares of 51 and 49 percent, respectively owned by the users/inhabitants who form a cooperative of rent-paying stakeholders, and by the Syndicate company. In this way, the residents retain autonomy over the decision-making processes regarding the development and administration of the property, while the participation of the Syndicate prevents attempts at exploitation or privatization. Land and premises are therefore fenced within a network of social control and are secured long-term as self-administered entities.[140] Another important contemporary experiment in withdrawing housing from the market and reclaiming it as a social right is the community land trust (CLT) model. Introduced in the United States by Robert Swann in 1969, the CLT model was conceived as a way to stem speculative development on farmlands. Since the 1980s, the CLT model has also been implemented in urban areas with the aim of protecting processes of allocation, continuity, and exchange.[141] The CLT model was based on the separation of land property from that of building, after which the land was to be retained by the CLT in perpetuity, thereby preventing land speculation while allowing housing units to be purchased with long-term ground leases. Nowadays, the model of the CLT is becoming more and more common in English-speaking areas, as well as in other European countries. This model represents one of the few viable alternatives to organize public plots without interference from private developers. In many European countries, this model of land acquisition is still in its initial phase, largely supported by public subsidies and therefore mainly addressing low-income citizens. However, its American version is much more advanced and able to provide—in addition to housing for everyone—a multitude of communal facilities such as emergency shelters, special-needs housing, and single-room-occupancy (SRO) housing for individuals with very low incomes.[142] In Switzerland, the success of the housing cooperative movement has been supported and made possible on the one hand by favorable legislation and on the other by financial assistance and land availability.

In London, the municipality has initiated and supported several programs in recent years that enable small plots of land in the hands of public authorities to be made available for small developers, housing associations, and community-led organizations through long-term lease contracts for the construction of alternative housing projects.

Today, as property prices rise and the hegemony of finance continues to expand, it becomes increasingly difficult to acquire land and finance a counterspeculative strategy for housing. In this light, contemporary forays into cooperative building should be reassessed in the neoliberal financialized condition. Cooperative building initiatives such as Baugruppen in Germany and Ryhmärakentaminen in Finland—where individuals self-organize to finance the construction of their buildings—appear successful in circumventing certain market mechanisms when it comes to housing. By effectively operating as its own developer, cooperative building cuts out the middleman in the development process, producing housing below market cost. While this process allows for the construction of alternative forms of housing and offers a degree of agency for residents in the arrangement of their domestic life, it is also limited to those with access to credit and capital. Because they operate essentially as individual business ventures, cooperative building assets are inevitably subject to some form of entrepreneurial calculus, promising either great returns on investment or at least stable housing costs amidst skyrocketing rents.

Without a mechanism to counter the speculative tendency, cooperative housing ventures risk only further entrenching the financialized condition of housing. In elaborating the contours of the contemporary housing condition, we hope to challenge contemporary approaches to housing affordability, and in turn begin to consider ways to mobilize and organize to confront what has by now become a globally systemic condition that calls for more than individualized responses—for a collectivized movement that actively contests the challenges of housing today.

CONCLUSION

The historical vicissitudes of housing remind us that far from being a private space, housing is political—which is to say that defining the housing system is always the outcome of struggles between different groups and classes. As David Madden and Peter Marcuse have argued, the enduring conflict in terms of housing is between its usefulness as lived space and its value as a means of profit. Exactly for this reason, it is crucial to rethink the role of the house beyond its understanding as a private space. This does not mean that the house as a space of privacy and family should be rejected, but that there is a need to break the logic of domesticity which binds together housing commodification and the privatization of reproductive labor. The recent renewed interest in forms of collective living does not seem to get to the core of the issue—namely, the possibility of sharing and collectivizing both the right to housing and its primary role, i.e., reproductive labor. In many recent housing projects, "sharing" and "collectivity" are terms that are applied, at best, to leisure facilities such as hobby rooms, meeting spaces, and the gym; they are hardly used to refer to forms of domestic labor such as care for children and the elderly, or to alternative forms of tenure to private ownership. Against the tropes of collectivity, the house must be considered as a space of work, in which both production and reproduction happen side by side. By not separating public from private, production from reproduction, housing has the potential to allow inhabitants to reorganize dwelling in a way that can be beneficial and self-valorizing. By countering the fragmentation of domestic space and its atomization into "private houses," architecture can support a scenario in which it is possible to share and thus minimize the burden of domestic labor, but also to enable the self-organization of working activities by cooperation and mutual help. In other words, collective living should not be fetishized as an image, but understood in its structural potential to democratize and decommodify the spaces of living and working.

1 Walter Benjamin, *The Arcades Project*, ed. Rolf Tiedemann, trans. Howard Eiland and Kevin McLaughlin (Cambridge, MA: Harvard University Press, 2002), 8.

2 In "Behind Marx's Hidden Abode," Nancy Fraser argues that the division between social reproduction and commodity production is not only central to capitalism but its artifact. Nancy Fraser, "Behind Marx's Hidden Abode," *New Left Review* 86 (2014): 55–72.

3 Maria Mies, *Patriarchy and Accumulation on a World Scale: Women in the International Division of Labor* (London: Zed Books, 2014), 104.

4 Peter J. Wilson, *The Domestication of the Human Species* (New Haven: Yale University Press, 1989), 50.

5 Mikhail I. Gladkih, Ninelj L. Kornietz, and Olga Soffer, "Mammoth-Bone Dwellings on the Russian Plain," *Scientific American* 254, no. 5 (1984): 164–175.

6 Klaus Schmidt, *Sie bauten die ersten Tempel: das rätselhafte Heiligtum der Steinzeitjäger: die archäologische Entdeckung am Göbekli Tepe* (Munich: Verlag C. H. Beck, 2006), 81.

7 Lewis R. Binford, "Willow Smoke and Dog's Tail: Hunter-Gatherers Settlement System and Archeological Site Formation," *American Antiquity* 45, no. 1 (January 1980): 4–20.

8 Wilson, *The Domestication of the Human Species*, 30.

9 Paul Memmott, *Gunyah, Goondie, and Wurley: The Aboriginal Architecture of Australia* (Brisbane: University of Queensland Press, 2008), 30–32.

10 David Graeber and David Wengrow, "How to Change the Course of Human History," *Eurozine*, March 2, 2018, https://www.eurozine.com/change-course-human-history/.

11 See Jerry D. Moore, *The Prehistory of Home* (Berkeley: University of California Press, 2012), 40–42.

12 See Leore Grosman, Hila Ashkenazy, and Anna Belfer-Cohen, "The Natufian Occupation of Nahal Oren, Mt. Carmel, Israel—The Lithic Evidence," *Paléorient* 31, no. 5 (2005): 5–26.

13 Wilson, *The Domestication of the Human Species*, 9.

14 See Wulf Schirmer, "Some Aspects of Building at the 'Aceramic-Neolithic' Settlement of Çayönü Tepesi," *World Archeology* 21, no. 3 (1990): 364–387.

15 Kent Flannery and Joyce Marcus, *The Creation of Inequality: How Our Ancestors Set the Stage for Monarchy, Slavery, and Empire* (Cambridge, MA: Harvard University Press, 2012), 137.

16 See Michael C. Robins, "House Types and Settlement Patterns: An Application of Ethology to Archeological Interpretation," *Minnesota Archeologist* 28, no. 1 (1966): 3–26.

17 See David Wengrow, "The Changing Face of Clay: Continuity and Change in the Transition from Village to Urban Life in the Near East," *Antiquity* 72 (1998): 790.

18 See Franziska Lang, "Structural Change in Archaic Greek Housing," in *Ancient Greek Houses and Households: Chronological, Regional and Social Diversity*, ed. Bradley A. Ault and Lisa C. Nevett (Philadelphia: University of Pennsylvania Press, 2005), 12–35.

19 Alexandra Coucouzeli, "From Megaron to Oikos at Zagora," *British School at Athens Studies* 15 (2007): 169–181.

20 Ibid., 170.

21 Aristotle, *The Politics*, trans. T. A. Sinclair (London: Penguin, 1981), 53–92.

22 Hannah Arendt, *The Human Condition* (1958; repr., Chicago: University of Chicago Press, 1998), 79–126.

23 Ruth Westgate, "The Greek House and the Ideology of Citizenship," *World Archeology* 39, no. 2 (June 2007): 229–245.

24 Ibid., 234.

25 Lang, "Structural Change in Archaic Greek Housing," 26.

26 Lisa C. Nevett, *Domestic Space in Classical Antiquity* (Cambridge: Cambridge University Press, 2010), 55.

27 Xenophon, *Oeconomicus*, trans. Ralph Doty (Bristol: Bristol Classic Press, 1998).

28 Aristotle, *The Politics*, 54.

29 See Shelley Hales, *The Roman House and Social Identity* (Cambridge: Cambridge University Press, 2003), 3.

30 Ibid.

31 On the symbolic relationship between paterfamilias and emperor see Judith B. Perkins, "The 'Passion of Perpetua': A Narrative of Empowerment," *Latomus* 53, fasc. 4 (October–November 1994): 837–847.

32 Andrew Wallace-Hadrill, "The Social Structure of the Roman House," *Papers of the British School at Rome* 56 (1988): 81–82.

33 Ibid., 73.

34 Ibid., 84.

35 See Kristina Sessa, "Christianity and the Cubiculum: Spiritual Politics and Domestic Space in Late Antique Rome," *Journal of Early Christian Studies* 15, no. 2 (Summer 2007): 171–204.

36 Peter Brown, *Treasures in Heaven: The Holy Poor in Early Christianity* (Charlottesville: University of Virginia Press, 2016), 77–95.

37 Roland Barthes, *How to Live Together: Novelistic Simulations of Some Everyday Spaces* (New York: Columbia University Press, 2013).

38 Ibid., 8.

39 See Svetlana Popović, "Dividing the Indivisible: The Monastery Space—Secular and Sacred," *Recueil des travaux de l'Institut d'études byzantines* 44 (2007): 52.

40 Giorgio Agamben, *The Highest Poverty: Monastic Rules and Form-of-Life* (Palo Alto: Stanford University Press, 2013).

41 See Walter Horn, "On the Origins of the Medieval Cloister," *Gesta* 12, no. 1–2 (1973): 13–52.

42 Ossa Raymond Sowers, "Medieval Monastic Planning: Its Origins in the East and Its Later Development in Western Europe" (PhD diss., Columbia University, 1952), 55.

43 Ibid., 487.

44 See Horn, "On the Origins of the Medieval Cloister," 27–33.

45 See Hastings Rashdal, *The Universities of Europe in the Middle Ages* (Oxford: Clarendon Press, 1985), vol. 1, 5–10; see also Robert Rait, *Life in the Medieval University* (Cambridge: Cambridge University Press, 1912).

46 Marson Korbi, "Nuove forme dell'abitare. Abitare collettivo dentro e oltre la città del capitalismo cognitivo" (PhD diss., Politecnico di Bari, 2020), 72–113.

47 Emanuela Ferretti, "La Sapienza di Siena nei disegni di Giuliano da Sangallo e Francesco di Giorgio Martini," in *Architetti a Siena. Testimonianze della Biblioteca comunale tra XV e XVIII secolo*, ed. Daniele Danesi, Milena Pagani, and Annalisa Pezzo (Milan: Silvana editoriale, 2009), 71–87.

48 See Philippe Contamine, "Peasant Hearth to Papal Palace: The Fourteenth and Fifteenth Centuries," in *A History of Private Life: Revelations of the Medieval World*, ed. Philippe Ariès and Georges Duby (Cambridge: Belknap Press of Harvard University Press, 1988), 448–449.

49 Jane Grenville, "Urban and Rural Houses and Households in the Late Middle Ages: A Case Study from Yorkshire," in *Medieval Domesticity: Home, Housing and Household in Medieval England*, ed. Maryanne Kowalesky and P. J. P. Goldberg (Cambridge: Cambridge University Press, 2008), 107–109.

50 See Fabio Redi, "Pisa medievale. Una lettura alternativa delle strutture esistenti. Architettura, cultura materiale, storia urbana, archeologia e topografia," in *D'une ville à l'autre. Structures matérielles et organisation de l'espace dans les villes européennes (XIIIe–XVIe siècle). Actes du colloque de Rome (Rome: Publications de l'École française de Rome*, 1989), 591–607.

51 Ibid., 593.

52 Ibid., 595.

53 Robert Fishman, *Bourgeois Utopias: The Rise and Fall of Suburbia* (New York: Basic Books, 1987), 21.

54 Felicity Riddy, "'Burgeis' domesticity in late-medieval England," in Kowalesky and Goldberg, *Medieval Domesticity*, 16–17.

55 Ibid., 23.

56 Ibid., 17.

57 Ibid., 34.

58 On the classical origins of the term see Guido Guerzoni, "Liberalitas, Magnificentia, Splendor: The Classic Origins of Italian Renaissance Lifestyles," in *History of Political Economy* 31, supplement (1999): 332–378.

59 See James R. Lindow, *The Renaissance Palace in Florence: Magnificence and Splendour in Fifteenth Century Italy* (Aldershot: Ashgate, 2007), 9–42.

60 Peter Thornton, *The Italian Renaissance Interior 1400–1600* (London: Weidenfeld and Nicolson, 1991), 284.

61 Ibid., 300–312.

62 Myra Nan Rosenfeld, ed., *Serlio on Domestic Architecture* (Mineola, NY: Dover, 1978).

63 Ibid., 50.

64 See Vaughan Hart, ed., *Sebastiano Serlio on Architecture*, vol. 2 (New Haven: Yale University Press, 2001), 157–385.

65 Ibid., 290–291.

66 Antoine Chrysostome Quatremère de Quincy, "Type," *Encyclopédie méthodique* 3, trans. Samir Younés, reprinted in *The Historical Dictionary of Architecture of Quatremère de Quincy* (London: Papadakis Publisher, 2000).

67 On the influence of Serlio's projects on the evolution of domestic space, especially in Paris, see Maria Shéhérazade Giudici, "Specific Spaces: Government and the Emergence of architecture d'accompagnement, 1584–1675," in *The City as a Project*, ed. Pier Vittorio Aureli (Berlin: Ruby Press, 2013), 143–169.

68 Leon Battista Alberti, *I libri della famiglia* (Turin: Einaudi, 1994), 25.

69 See Stefan Muthesius, *The English Terraced House* (New Haven: Yale University Press, 1982), 5.
70 Ibid., 31–37.
71 Mies, *Patriarchy and Accumulation on a World Scale*, 100–111.
72 Ibid., 83.
73 Part of this paragraph was previously published in our essay Dogma, "The Home at Work: A Genealogy of Housing for the Laboring Classes," *Harvard Design Magazine*, no. 46 (2018): 194–202.
74 Renato de Fusco and Alberto Terminio, *Company towns in Europa dal XVI al XX secolo* (Milan: Franco Angeli, 2017), 21–30.
75 Benjamin Scheller, *Memoria an der Zeitenwende: Die Stiftungen Jakob Fuggers des Reichen vor und während der Reformation* (Berlin: De Gruyter, 2004), 225–238.
76 Mark Häberlein, *The Fuggers of Augsburg: Pursuing Wealth and Honor in Renaissance Germany* (Charlottesville: University of Virginia Press, 2006), 157–158.
77 Ibid., 157.
78 Ibid., 158.
79 Max Weber, *The Protestant Ethic and the Spirit of Capitalism* (1905; repr., New York: Penguin Books, 2002).
80 John Wood the Younger, *A Series of Plans for Cottages or Habitations of the Labourer, Either in Husbandry, or the Mechanic Arts* (1781; repr., London: T. Bensley, 1806).
81 Daniel Maudin, "Habitations of the Labourer: Improvement, Reform and the Neoclassical Cottage in Eighteenth-Century Britain," *Journal of Design History* 23, no. 1 (2010): 7–20.
82 See Robin Evans, *Translations from Drawing to Building and Other Essays* (Cambridge, MA: MIT Press, 1997), 93–117.
83 Henry Roberts, *The Dwellings of the Labouring Classes. Their Arrangement and Construction* (London: n.p., 1850).
84 Mies, *Patriarchy and Accumulation on a World Scale*, 106.
85 Ibid.
86 On the political context of the project in Hellerau, see Marynel Ryan Van Zee, "Form and Reform: The Garden City of Hellerau-bei-Dresden, Germany, between Company Town and Model Town," in *Company Towns: Labor, Space, and Power Relations across Time and Continents*, ed. Susana B. Torres and Marcelo J. Borges (New York: Palgrave Macmillan, 2012), 41–67.
87 Ibid., 51.
88 See Didem Ekici, "In Praise of Poverty: The Middle-Class Dwelling and Asceticism in Early Twentieth-Century Germany," *Journal of Architecture* 18, no. 3 (2013): 368–374.
89 Charles Fourier, *The Theory of the Four Movements*, ed. and trans. Gareth Stedman Jones and Ian Patterson (Cambridge: Cambridge University Press, 1996).
90 Dolores Hayden, *Seven American Utopias: The Architecture of Communitarian Socialism, 1790–1976* (Cambridge, MA: MIT Press, 1976), 149–185.
91 David P. Handlin, *The American Home: Architecture and Society 1815–1915* (Boston: Little, Brown, 1979), 4–81.
92 Hayden, *Seven American Utopias*, 159.
93 Ibid., 186–223.
94 Dolores Hayden, "Two Utopian Feminists and Their Campaigns for Kitchenless Houses," *Signs* 4, no. 2 (Winter 1978): 274–290.
95 Paul Groth, *Living Downtown: The History of Residential Hotels in the United States* (Berkeley: University of California Press, 1994), 38.
96 For a comprehensive history of boarding see Wendy Gamber, *The Boarding House in Nineteenth-Century America* (Baltimore: Johns Hopkins University Press, 2007).
97 Anna Puigjaner, "Ciudad sin cocina: El Waldorf Astoria, apartamentos con servicios domésticos colectivos en Nueva York, 1871–1929" (PhD diss., Universitat Politècnica de Catalunya, 2014).
98 Dogma, *Loveless: The Minimum Dwelling and Its Discontents* (Milan: Black Square, 2019), 56–57.
99 For an overview of early communal housing in Europe see Norbert Schoenauer, "Early European Collective Habitation: From Utopian Ideal to Reality," in *New Households, New Housing*, ed. Karen A. Franck and Sherry Ahrentzen (New York: Van Nostrand Reinhold, 1991), 47–70.
100 Ibid., 50–53.
101 Karel Teige, *The Minimum Dwelling*, trans. Eric Dluhosch (Cambridge, MA: MIT Press, 2002). On Teige's minimum dwelling we published an earlier book; see Dogma, *Loveless*.
102 Teige, *The Minimum Dwelling*, 350–377.
103 For an overview of the work of OSA see Anatole Kopp, *Town and Revolution: Soviet Architecture and City Planning, 1917–1935* (New York: George Braziller, 1970), 63–100; see also Guido Canella and Maurizio Meriggi, *SA, Sovremennaja arkhitektura 1926–1930* (Rome: Dedalo, 2007); and Vieri Quilici, *Il costruttivismo* (Bari: Laterza, 1991).
104 Leon Trotsky, *Problems of Everyday Life: and Other Writings on Culture and Science* (New York: Ed Conroy Bookseller, 1994).
105 Marco De Michelis, "L'organizzazione della città industriale nel primo piano quinquennale," in *Socialismo città architettura URSS 1917–1937. Il contributo degli architetti europei*, ed. Manfredo Tafuri et al. (Rome: Officina, 1971), 153.
106 Charles Hoc and Robert A. Slayton, *New Homeless and Old: Community and the Skid Row Hotel* (Philadelphia: Temple University Press, 1984), 62–86.
107 Ibid., 69–70.
108 Ibid., 70–71.
109 Groth, *Living Downtown*, 220.
110 Anna Granath Hansson and Björn Lundgren, "Defining Social Housing: A Discussion on the Suitable Criteria," *Housing, Theory and Society* 36, no. 2 (2019): 149.
111 Quoted in ibid., 111.
112 Gilles Deleuze and David Lapoujade, *Two Regimes of Madness: Texts and Interviews 1975–1995* (Cambridge MA: MIT Press, 2006), 113–121.
113 Martin Stilwell, "Housing the Workers in London: Housing Legislation 1850–1914," http://www.socialhousinghistory.uk/wp/wp-content/uploads/2017/10/Early_LCC_Housing_Part_4.pdf
114 Irina Davidovici, "The Depth of the Street," *AA Files*, no. 70 (2015): 103–123.
115 Ibid., 109.
116 Ibid., 114.
117 Mies, *Patriarchy and Accumulation on a World Scale*, 106.
118 Ibid.
119 Roger Guerrand, *Le origini della questione delle abitazioni in Francia 1850–1894*, ed. Georges Teyssot (Rome: Officina, 1981), 288–312.
120 Ibid., 496.
121 W. Brian Newsome, "The Rise of the Grands Ensembles: Government, Business, and Housing in Postwar France," *Historian* 66, no. 4 (Winter 2004): 794–795.
122 As quoted in Ann-Louise Shapiro, "Housing Reform in Paris: Social Space and Social Control," *French Historical Studies* 12, no. 4 (Autumn 1982): 496.
123 Nancy Stieber, *Housing Design and Society in Amsterdam: Reconfiguring Urban Order and Identity, 1900–1920* (Chicago: University of Chicago Press, 1998), 15–46.
124 Ibid., 73–96.
125 Lars Lerup, *After the City* (Cambridge, MA: MIT Press, 2000), 182.
126 See Silvia Federici, *Wages against Housework* (Bristol: Falling Wall Press, 1975).
127 Kathi Weeks, *The Problem with Work: Feminism, Marxism, Anti-Work Politics, and Post-Work Imaginaries* (Durham: Duke University Press, 2011), 37–76.
128 Jeremy Hoskyn and Tanja Schrag, eds., *Grundrissfibel. 50 Wettbewerbe im gemeinnutzigen Wohnungsbau* (Zurich: Hochparterre, 2014).
129 Federico Coricelli, "A New Domestic Rentscape: A Critical Inquiry into Middle-Class Housing" (PhD diss., Politecnico di Torino, 2020), 137–149.
130 Melinda Cooper, *Family Values: Between Neoliberalism and the New Social Conservatism* (New York: Zone Books, 2017).
131 Frances Hollis, *Beyond Live/Work: The Architecture of Home-Based Work* (New York: Routledge, 2015), 13–14.
132 Ibid., 18–19.
133 Cosimo Campani, "Redneck Urbanism: The Architecture of the Fabbrichetta" (PhD diss., Università di Roma Tre, 2021).
134 Elena Palacios Carral, "The Studiofication of the Home: The Freelance Artist's Studio in Western Europe and USA, from 1600 to the Present" (PhD diss., Architectural Association, London, 2022), 14–15.
135 Sharon Zukin, *Loft Living: Culture and Capital in Urban Change* (New Brunswick: Rutgers University Press; 2015).
136 Board of Supervisors of San Francisco, "Industrial Protection Zones, Live/Work Projects and Community Plans," https://sfbos.org/industrial-protection-zones-livework-projects-and-community-plans.
137 Jackie Barshak, "Live/Work Spaces for Artists: A Historical Perspective," in *Found SF*, https://www.foundsf.org/index.php?title=Live/Work_Spaces_for_Artists:_A_Historical_Perspective.
138 James DeFilippis, *Unmaking Goliath: Community Control in the Face of Global Capital* (New York: Routledge, 2004).
139 Dogma and Realism Working Group, *Communal Villa: Production and Re-production in Artists' Housing* (Leipzig: Spector Books, 2015), 82–83.
140 Ibid.
141 Robert S. Swann, Shimon Gottschalk, Erick S. Hansch, and Edward Webster, *The Community Land Trust—A Guide to a New Model for Land Tenure in America* (Cambridge: Center for Community Economic Development, 1972).
142 DeFilippis, *Unmaking Goliath*.

LIVE FOREVER: THE RETURN OF THE FACTORY (2013)

This proposal was developed as a response to an invitation to intervene in the area of the Balti Station, one of the most notable public landmarks built during socialism in Tallinn, Estonia. Rather than on the station building, we focused on the large area along the tracks on the edge of the Telliskivi Creative City, an area currently prime for real estate development. Against the speculative development that would characterize this site, we put forward an alternative scenario in which the current owner—the national railway company—rather than selling the land to private developers, would lease it to the city in order to build social housing. This strategy is motivated by the fact that land is the fundamental factor in the development of affordable housing. Historically, rising land values have been the main cause of the growing wealth gap between those who own property and those who must rent it. Therefore, the building of social housing is strictly dependent on the capacity (and political will) of the public sector to retain public land for social purposes. Given the fact that in many European cities there is a lot of unused land along railway tracks, and this land is generally owned by railway companies, our proposal is applicable to other similar situations.

Live Forever is a building for 1600 inhabitants that contains both living and working spaces. The building makes explicit reference to the Unité d'Habitation (1947–1952), a large slab that Le Corbusier proposed as a model for mass housing. The most remarkable aspect of this model was the proportions of the apartments with their narrow and elongated plan and the dramatic double height of the living room, which opens up to a monumental window balcony. Another impressive feature was the wealth of social spaces, culminating with the roof terrace. The Unité put forward a housing model based on self-sufficiency and monumental scale in which the "mass" of social housing was made tangible in the most readable terms. As noted by architectural historian Tim Benton, the assertive verticality of the block of flats was meant to recall Le Corbusier's obsession with the duality of vertical versus horizontal, or building versus nature.[1]

In our Unité in Tallinn this duality is reinterpreted in terms of form and economy. The stark contrast between the block and the rest of the city is meant to manifest in a monumental way the decommodified status of this building as a "machine for living and working." Unlike its illustrious predecessor, Live Forever is not made of apartments and collective spaces, but rather of an open and adjustable system of cores and partitions in which living and working, collective and individual spaces can be constantly negotiated and adapted to contingent conditions of use. The basic housing unit is a room that measures 6 x 6 x 6 meters. This room is also the basic three-dimensional module of the concrete load-bearing structure. The room can function as a cell for one or two persons and can be used as both living and working space. The generous height of the room allows its vertical subdivision into two floors. The structural module allows for easy aggregation of rooms into larger units. This means that rooms can be combined vertically and horizontally into larger households. Here lies an important principle that we have tried to apply in other housing projects: the basic housing unit is not the apartment, but the room for one or two persons. This principle is meant to guarantee to each inhabitant their right to solitude, while challenging any predefined idea of household.

Vertical subdivision and the linking of units are possible thanks to the use of light timber slabs and prefabricated partitions that can be easily added or removed. The clear differentiation of structure and partition manifested by the bay system is meant to allow inhabitants to immediately understand what is fixed and what can be moved.

Each room is to be equipped with a core that contains basic utilities: a bathroom, storage, and a kitchenette. The core acts as a platform that can support a large bed accessible by a small staircase. Every fifth core contains the vertical circulation. The circulation core defines the collective space that acts as a shared living room. The uniformity of spaces and the flexibility of the structure aim to make residential and working spaces interchangeable. These ad hoc transformations are allowed by a tenancy system in which inhabitants do not rent space but a share of the building. In this way the distribution of spaces follows an evolvable model in which house dimensions are determined by the inhabitant's needs rather than by a fixed standard.

The simplicity of the floor plan and of the section recuperates the typical plan of the factory in which the structure is minimized in order allow maximum flexibility. The visibility of the structure and its relentless modularity are meant to establish a common rhythm within the different spaces. Such structure aims to become a visible notation, a legible score that orchestrates a multitude of uses without imposing a rigid and predefined organization. The project's goal is to recognize not only the ephemeral boundaries between living and working, but also—and especially—the productive character of housing itself. It is for this reason that this project postulates the return of the factory as both practical and symbolic space in which the social and productive dimensions of life become spatially and physically tangible.

1 Tim Benton, "Marseille: Unité d'Habitation, or the Company of Clouds, the Sky, or the Stars," in *Le Corbusier: An Atlas of Modern Landscapes*, ed. Jean-Louis Cohen (New York: MoMA, 2013).

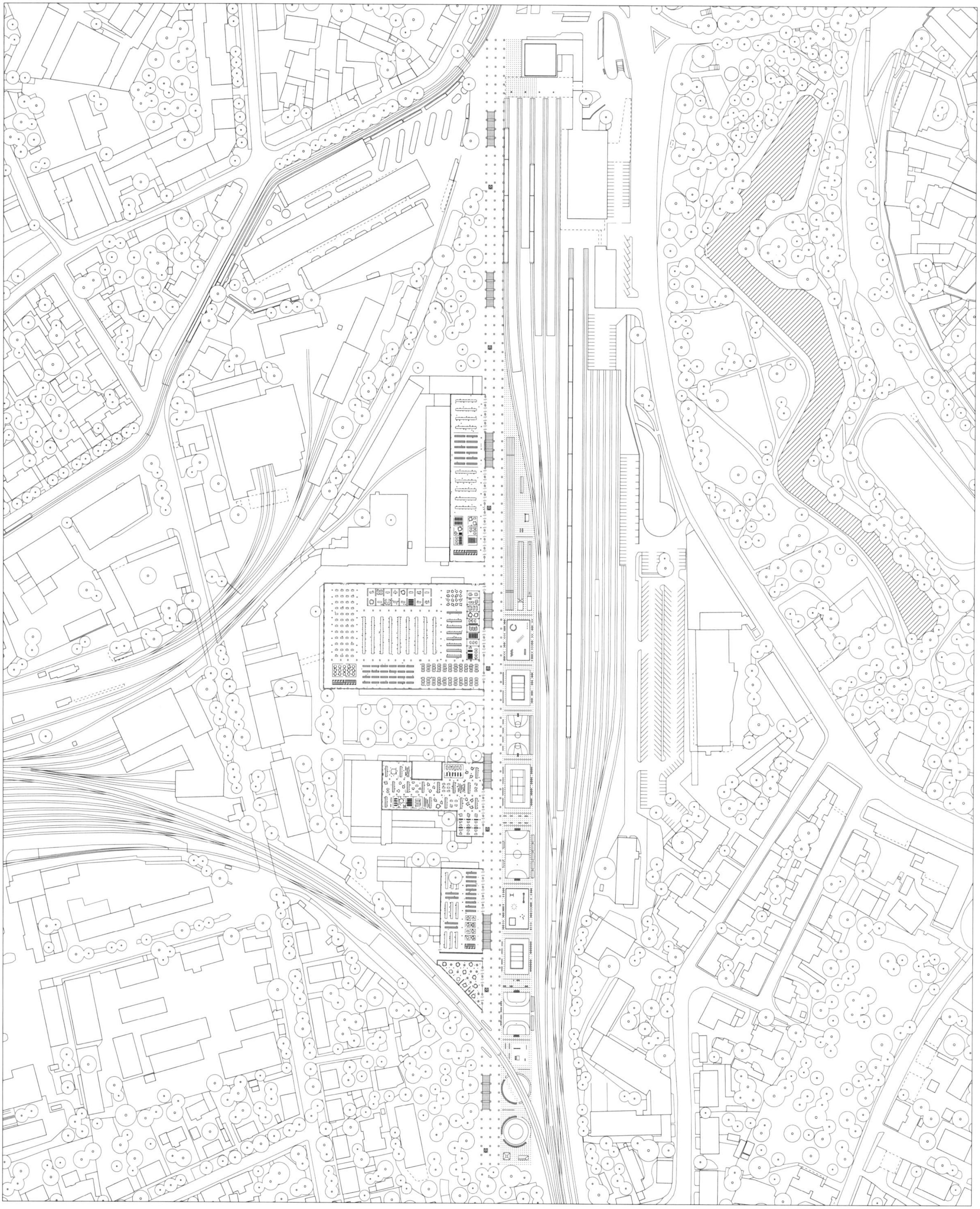

50 m

Ground-floor plan

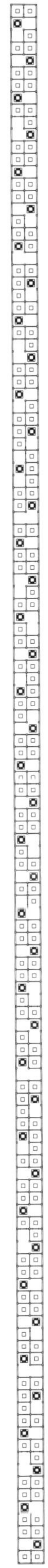

Typical plan

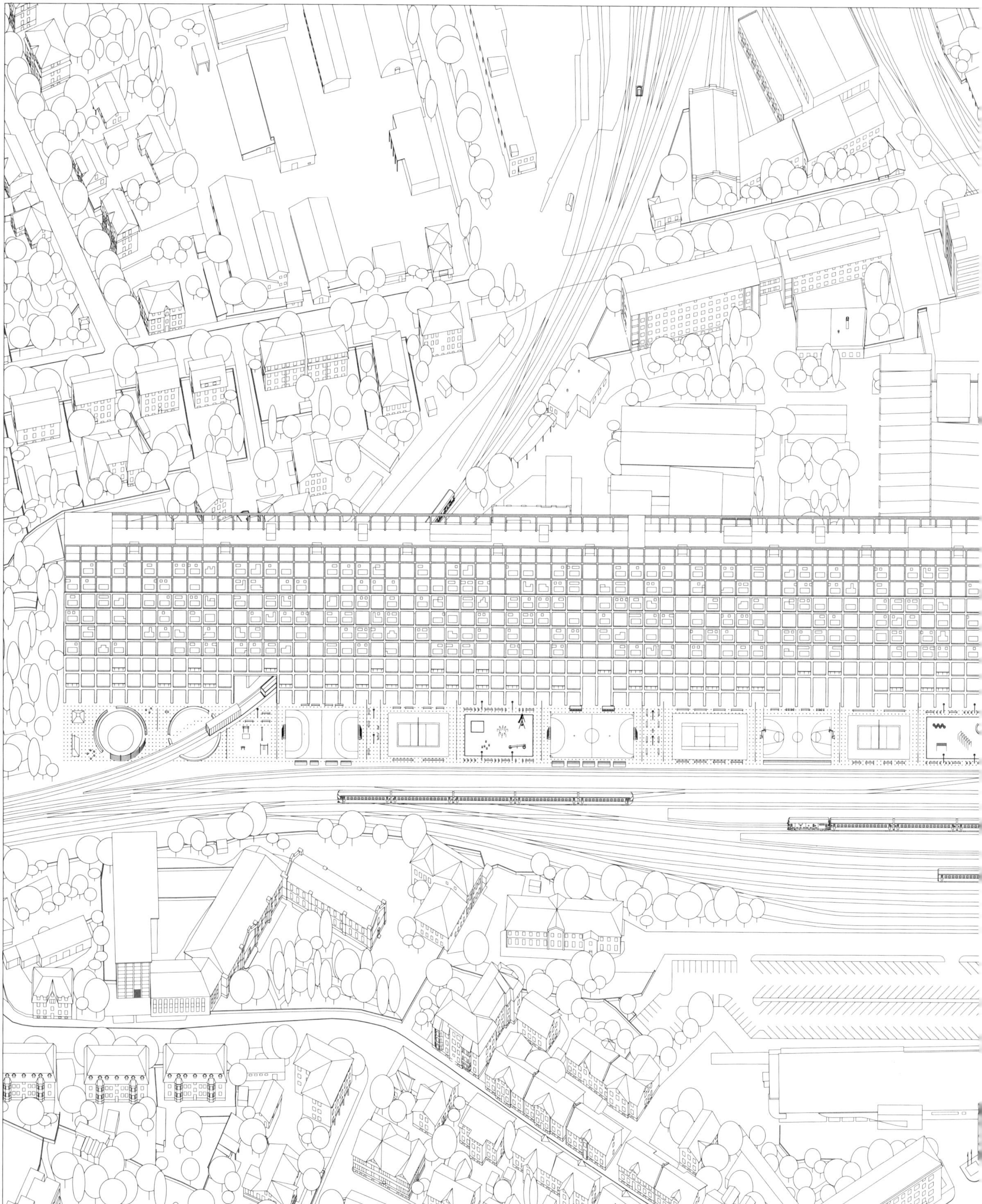

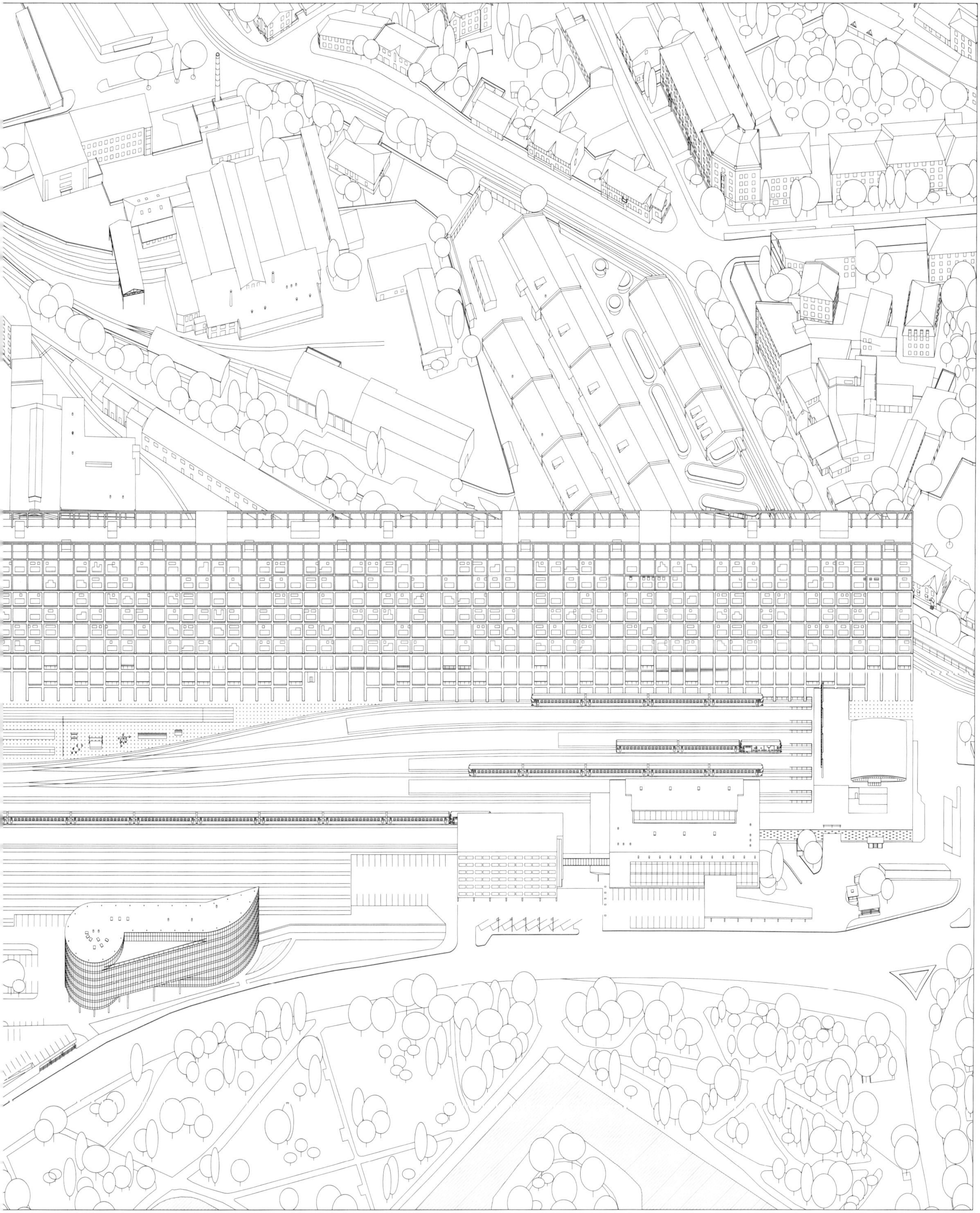

Section

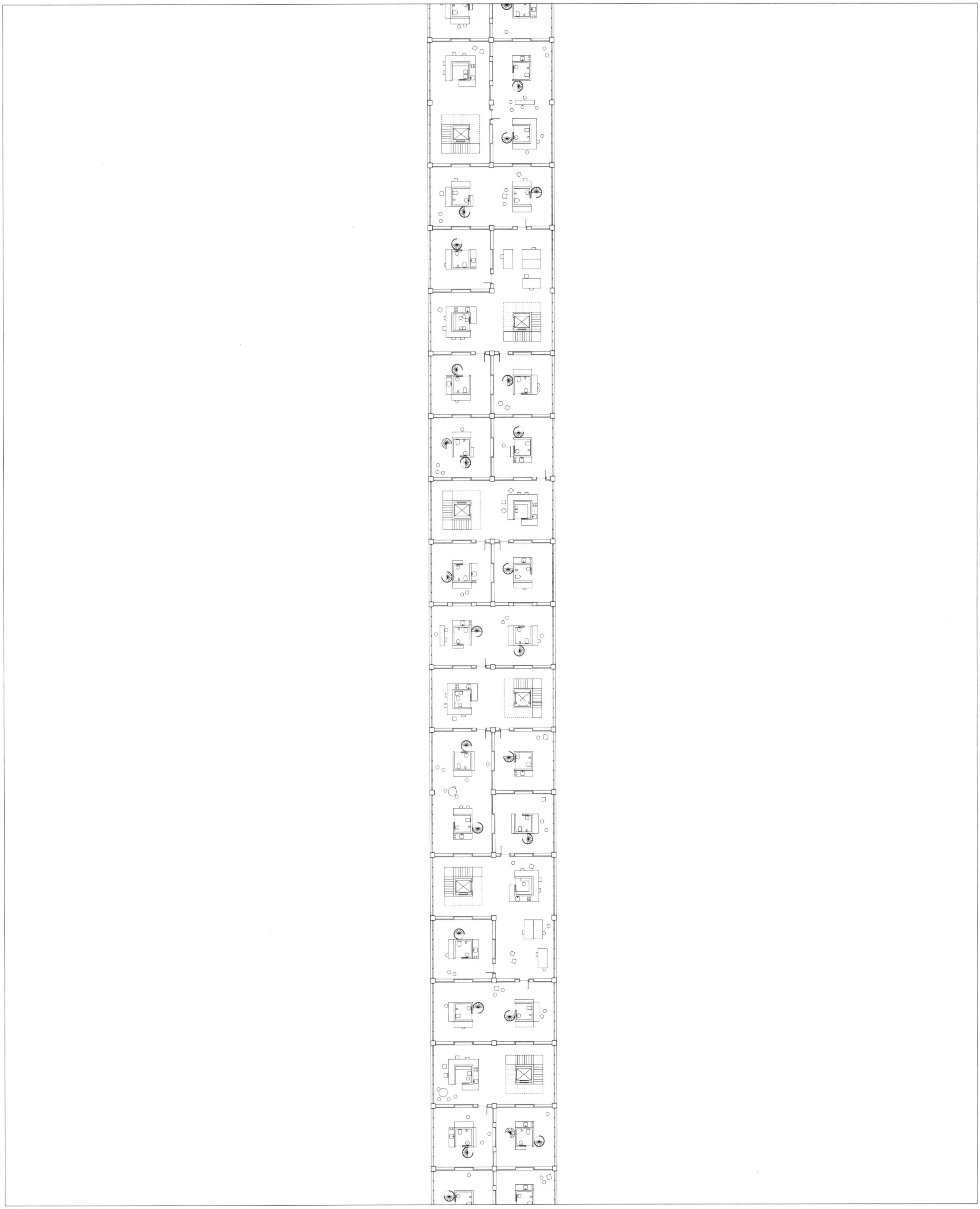

10 m

Detail of the typical plan

AFTER HILBERSEIMER (2014)

In the early 1950s Ludwig Hilberseimer developed a proposal for the neighborhood of Marquette Park in Chicago; the layout of Hilberseimer's design was based on the transformation of the typical settlement gridiron into what Albert Pope later called the "ladder." In his book *Entfaltung einer Planungsidee* (1963), the German architect dedicated a chapter to Marquette Park in which he pointed out two alternative strategies to change the contemporary city.[1] The first involved working outside of the city itself, addressing the surrounding unbuilt territory with an expansive project. The second was of a more complicated nature, as it aimed at tackling the city from the inside, through the gradual transformation of what was already there. Such an approach requires first the identification of the most important elements of the city, such as the houses, the blocks, the parks, the streets, and its structuring systems such as its infrastructure and road networks; and then the design of their gradual transformation. Hilberseimer's proposal for Marquette Park is a seminal representation of the inside-out approach, and the first of a series of studies in which he tried to tackle the gradual transformation of the existing American city with the aim of implementing his idea of the settlement unit.

The neighborhood of Marquette Park, about three square miles and located adjacent to the largest public park on the southwest side of Chicago, was in those years at the center of the architect's reflections, as revealed also by the work of his students at IIT, which gravitated to the same topic. In the 1960s, the park would eventually became well known as the place of Black Americans' civil rights protests such as those led by Dr. Martin Luther King. As these protests often tackled the right to decent housing conditions, our proposal is an attempt to rethink Hilberseimer's method not by reducing but rather by increasing housing density.

Hilberseimer's proposal for Marquette Park is contained in three schematic plan drawings stitched and folded together. This set of abstract drawings presents the three phases of the gradual transformation of the area and clarifies the scope of the project, namely the opening of the blocks and the establishment of a new relationship with the park. The first drawing simply presents the existing situation of the neighborhood, the second the closing and the erasure of certain roads, and the third the removal of certain blocks and the consequent enlargement of the park in the space made available through demolition. In this way, the park not only would acquire a central role, but its importance would also be enhanced by the insertion of a series of public buildings and educational facilities that could therefore be reached from each house of the neighborhood without having to cross any street.

Despite these good intentions, Hilberseimer's proposal was considered problematic as it represented an archetypical manifestation of the suburban cul-de-sac urban structure.[2] Yet, little attention has been given to two positive aspects of this scheme. The first is the extension of the park into the neighborhood, and the second is the depth of the housing strip, which, although ignored by Hilberseimer, allows for gradual densification and retrofitting. Our proposal departs from the last of the three phases of Hilberseimer's project and tries to push densification to the extreme, maintaining the one-story height of the houses. While Hilberseimer focused primarily on the infrastructure, without imagining a radical rethinking of the single-family houses and the traditional separation between living and working activities that dominated that part of the city, in our proposal we imagine the gradual replacement of the typical American suburban house with long and narrow courtyard houses that occupy the entirety of the strips in between the roads. Given the absence of windows on the two elevations that do not face the street, these long houses can be placed next to each other, forming a very dense built pattern. This proposal is based on a reinterpretation of the shophouse, a building type generally serving both as a residence and commercial premises; the shophouse's store opens onto the sidewalk and also functions as entrance to the house. Similarly to our proposal, shophouses were often designed to be narrow and deep so that many businesses could be accommodated along a street. Although traditionally the residential space occupied a floor above the shop, in our proposal the houses are organized on a single level through a sequence of indoor and outdoor rooms. A service wall runs along the whole house, containing bathrooms, storage, shelves, kitchens, and even bed alcoves. This linear spatial organization allows the residents to use the rooms closer to the street as workshop, shop, office, or for any work-related activities, and the rooms at the back for residential purposes, without predetermining a rigid functional organization since all services are contained in the service wall and are independent of the rooms. These houses can therefore be used for living and working while allowing different combinations of these two conditions. While the courtyards have the role of separating the rooms of the house from each other and offer a buffer space in between them, they can also easily be covered through the construction of a light roof structure between the two service walls, thus providing a single interior space that could potentially expand all the way to the back of the plot.

1 Ludwig Hilberseimer, *Entfaltung einer Planungsidee* (Berlin: Ullstein, 1963).

2 Christopher Alexander, "The City Is Not a Tree," *Architectural Forum* 122, no. 1–2 (April–May 1965): 62.

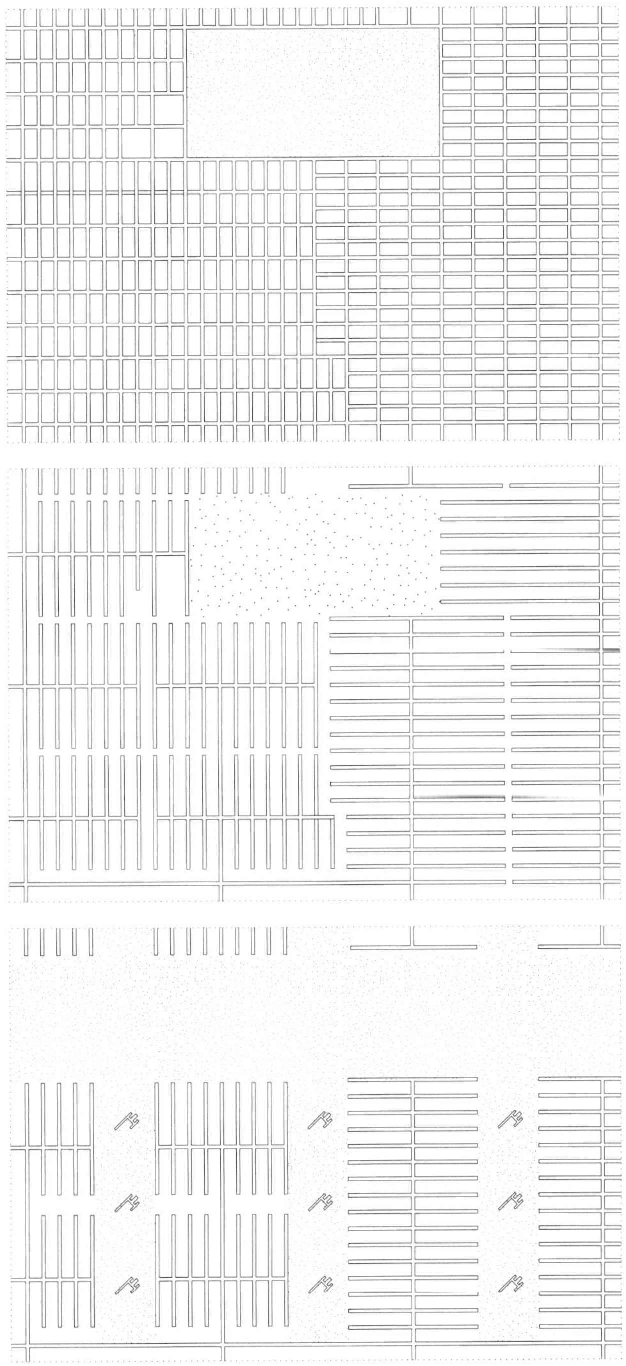

Ludwig Hilberseimer, proposal for the transformation of Marquette Park, Chicago, 1955

150 m

Ludwig Hilberseimer, a new settlement unit (from *The New City*, 1944)

Retrofitting of Hilberseimer's settlement unit: suburban houses are replaced by shophouses

View of the retrofitted settlement unit

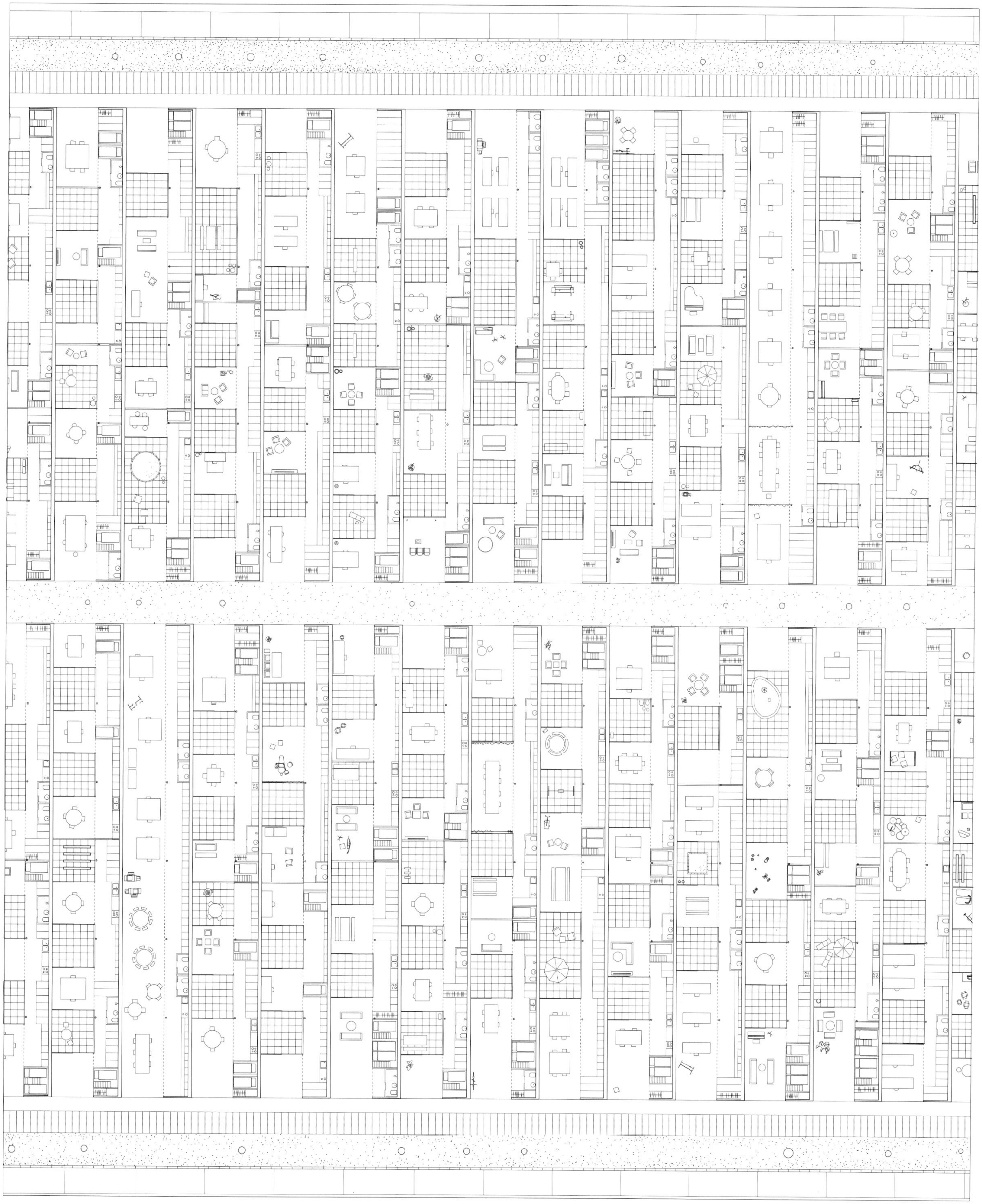

5 m

Plan of the retrofitted settlement unit

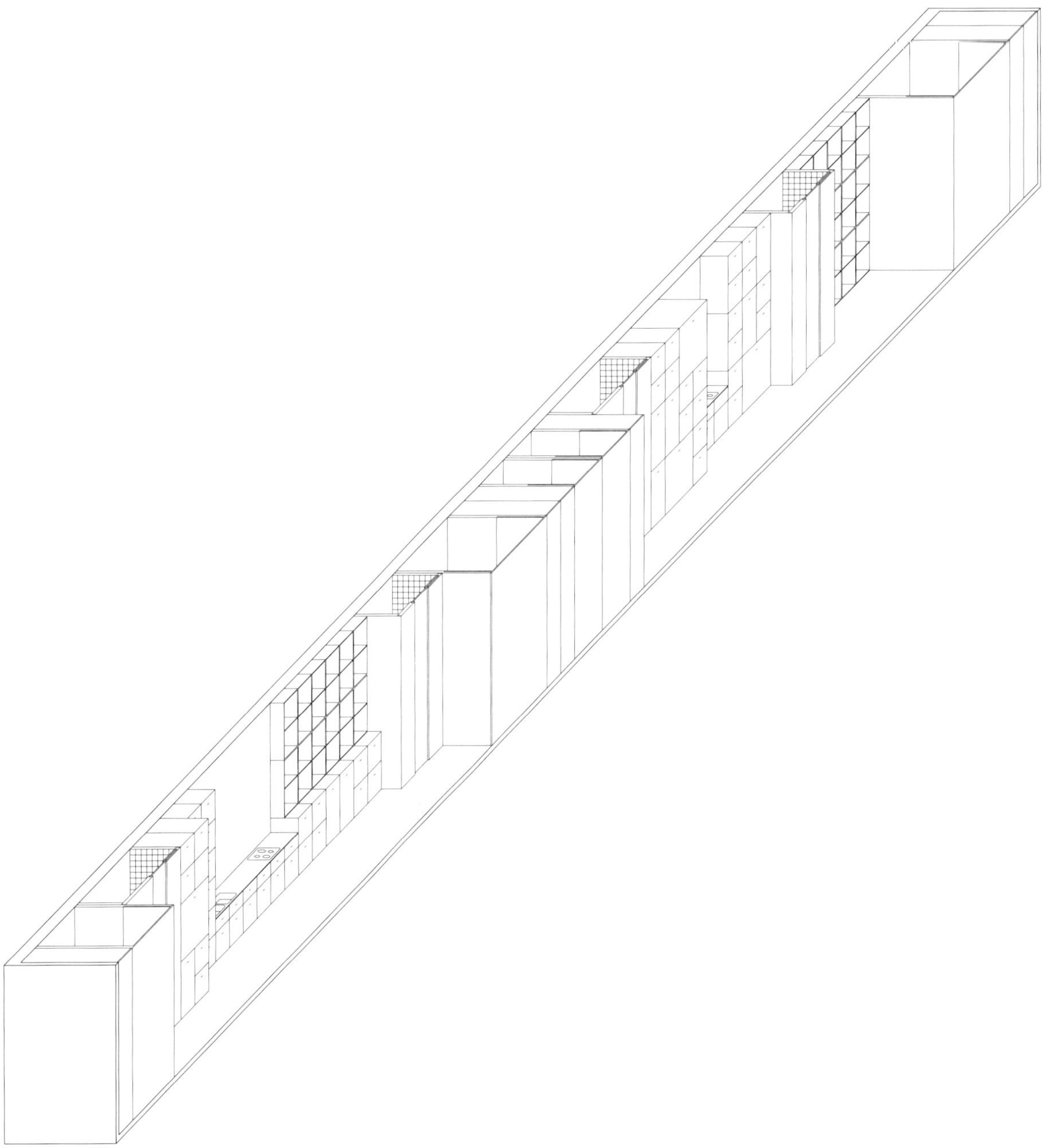

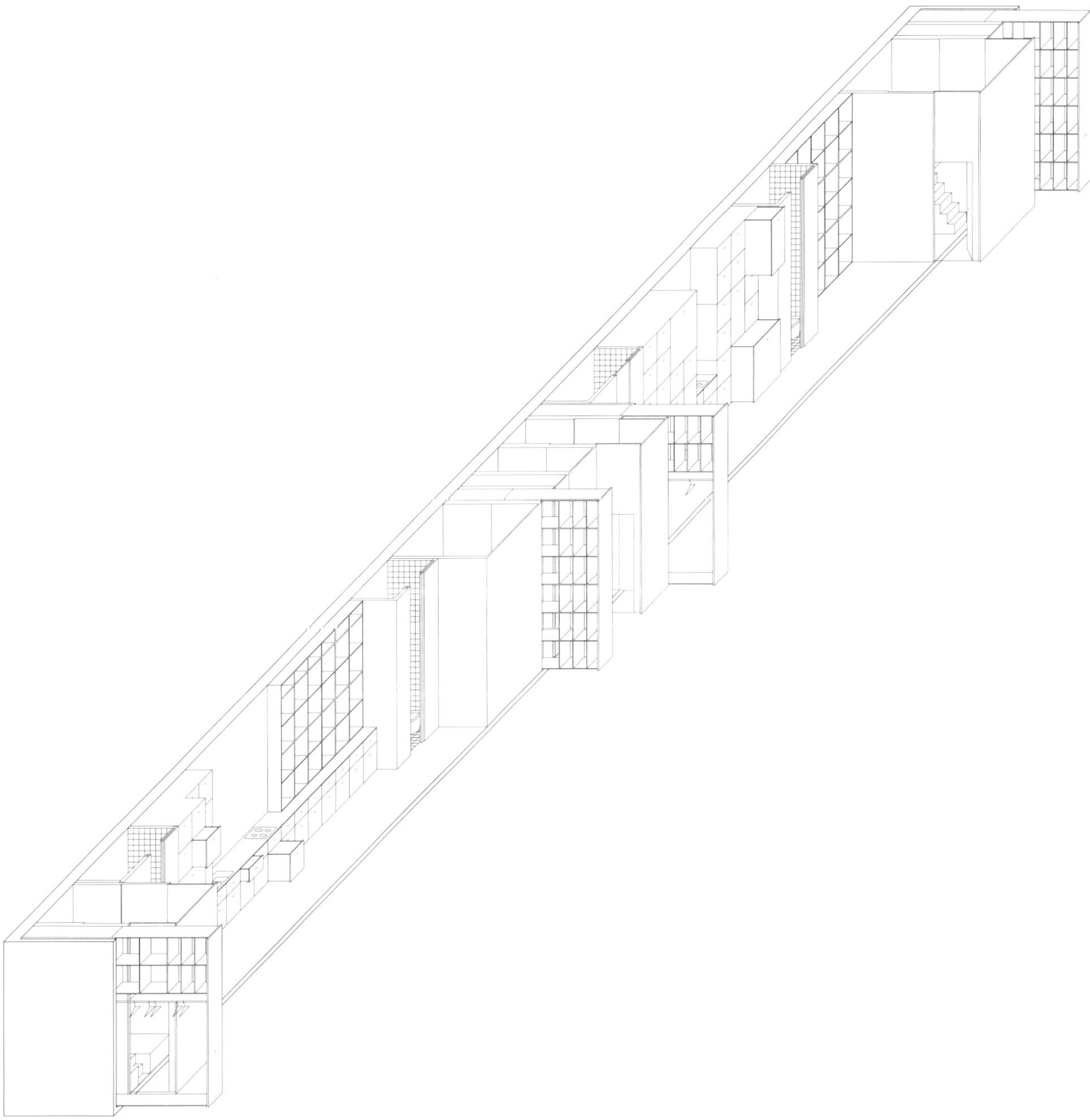

PRETTY VACANT (2014)

Recent studies demonstrate that in many European cities there is a huge demand for studio flats.[1] Because the availability of this type is scarce, renting them is expensive. Moreover, newly built studio flats are often too small, ill-designed, and difficult to furnish. In the 2010s there has been a surge of companies specializing in renting rooms within premises that include shared facilities, and yet real estate pressure and restrictive building codes have made their offerings extremely high-priced. These companies generally target young professionals, excluding other people in need of these types of dwellings, such as people with disabilities and elderly people. Single people today are expected to live alone in conventional apartments or houses or to share these with other people. Our project proposes a model for affordable housing not made of family apartments but of single-room occupancies (SROs). This type of habitation thrived in the United States and Europe in the nineteenth and the early twentieth century and comprised a variety of housing accommodations ranging from residential hotels to rooming houses to "efficiency apartments." In many cases, SROs resulted from dividing large private residences into smaller units. Although SROs were used by a wide variety of urban dwellers, the public attitude toward these accommodations became increasingly hostile as they were considered both an antifamily type of habitation and a threat to the more lucrative market of homeownership. As a result, in the United States and Europe there was a crusade against long-term residential hotels led by city authorities often under the spell of real estate lobbies, and by the 1980s they had disappeared from the market, converted into tourist hotels or destroyed altogether.[2] This project seeks a way to resurrect single-room occupancy at a large scale so that mass production may drastically reduce the type's cost and make it accessible to anyone. Therefore we envisage this proposal not as a private venture but a public initiative, within a larger program to build housing.

Due to Brussels's role as an administrative and political center, the city has witnessed a dramatic increase of office space over the past thirty years. Today, a large part of this stock is vacant as is especially visible in the Quartier Léopold, just east of the inner ring road, where almost all the major EU administrative buildings and associated organizations are located. We propose to transform office space into SROs supported by a multitude of shared facilities and working spaces. Our intention is to intervene in a molecular way, building by building, giving priority to premises whose prolonged vacancy has deeply affected their market value and which are thus affordable for the municipality to purchase.

Architecturally, the office plan offers a generic building layout. Typically organized as unobstructed space with a minimum number of vertical supports and with vertical circulation and clustered services, the office plan can easily be adapted to any use and occupation. In his essay "Typical Plan" (1995), Rem Koolhaas celebrated the conventional office plan as zero-degree architecture, "stripped of all traces of uniqueness and specificity."[3] With its radical abstraction, the "typical plan" approximates and gives spatial form to what Marx understood as the most generic faculty of the human being: the potential to produce. For this reason, to transform offices into housing is not only an act of recycling an increasingly underused typology, but a chance to give tangible and spatial form to the contemporary condition of labor in which work, domestic labor, socialization, rest, and exchange are understood no longer as separate spheres but as part of the same productive stream.

To repurpose office space for dwelling space also means to take advantage of the abstraction of the office plan to invent alternative housing configurations. While in apartment buildings the load-bearing structure is often combined with the walls that separate rooms, in the office building this structure is usually independent of the partitions. Within the office building it is therefore easier to organize a more flexible collective and shared mode of living both in social and economic terms.

After demolishing all non-load-bearing partitions, "inhabitable walls" are inserted into the office floor perpendicular to the exterior walls. These walls contain all standard services: storage, a bathroom, a bed alcove, and a kitchenette. The row of inhabitable walls divides the floor into two parts: a more private realm and a more collective one, respectively dedicated to living and social activities. In the middle, each inhabitable wall acts as a poché space and supports the needs of the inhabitants. Eventually, the more private segments of the walls can be opened up by the inhabitants and shared. Rather than being a sequence of rigidly separated conditions, housing becomes a sequence of spaces where being alone or together can be negotiated constantly by the inhabitants.

At the scale of the block, the inner courtyard is liberated from the extensions that have occupied this space over time, and is transformed into an inner collective area, accessible from the surrounding streets through four entrances (one for each side). By adding a light steel structure along the inner elevations, a continuous system of balconies grants accessibility to each floor of all the buildings, becoming itself an adaptable meeting or gathering place. Within each block, small and decaying buildings are demolished and replaced by slim, high towers. These towers offer large storage spaces on the first levels and host a dense system of temporary living units on the higher floors. Ultimately this project aims to create an entire district of SROs which can host all kind of households previously unsuited to the very traditional domestic landscape of Belgian cities.

1 Christian Dessouroux et al., "Housing in Brussels: Diagnosis and Challenges," *Brussels Studies*, no. 99 (June 2016): 4–5.

2 As in the case of San Francisco. See James Tracy, *Dispatches against Displacement: Field Notes from San Francisco's Housing Wars* (Oakland: AK Press, 2014), 39–50.

3 Rem Koolhaas, "Typical Plan," in Rem Koolhaas and Bruce Mau, *S,M,L,XL* (Rotterdam: 010), 335.

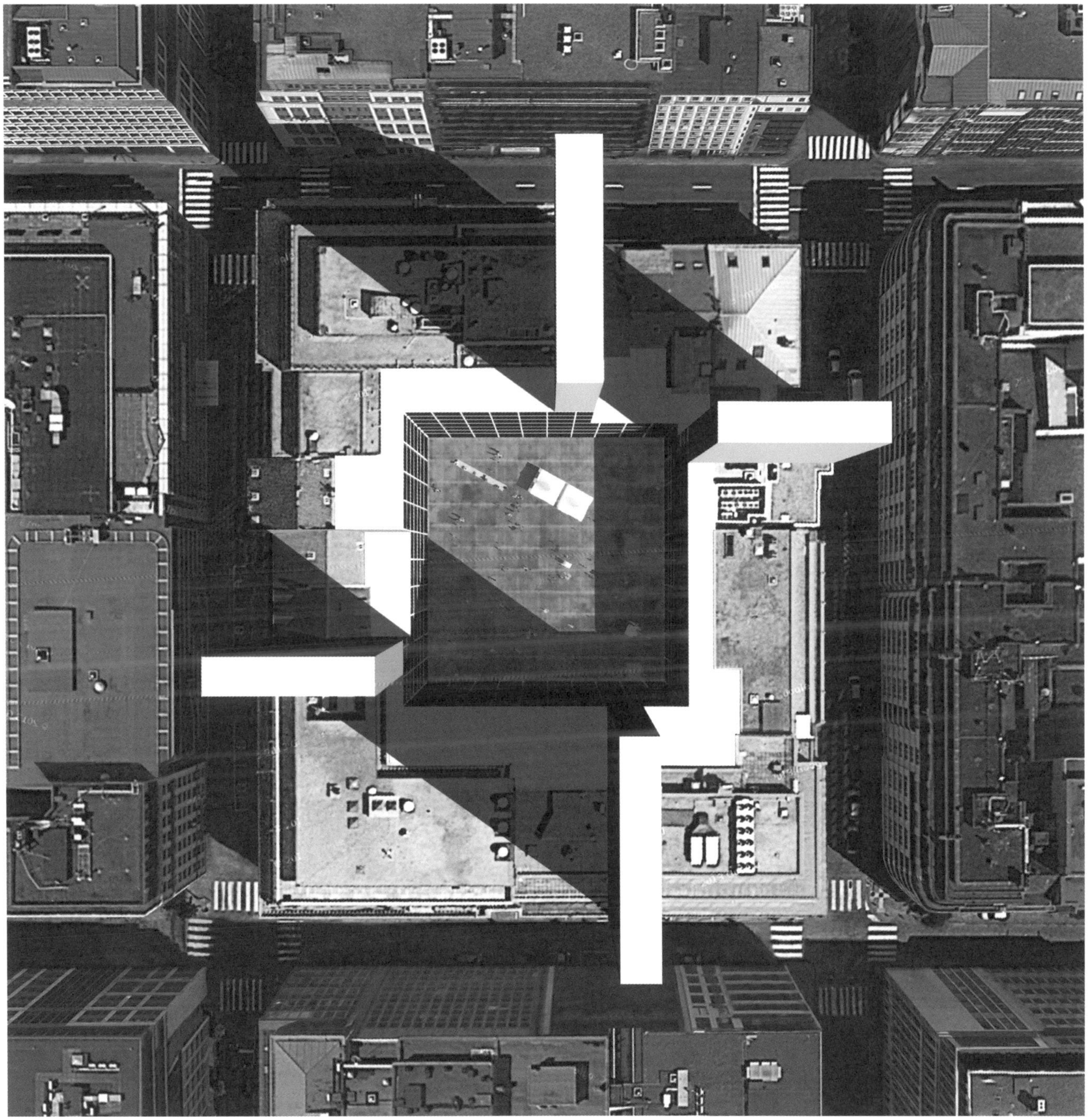

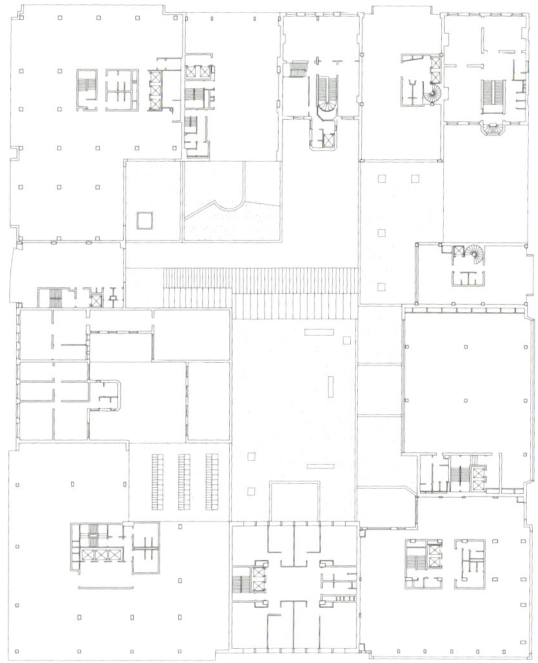

Existing typical plan

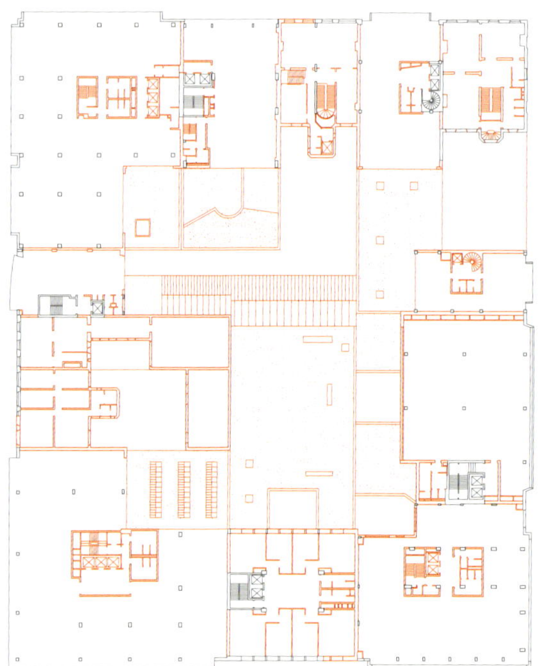

Demolition plan, phase 1

20 m

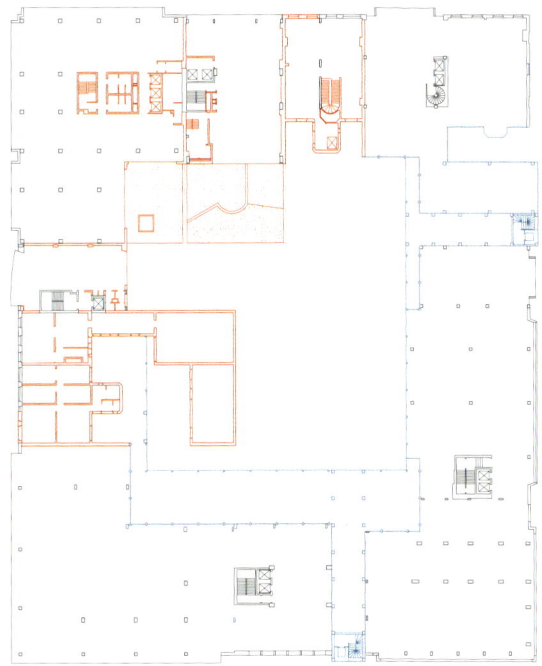

Demolition and construction plan, phase 2

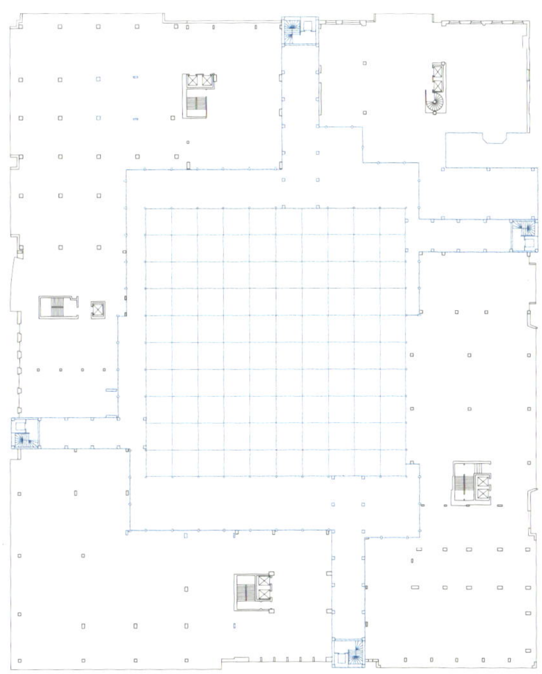

Construction plan, phase 3

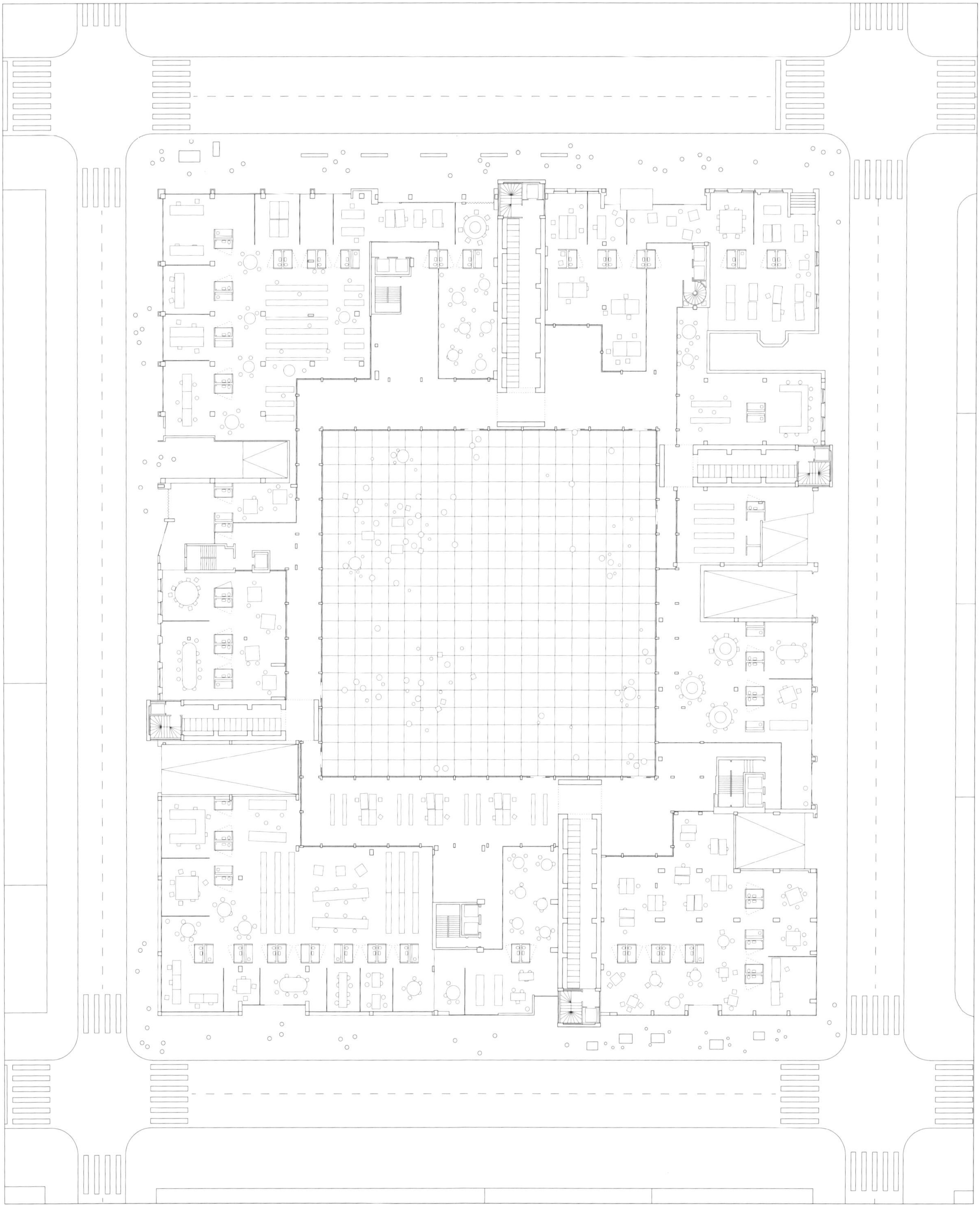

10 m

Ground-floor plan with workplaces and services.
The alignment of service cores defines two areas: secluded toward the street, open toward the courtyard

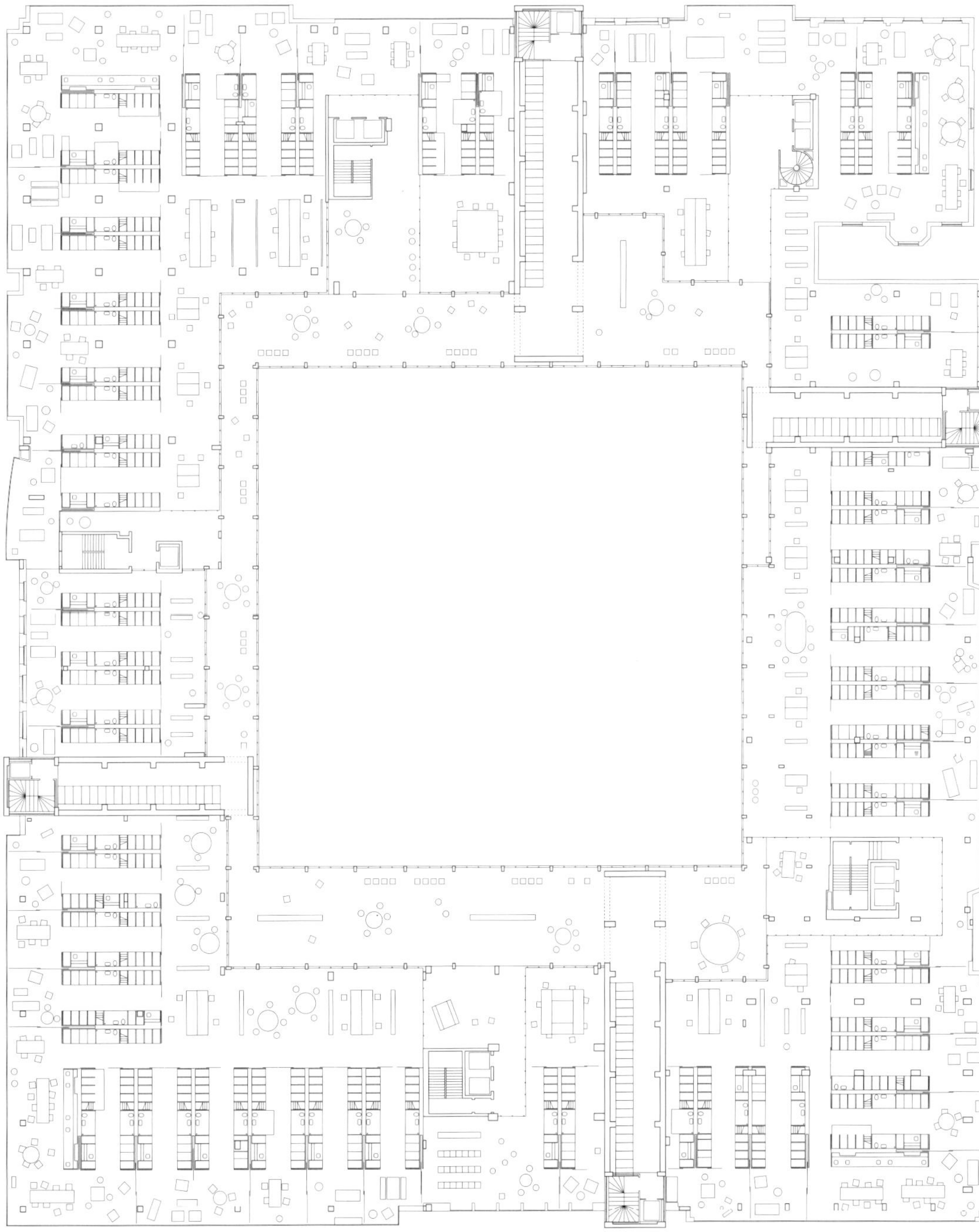

Typical plan with lodgings and collective spaces.
The alignment of service cores defines two areas: private toward the street, communal toward the courtyard

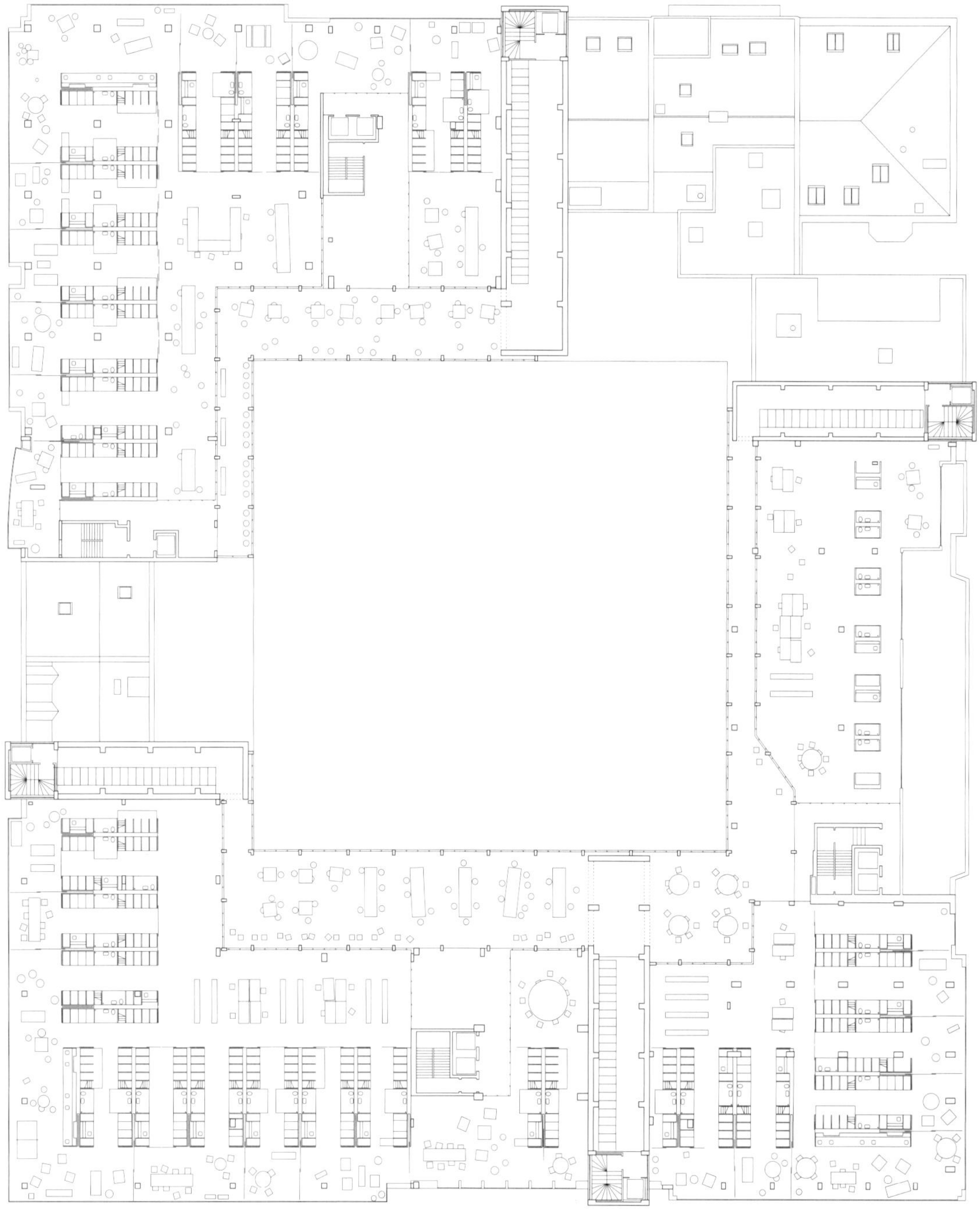

10 m

Plan of the last floor of the block, hosting lodgings and collective spaces

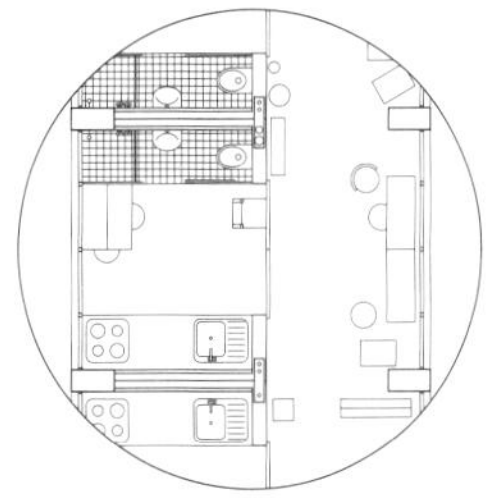

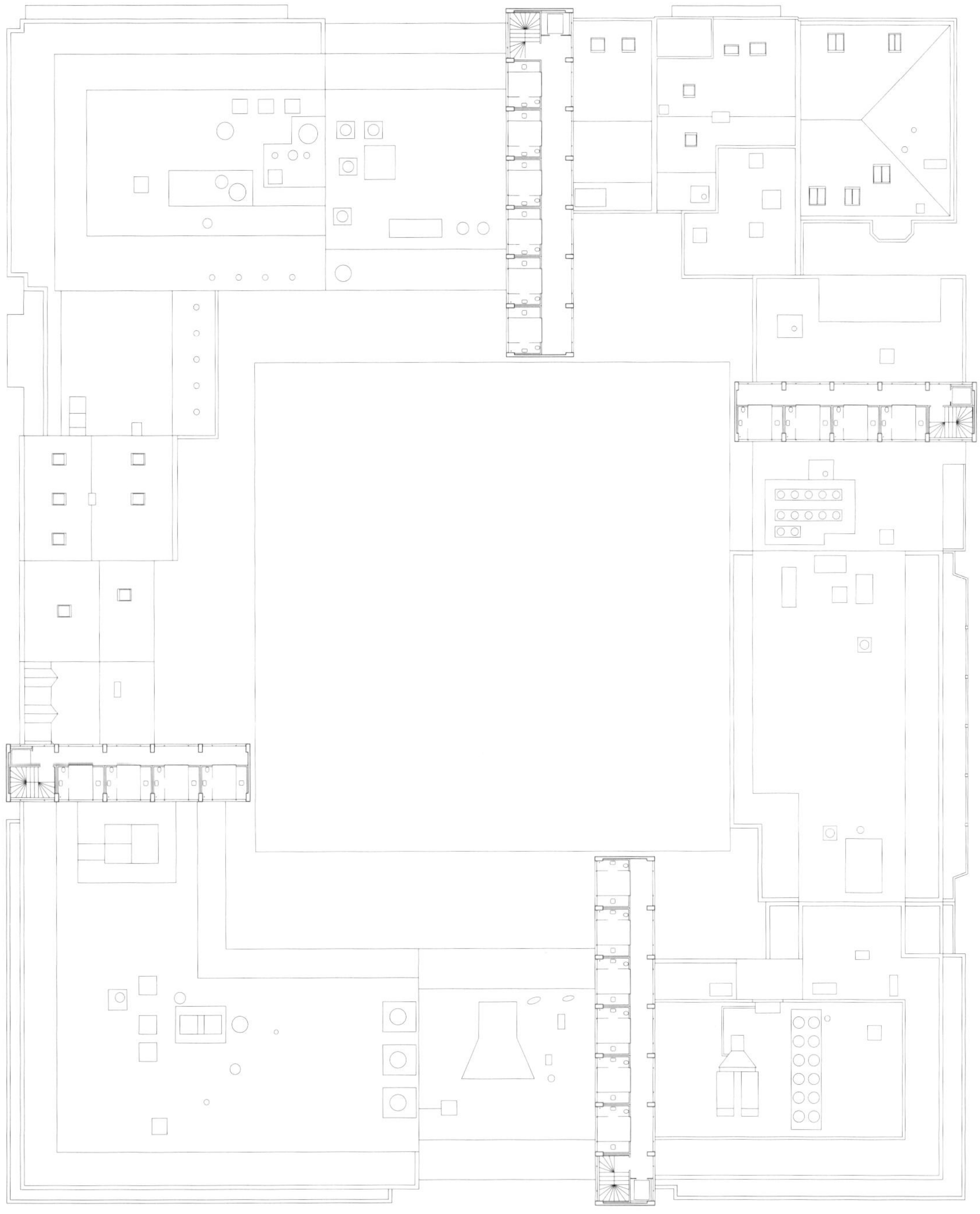

Typical plan of the towers, hosting studios for short stay periods

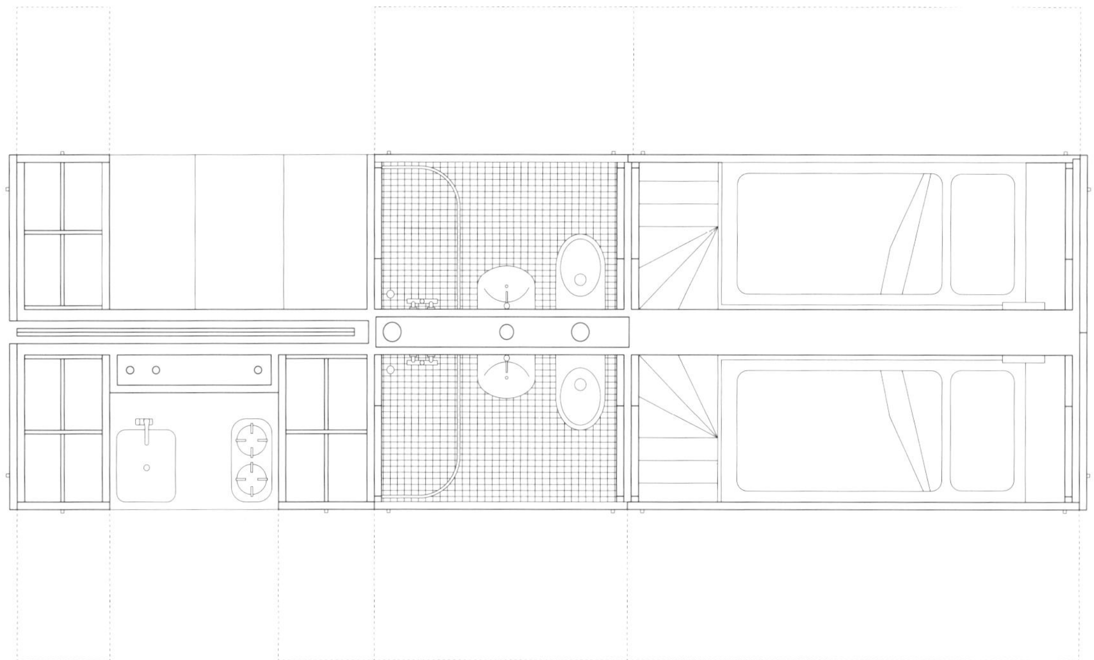

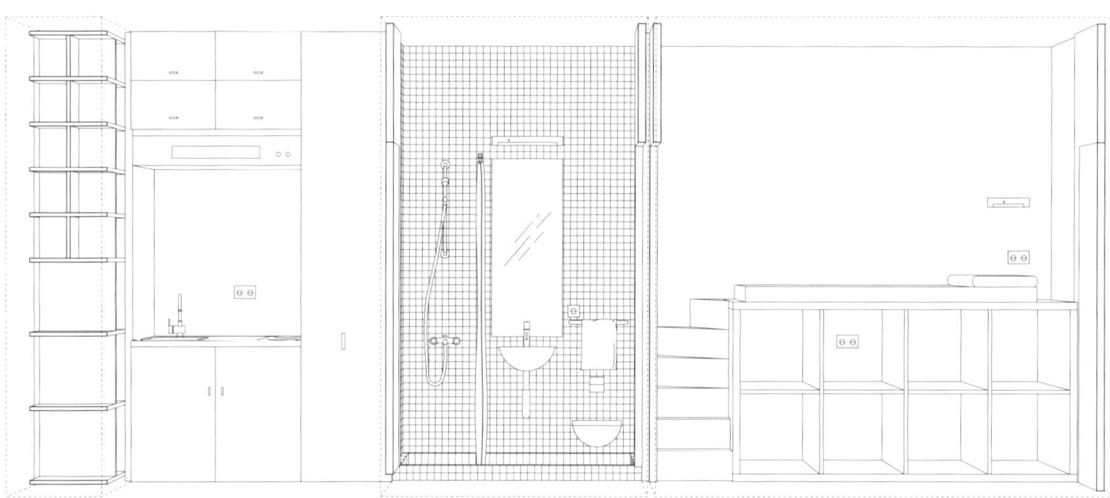

Plan, elevation, and section of the service core

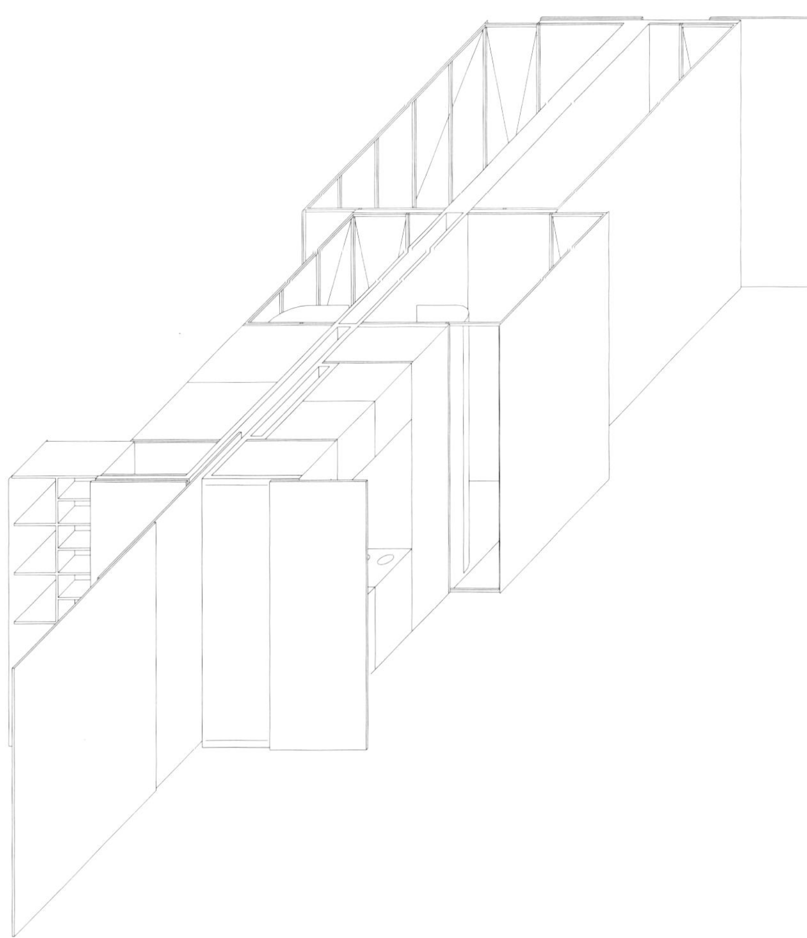

TOWER AND PLINTH (2014)

This project concerns a study for the development of an area around Merihaka, a residential neighborhood in central Helsinki consisting of large high-rise housing blocks built during the 1970s and 1980s on reclaimed land. Due to its strategic location and visibility, the site offers an ideal opportunity to introduce both affordable housing and working spaces in proximity to the center of the city. Rather than just accommodating these functions into a generic hybrid building, our proposal attempts to define a new urban live/work archetype. The starting point of the proposal is the observation that despite the stigma that affects late modernist housing complexes, Merihaka is a very valuable intervention within the city of Helsinki. The anonymity of its architecture dignifies the area and highlights the qualities of the surrounding landscape. The area is serene and slightly melancholic, an aspect that can be considered a quality rather than a problem. While the Merihaka housing complex exemplifies the typical "dormitory" character of twentieth-century mass housing, the extension we propose drastically changes this condition by recreating the premodern model where housing and working spaces are superimposed on each other.

The proposal sets out from the elaboration of a simple prototype, reinterpreting the tower and plinth of the existing Merihaka housing complex. While this architecture uses the plinth as a large, multistory parking space, in our proposal the plinth becomes an integral part of the living and working functions that are to be accommodated in the new complex, hosting a multiplicity of working and commercial activities and contributing to bringing social activity to the space of the street. The two-story plinth is regularly pierced by patio spaces and by the cores of the towers. While the patios offer a protected outdoor area, and provide daylight to the interior spaces of the plinth, the towers' cores become the magnet around which all services and facilities are placed. Circulation and accessibility to the facilities contained in the plinth are provided by an orthogonal system of double-height galleries that stretch between the towers and patios and are lit by linear skylight windows. Our proposal implicitly criticizes the open-ended spatial character of the typical office plan, without renouncing its flexibility. Even though the structure of the plinth offers the potential of an open space minimally obstructed by load-bearing structure, the space is divided and differentiated by the position of the cores, patios, and internal galleries, and rhythmed by the arrangement of the blocks that contain the services, stairs, and storage. In this way, it is possible to obtain spaces of different size that are supported by all the necessary services while keeping these services independently accessible. In contrast to the plinth, the towers are typically dedicated to residential functions. The living units in the towers are the result of a simple and strategic spatial organization. The floor plan is organized as a concentric sequence of layers that goes from the outer space for living, to the intermediate ribbon of services, to the inner vertical core. In this way each floor can host various types of residential units that can be arranged in multiple ways. Due to the flexibility of this spatial organization, working spaces can also be accommodated next to, or in lieu of, residential units. By clearly separating served and servant spaces, each living unit can take maximum advantage of the view toward the surrounding landscape, while retaining the possibility of being typologically configured in various ways, from large studio to multiroom apartment. As a result, inhabitants are offered a variety of spaces for different uses in which living and working activities can coexist in different manners.

From an urban point of view, our proposal interprets the district as a threshold between the city center and the first periphery, and it attempts to tackle two unresolved aspects of Merihaka, namely its lack of relationship with the adjacent thoroughfare leading across the bridge into the city center, and more generally the residual condition of the many open spaces adjacent to the modernist housing estate. A bridge reconstruction is planned for the coming years, together with the reconfiguration of the important traffic artery crossing the extension we propose; these works, along with a very high demand for affordable housing in the city, represent an opportunity to solve the relationship between the estate and the street. Our proposal thus aims to complete the Merihaka housing complex by adjusting its relationship with the urban context and establishing a clear relationship between the plinth and the street. As for the open spaces located along the main thoroughfare and facing the water—some of them green areas and others temporary parking lots—these are identified as an opportunity for the long-term densification of this part of the city through the same urban live/work archetype. Yet, distinct from the rigid geometry of its predecessor, the proposed plinth adjusts itself to the geometry of the street while revealing its abstract orthogonal logic toward the water. In this way, the proposed archetype defines a streetscape with commercial and production spaces along the street front, whose social intensity is offset by the more intimate, protected gardens and patios toward the waterfront. Like its predecessor, our proposal is based on an architectural presence which, rather than being an iconic gesture, aims to be a structuring framework that offers the Merihaka site a readable formal definition.

86

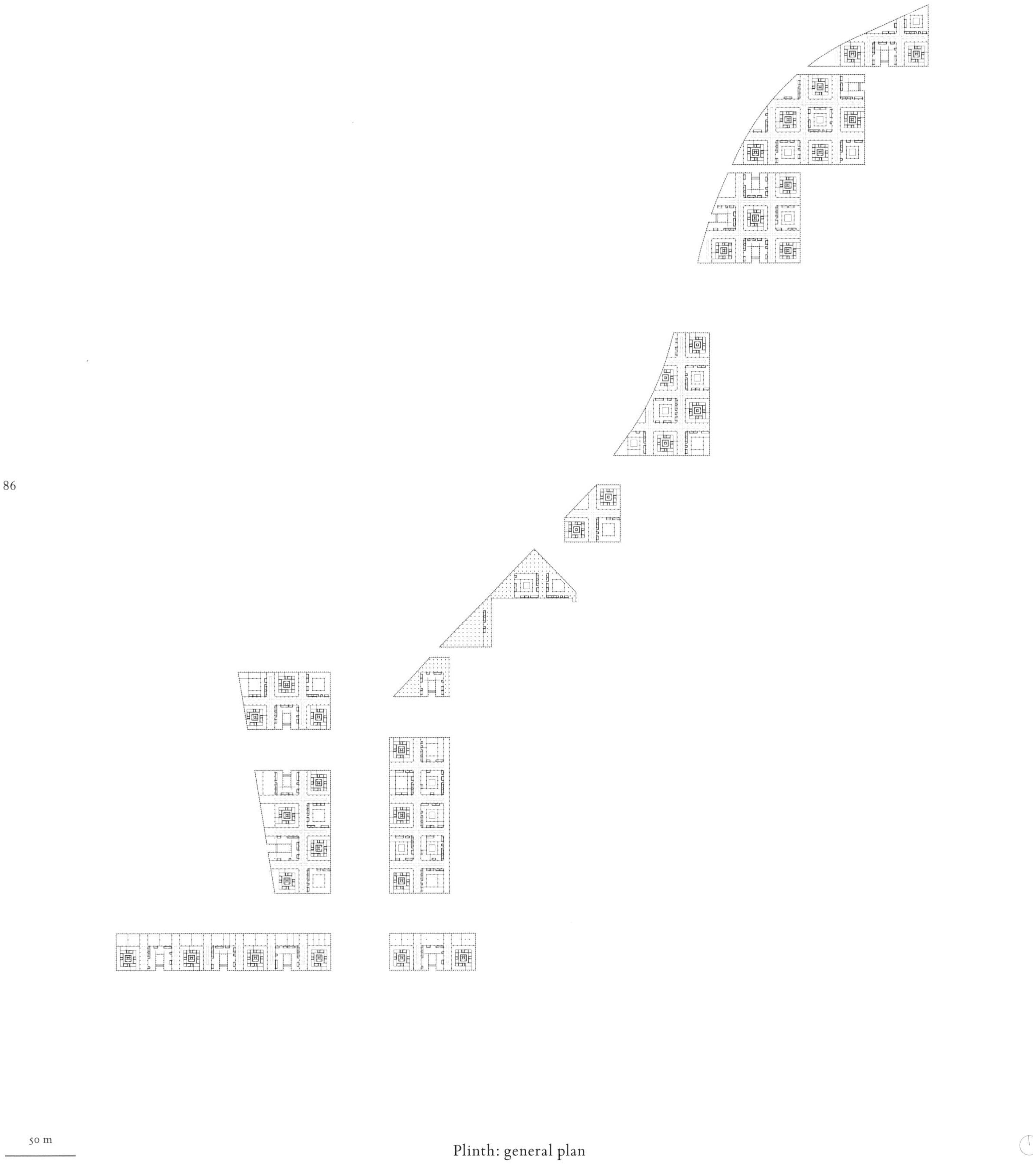

Plinth: general plan

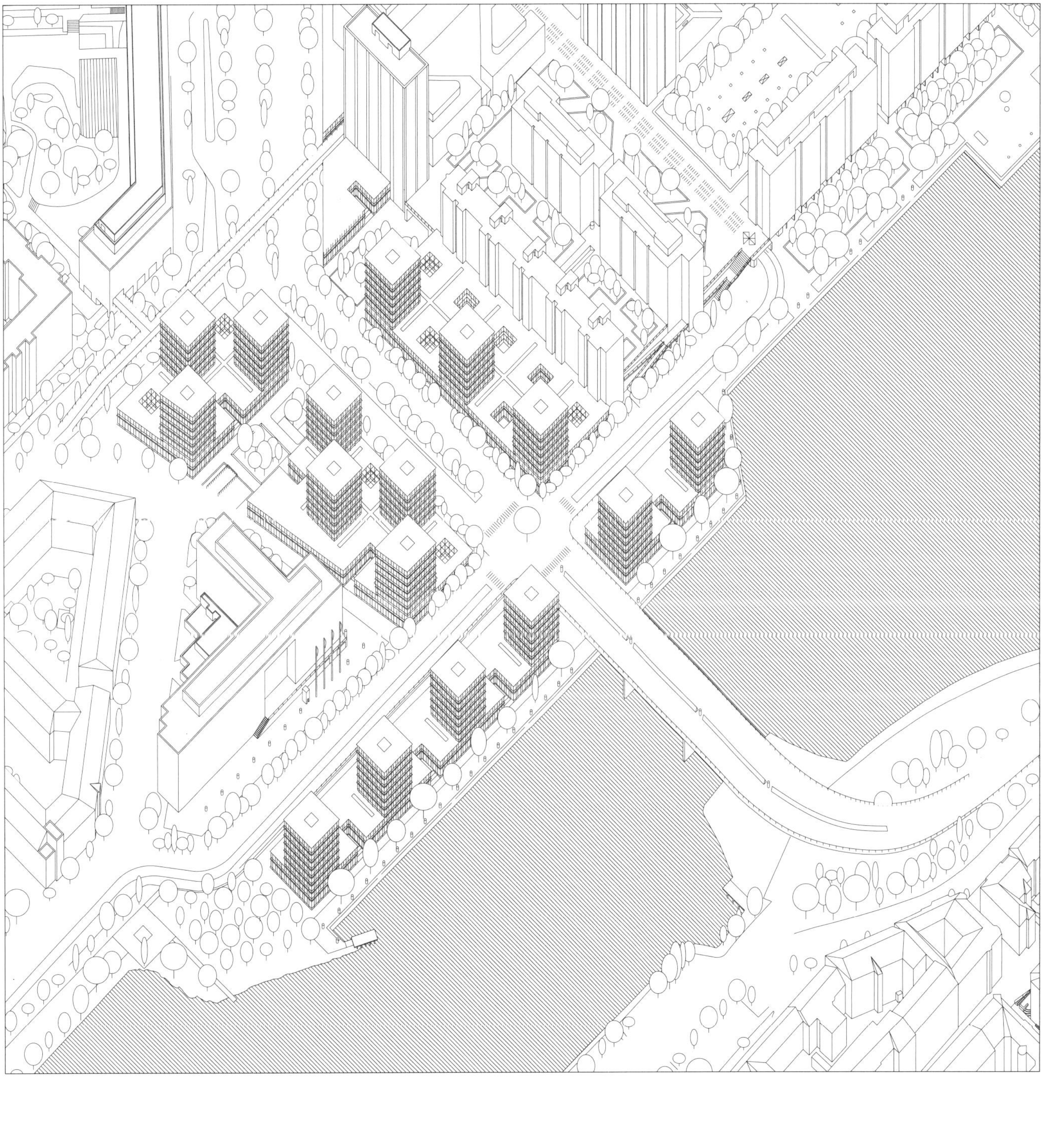

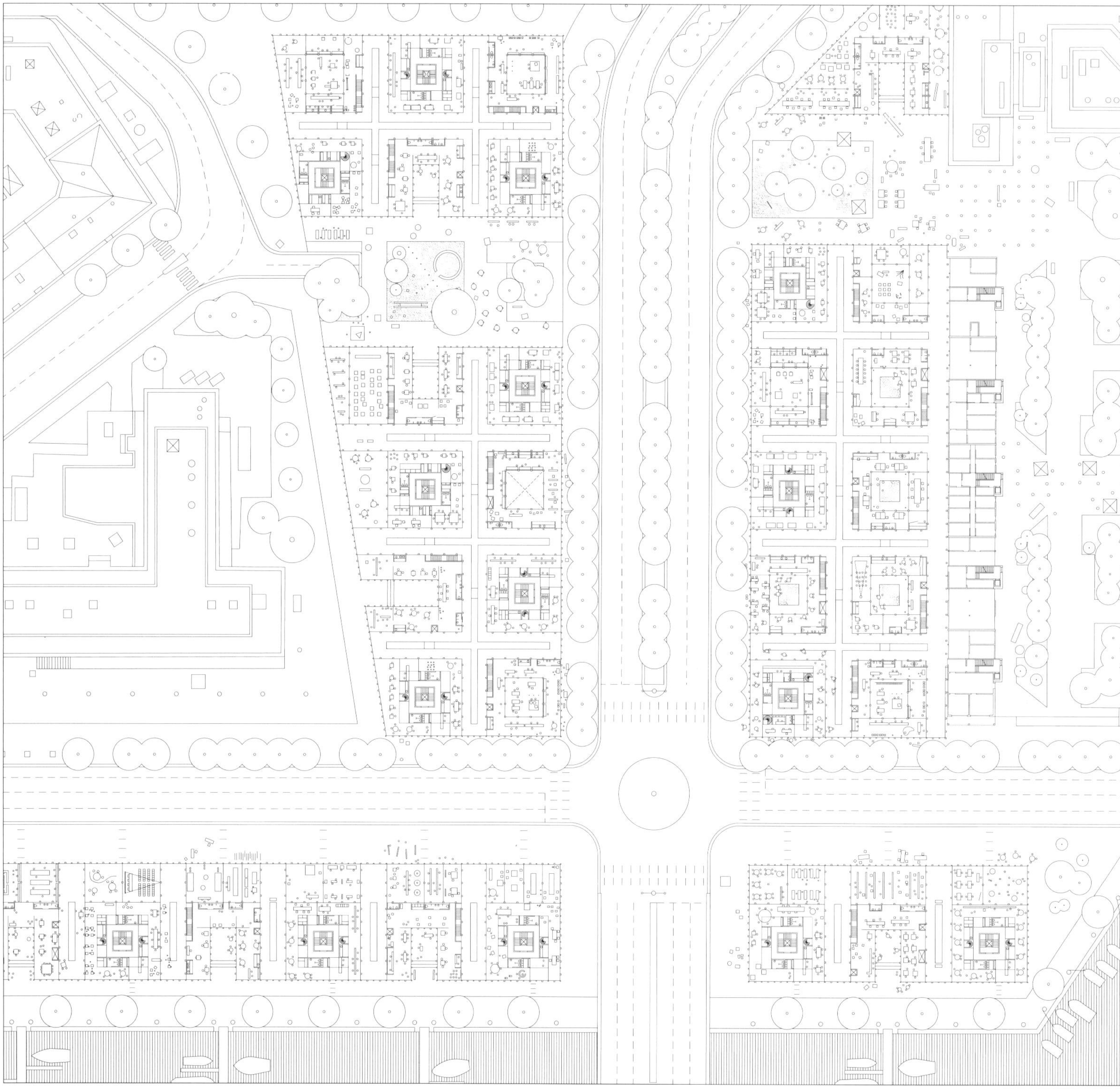

Ground-floor plan with workspaces and collective services

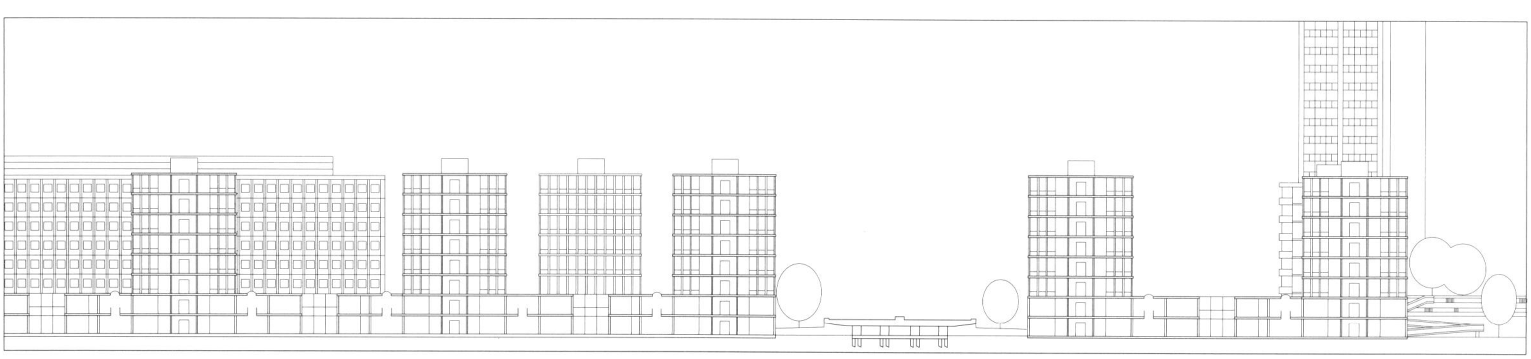

20 m

Section

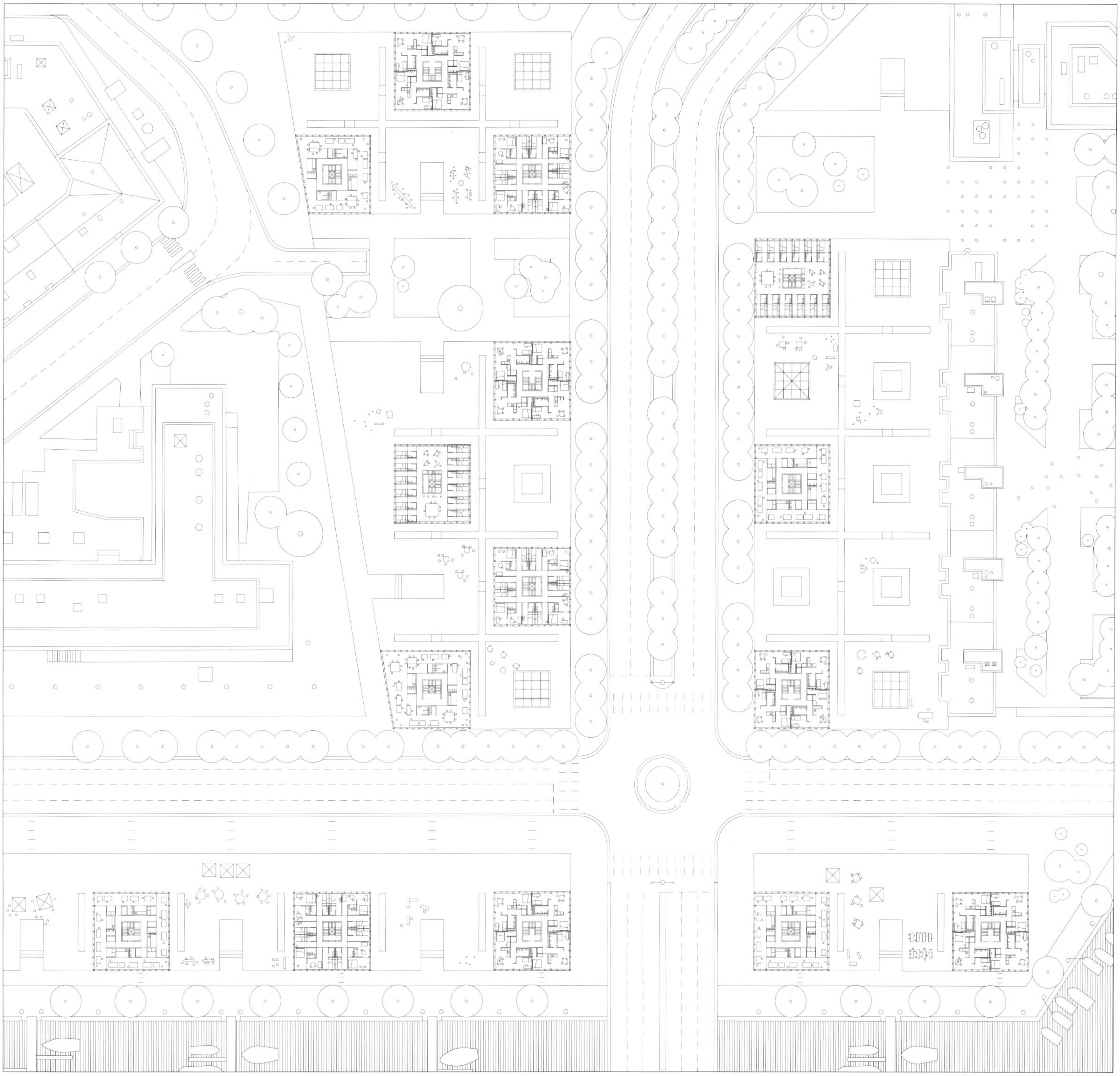

Typical floor plan of the towers

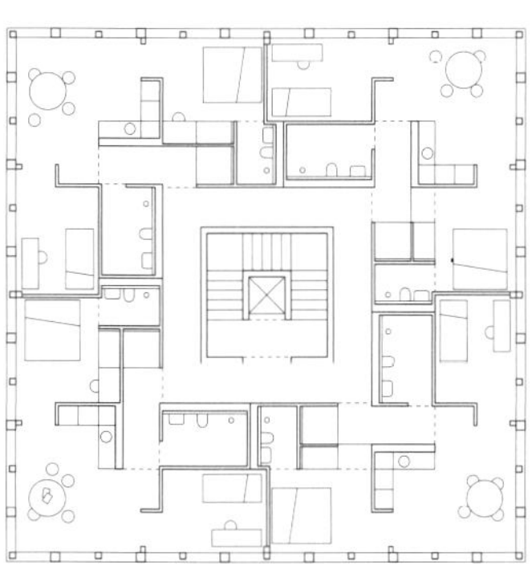

Apartments

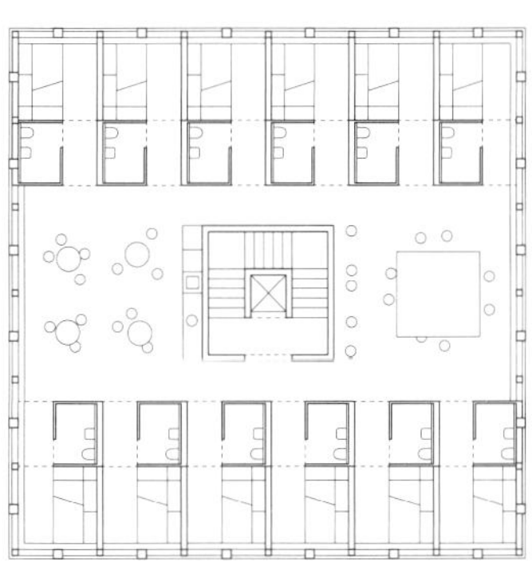

Hostel

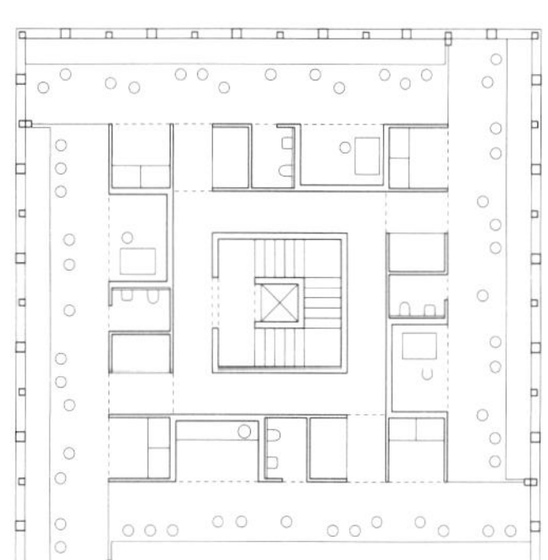

Offices

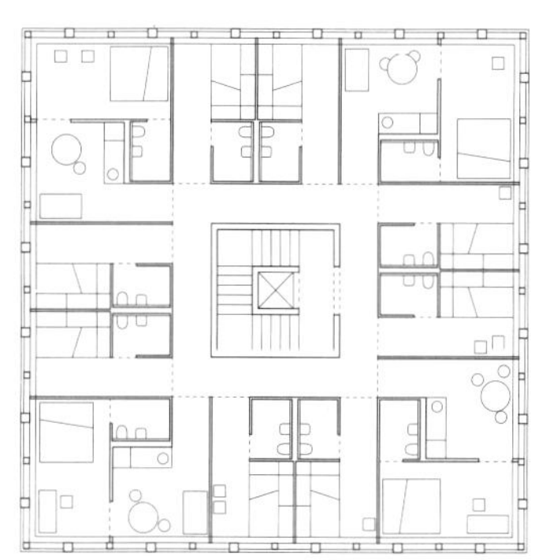

Apartments/offices

EVERYDAY IS LIKE SUNDAY (2015)

While the environments of the park and the industrial site seem antithetical, in the twentieth century their overlapping became one of the most important paradigms of contemporary urbanization. The industrial park is a cluster of production facilities in green spaces, often located in a suburban setting, and it symbolizes how, in the context of modernization, "nature" is no longer the antithesis to "civilization" but its very ideological and spatial archetype. In the eighteenth century, reconstructing nature—either in the form of a park or in the form of the picturesque garden—became a widespread development tactic in cities. As a result of this, the image of "nature" is now driven by two objectives: on one hand, nature must calm and dampen the hectic rhythms that industrial production imposes on urban dwellers; and on the other, nature is invoked by the ruling class as a condition that naturalizes (or legitimizes) the power relationships brought about by new forms of production.[1] Nature as a form of "landscape" within urban development is not only ideological but evoked to create a profitable framework for urban development. The industrial park represents the possibility of developing industry not as an ad hoc concentration of people and machines, but as a carefully orchestrated environment liberated from the social constraints caused by production in the city—it is no coincidence that the industrial park was born after the wave of labor struggles that characterized late nineteenth- and early twentieth-century capitalism.

THE RISE OF THE INDUSTRIAL PARK

Despite their projected image of openness, parks were introduced in the early eighteenth century as enclosed spaces. Etymologically, park has cognates in the West Germanic term *parruk*, or "enclosed tract of land," and the Old High German *pfarrih*, which means "fencing, enclosure." The industrial park thus originates as a compound separated from its surroundings and accessible only via infrastructure such as a road or railway. As a clearly delimited portion of land, the park functions not only as an efficient compound, but also as the image of an uncorrupted landscape where production and "life in nature" are reconciled. The image invoked by the industrial park is that of the "arcadia," the longed-for place of harmony, that nevertheless is invested in the pragmatic goal of making production as efficient as possible.

For this reason it is possible to argue that an ancestor of the industrial park is the villa. The best illustrations of this type are Palladio's villas in Venice's *terraferma*. Inspired by Alvise Cornaro's praise of the countryside as the locus of the good life, Palladio's designs were in fact hybrids of a palazzo and a farm expressed through the unprecedented combination of the classicist pediment of the central house and the rustic architecture of the flanking *barchesse*.[2] The Palladian ethos that combines the logic of the proprietor with bucolic asceticism was reinterpreted by Thomas Jefferson as the only genuine and safe way of living. To an extent the ideology of the "industrial park" is deeply rooted in these ideas, which took on newfound urgency at the moment the overcongested and filthy metropolis started to backfire and contradict capitalism's self-promotion as rational system. The industrial park, followed by the office campus, the office park, the science park, and the business park, are all variations on a theme of the pastoral image where "nature" is an incentive for hard work and the site for relaxed and "thoughtful" social behavior. Like the Palladian villa, the industrial park tames the reality of hard labor with the reassuring image of nature.

The prototype for this kind of industrial park is the warehouse and administrative facility for Sears Roebuck & Company designed by George Nimmons in Chicago in 1906, which juxtaposed the workplace and amenities such as gardens, sport fields, and ball courts. In placing work and leisure next each other, Nimmons was attempting to balance the ethos of production with its seeming opposite: play and free time. As a result, the industrial park introduced a new subjectivity within the sphere of production which architectural historian Louise Mozingo has defined as "pastoral capitalism."[3] For Mozingo the rise of pastoral capitalism has its roots in Andrew Jackson Downing's advocacy of suburban development as the antithesis to the congestion of big cities.[4] Downing favored the expansion of cities, but he also realized that the pressure of the industrial metropolis could be alleviated by introducing the possibility of retreat into the calming landscape of the countryside. This vision was already a familiar American trope, established by Jefferson's vision of the American nation as rural and Ralph Waldo Emerson's and Henry David Thoreau's lyrical exaltations of nature as the American way of life. By the time of Sears Roebuck, the United States had become a country where greenness was the most convincing image of capitalism's goodness. This understanding of the park as a green space where nature and urbanization could peacefully coexist became the framework for bringing together urban reform, speculative real estate, marketing, and a moral interpretation of the "good life"—a balance of hard work and bucolic living. While the heavy logistics of manufacturing processes made the combination of production and green space difficult to achieve, the factory became an ideal model as industrial labor gave way

Keiberg Office Park,
Zaventem, 1985

Keiberg 1,
Zaventem, 1985

Ikaros Business Park,
Zaventem, 1990

Amadeus Square,
Anderlecht, 1999

Amadeus Square,
Anderlecht, 1999

Green Hill Campus,
Leuven, 2000

Imperial,
Zaventem, 1990

Fountain Business Park,
Bornem, 1991

Sphere Business Park,
Zellik, 1992

to "immaterial" labor; hence the office park—a space where the smooth politics of "clerical" work found its appropriate locus in the Arcadian look of the domesticated "green" landscape.

FROM THE CORPORATE OFFICE PARK TO THE RESEARCH PARK

In the United States the success and diffusion of the office park was triggered immediately after the Second World War by the increasing importance of managerial work in an advancing capitalist economy. And the absolute protagonist of the managerial revolution was the corporation, the large-scale ensemble of material and immaterial productive activities whose paternalistic approach to employees found its ideal spatial form in the constructed "pastoralism" of green landscape. It was precisely to avoid the political effects of a big concentration of workers in the city that capitalists introduced the office park as a safer and more controllable enclave for production. Within this context the white-collar worker emerged as dedicated employee indifferent to politics and skeptical toward class solidarity and the possibility of unionizing against the bosses—a stark contrast to the blue-collar worker he replaced.[5] There are two kinds of white-collar workers: the specialized technician whose main job is research, and the service manager whose job consists of clerical activities such as the organization and transmission of information. Given the increasing importance of technological innovation as a competitive factor within the capitalistic economy, the training of the researcher is an important concern for corporations. It is for this reason that the office park came to resemble the university campus: enter the research park, the most emblematic example of which is the Stanford Research Park, the embryo of Silicon Valley. A fundamental aspect of this research campus was its strategic proximity to the university, which significantly altered the traditional isolation of the corporate enclave. The Stanford Research Park initiated a new tradition of a workplace dominated by the image of the "casual" transfer of knowledge among workers and companies. As Mozingo has noted, it was here that the promise of the pastoral workplace was finally fulfilled. In an environment characterized by the eternal California spring and the increasing informality of working relationships, the research park initiated the idea of the workplace as "playground," where work and free time casually mix in an environment that is less corporate and more entrepreneurial. And yet a crucial aspect of the success of the research park is its link with the university, which works not only spatially but also through continuous exchange between research and business.

Within this milieu, the entrepreneurial worker took form, and so too a post-Fordist method of production. For in the context of this model, capital no longer relies solely on the means of production, but on the workers' subjective ability to adapt to conditions that are less and less organized by the conventional nine-to-five office schedule. Today, the legacy of the research park has been absorbed and "interiorized" by the Google campus model in which interiors are made up of both endless factory spaces and theme park playfulness. In this late interpretation of the research park, the interior has replaced the exterior by offering an abundance of amenities within the office buildings and reducing the surroundings to a thin green space to be seen only from the office interior.

THE BUSINESS PARK IN THE OUTSKIRTS OF THE EUROPEAN CITY

Paradoxically, the widespread success of the office park coincides with its crisis. Since the 1970s the office park has been exported to other countries around the world, especially throughout Europe, as the service industry has become a leading economic sector. However, compared to the corporate logic that gave birth to the postwar American office park, the European model was built on a more volatile economic structure. Rather than developing as specific company headquarters, European office parks have mainly developed as venture capital speculations and are quickly rented to companies searching for a local base in the ever-expanding network of transnational trade. It could be argued that the diffusion of the office park in the 1980s and 1990s in Europe is tied to the rise in risk capital investment typical of a neoliberal economy. Not surprisingly, the Europeanized version of the American office park proliferated by taking advantage of Margaret Thatcher's 1987 deregulation of the zoning code, and is perhaps best represented by the Cambridge Science Park. Founded in the 1970s by Trinity College as a place for scientific enterprise, it was developed following the university campus model. However, its success led to the development of major business parks in the same area, and later of an ever-growing constellation of anonymous office clusters. The Cambridge development shows a compressed view of the rise and fall of the office park: from its rise as a "campus" to its fall as a suburban cluster of generic "boxes." The rental purpose of the office park had a major impact on its architectural and urban qualities. No longer the unique premises of the company headquarters, by the 1980s the office park had become a compound of rentable office space. Known as a business park, this reduced version of the American office park offered office space located within close proximity to important traffic nodes and airports. Thus strategic placement supplanted the landscape quality of the traditional office park. Indeed, in many business parks built across Europe in the last thirty years, the green landscape has altogether disappeared to be replaced by parking facilities and occasional flowerbeds. This is the case for several office parks developed around Brussels and cities in Flanders between the 1980s and early 1990s. Since the 1970s Flanders had been a site for international trade—this is also thanks to its location at the heart of the Benelux countries and the most advanced regions of the European Union. In the early 2000s, when Brussels became the official capital of the European Union, developers raced to build more office space inside and outside the city. But the result was low-quality architecture far distant from the "American Versailles" that served as the model for postwar office parks in the United States. Stripped of landscape attributes, the generic office park has come to embody the volatility of an economy increasingly tied to risk investment. The last gasp for office park development coincided with the dot-com boom of the late 1990s, which sparked a mini-renaissance of the office park and a return to the corporate ambition of placemaking—for example some office parks built near Brussels during this time were more carefully designed with more generous landscape features. But the moment was short-lived, and since the mid-2000s the office park has entered a slow but irreversible agony, analogous to the economic restructuring that resulted after the 2007 recession.

Indeed it is possible to argue that the crisis of the business park is the result of the larger crisis of the service economy. Business parks once provided the most efficient location for housing a type of labor that was mainly reliant on the management and transfer of information while being independent of the traditional forms of social encounter that are typical of the dense city. But today their distance, both from the city and the university, makes them vulnerable vis-à-vis the increasing importance of informal socialization within contemporary forms of production. Moreover, because they are developed to be rented in large quantities of square meters, office parks do not accommodate an increasing number of small-scale companies.

THE TRANSFORMATION OF THE OFFICE PARK

The office park crisis represents an opportunity for radical reinvention. Our proposal for their transformation does not follow a problem-solving approach, but rather looks to the real issue at stake: the housing crisis. It has been estimated that by 2030 Flanders will need more than 300,000 new residences. Where will these be located? What sort of urban form will this amount of new housing produce? Above all, what sort of houses should be built? The typical response is to increase the density of cities in order to spare the territory between them from further urbanization. While this position seems reasonable, it often puts the existing and already dense city under pressure by making it the only place where urban life is possible. This "return to the city" also does not account for the many areas in between cities (and this is especially true for Flanders) that are already densely urbanized and well connected by public transport. Flanders offers a chance to retrofit suburbia as a place for living and working. Office parks can function as the pilot project for this idea. The advantage of office parks is that as "parks" they are a clearly delimited area, and due to the abundance of parking lots the sites are ripe for development. This condition offers the possibility of using the office park area as a clear compound for living and working space. While existing office buildings can serve both as working and community facilities, the entire site of the office park can be filled with housing. In this way existing office space becomes a shared space of living—a luxury that would hardly be possible in the city. The housing system we propose maintains the privacy of rooms while increasing collective facilities. In this way the overall private domain is still essential and reduced to a minimum, allowing a multiplicity of subjects—users, inhabitants, families—to live together, limiting the burdens of traditional housekeeping.

The governing principle of our housing system is the room not the house. Distribution logic allows each room to function as an independent microflat while directly connecting to shared facilities as part of one generous domestic space. The arrangement of the rooms and shared spaces allows inhabitants to choose and negotiate how to live together and what degree of sharing they can or want to accept. A fundamental objective of our proposal is to counter the ideology of the park by making explicit the productive aspect of housing itself. The separation of housing from office space suggests that reproduction within the residence is inconsequential for production in general. An inhabited office park makes the interrelation between work and life explicit. To an extent our proposal revisits the Palladian hybrid of life and work enacted by the combination of the house and the barn as one single dwelling, but unlike the Palladian villa, whose architecture celebrated the mastery of the landowner over territory, the inhabited office park celebrates communal life freed from the traditional hierarchies of homeownership.

This transformation of the office park into a live-work compound is based on an economic scenario that sees the office park's loss of rent value as a possibility for a radical redistribution, meaning that these properties can be acquired at lower prices by organizations such as cooperatives or the Community Land Trust. Housing cooperatives seem to have a lot of potential, since they would also be supportive of the possibility of residents sharing facilities and other resources linked to their specific form of production, such as machinery, production spaces, and human resources. These models would make it possible to operate within an economic framework, but one in which the individual tenant is replaced by the collective tenant—a model that effectively withdraws properties from their commodity status, protecting them from hostile market takeover. Our proposal seeks to define an architectural transformation of the office park that could accommodate the collective use of this typology. We appropriate and twist the same ideological impetus that animated the villa, the park, and later the industrial park as harbingers not only of a new economic organization, but also of a new ethos.

The main goal of our design is to create space that is indifferent to the distinctions between living space and working space. Our proposal is neither home nor office, workshop nor factory, but a living space open to a multiplicity of uses with the ability to accommodate companies of up to six employees. For this reason we are putting forward an overall spatial order that can easily be divided into small units without losing the generosity of the whole. We aim to create conditions for inhabitants to negotiate their shared space without renouncing individual privacy. In order to achieve this, we adopted the "equal rooms" principle whereby all new spaces are made up of rooms that are equal in size and can be united to form larger rooms. Our proposal consists of three strategies ranging from the transformation of the existing office buildings to the addition of new buildings that help to increase the density of office park areas.

STRATEGY 1: CELL

The first strategy transforms the typical office building into large communal houses. Existing buildings are emptied of non-load-bearing walls including the façade. Circulation is added in the form of a ring that encloses the existing structure. A generous storage space is located at the core of the existing building, while all living and working spaces are located in the remaining area (between the storage and the ring). In this way the entire plan of the office building is reorganized as a sequence of concentric strips (as opposed to a composition of different rooms) spanning from the storage at the core to the private spaces on the edge. The space between the cells and the core can be divided by light partitions or remain open and can be used as workspace, living space, or both. Steel cells for single dwellers—conceived as individual alcoves with a generous personal bathroom—are stacked as towers and attached to the circulation structure. All internal elements, such as the closet, bed, and the wall separating the bed and bathroom, are made of plywood.

STRATEGY 2: EDGE

The second strategy involves enclosing the entire area of the office park with a multistory "wall" of rooms. They are organized as "terraced houses" in which all service spaces (vertical circulation, alcove, bathroom, storage, and kitchen) are placed at the back to form a deep service wall that frees the inhabitable space from functional constraints. We propose two types of this housing solution: the first, Type A, consists of two superimposed single rooms that share a collective space on the ground floor. This type can be a home shared by two (or more) tenants or a family home. The second, Type B, is also made of single rooms, but these are accessible from a large staircase and corridors at the back serving 36 rooms. Thus Type B is more like a hotel, with a large collective area for facilities located on the ground floor. Both types are made of rooms that work as generous balconies opening toward the office park, enclosing the space and thus returning to the very original etymological concept of a fenced plot of land. The existing office buildings remain workplaces, but their interiors are transformed in the same way as illustrated in the first strategy, minus living cells. We have called this strategy "edge" because the main concept is to occupy only the border of the office park. The strategy is best suited to office parks whose area is taken up almost entirely by existing office space.

STRATEGY 3: FIELD

In the third strategy, the density of unbuilt areas of the office park is increased with housing but without compromising the parklike nature of the site. Office parks are often characterized by low density and an abundance of parking lots, which make them very flat. This condition offers the chance to fill the space between buildings with rows of housing that serves as a sort of poché to absorb all the existing office buildings and create community facilities and working spaces. Within the field of housing, the banal layout of office buildings creates interesting incidents while the monotonous rows of housing are interrupted in unexpected ways. The houses are developed as one single space lightly divided by mezzanines. In this way the space of the house is made both generous and flexible.

1 Manfredo Tafuri, *Architecture and Utopia: Design and Capitalist Development* (Cambridge, MA: MIT Press, 1979).
2 James S. Ackerman, *Palladio* (London: Penguin, 1974).
3 Louise A. Mozingo, *Pastoral Capitalism: A History of Suburban Corporate Landscape* (Cambridge, MA: MIT Press, 2014).
4 David Schuyler, *Apostle of Taste: Andrew Jackson Downing, 1815–1852* (Baltimore: Johns Hopkins University Press, 1996).
5 James Burnham, *The Managerial Revolution: What Is Happening in the World* (New York: Praeger, 1972); see also Reinhold Martin, *The Organizational Complex: Architecture, Media, and Corporate Space* (Cambridge, MA: MIT Press, 2005).

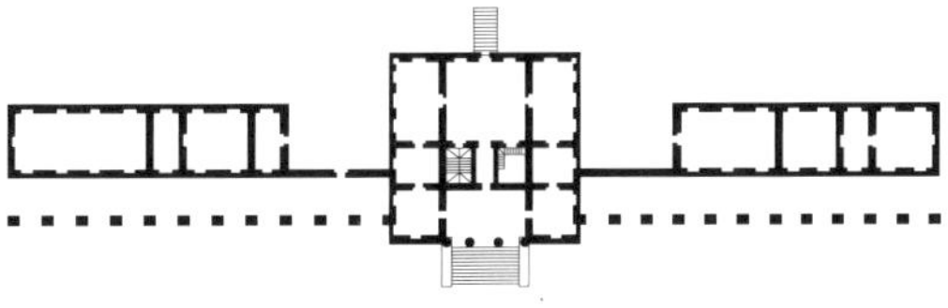

Plan of Villa Emo,
Fanzolo, 1559
architect: Andrea Palladio
(adapted from Andrea Palladio, 1570)

25 m

Plan of Union Carbide Headquarters,
Danbury, Connecticut, 1982
architect: Kevin Roche

25 m

Plan of Stanford Research Park,
Stanford, California, established 1951

150 m

1985–1992

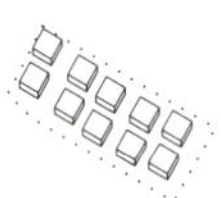

Ladder

1992–2000

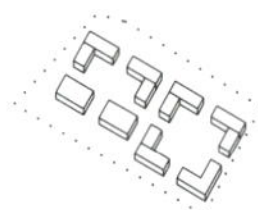

Courtyard

1

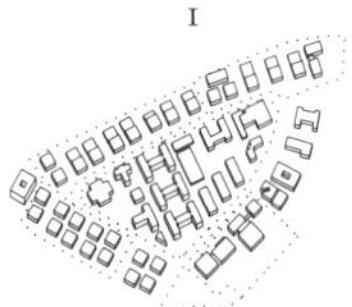

Keiberg
1985, Zaventem

2

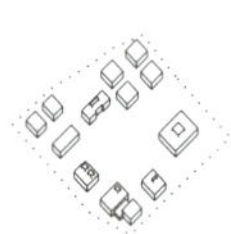

Imperial
1987, Zaventem

3

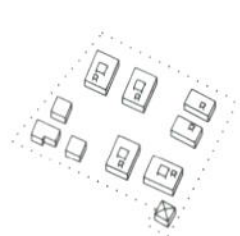

Minerva
1989, Zaventem

4

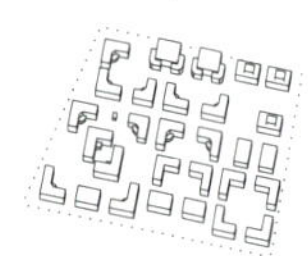

Ikaros Business Park
1990, Zaventem

5

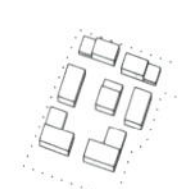

Atlas Park
1990, Zaventem

6

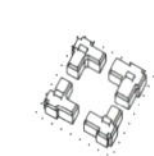

Fountain Plaza
1991, Zaventem

7

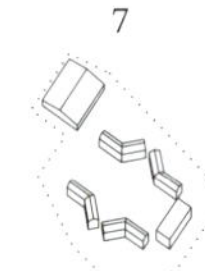

Fountain Business Park, 1991, Bornem

8

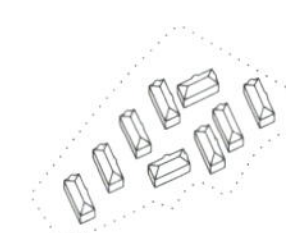

Riverside Business Park, 1991, Anderlecht

9

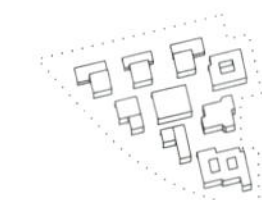

Sphere Business Park
1992, Zellik

19

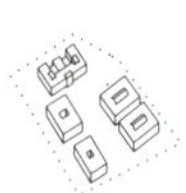

Millenium Park
1996, Diegem

20

Clinton Park
1996, Roeselare

21

Astra Gardens
1997, Zaventem

22

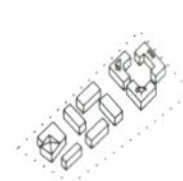

Veldkant Park
1998, Kontich

23

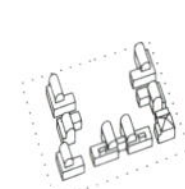

Park Lane
1999, Diegem

24

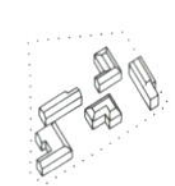

Twin Square Madison
1999, Woluwe

25

Cluster Park
1999, Woluwe

26

Amadeus Square
1999, Anderlecht

27

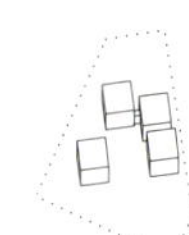

Da Vinci Park
2000, Diegem

37

Corda Campus
2002, Hasselt

38

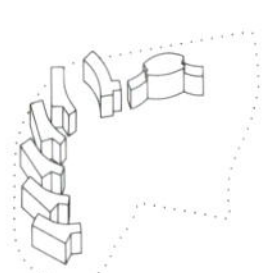

The Corporate Village
2002, Zaventem

39

Ragheno Business Park, 2003, Mechelen

40

Greenland
2004, Jette

41

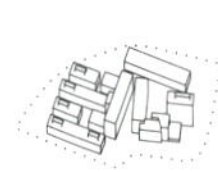

Zuidepoort Office Park, 2004, Ghent

42

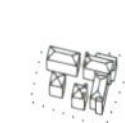

Heysel Office Park
2004, Strombeek

43

Intercity Access Park
2004, Bijgaarden

44

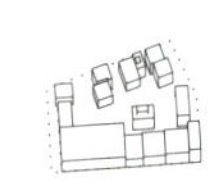

Everest
2005, Vilvoorde

45

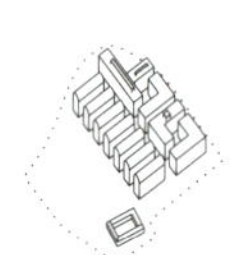

Axxes Business Park
2005, Ghent

Chronological atlas of office parks in Flanders

2000–2007

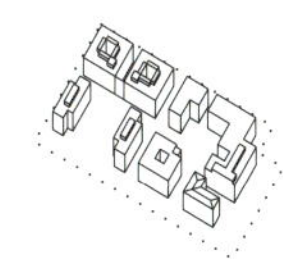

Dense Courtyard

2007–2015

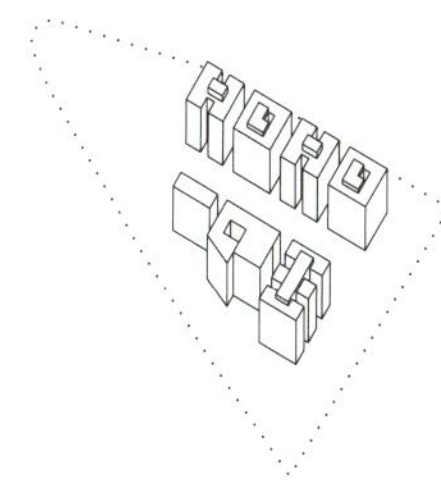

Park

10

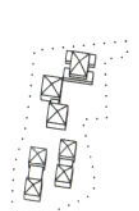

Park Hill
1992, Zaventem

11

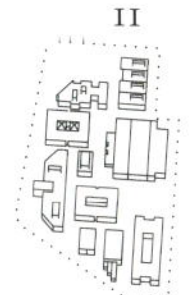

Intercity Business Park
1993, Mechelen

12

Ring Business Park
1993, Kortrijk

13

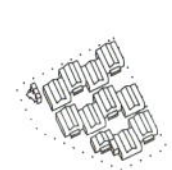

Ghent Port Side
1993, Ghent

14

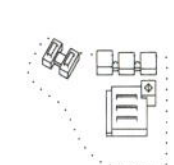

Astrid Business Park
1993, Wemmel

15

Zellik Park
1994, Zellik

16

Rozendael
Business Park
1994, Rozendael

17

Latem Business Park
1995, Ghent

18

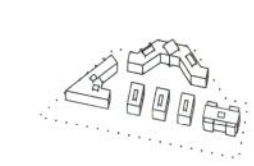

Airway Park
1995, Sint-Stevens-Woluwe

28

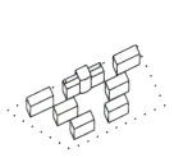

Potvlietlaan
2000, Antwerp

29

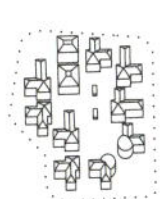

Mechelen Campus
2000, Mechelen

30

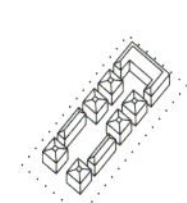

Green Hill Campus
2000, Leuven

31

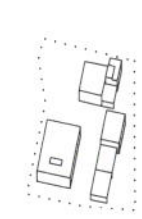

Mercure Center
2001, Zaventem

32

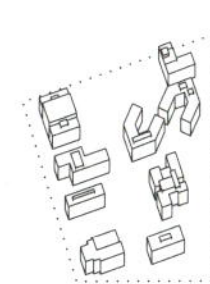

Diegem Campus
2001, Diegem

33

Green Square
2001, Diegem

34

Clinton Park
2001, Aalst

35

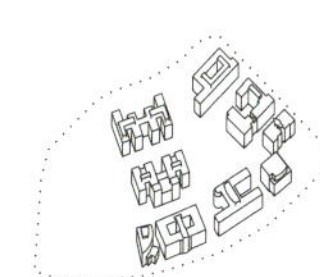

Pegasus Park
2001, Diegem

36

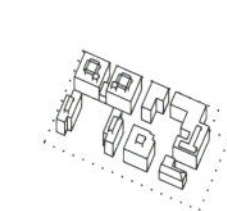

Business & Media Park
2002, Vilvoorde

46

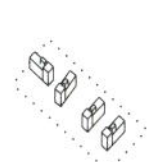

Zenith Business Park
2006, Mechelen

47

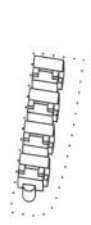

Namur Office Park
2007, Namur

48

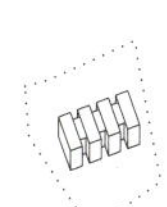

City Link
2007, Antwerpen

49

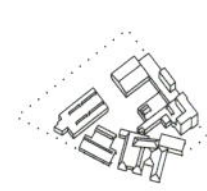

Twaalfapostelen
2008, Ghent

50

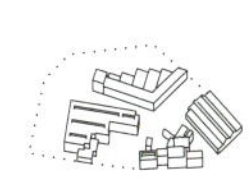

Buchten Park
2009, Ghent

51

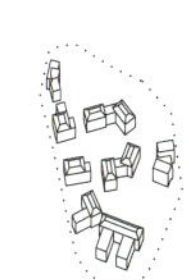

Alliance Business Park
2010, Braine L'Alleud

52

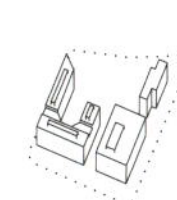

Leopold Park
2010, Zaventem

53

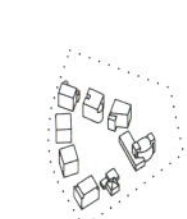

Ilgat Business Park
2011, Hasselt

54

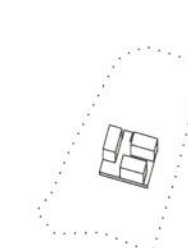

Rijvissche Park
2012, Ghent

City — Main road — Railway — River

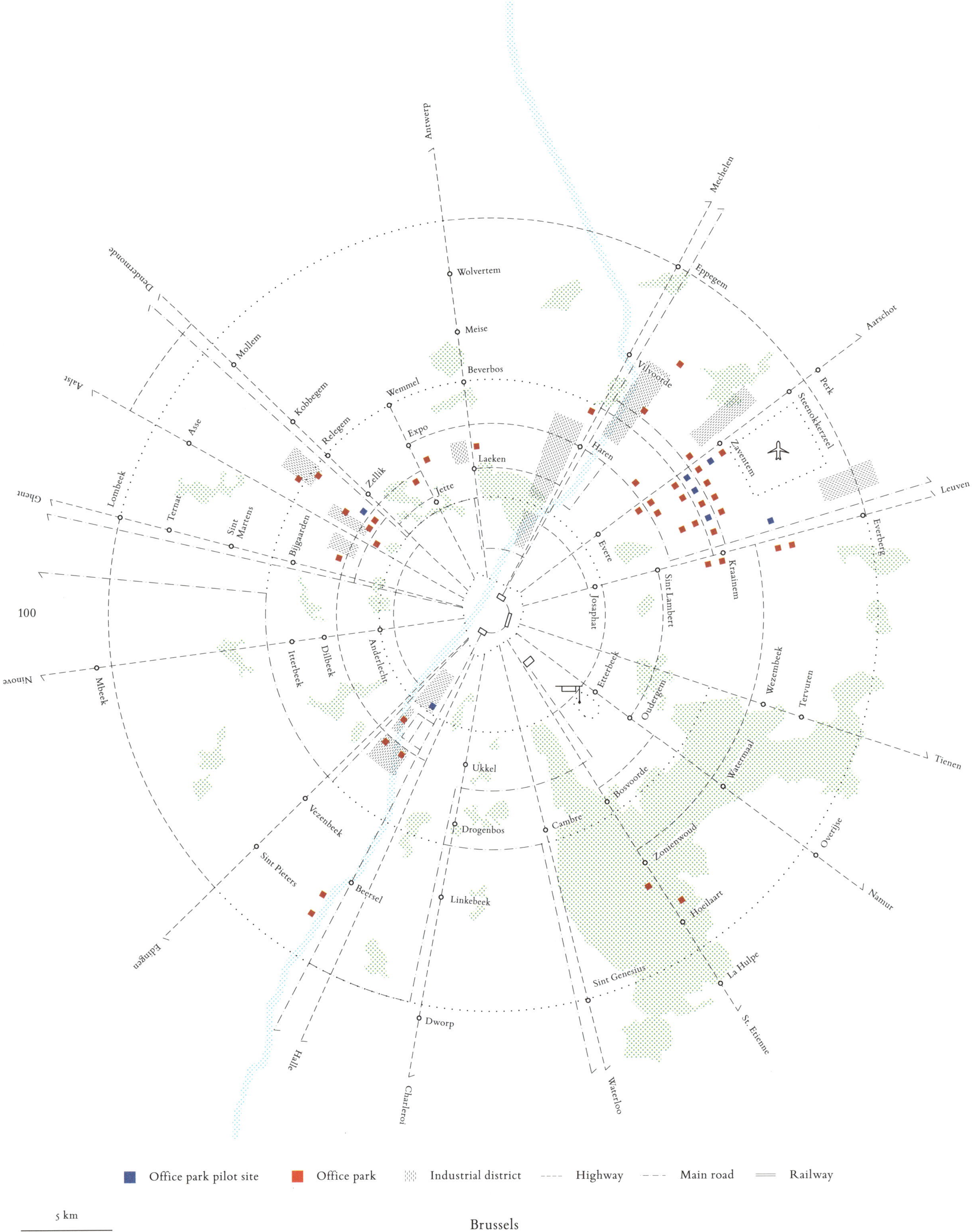

Antwerp
Mechelen
Dendermonde
Wolvertem
Eppegem
Meise
Aarschot
Mollem
Aalst
Beverbos
Vilvoorde
Perk
Wemmel
Steenokkerzeel
Kobbegem
Asse
Relegem
Expo
Haren
Zaventem
Laeken
Zellik
Jette
Ghent
Lombeek
Ternat
Sint Martens
Bijgaarden
Leuven
Everberg
Evere
Kraainem
Sint Lambert
Josaphat
Itterbeek
Dilbeek
Anderlecht
Ninove
Mbeek
Etterbeek
Oudergem
Wezembeek
Tervuren
Tienen
Watermaal
Ukkel
Bosvoorde
Vezenbeek
Drogenbos
Cambre
Zonienwoud
Overijse
Sint Pieters
Namur
Beersel
Linkebeek
Hoeilaart
Edingen
La Hulpe
Sint Genesius
Dworp
St. Etienne
Halle
Charleroi
Waterloo
Office park pilot site
Office park
Industrial district
Highway
Main road
Railway
5 km

Brussels

Wechtebeke
Zomergem
Vinderhoute
Zeehaven
Oostaker
Lokeren
Mariakerke
Antwerp
Heusden
Destelbergen
Nevele
St. Martens
Drongen
Afsnee
De Pinte
Deinze
Melle
Aalst
Zwijnaarde
Zevergem
Merelbeke
Nazareth
Gavere
Office park pilot site
Office park
Industrial district
Highway
Main road
Railway
5 km

Ghent

Keiberg I, Zaventem, 1985

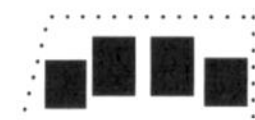

Latem Business Park, Ghent, 1995

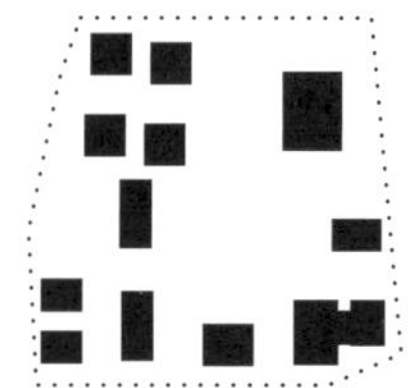

Minerva, Zaventem, 1990

Imperial, Zaventem, 1990

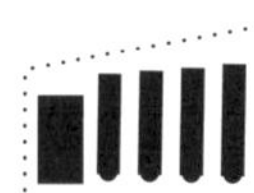

Amadeus Square, Anderlecht, 1999

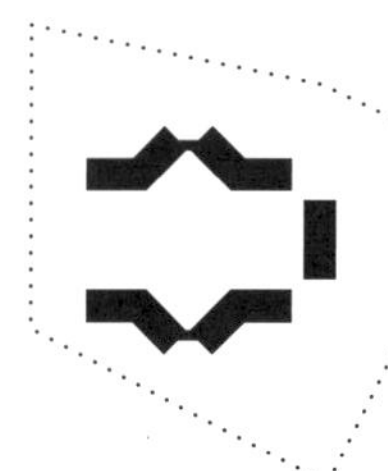

Fountain Business Park, Bornem, 1991

Ikaros Business Park, Zaventem, 1990

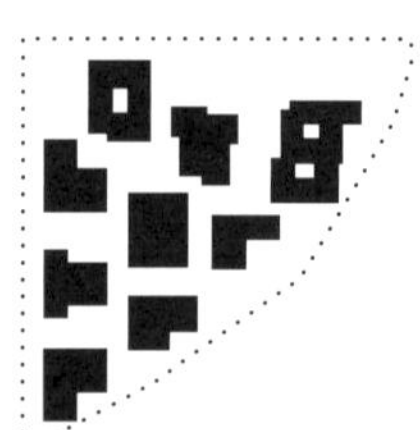

Sphere Business Park, Zellik, 1992

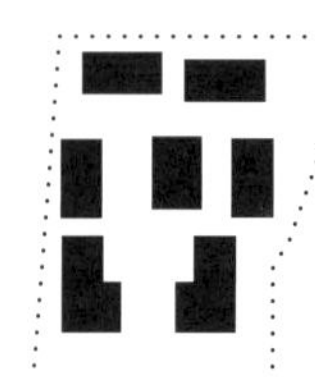

Atlas Park, Zaventem, 1990

Pilot sites, existing building footprint

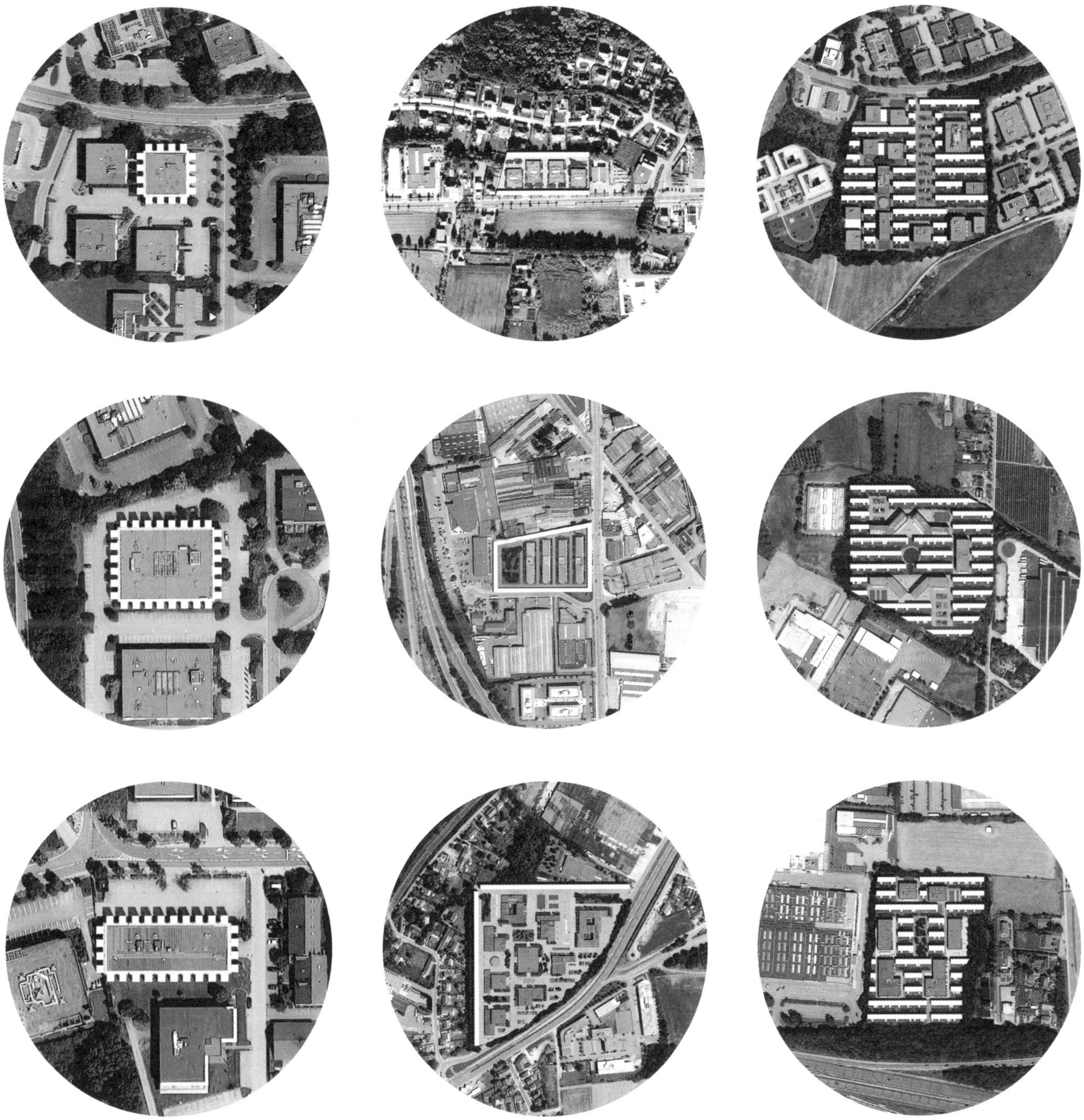

Cell | Edge | Field

Pilot sites, transformation strategies

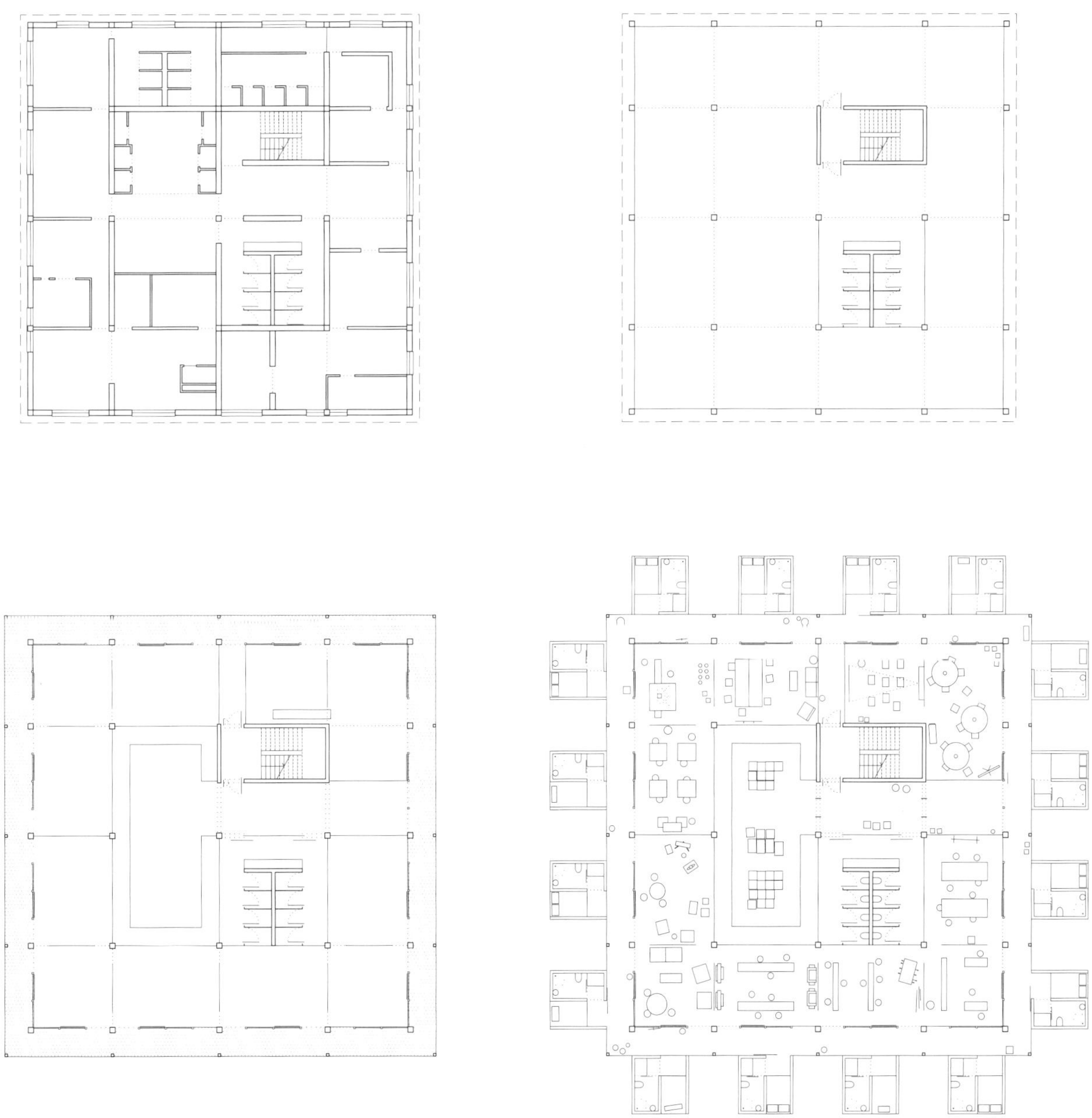

Strategy 1: Cell
Transformation phases, from typical office building to communal house

15 m

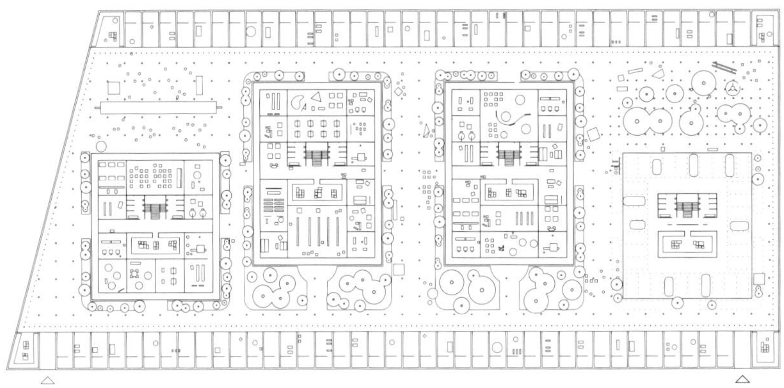

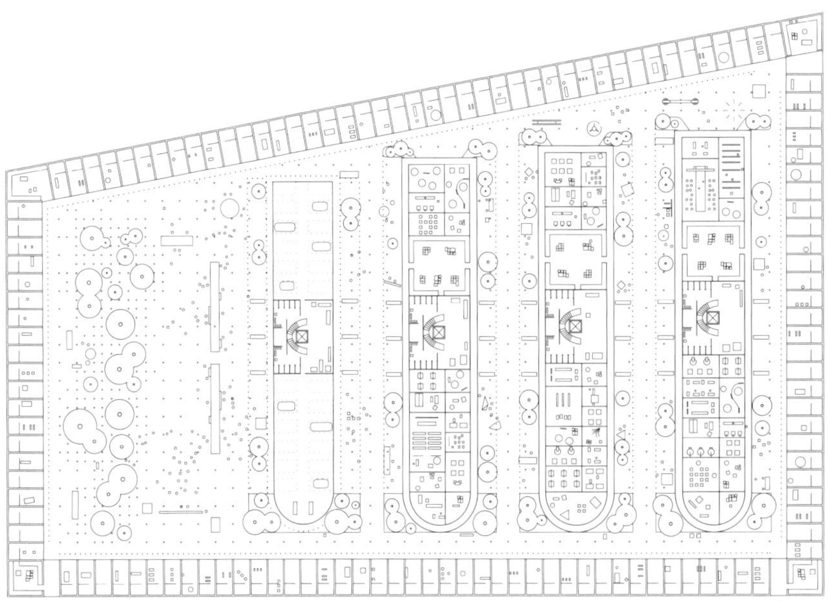

Strategy 2: Edge
Plan of retrofitted Amadeus Square, Anderlecht
Plan of retrofitted Latem Business Park, Ghent

30 m

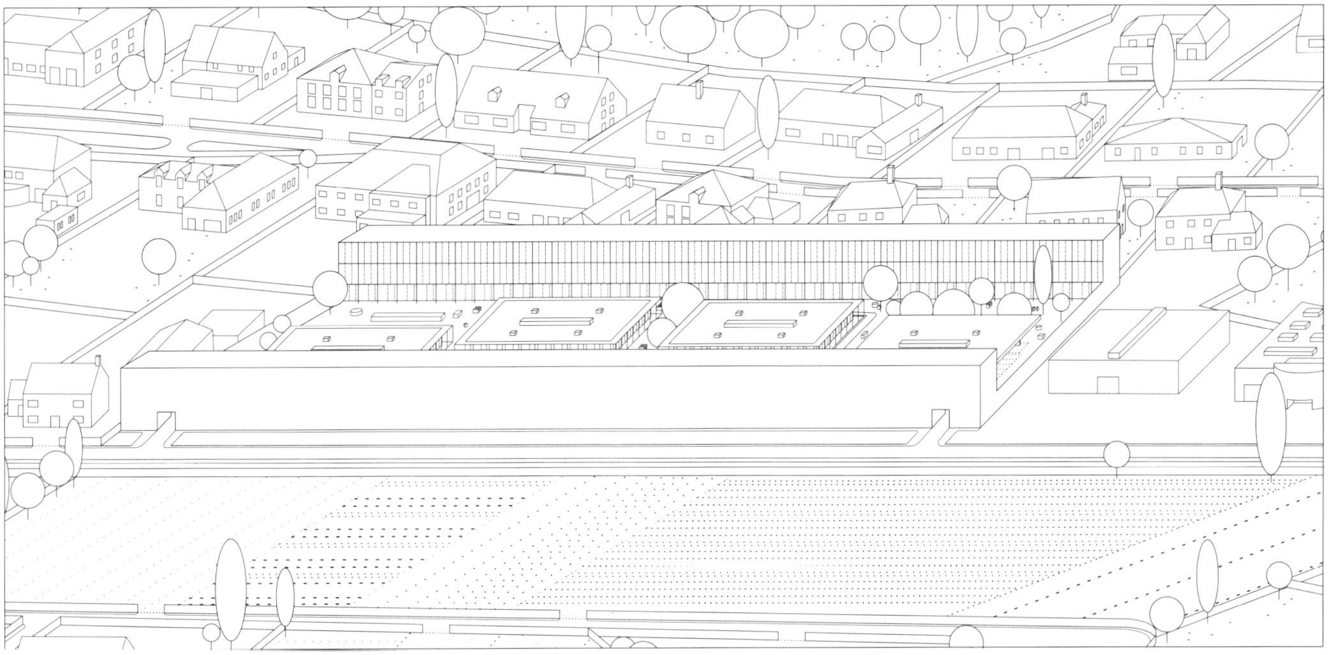

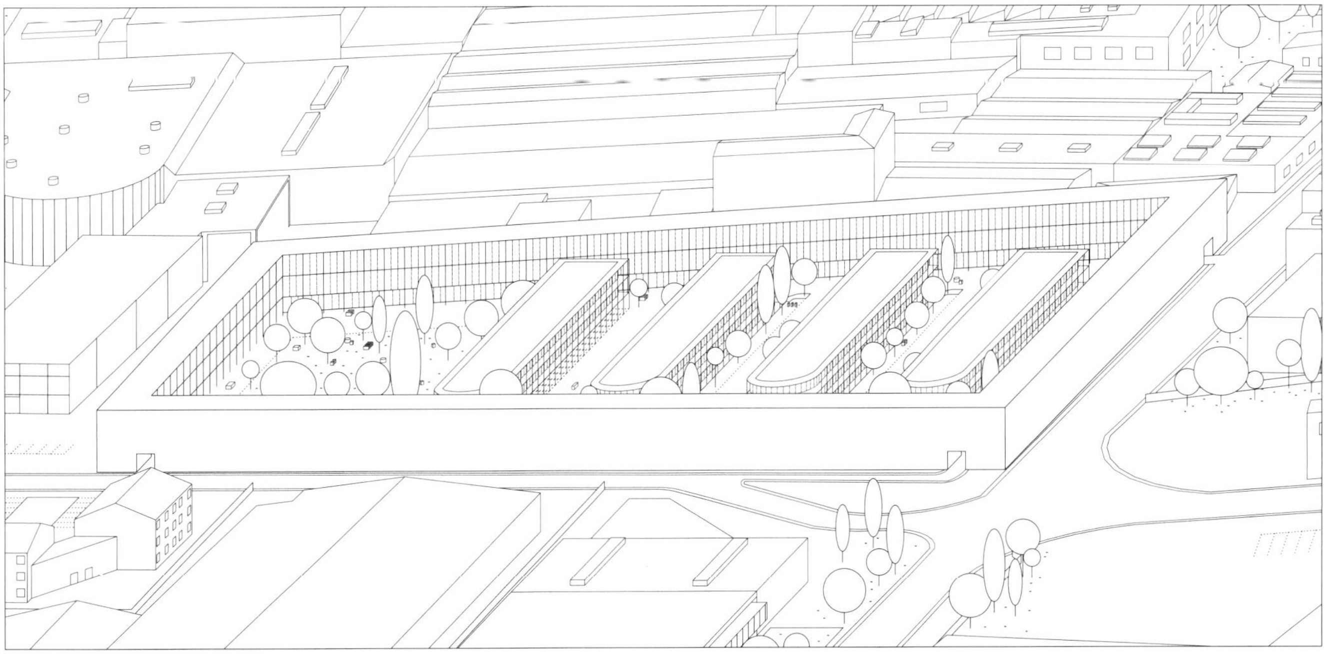

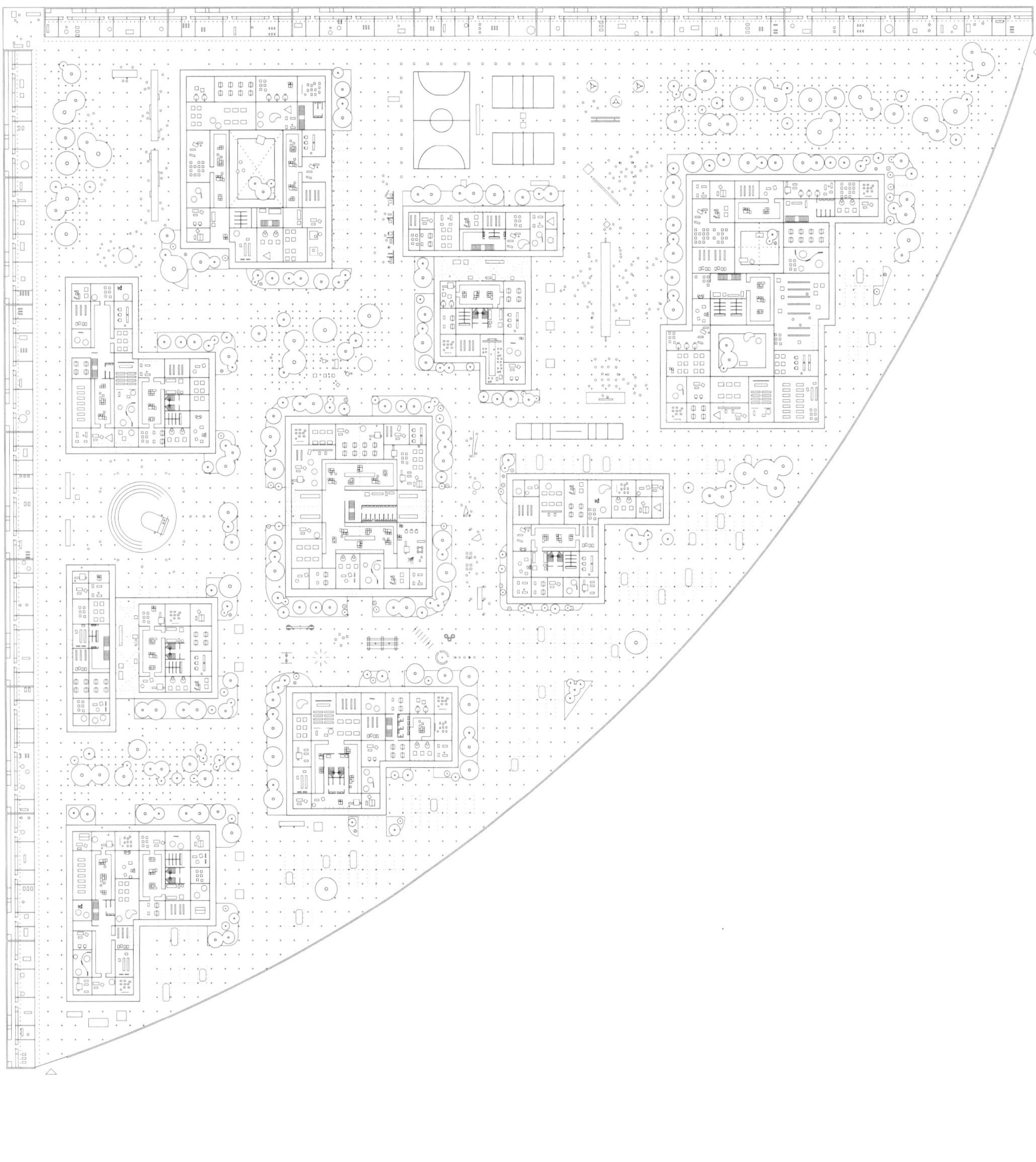

Strategy 2: Edge
Plan of retrofitted Sphere Business Park, Zellik

30 m

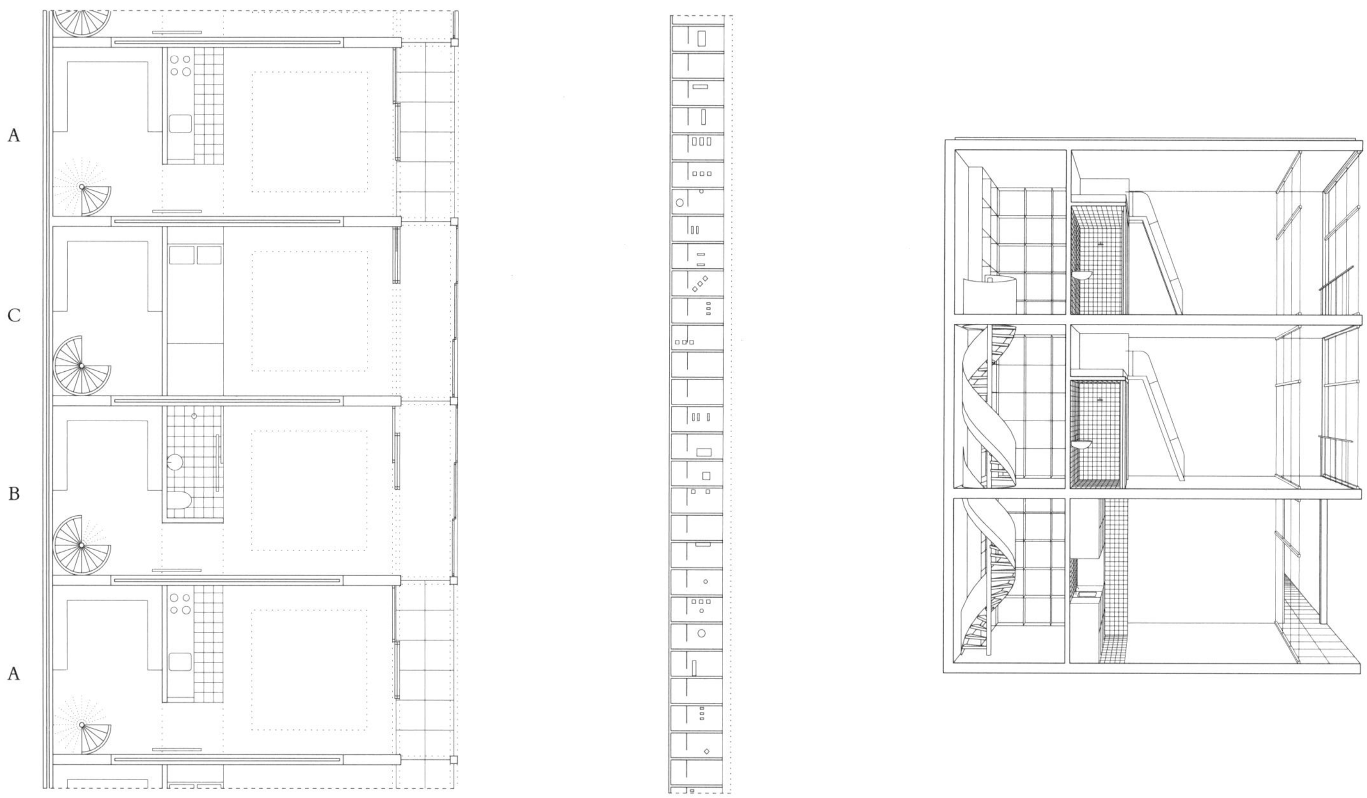

Type A: townhouse

(A) ground floor, (B) second floor, (C) mezzanine bedroom

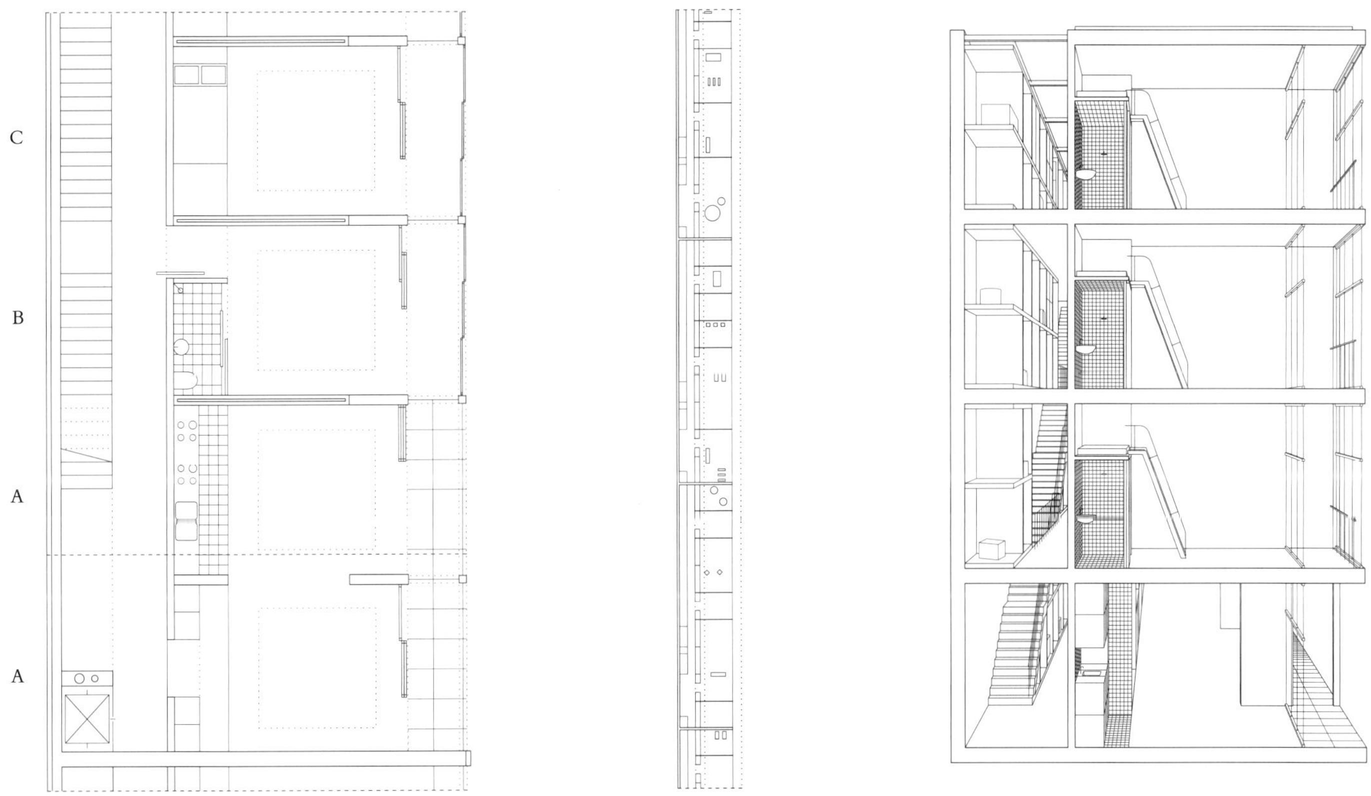

Type B: gallery housing

(A) ground floor, (B) second floor, (C) mezzanine bedroom

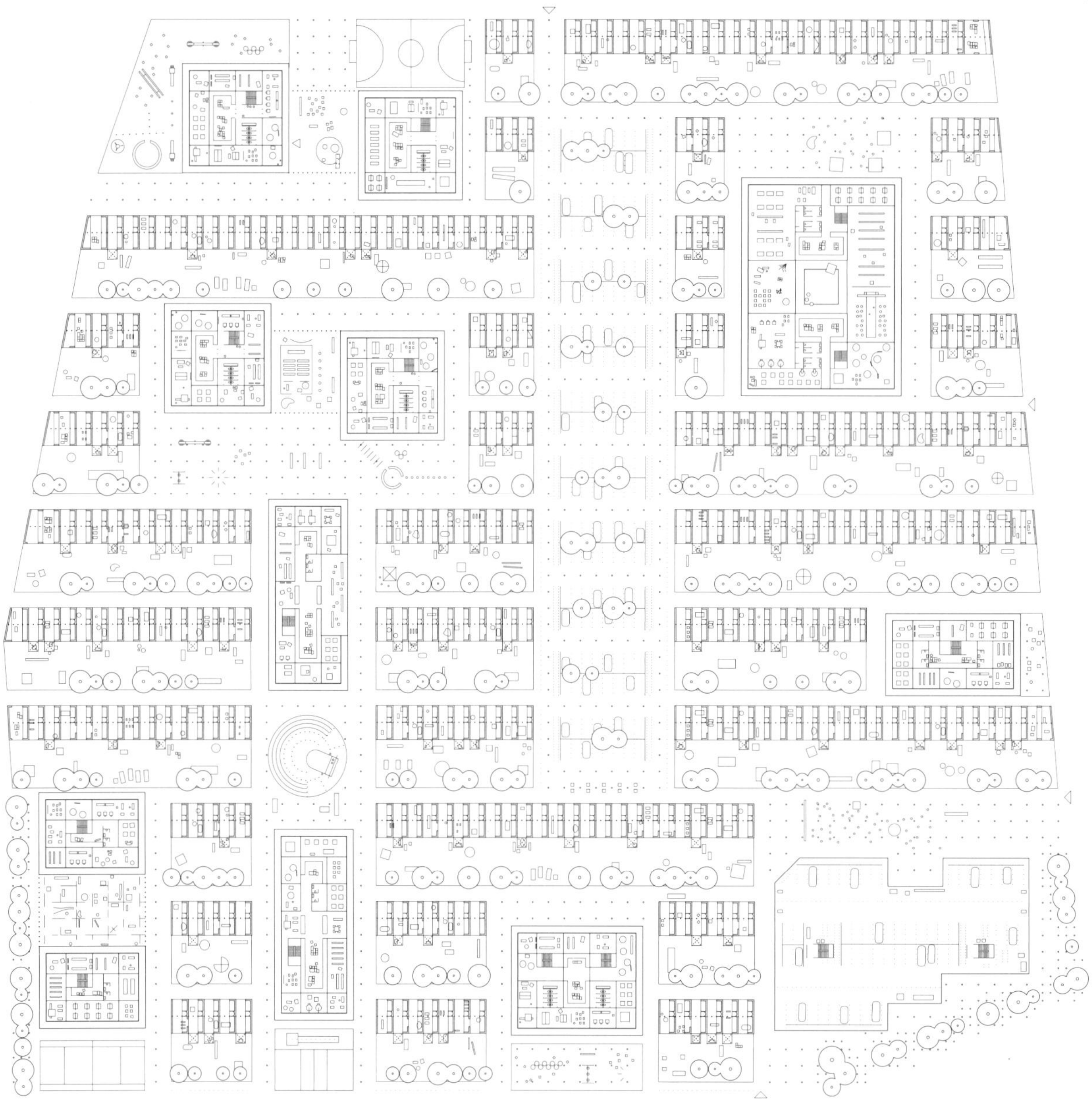

Strategy 3: Field
Plan of retrofitted Minerva, Zaventem

30 m

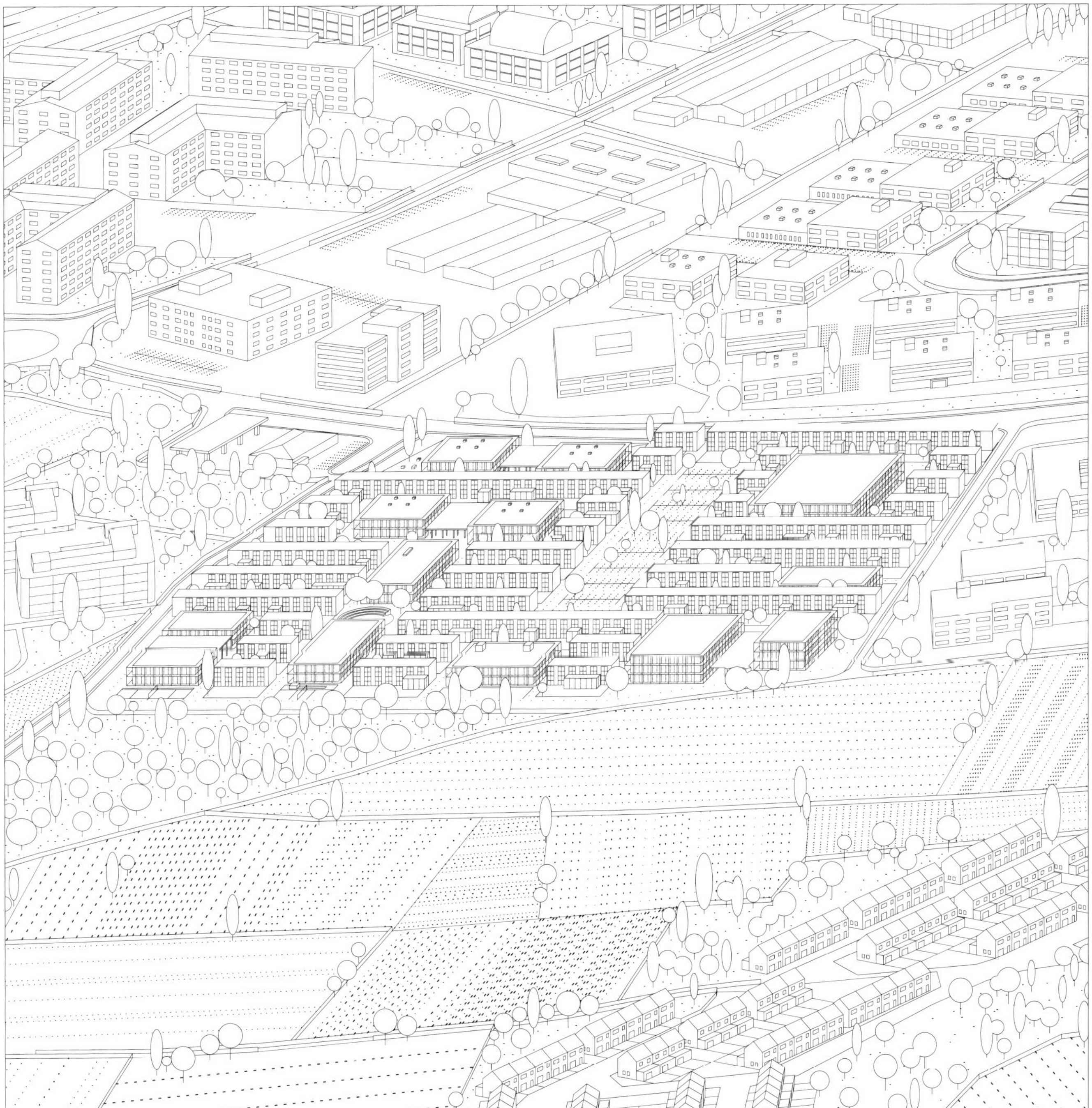

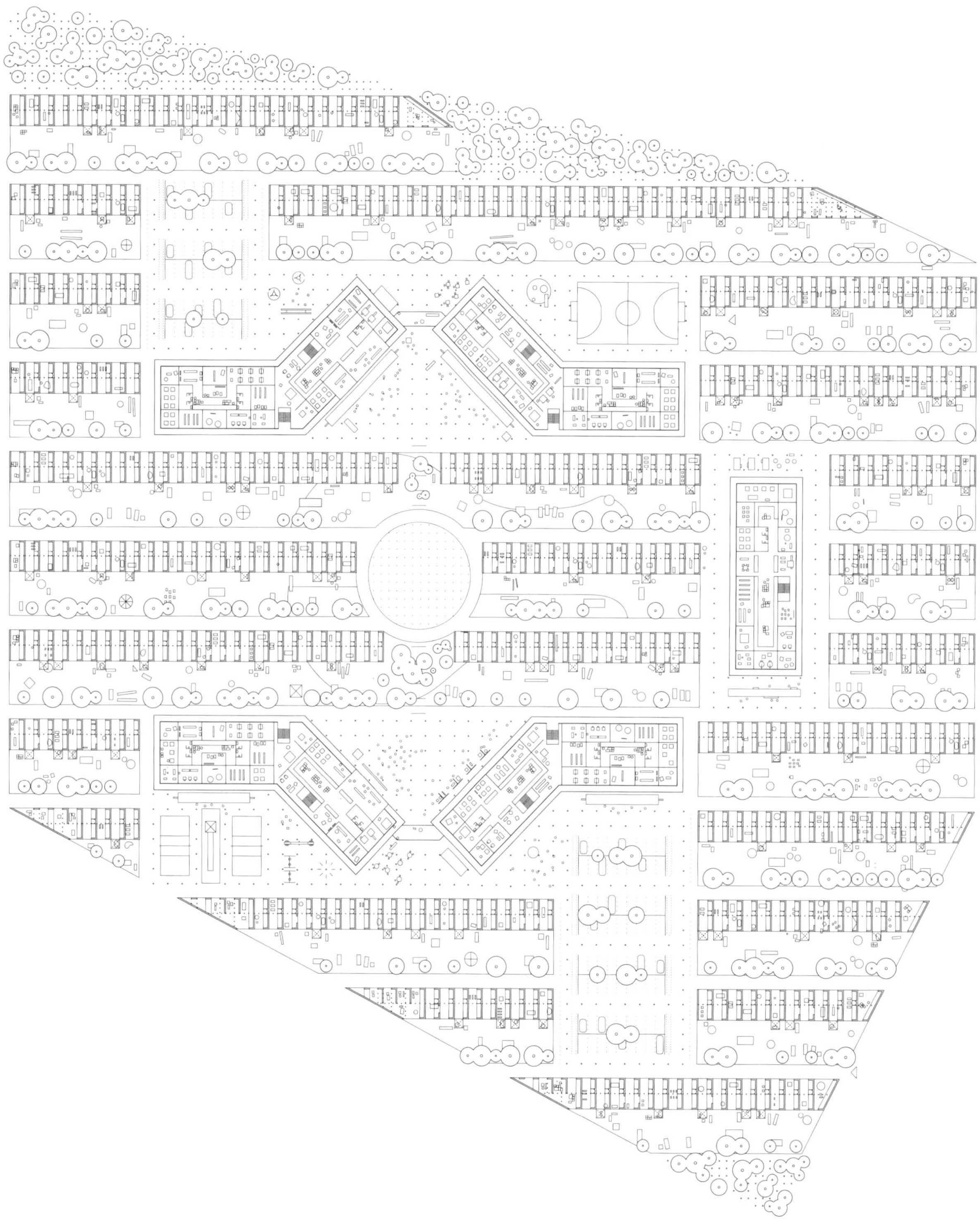

Strategy 3: Field
Plan of retrofitted Fountain Business Park, Bornem

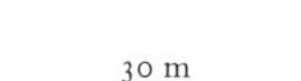

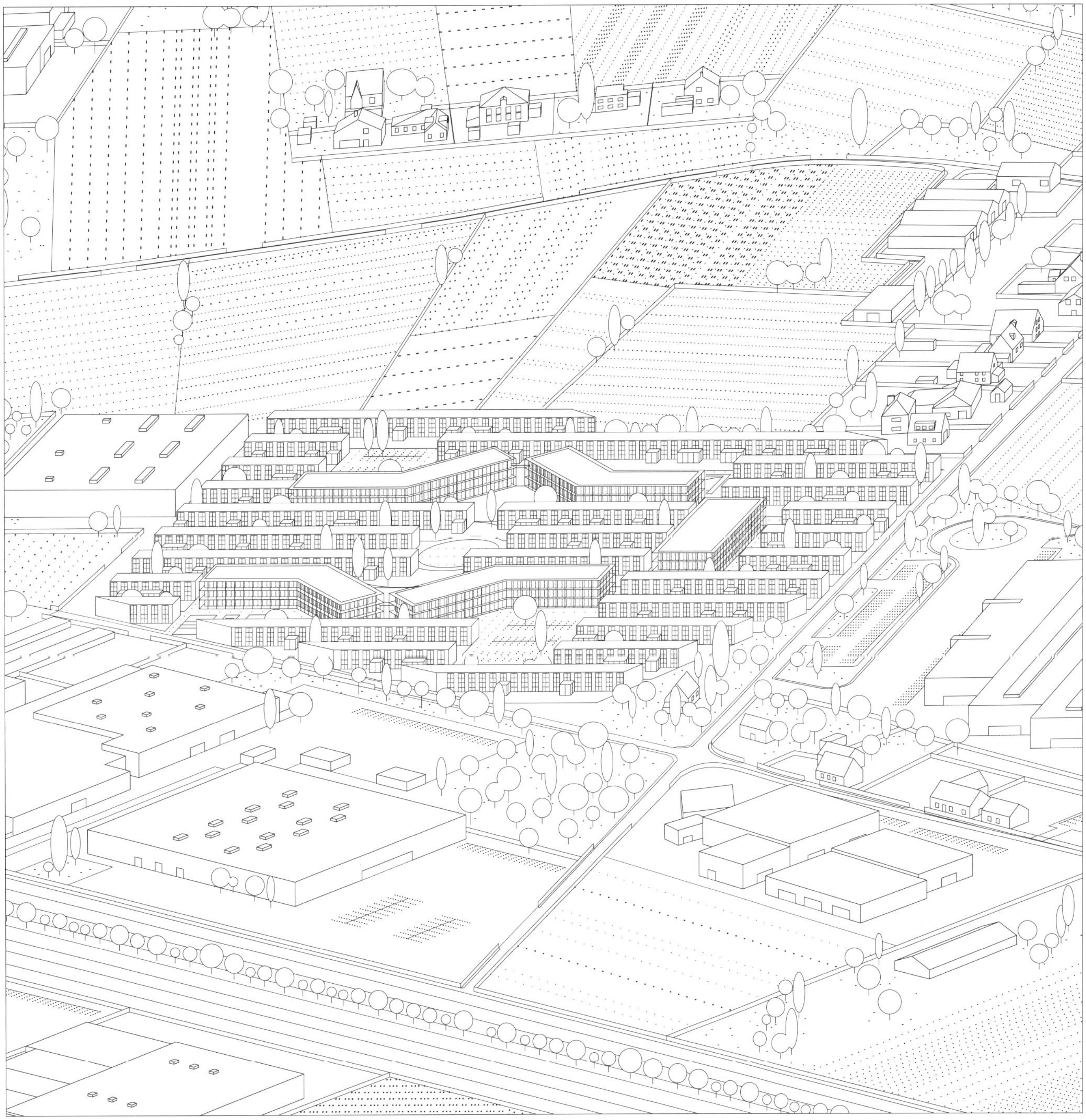

115

15 m

Detail of the retrofitted Fountain Business Park, Bornem

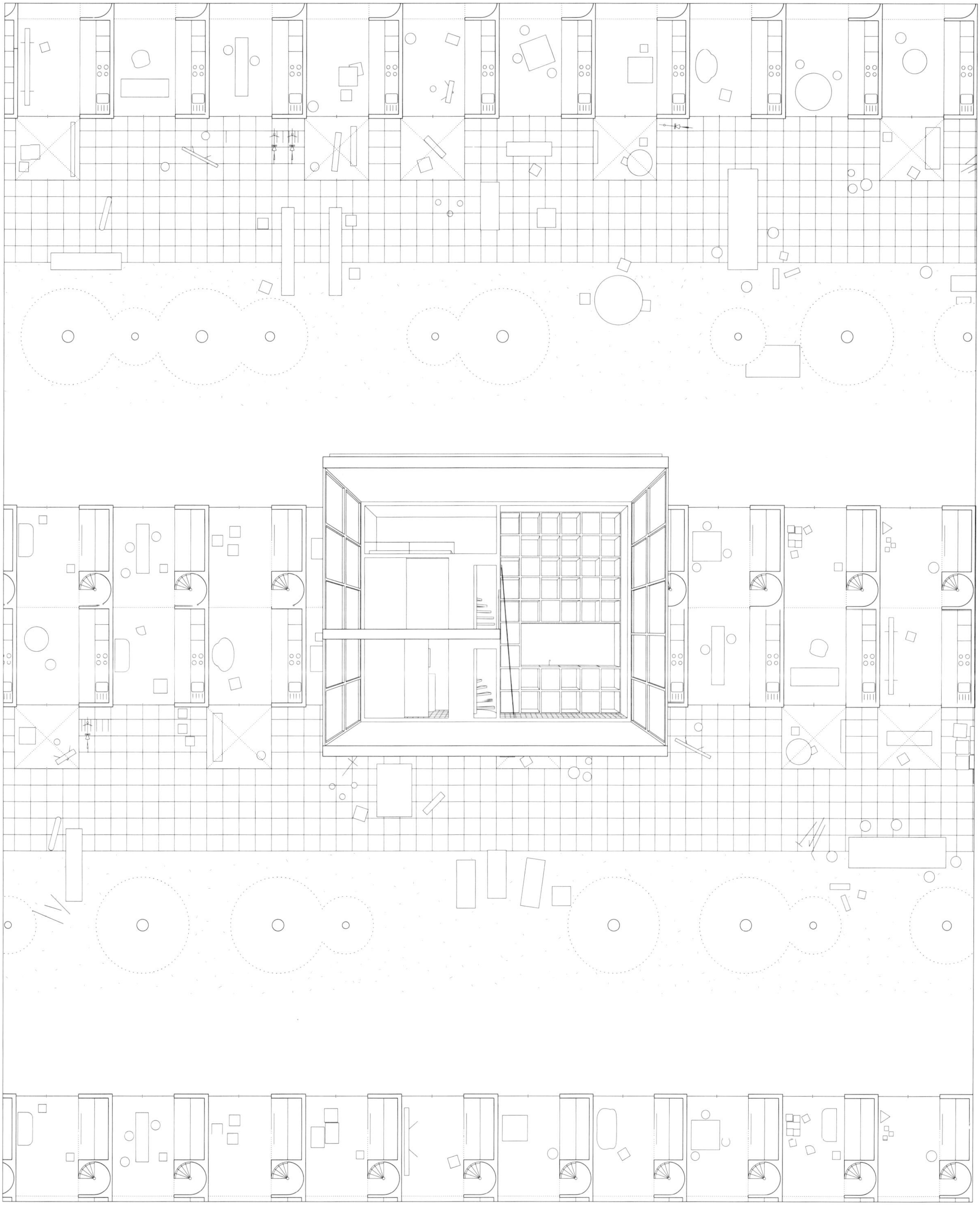

5 m

Type C: terraced house

COMMUNAL VILLA (2015)

In their seminal book *The Villa as Hegemonic Architecture* Reinhard Bentmann and Michael Müller argued that the villa is a "negative utopia," since it attempts to construct an idyllic image of living freed both from the pressure of the city and the burden of productive and reproductive work.[1] The villa is not a modern invention: it originates from the "dream of countryside" and the flight from cities cultivated by many elites of the ancient world.

If the ancient Greeks invented the agora as the core of the polis and as the proper space of politics, the ancient Romans (who were less inclined toward politics than the Greeks were) invented the villa as an economically efficient retreat. Since its invention in antiquity, the villa has always pretended to be a *locus solus*, somewhere to retreat away from the city. However, to support its self-sufficiency, the villa in reality is an urban compound strategically linked to the city and fully equipped with all necessary infrastructures for living.[2]

GENEALOGY OF THE VILLA AS "NEGATIVE UTOPIA"

We can trace the origin of the villa to the farm. The rise of the villa is linked with the importance of the countryside within the Roman Empire. After the civil wars that brought Augustus to power, farmers were expropriated of their land by wealthy landowners.[3] Family farms were thus replaced by the villa, which included both the residence of the proprietor and facilities for farming.

Both farm and villa radicalize the paternalistic nature of the house by disconnecting the latter from the city. However, while the farm is an ostensibly utilitarian structure, the villa upgrades the rustic nature of the farm into a luxury retreat. It is for this reason that the villa represents a radically ideological architecture: its role was to construct the pastoral myth of living free from the burden of the city while concealing the fact that such a fantasy was possible only if supported by the laboring classes or slaves. The villa thus introduces a narrative tradition that projects the countryside as a place of innocence, virtue, and even pleasure. A famous celebration of this idea of the countryside at the time of Augustus was Virgil's famous *Eclogues*, still the quintessential vision of the idyll of the countryside. However, as has been noted, such celebration is the idealist representation of a very practical and political problem for the landowners: the management of farming and the control of the labor force necessary for it to function. What lies behind the representation of the virtue of the countryside is the passage from the self-organization of the family farm to the great estate ruled by aristocrats. From this moment on, the villa is always associated with economic wealth and functions as a visual reminder of the economic power of the ruling class. The conflict between the villa as a luxury retreat and the villa as a productive space is exemplified by the difference between the *villa rustica* which contained all the necessary functions for agricultural work (including the dormitory for the slaves) and the *villa urbana* which contained winter and summer apartments, baths and other luxurious amenities for the proprietor. The villa thus exemplifies the contradictions implicit in domestic space, since it conflates the house as the place for *otium*, the pleasure of living a life freed from domestic chores, and the house as a productive and reproductive machine. This dichotomous nature is perhaps most starkly visible in the Villa San Rocco in Francolise, in which the *villa urbana* and the *villa rustica* are juxtaposed as twin entities. While the *villa urbana* is composed of space exclusively devoted to the pleasure of the residents, the *villa rustica* is strictly devoted to work. Moreover while the *villa urbana* opens up toward the lanscape thanks to a generous portico, the *villa rustica* is hidden behind a garden.[4]

It was precisely the combination of idealization and ruthless enforcement of private property that made the Roman villa an archetype of colonial logic; and it was for this reason that it was rediscovered in fifteenth-century Italy, at the dawn of capitalism, when it became the perfect settlement form through which the European elite gentrified rural territories, effectively inventing the idea of countryside as the place of respite from the city, but also of exploitation of rural communities. An early and outstanding example of this resurrection of the Roman villa as a colonial project are the estates created by the Medici family around Florence.[5] By building these villas the Medici expanded their influence beyond the city and reinvested their financial gains into landownership. Another influential example are the villas designed by Andrea Palladio for the aristocracy of the Serenissima, a class desperate to switch to agricultural economy after the discovery of the New World in the west and the demise of Venice's maritime economy decreed by the Ottoman blockade in the east. Like their Roman precedents, Renaissance villas were not mere buildings, but rather villages that included all the necessary infrastructure to support both living and working outside the city. Indeed, a seventeenth-century Italian dictionary defined the villa as "estate with house,"[6] and during the Renaissance the term villa was interchangeable with "countryside possession," hamlet, small town, and even *contado* or county. Palladio called his villas "case di villa," making clear that the villa is not the house, but the village near which the landowner's house is built.[7] These definitions of villa demonstrate that, as much as it stresses its image as a finite island, the villa is rather an expanded territorial domain, often strategically located next to a village or a small rural town so as to exploit its resources. When the villa is located in a more remote region, it has to build its own village or town, as in the case of the Latin American haciendas which were a colonial reinvention of the Roman large rural estates known as *latifundia*. And yet besides its complex spatial and functional organization, going far beyond the scale of architecture, the villa had to become an unequivocal archetype whose form was often embodied by the owner's house. For example in the Villa Medici at Poggio a Caiano, near Florence, the family residence assumes the perfectly symmetrical form of a palace clearly distinguished from the surrounding estate. Elevated on a plinth and fronted by a loggia topped by a pediment, the owner's residence is sublimated in the image of a sanctuary/temple whose iconic power irradiates the surrounding rural setting. The villa is here reinvented as pure semantic sign, whose archetypical image is meant to transform the rural landscape into a gentry's phantasmagoria.[8]

One of the most powerful and influential representations of the villa as sign is Andrea Palladio's Villa Capra, known as the Rotonda due to the perfect axial symmetry that governs its architecture.[9] The Rotonda can be understood as the reenactment of the *villa suburbana*, a retreat situated near the city (Vicenza) but not linked to agriculture. Inspired by Palladio's reconstruction of the hilltop temple in the Sanctuary of Fortuna Primigenia in Palestrina, the Rotonda, for its time, was a strange building. The abundance and monumentality of its porticos topped with pediments and a dome make it look more like a religious building than a house. Although it sits atop a hill like a castle or a manor house, the Rotonda is completely open to the surrounding landscape and, as its generous entranceways make clear, the building is more a celebration of the landscape around it than of the architecture itself. Here the semantics of the villa is at its most powerful: the building becomes a secular temple that sanctifies rural life, by projecting on the latter a timeless uncorrupted image. The building is like a house that seems devoid of all utilitarian functions. Yet the section of the building reveals the trick, demonstrating how all the service areas are concealed in the plinth that supports the piano nobile (the main floor). In this sense, Palladio's Rotonda might be understood as a semantic gentrification of the countryside: what was once a rustic environment inhabited by humble peasants is now reclaimed as a landscape fit for the gentry.

Yet Palladio was responsible for reinventing the villa by collapsing within the same form the patrician palace and the farmyard barns. Unlike the Rotonda, in his villas—and notably at the Villa Emo—the function of the villa as a workplace is not concealed but made as visible as possible in the *barchesse*, porticos which flank the patrician house. The *barchesse*, which hold no place in classical architecture but were borrowed from the tradition of modest farm buildings, have a utilitarian function in Palladio's architecture. By combining the patrician palace with the *barchesse* tradition, the Palladian villa reveals its true political essence as the patrician's attempt to patronize peasant culture and make the countryside, as a truly urban condition, no longer stand in opposition to the city. Within the logic of the Palladian villa, the territory becomes an expanded city to be governed by a strategic alliance between high and low culture, patricians and peasants. Thus the Palladian villa, for the first time in the history of this typology, disrupted the image of the villa as a space freed from the burden of labor. This becomes evident in what can be considered the most radical example among Palladio's villas, the Villa Repeta. The logic of the *barchesse* takes over the development of the villa itself to the point that there is almost no visual difference between the proprietor's residence and the barns. Here we see the opposite ideology to that at work in the Roman villa or in the French château: the Palladian villa seeks to appropriate and celebrate the language of (agricultural) production rather than to hide it behind the image of hedonistic living, as seen in the Rotonda. This strategy will be short-lived. Already in the United States, the founding father Thomas Jefferson's reinterpretation of the Palladian villa for his own residence of Monticello keenly distinguished the proprietor's house from the other buildings that accommodated the cohort of slaves who worked on the plantation.[10]

Jefferson's Monticello is perhaps the most acute representation of the contradictions implied in the pastoral politics of the "return to nature" that the villa has always represented. An ardent supporter of democracy and the individual right to happiness, Jefferson built Monticello as the embodiment of personal ideals. The celebration of nature, the recuperation of classicism, and, above all, the idea of living away from the city were all intended to revive the Roman ideology of the countryside as the place of virtue. Yet such virtue could only be supported by recreating the totalitarian household, which the villa as an estate that drives the economic machine has always been since its origin. Above all, Jefferson's reinterpretation of the villa was instrumental to his political vision for the United States, as a country that would resist industrialization and embrace agriculture as the main force of its economy. And even if the country has not evolved along these lines, Jefferson was successful in feeding the myth of pastoral living, which in spite of the country's later heavy industrialization was to become one of the most powerful urban ideologies of the nineteenth and twentieth centuries. There is not enough space here to revisit the history of suburbia in America; suffice it to say that it can be seen as the final accomplishment of the American villa ideal, where the fundamental aspect of the suburban landscape was the democratization of villa living and the structure itself evolved from luxury mansion to humble cottage. However, the democratization of the villa cannot be understood apart from the rise of the class struggle as the main political consequence of capitalist development. The more the city became an explosive concentration of workers, the more pastoralism and the dream of the individual family house would be pushed to the forefront as a most powerful preemptive strategy in the hands of capitalist landowners and governments.

One way to better understand this coupling of conflict with suburbia is through Gilles Deleuze and Félix Guattari's concept of deterritorialization and reterritorialization.[11] Deterritorialization is the process of uprooting and opening up social relationships, which is typical of capitalistic processes of production. Industrialization, for example, implied the mass mobilization of workers, which thus freed their subjectivity from traditional ties—think of the role of the pioneers of the Wild West in the history of the United States or the massive movement of workers to industrial cities.

This is why even capitalist exploitation runs the risk of violently opening up its contradictions and dissolving itself. And it is also for this reason that capitalism constantly reterritorializes itself by "recomposing" its contradictions and thus organizing subtler but stronger ties for its subjects. We can therefore reread modern domestic space, and especially the democratization of the villa in the form of the single-family house, a powerful process of reterritorialization. It is not by chance that one of the most important waves of suburbanization in the United States, in terms of both quantity and quality, happened after the Second World War. The period between the New Deal and the war saw a massive and unprecedented process of reorganization of labor power, which explicitly and implicitly recognized the latter as the true protagonist of capitalist development. Welfare, union rights, rising wages, and especially the entrance of more women into the workplace were the price that capitalism paid in order to resurrect itself after the Depression era. It is precisely against the potential side effects of the "capitalistic revolution" seen in the New Deal that the American government introduced the suburban home as a reterritorialization process. Although funded through private investment, the development of the single-family house in the United States was orchestrated by federal legislation in favor of private property, which enabled millions of Americans to buy their own homes. Equipped with a large kitchen, generous lawn, and private parking and organized around a strict family-oriented layout, the American single-family house represents the ultimate incarnation of domestic space as a safe haven, completely removed from the promiscuity of the world of labor. The "domestic" was where family members could reunite within the strict format of the nuclear family and its specific gender and racial orientations. However, it is a mistake to think that the domesticity that emerged from American suburbia was a merely suburban affair, since it became a template for domestic space that transcends the distinction between suburbia and the city. The family apartment, the studio flat, and the condo with its hermetic isolation can all be understood as suburban typologies that have colonized the city itself.

The phenomenon of suburban living sucked in the majority of the middle class, giving them access both to property and to an economic and financial regime that reduced the owner to a permanent debtor. It is not by chance that a major symptom of the 2008 banking crisis was the credit crunch, a crisis that was brought about by deliberately careless mortgage lending by banks offering unrealistic loans to people to purchase property, especially houses. Access to credit was an aspiration triggered especially by the suburban dream, and the family home an ideal propagated for many years by the middle class. The financial crisis has demonstrated once again the fundamental link between the financial economy and domestic subjectivity. In other words, the way in which the oikos has been constructed—with its values, images, and spatial hierarchies—is directly linked to the way in which economic frameworks have been orchestrated.

The villa can be seen as the place in which the oikos has been pushed to its totalitarian limits, where the horror of individualism, isolation, commodification, and debt have been masked by the idyllic image of living the pastoral ideal. So, then, why resurrect the villa type for a project that attempts to challenge the very ideological premises that the villa has historically embodied? In his 1803 poem "Patmos," Friedrich Hölderlin famously wrote, "Where the danger is, also grows the saving power";[12] similarly, we hope perhaps to appropriate the "negative utopia" of the villa and twist it against its own premises. What was once the symbol of privilege and strict domestic hierarchy is transformed into a space in which communal life can be organized; a space where domestic labor was concealed now becomes a space in which sharing and solidarity reduce rather than exacerbate the burden of work for the individual, in the process of reappropriating what was once a symbol of private property as a space where collective ownership is finally realized.

TOWARD THE URBAN VILLA

In the summer of 1977, a group of architects and students lead by Oswald Mathias Ungers proposed an ambitious project for the reurbanization of Berlin based on the typology of the urban villa.[13] This proposal may sound paradoxical since the villa is the quintessential family home and in its modern version, as a cottage, is the symbol of low-density suburbia. But against this tradition, Ungers and his collaborators reinterpreted the villa as a multifamily dwelling type and thus as a prototype of an inner-city residence. Ungers's project began with the consideration that designs for houses at the time were of two residential types: the single-family house and the apartment. He intended the urban villa to offer an alternative to these typologies and become a collective form of housing, neither too big nor too small. According to Ungers, the urban villa would contain between six and ten apartments and would be no more than four stories tall. Rather than providing only housing, the urban villa would also include small office spaces, a kindergarten, schools, studios, etc. Special urban villas would be planned as small hotels, clinics, ateliers, or rooming houses. Ungers saw the urban villa as a way to promote small-scale construction, a backlash against the large-scale developments of mass housing that only the state or large private companies were able to operate. In terms of ecology, a medium-size housing type such as the urban villa was assumed as the ideal for energy-saving methods and for reducing technological waste. Due to its dimensions, to Ungers the urban villa was easily adaptable to any context, and thus it was seen as complementary to urban environments rather than replacing them. Ungers insisted that the urban villa would be the ideal type to promote a democratic and pluralistic city, although the political role of his project remains ambiguous. Indeed he promoted the urban villa as a way to encourage private homeownership and commercial enterprise, which was his response to the crisis of welfare housing that was becoming evident in the 1970s. We should not forget that the urban villa is the quintessential bourgeois domestic typology. Heir to the most aristocratic villa, in the nineteenth century the urban villa gave up its illustrious predecessor's detachment from the city to become one of the most widespread models of the urbanization of the city's periphery. It is for this reason that the urban villa developed as a speculative building, the main goal of which was to balance the Arcadian atmosphere of the villa with the necessity of urban densification. Regional variation of this type can be found in the Italian *palazzina* and the Greek *polikatoikia*, two building types that embody perfectly the petit bourgeois way of life in the golden age of the postwar urban boom. Indeed Ungers's reappropriation of the urban villa in the 1970s reflected the increasing affluence of Europe and the trend toward suburbanization that motivated the middle class to demand more than just a tiny flat within a social housing block.

Today, in an age when affluence is increasing only for a select few, it seems to us that the urban villa remains a valid housing type, offering a radical alternative to current solutions to the housing crisis. However, in contrast to Ungers's urban villa concept, we believe that the villa typology can go beyond the single family as its main subject and address a community of people. In this way, the advantages of the urban villa highlighted by Ungers can become the springboard for the development of a building type that goes beyond the framework of speculative real estate. Perhaps it is precisely when the bourgeois way of life has lost its ideological confidence and entered into an epochal crisis that the reappropriation of the urban villa as a collective living space will challenge the spatial premises of private homeownership.

THE COMMUNAL VILLA

Our proposal for a Communal Villa focuses on a realist housing model for artists who have chosen to live together. The program, ownership model, and potential number of inhabitants for each villa were developed in collaboration with a group of artists gathered within the Realism Working Group whose focus is the housing condition in heavily gentrified German cities such as Frankfurt am Main and Berlin. Communal Villa consists of the development of two villa types—the *villa suburbana* and the *villa urbana*—both of which are designed with the capacity to hold on average fifty inhabitants, a number considered neither too big nor too small and suitable for forms of communal living. Our interventions are not specific to the current project but, following specific criteria, they put forward a prototype realizable in many different contexts. 123

The first important criterion is that the villa should be a communal house organized within principles such as those of the Mietshäuser Syndikat (Syndicate of Tenements). This organization, which has existed in Germany for over twenty years, has as its main purpose to withdraw housing from the commercial real estate market. Once a building is appropriated in the model of the Syndicate of Tenements it is part of a collective-ownership structure of currently 166 house projects (in Germany). The Syndicate has the right to veto any attempts to sell or reprivatize the building. As a consequence, the house remains a project of collective living, even as individual residents move in and out. The Syndicate thus prevents real estate speculation or hostile takeovers and guarantees stable accommodation and affordable rents.[14] It is important to say that our endorsement of the villa aims to reflect the nature of the Syndicate of Tenements as composed of medium-size communities that seek a collective self-organization of dwelling. The villa thus offers a tangible architectural response to a phenomenon that is already happening: the increase of Syndicate projects in recent years. While trying to adapt existing buildings to the Syndicate model may compromise the egalitarian nature that this model requires, proposing a new spatial layout offers the possibility of directly translating into spatial terms the economic structure of the Syndicate model. For this reason we decided to propose a spatial and structural organization that facilitates sharing while also making it impossible to return to its traditional domestic setting of single-family occupancy.

Another important criterion lies in the sites on which the villas are built. If, historically, the villa represented the celebration of private property, in the current project we seek to use this type precisely against the idea of private property for both the house and the land it occupies. We propose to build the villas on what are currently unused plots, which even in the current urban master plan are not earmarked for any other program (residential, industrial, green space, agricultural, etc.). This type of land, which is often abundant within cities and their surrounding regions, is frequently located on the margins of residential areas or along railway infrastructure. Generally, the majority of this land belongs to the municipality or to other public bodies (such as railway companies). In Berlin there are large amounts of unused land that would be suitable for the development of affordable housing and studios. However, at present there is no complete cadastral mapping of this type of land, and it would take a survey (and the political will) to mark it out for social use. Yet, as we noticed during one of our surveys in Berlin, this land often has an "accidental" beauty, a quality that reevokes the picturesque setting of the historical villa in a somewhat ironic way, since many of the unused locations are unlikely places for a "villa." Often these areas (at least those we selected to test our prototype) are in close proximity to train and metro stations and, although in relatively remote locations, are frequently connected to the urban center. According to our hypothesis, land of this sort could be released to the Syndicate of Tenements either at no cost or on a subsidized lease. In cases where plots are in the hands of private owners, the city could trade fiscal incentives in exchange for a twenty- or thirty-year lease.

As available land parcels are frequently characterized by an irregular shape, the two versions of the villa proposed—the *villa suburbana* and the *villa urbana*—are ideal for their versatility. While the *villa suburbana* presupposes a larger site than the *villa urbana*, the latter is more introverted and adaptable to narrower and denser conditions. However, the form of the villa is deliberately indifferent to its context so that it can be adapted to different situations.

The third criterion concerns the construction technique of the villa. In order to reduce costs, the villa is imagined as a simple industrial building, based on prefabricated-steel construction in the case of the *villa suburbana*, and prefabricated concrete in the case of the *villa urbana*. Industrial buildings are obviously cheaper to build than residential, because although industrial building structures are often larger than residential ones, the price difference between the two is due to the large sums needed for the finishing and furnishing of residential architecture. The traditional construction process of residential architecture can be seen as a succession of three different phases—the structure, finishing, and furnishing—but in our villa we have decided to get rid of the finishing phase. We tried to imagine a residential building where the structure can be simply furnished to create a comfortable living space. In this way, instead of expensive residential units, which once bought or rented need furnishing, we offer inhabitants already-furnished affordable living spaces, ready to move into. Additionally, cheap construction, of course, translates into affordable rents.

Both villas comprise individual spaces (cells) and collective spaces (artists' studios, workshops, kitchens, sauna, sound studio, kindergarten, etc.). This organization aims at maximizing collective space and minimizing individual space, so that the latter can become a true space of refuge while at the same time encouraging tenants to dwell in the collective space. In both villas, the structure is based on the same module: 7.5 m x 7.5 m x 5 m. The module is based on the measurements of one cell (45 sq m). The prefabricated (concrete or steel) structure remains visible in order to allow the inhabitants to discern the load-bearing elements should they want to modify or transform the building in the future. All the partitions are made of timber and are movable. The only fixed partitions are those of the "inhabitable walls" that divide the individual cells from the collective space.

The industrial nature of the villas renders them more abstract and generic and thus able to reject the traditional "domesticity" of housing architecture. Each cell has an "inhabitable wall," an element designed to blur the distinction between furniture and architecture. Made of plywood, the inhabitable wall contains all the necessities for living: storage, bathroom, and sleeping alcove with bookshelves. Toward the outside, the inhabitable wall becomes a large storage area for collective use. The collective nature of our villa is emphasized by the abstraction of its architecture. If style, decoration, character, and representation in architecture have always made homes the space of the individuation of the subject (male, female, father, mother, son, etc.), with the villa we aim to create an architecture of deindividuation where every member of the community, whether adult or child, has an equal amount of space and facilities. Each villa allows individual dwellers a total of 80 sq m, including the individual space (the cell) and the different collective spaces.

Thanks to the flexible layout of the villa, where most communal spaces are multifunctional and not rigidly defined, there is potential for equality of space that will allow inhabitants to negotiate for space according to their different needs.

An organization of this type challenges the artist's specialized role within society, and allows multiple interpretations of the meaning of (artistic) production. Above all, the villa emphasizes the collective nature of art production by challenging the idea of the artist as a solitary person confined to her or his studio.

We conceived the villa's organization as aiming to disrupt the idealization of the studio as a space removed from domestic chores while also offering a generous open space for collective negotiation of everyday activities. While the plan separates noisy and quiet zones and rooms for toxic or dirty activities (such as a spray room, or metal workshop) from the rest of the studios, the flexibility of the central space invites different combinations of use that do not rigidly identify "production" and "reproduction." Thanks to movable partitions, the generous central space can be organized in multiple ways, from a set of independent rooms to one large, open, shared space.

Each villa is completely autonomous from its surroundings, and its form is indifferent to its context. As we have seen, historically the villa implied an escape from the city; but since now we live in conditions where "outside" is shrinking, where the countryside is becoming rapidly urbanized, such escape is becoming ever less possible. We live in a period in which density and the fetish of the "city" are attracting a lot of people to the urban center. By now, we are all familiar with how this process uses art and artists as a sort of pioneering force at the service of gentrification. Moreover, this tendency seems to leave little choice in terms of where one wants to live. To live in the city often seems more a necessity than a desire. Paradoxically, the ideological power of the villa as a "utopian" place can now be used against the commodification of living, which we see happening within all cities, where every activity is immediately exploited in order to create profit. Like Charles Fourier's self-sufficient Phalanx model, the villa, with its monumentality and autonomy from the fabric of the city, can offer the spatial template for a radical reorganization of living and working conditions.

Moreover, as we have seen, while the traditional villa occupied a position of dominion and control of the land around it, our villas occupy areas that are neither residential nor rural. Undeniably, the architecture of the villas is deliberately Palladian, organized according to the principle of axial symmetry. However, while the symmetry of the Palladian villa is at the service of social hierarchy (the center for the proprietor's palace, the peripheral areas for the servants), in our villas symmetrical organization aims to make the space legible. Here spatial legibility becomes a supportive structure for collective self-organization and self-determination, toward a space where cooperation and solidarity become the true fulcrum of dwelling.

1 Reinhard Bentmann and Michael Müller, *The Villa as Hegemonic Architecture* (Atlantic Highlands, NJ: Humanities Press, 1992), 15.

2 See James S. Ackerman, *The Villa: Form and Ideology of Country Houses* (London: Thames and Hudson, 1990).

3 Ibid., 43.

4 See ibid., 35–61.

5 See Raffaella Fabiani Giannetto, *Medici Gardens: From Making to Design* (Philadelphia: University of Pennsylvania Press, 2008).

6 See Howard Burns, *La villa italiana del Rinascimento* (Vicenza: Angelo Colla Editore, 2012), 16–17.

7 Ibid., 18.

8 See Howard Burns, "Giuliano da Sangallo and the Renewal of Residential Architecture," in *Giuliano da Sangallo*, ed. Amedeo Belluzzi, Carolina Elam, and Francesco Paolo Fiore (Milan: Officina Libraria, 2017), 89–95.

9 It is important to note that Villa Capra was not considered a villa since in his *Four Books on Architecture* Palladio placed it in the book on palaces. See Andrea Palladio, *The Four Books on Architecture*, trans. Robert Tavernor and Richard Schofield (Cambridge, MA: MIT Press, 2002), 45.

10 See Ackerman, *The Villa*, 185–211.

11 See Gilles Deleuze and Félix Guattari, *Anti-Oedipus: Capitalism and Schizophrenia* (Minneapolis: University of Minnesota Press, 1983).

12 Friedrich Hölderlin, *Selected Poems and Fragments*, translated by Michael Hamburger (London: Penguin, 1994), 231.

13 See Oswald Mathias Ungers, Hans Kollhoff, and Arthur Ovaska, *The Urban Villa: A Multi-Family Dwelling Type* (Cologne: Studio Press for Architecture, 1977).

14 The Syndicate of Tenements offers advice, financial support, and helps with the overall organization of the project. Essential to the Syndicate's model is that the residents themselves decide on all matters concerning the house, but they don't privately own any of its space. The official owner of the house is a limited liability company (in German: Gesellschaft mit beschränkter Haftung, or GmbH), whose shareholders are on the one hand the collective association of rent-paying tenants, and on the other hand the Syndicate as the association of all the other such house projects. See Lina Hurlin, "Mietshäuser Syndikat: Collective Ownership, the 'Housing Question' and Degrowth," in *Housing for Degrowth: Principles, Models, Challenges and Opportunities*, ed. Anitra Nelson and François Schneider (London: Routledge, 2019).

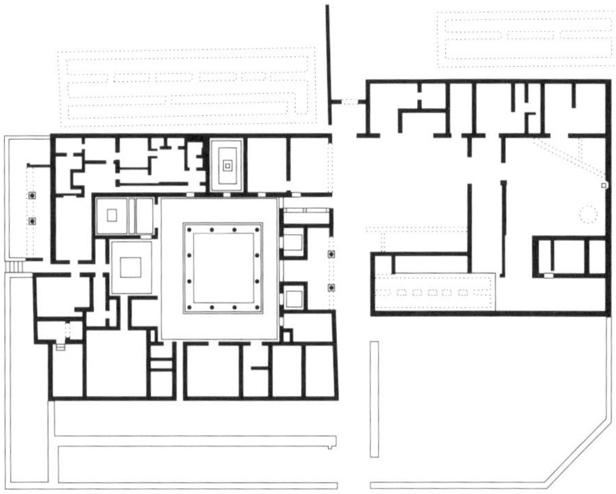

Plan of Villa San Rocco,
Francolise, 30 BCE

10 m

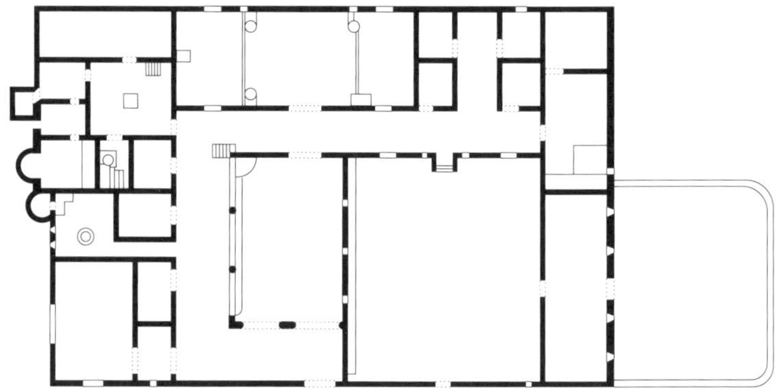

Plan of Villa della Pisanella,
Boscoreale, late first century CE

10 m

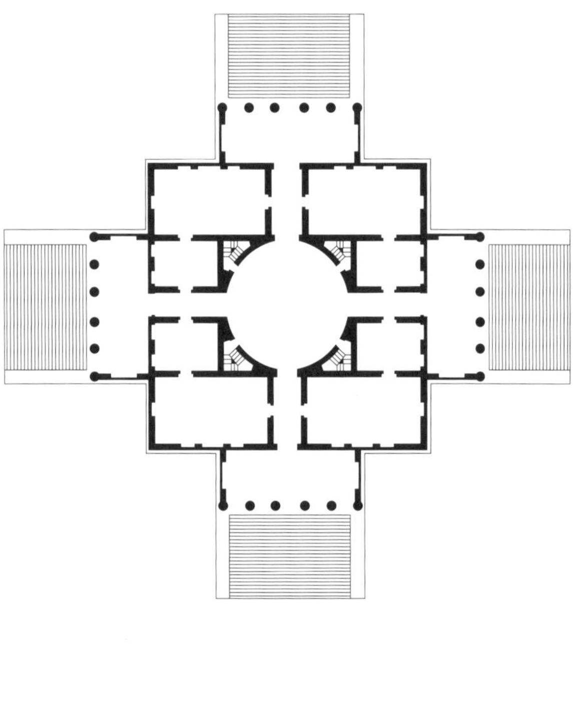

Plan of Villa Capra, known as "La Rotonda,"
near Vicenza, 1566
architect: Andrea Palladio
(adapted from Andrea Palladio, 1570)

10 m

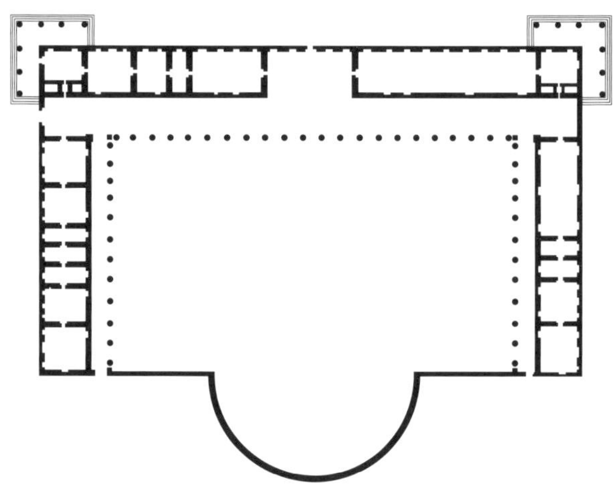

Plan of Villa Repeta,
Campiglia, 1557
architect: Andrea Palladio
(adapted from Andrea Palladio, 1570)

10 m

Clockwise: Block Villa, Courtyard Villa, Sandwich Villa, Double Nave Villa, student projects from the "Urban Villa" Summer School, Berlin, 1977 (adapted from Oswald Mathias Ungers, Hans Kollhoff, Athur Ovaska, 1977)

2 m

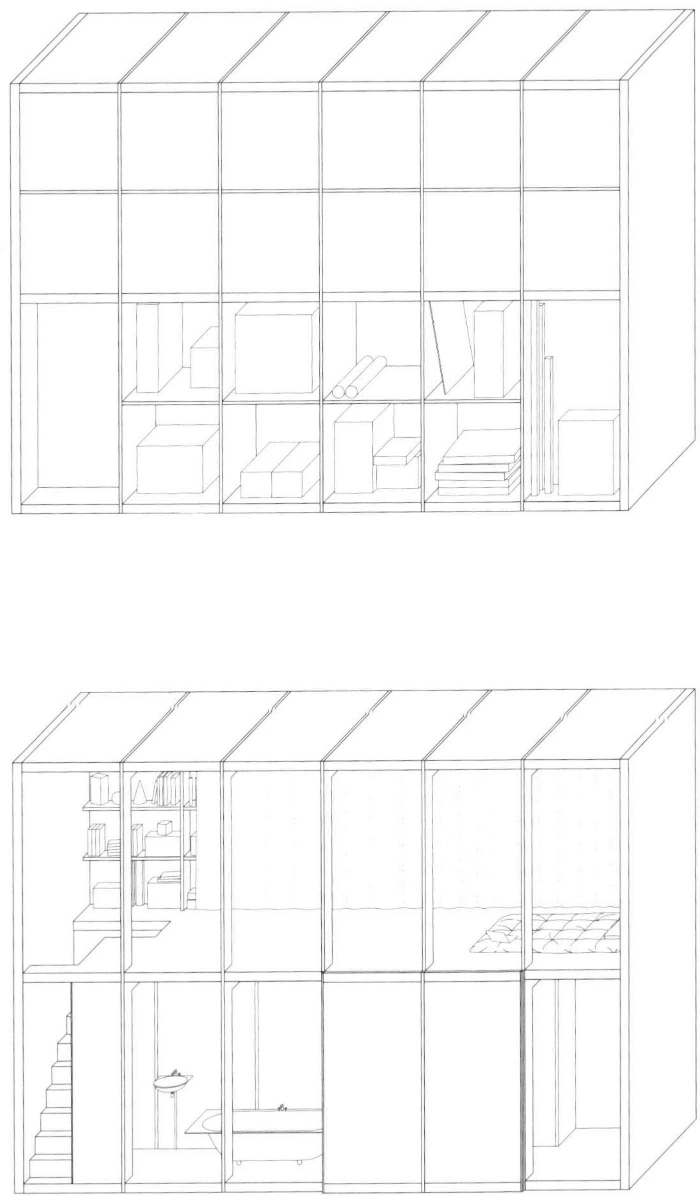

The inhabitable wall, view from the collective space (above) and from the room (below)

131

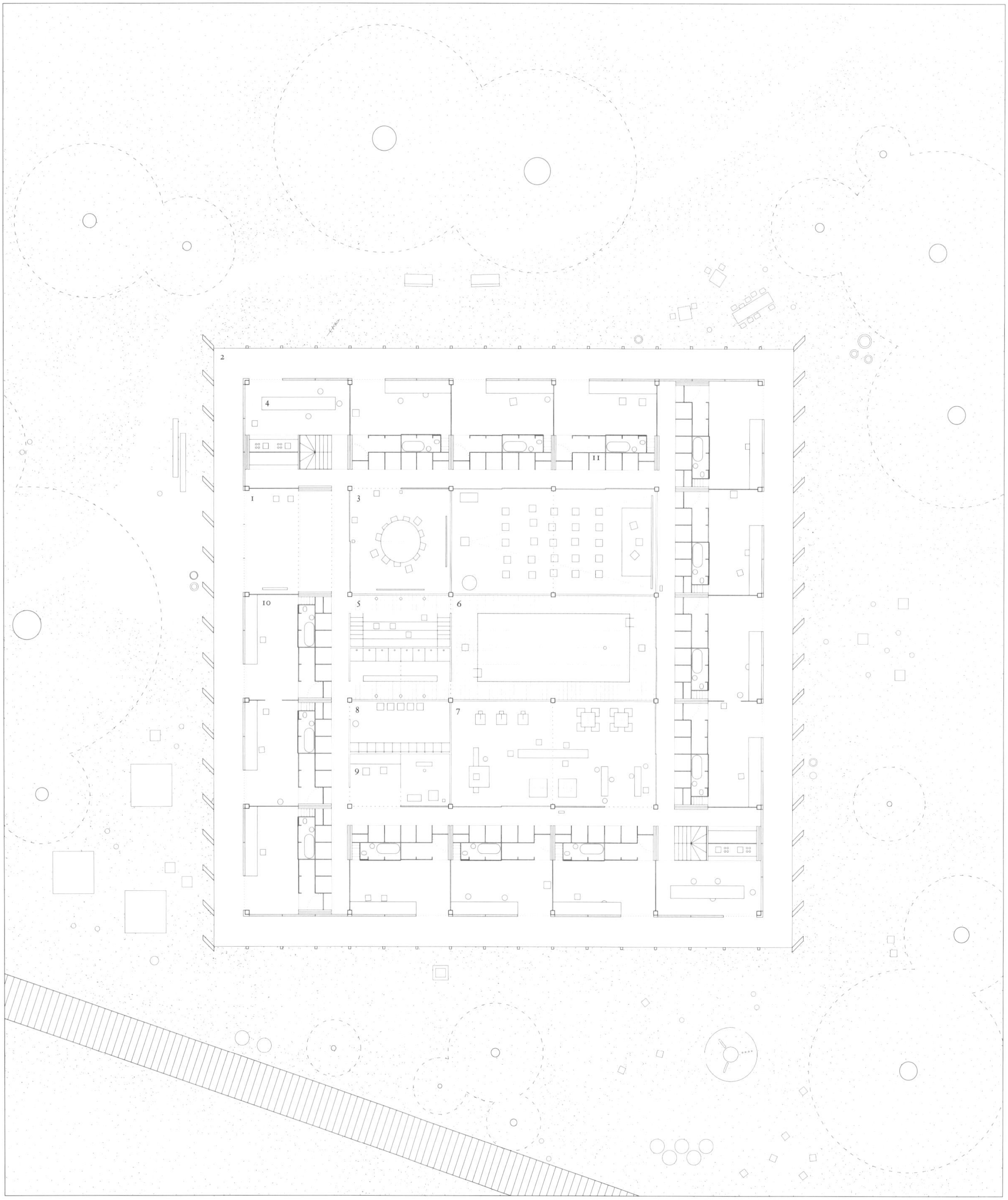

Villa Suburbana, ground-floor plan

5 m

(1) entrance, (2) loggia, (3) meeting and seminar room, (4) kitchen, (5) sauna, (6) pool, (7) noisy workshop, (8) recording studio, (9) laundry, (10) room for one person, (11) storage

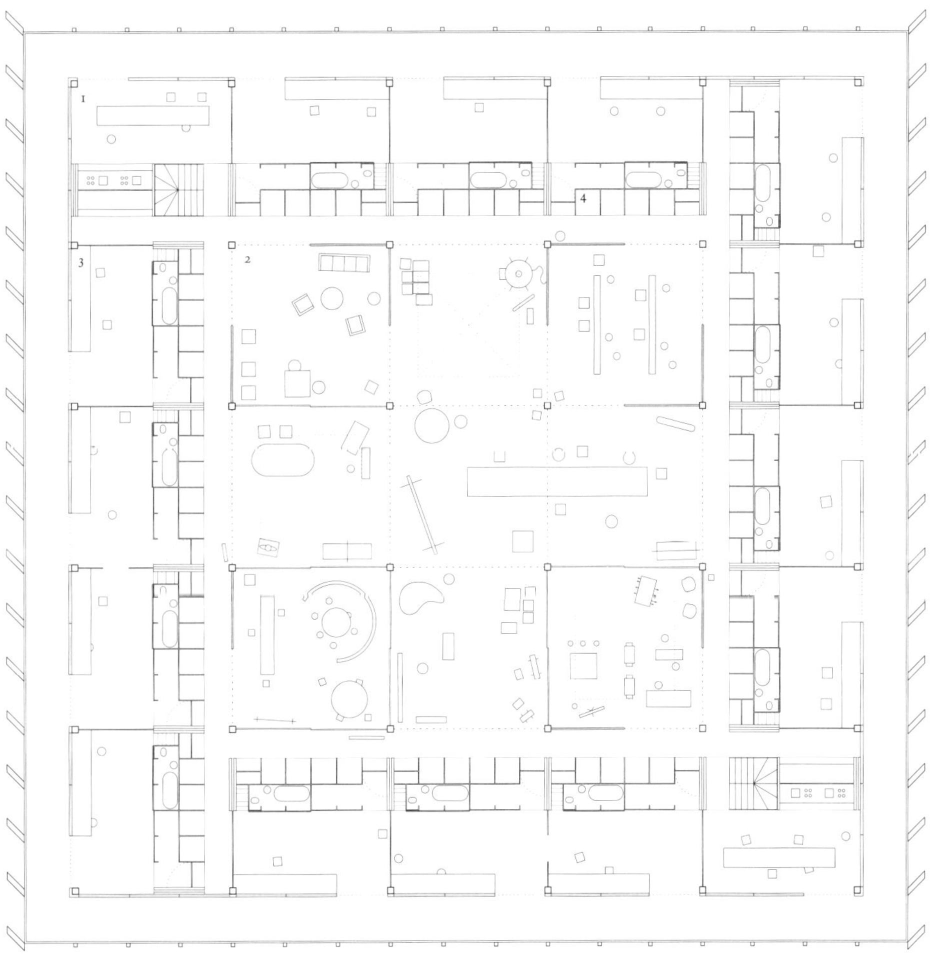

Villa Suburbana, first-floor plan

(1) kitchen, (2) collective multipurpose space, (3) room, (4) storage

138

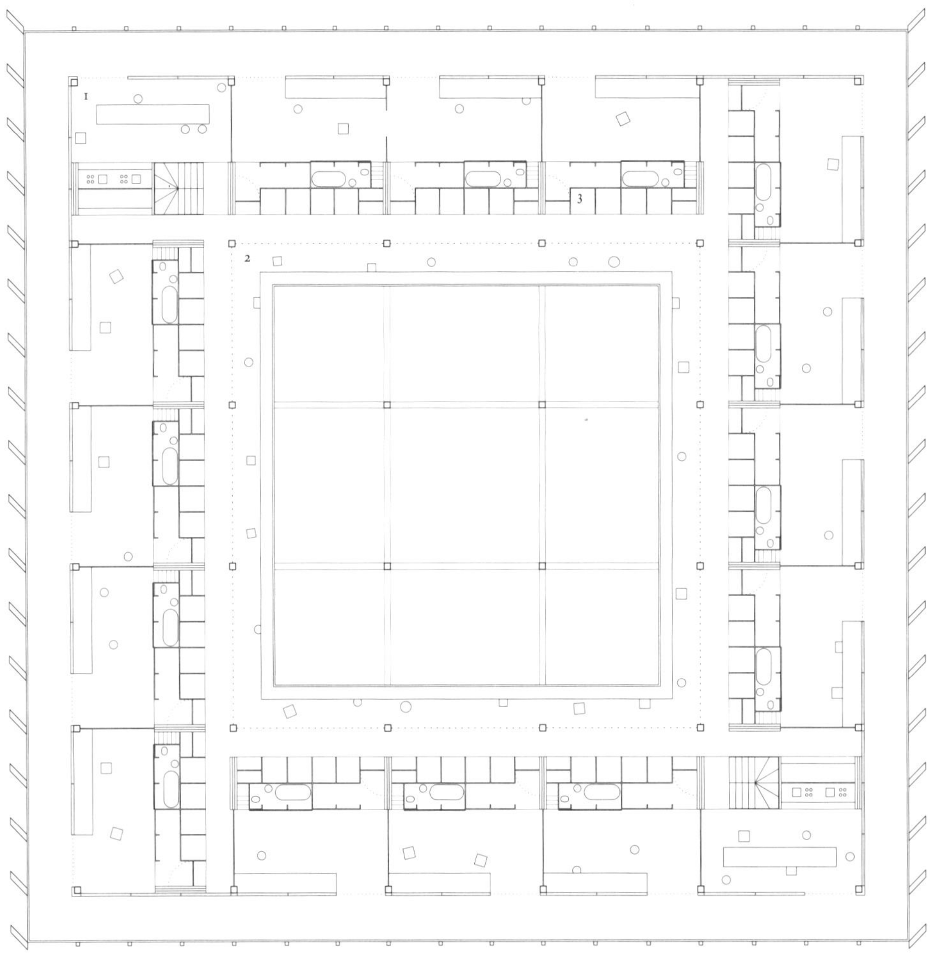

Villa Suburbana, second-floor plan

(1) kitchen, (2) gallery studio, (3) storage

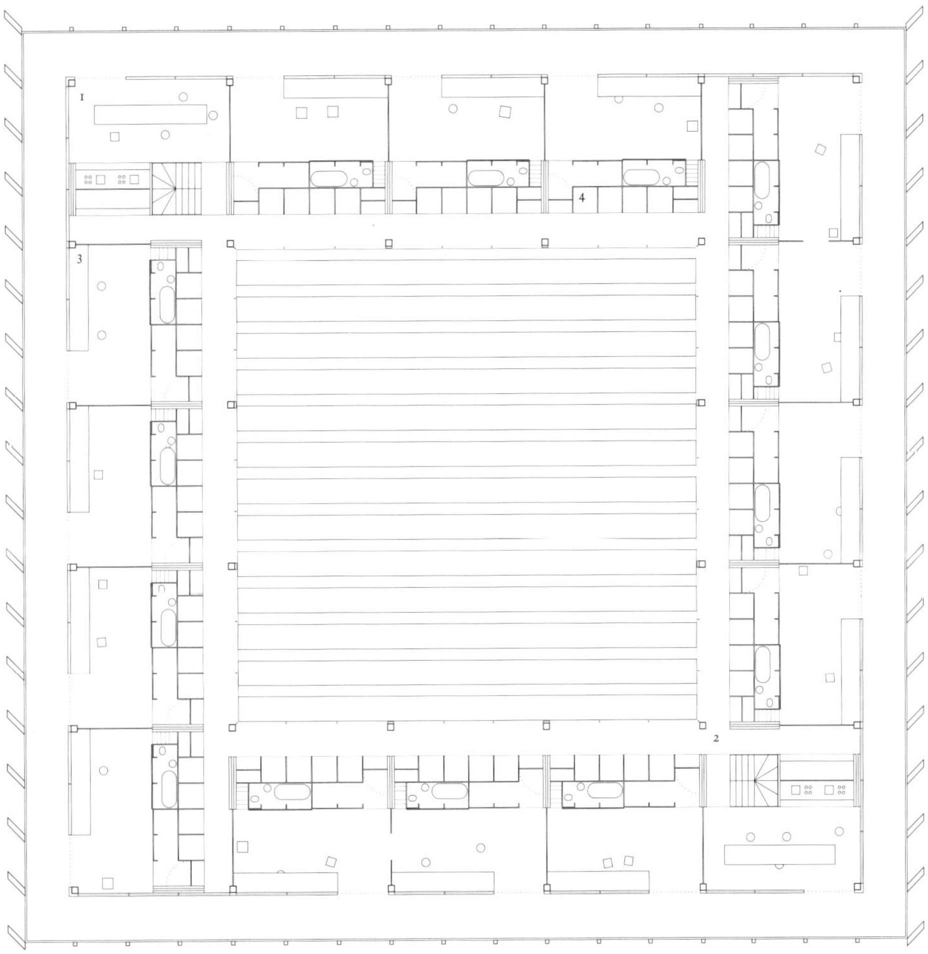

Villa Suburbana, third-floor plan

(1) kitchen, (2) gallery, (3) rooms, (4) storage

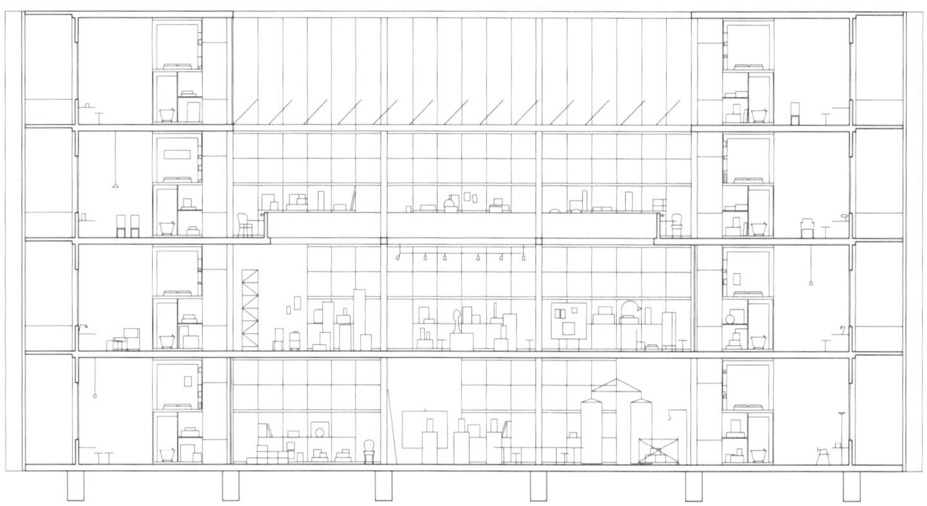

Villa Suburbana, section

5 m

The Villa Suburbana is constructed as an industrial steel building. Horizontal slabs are made of corrugated steel deck, a consolidating layer of reinforced concrete cast on site, insulation/impermeabilization/heating, and a final cement screed; the building façade is made of standard prefabricated insulated metal panels hung onto the building's primary structure; external parapets, vertical shading elements, and external columns are standardized metal profiles; staircases are in prefabricated concrete; the inhabitable wall is a self-supporting element built in plywood. Installations and finishing are also those typical of an industrial building, with plumbing partially visible and horizontal surfaces made of solid exposed material.

Villa Suburbana, construction detail

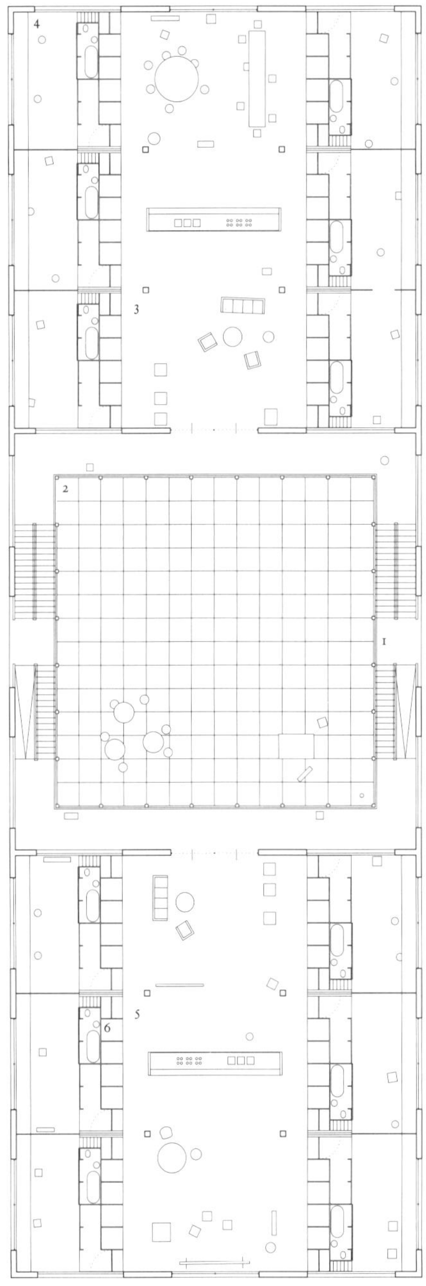

Villa Urbana, ground-floor plan

(1) entrance, (2) courtyard, (3) multipurpose space, (4) room, (5) kitchen, (6) storage

The Villa Urbana, unlike the Villa Suburbana, is built in concrete. Columns and staircases are prefabricated concrete elements put in place on site; horizontal slabs are the result of the combination of horizontal prefabricated trussed joists and prefabricated hollow-core concrete slabs, all reinforced with a horizontal completing reinforced concrete layer, poured on site. The building façade is made of standardized prefabricated reinforced, insulated concrete panels hung onto the building's primary structure; the inhabitable wall is a self-supporting element built in plywood. Installation and finishing are those typical of an industrial building, with plumbing partially visible and horizontal surfaces made of solid exposed material (cement screed).

Villa Urbana, construction detail

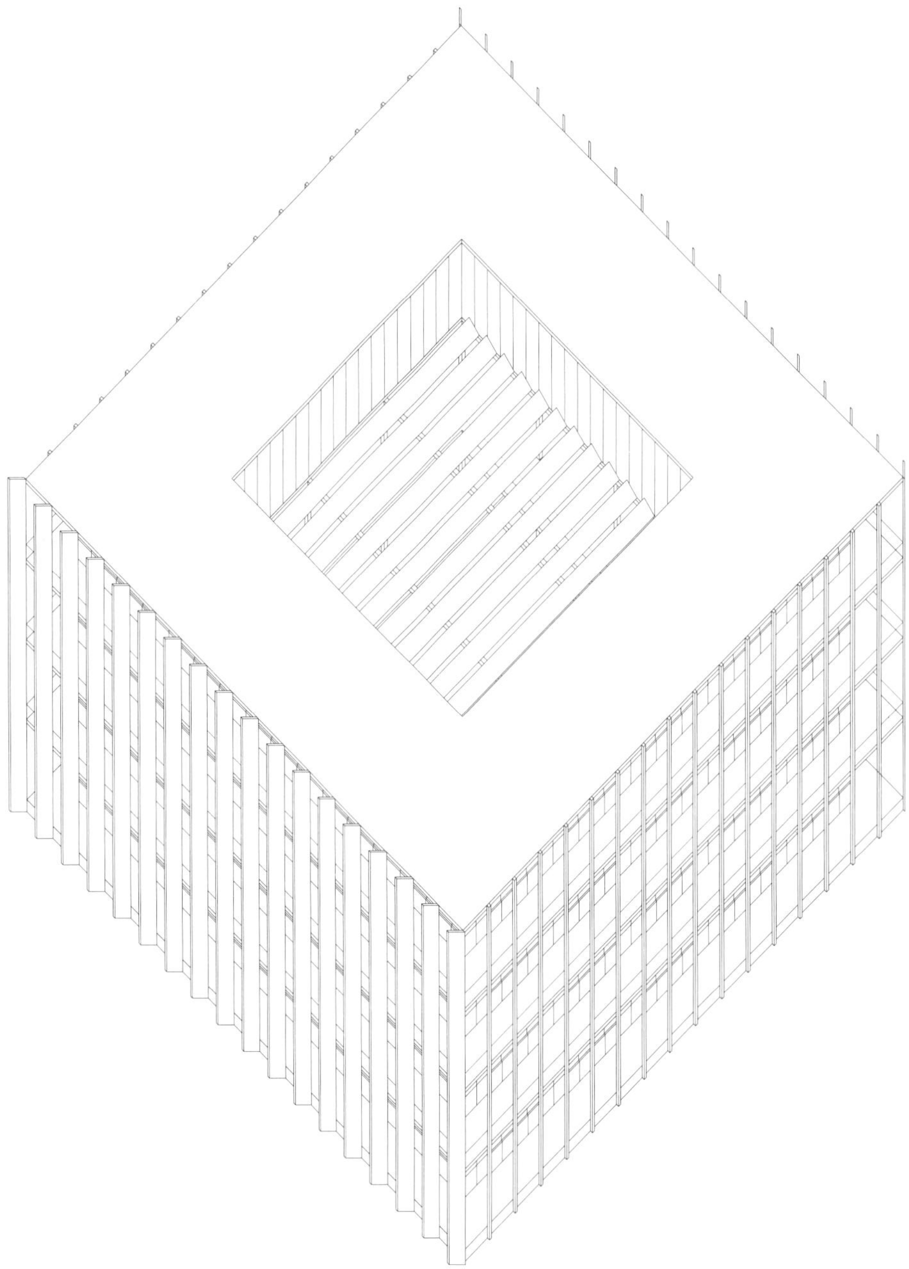

Villa Suburbana

Villa Urbana

Unused land as potential sites for the communal villa in Berlin

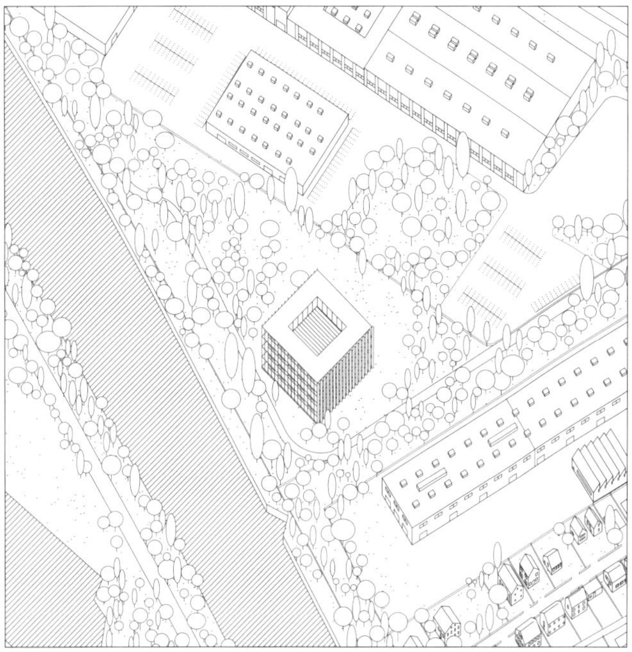

Haselhorst

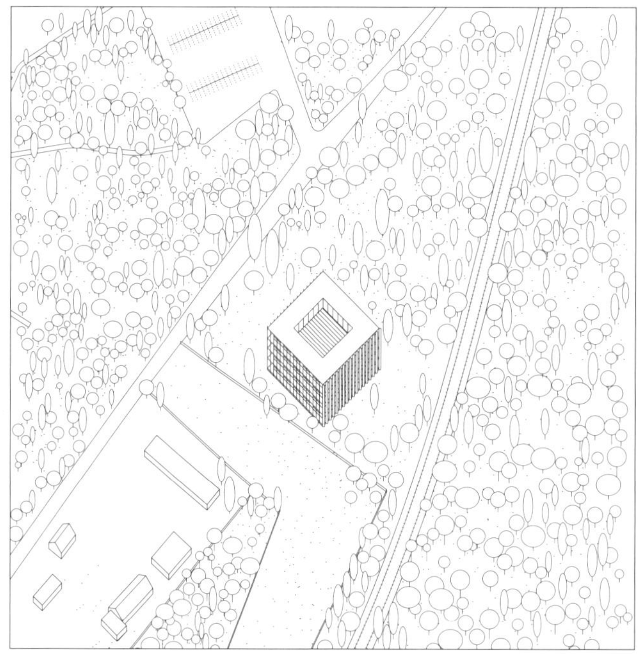

Wuhlheide

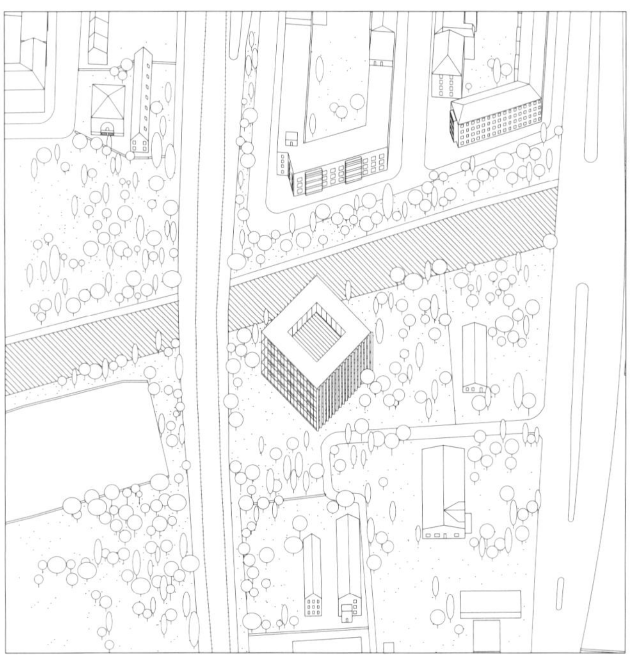

Baumschulenweg

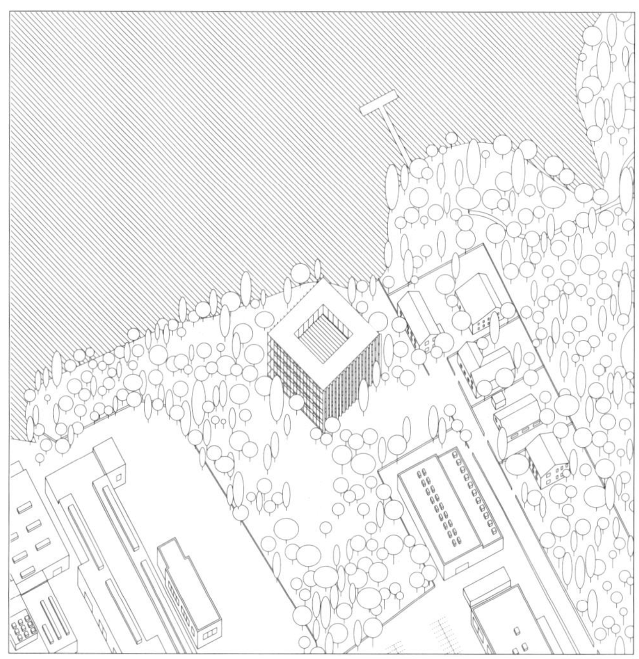

Haselhorst

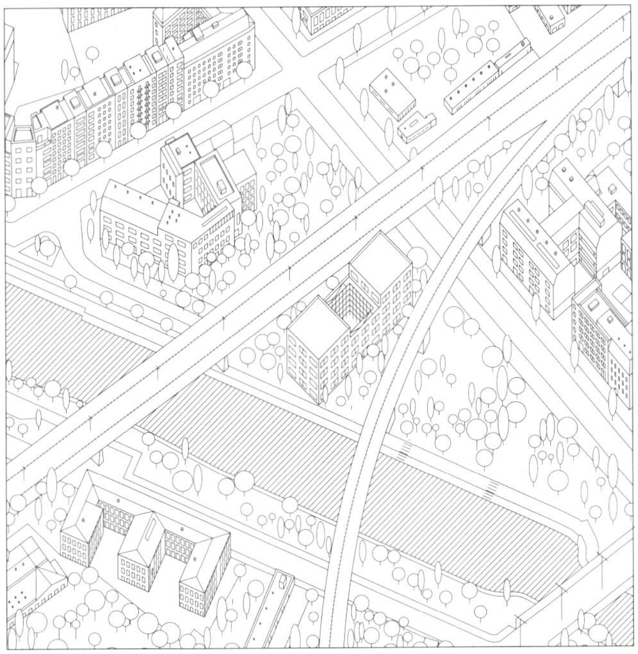

Mettmannplatz

Yorckstraße

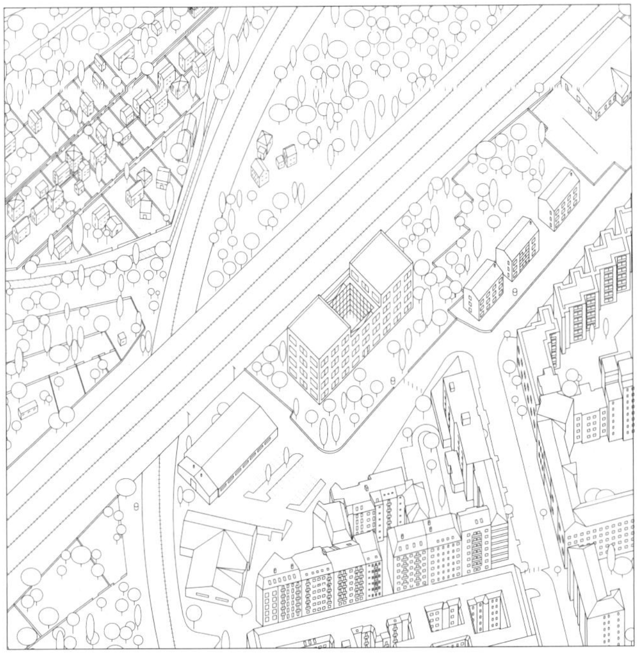

Westkreuz

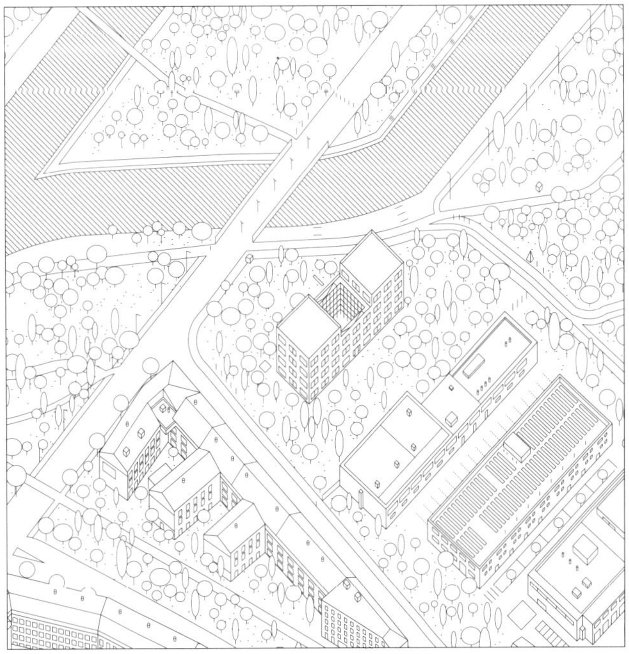

Treptower Brücke

LIKE A ROLLING STONE (2016)

This proposal is a prototype for a house meant to host a dweller for a limited length of time where domestic chores such as housekeeping and meal preparation are collectivized and professionalized. The prototype can be applied on sites of different configurations as it is based on an adaptable, modular concrete skeleton with prefabricated concrete slabs. Outer elevations are clad with light insulated-metal paneling and fitted with metal frame windows. Vertical circulation varies according to the conditions of the site and the overall dimensions of the prototype—some of them have an internal staircase, others an external prefabricated staircase and lift. All interiors are based on the repetition of the same inhabitable core to be placed at the center of the structural module. The inhabitable cores are prefabricated and stacked on top of each other with the help of a crane once the concrete skeleton and slabs are completed. These cores contain bathroom, storage, and a small kitchen surface on the lower level, and a generous sleeping alcove for up to two persons on the upper level. This individual space can be seen as a self-sufficient interior, as the access to the upper level is contained within the core itself, behind a door that can be closed to isolate the user from the noise of any surrounding activities. In this way, the bathroom can be accessed directly from the upper level, which is imagined as an intimate, quiet space—a soft platform to sleep, read, watch videos; a large round window gives the upper level air, light, and a view.

Because these cores are stacked, pipes and cables are contained within a vertical shaft placed at the corner of each core that can serve the whole column of units. Inhabitable cores are the most technological components of the prototype, and their production inside factories rather than on site is meant to simplify the construction process, improve quality, and reduce costs. Around the core, double-height shared spaces can be used by inhabitants as living rooms or working space depending on their preferences. This space is equipped with built-in furniture such as sofas and tables to be placed in the bow windows along the elevations. These elements—together with the part of the core that is completely open to this communal space such as the working ledge equipped with sink and a hot plate—reduce the need of inhabitants to purchase any kind of furniture that they might not be able to take along with them once they decide to move out. Besides responding to the need for housing of temporary inhabitants, the aim of this prototype is to undomesticate housing and thus challenge the ideology of domestic space as an enclosed and privatized household.

This housing proposal can be understood as an attempt to revisit the model of the boardinghouse. In this type of lodging, which was popular in the nineteenth century, dwellers could rent their space for a limited amount of time. The boardinghouse distinguishes itself from both hotel and rental flat because all chores pertaining to domestic labor (cleaning and cooking) are conceived as work, professionally offered by those who run the house, and paid for by the tenants. The boardinghouse emerged in the mid-1800s as a response to the large influx of foreign workers in newly industrialized cities. This domestic arrangement was to be found on both sides of the Atlantic, but it was particularly pervasive in North America where by mid-century 30 to 50 percent of households kept boarders. A distinct advantage of this kind of housing was its flexibility, which allowed workers to move from city to city following various job opportunities. Boardinghouses came in all sizes—from a few rooms run by a widow and a servant, to large buildings manned by a full team of maids, cooks, and handymen. Because of their popularity and because they threatened the idea of the family household as the site of unpaid domestic labor offered by married women, housing reformers and city authorities in the United States and elsewhere halted their proliferation. Today a caricature of the boardinghouse has returned in the plethora of initiatives focused on transient living such as WeLive or The Collective. Yet unlike their predecessors, these new accommodations are very expensive, often because in the places where they are most needed, land value is very high.

In our proposal, we put forward a scenario in which a multitude of affordable boardinghouses are built on sites in London that today have no clear use as they are vacant or are residual parcels. These sites should be in proximity to major transport infrastructure, as the users of such a type would need to be highly mobile; we traced a constellation of possible sites around the Crossrail line, cutting an east-west section through London and touching upon very diverse urban conditions. These sites could be leased or obtained by nonprofit associations at lower rates from either public or private owners through special planning agreements that would support forms of affordable housing in the city by making public parcels available to alternative housing initiatives. Time-limited building permissions could be granted in exchange for rent-controlled boardinghouses.

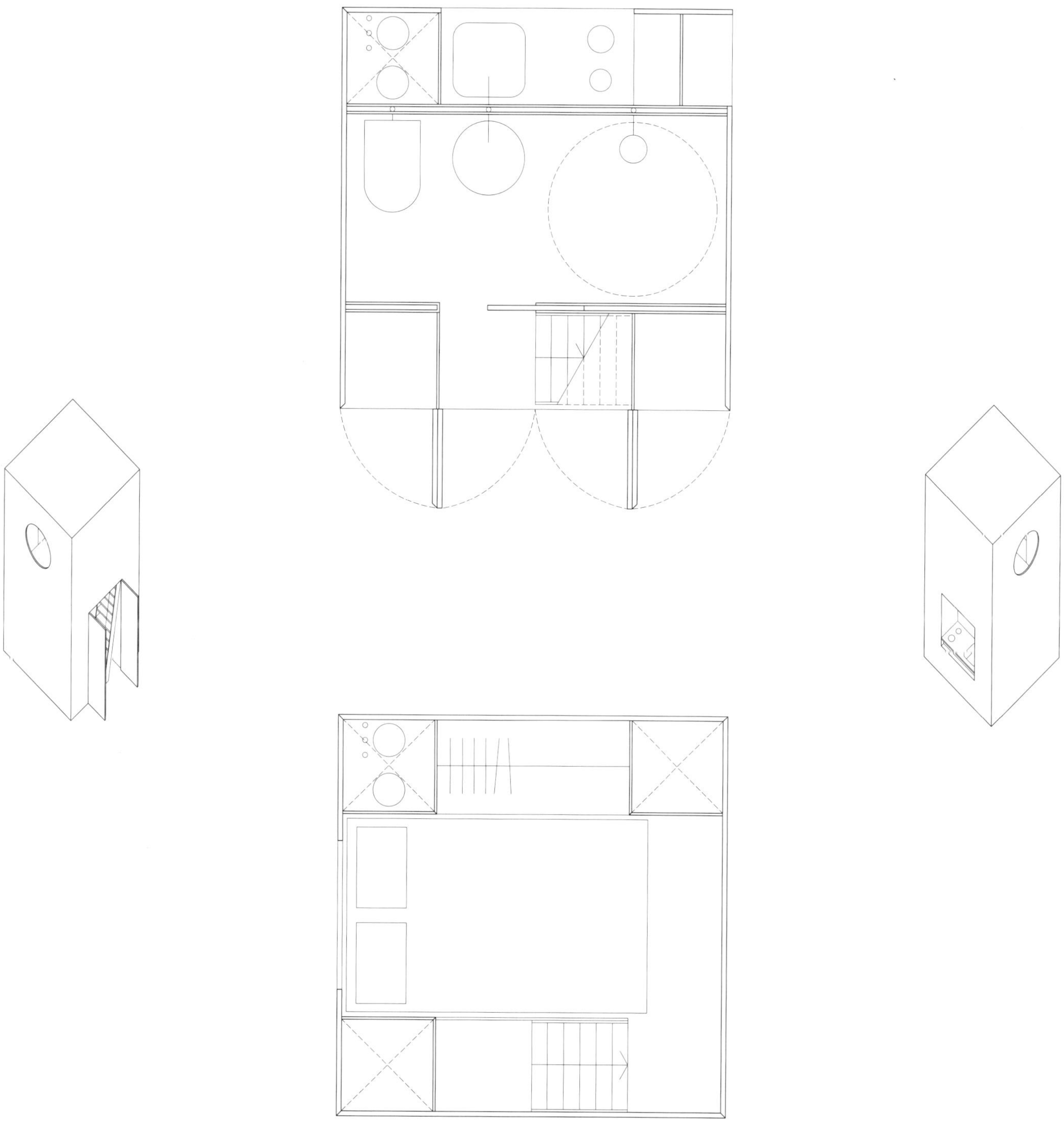

Inhabitable core: plan of the first level (above) and second level (below)

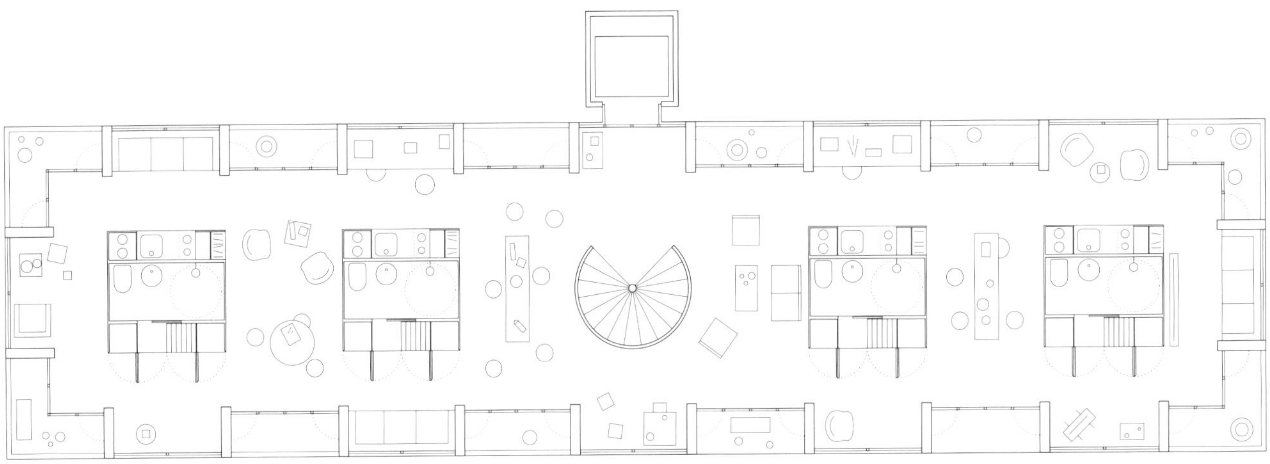

Typical plan

3 m

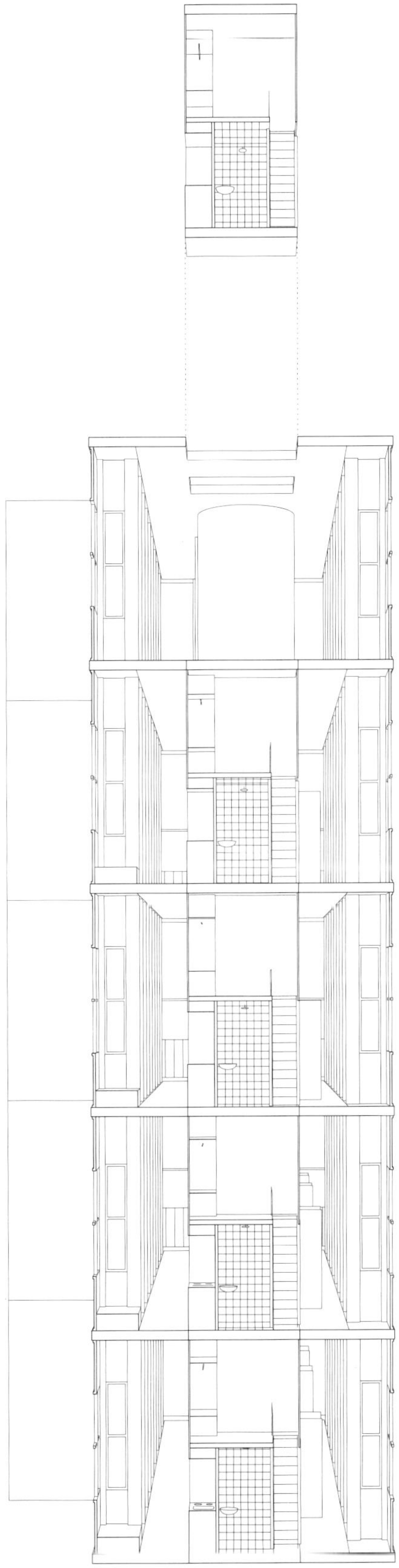

Section

162

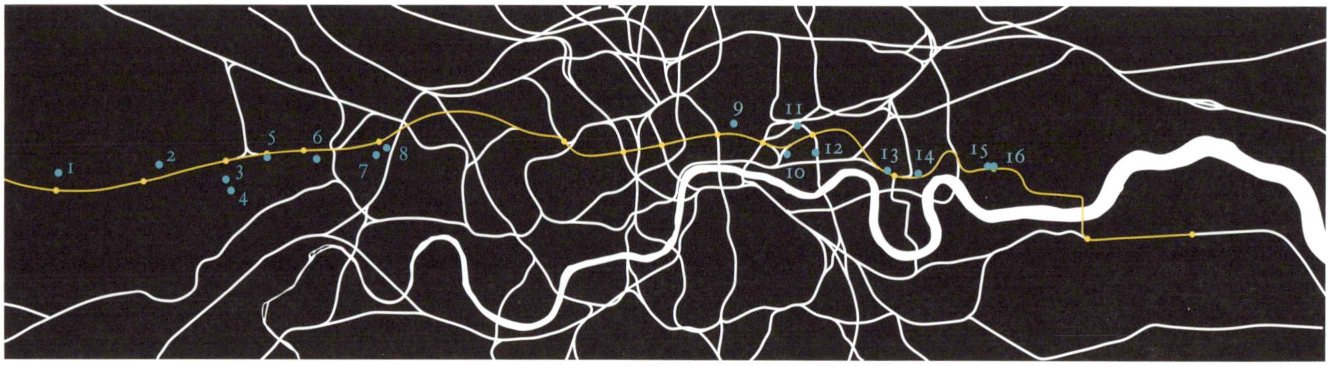

5 km

Unused land in proximity to London's Crossrail as sites for the boardinghouse

1. Hayes Harlington, Botwell Lane

2. Southall, Uxbridge Road

3. Hanwell, Lower Boston Road

4. Hanwell, Rosebank Road

5. West Ealing, Manor Road

6. Ealing Broadway, Florence Road

7. Acton Main Line, Essex Road

8. Acton Main Line, Emanuel Avenue

9. Farringdon, Clerkenwell Road

10. Liverpool Street, St. Botolph Street

11. Whitechapel, Pedley Street

12. Whitechapel, Nelson Street

13. Canary Wharf, Salter Street

14. Canary Wharf, Newby Place

15. Canary Wharf, Boreham Avenue

16. Canary Wharf, Coolfin Road

The basic system, composed of a load-bearing skeleton hosting regularly distributed cores, can be adapted to different conditions. Depending on the available space, the modular structure can develop in a variety of urban morphologies by expanding both vertically and horizontally. The frame is stable enough to support a mid-rise tower, while the staircases are part of the pattern of cores. Lifts can be attached to the façade as add-on elements. If the site allows it, the boardinghouse can frame a courtyard, offering a shared, open cloister to the guests. In some cases, the prototype can take over a whole block and be deployed as a sequence of linear buildings separated by gardens.

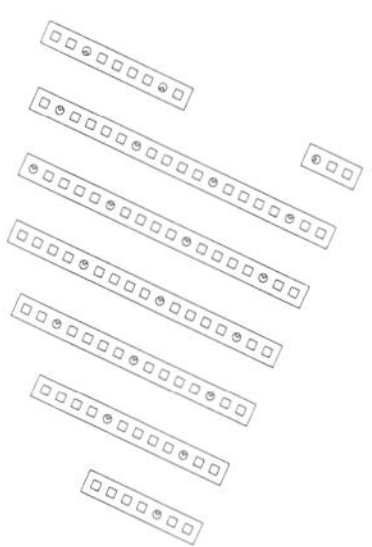

1. Hayes Harlington, Botwell Lane

2. Southall, Uxbridge Road

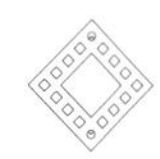

3. Hanwell, Lower Boston Road

4. Hanwell, Rosebank Road

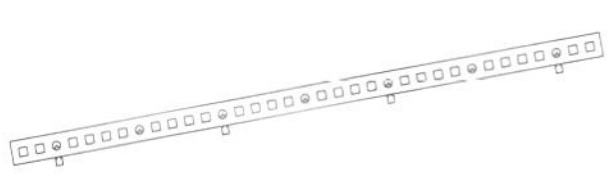

5. West Ealing, Manor Road

6. Ealing Broadway, Florence Road

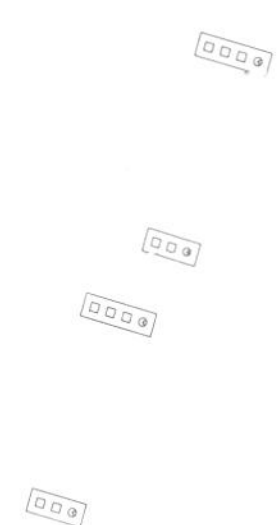

7. Acton Main Line, Essex Road

8. Acton Main Line, Emanuel Avenue

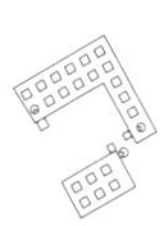

9. Farringdon, Clerkenwell Road

10. Liverpool Street, St. Botolph Street

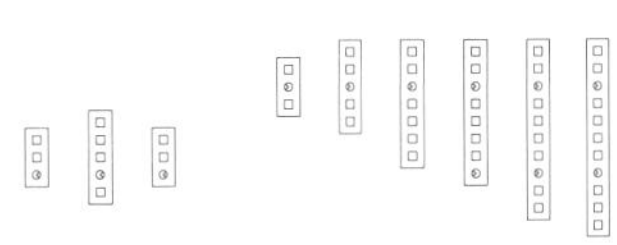

11. Whitechapel, Pedley Street

12. Whitechapel, Nelson Street

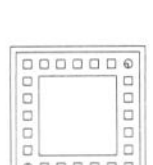

13. Canary Wharf, Salter Street

14. Canary Wharf, Newby Place

15. Canary Wharf, Boreham Avenue

16. Canary Wharf, Coolfin Road

PARK CITY (2016)

Flanders has a high number of homeowners and single-family houses: 70 percent of households own their house and almost 80 percent of the housing stock is made up of single-family houses.[1] This situation is rather unique in Europe and reflects the history of Belgium as a state whose politics have consistently supported homeownership. Since the late nineteenth century, Belgium's housing condition has been characterized by the hegemony of the single-family home as a way of life—a condition created by the long-standing "anti-city" policy promoted by the Belgian government.[2] After its rise as an independent nation-state, Belgium went through a rampant process of industrialization, which triggered several social conflicts. Fearing a high concentration of urban-dwelling workers, the Liberal-Catholic government pursued a policy of dispersing the labor force throughout the rural territory by promoting homeownership and affordable railway transport.[3] Urban sprawl in Belgium was a carefully orchestrated political project with a threefold objective: the ruralization of industrial workers, the promotion of homeownership, and the reinforcement of family values.[4] The state's promotion of homeownership was an especially successful tactic that enabled the social, political, and above all ideological integration of the working class into the capitalist system.[5] This was achieved by creating an institutional framework that allowed workers to obtain an adequate financial base through local savings and loan associations.[6] The ease of obtaining funding for homeownership was reflected by the availability of domestic typologies, which combined affordability and the possibility of a family dwelling freed from the hectic rhythms of metropolitan concentrations.

SUBURBAN POLICIES

If one of the major tendencies in housing since the nineteenth century was the splitting of living and working functions, then within the Belgian housing condition the separation between the workplace and the home became even more radical: work was limited to cities, and living to the countryside. Suburban living was promoted not just as a housing solution, but as a way of life—the once-struggling family was suddenly unburdened from the toil and promiscuity of wage-laboring activities. The state reinforced this ideology by promoting and financing a whole spectrum of nonprofit social organizations such as trade unions, farmers' associations, and women's collectives whose overarching goal was to educate dwellers in the virtues of family living.[7] The activities of these organizations focused on every aspect of domestic living, including architecture. There was an urgency to emphasize certain aspects of a domestic space such as the representative role of the living room, replete with outstanding fireplace, and the generous provision of bedrooms to individuate and define the role of each family member. In addition, both government institutions and social organizations were keen to emphasize the private garden (an important complement to the single-family house), sweetening their idea of domestic life by connecting home to land. Yet gardens were also important as instruments of housekeeping—they provided space for domestic chores, such as washing and drying laundry, and for the cultivation of the kitchen's herb and vegetable patches. Above all the garden played an important role as a form of recreation, discouraging life in denser urban centers. In the imagination of the home, the garden is a symbol of conforming to the local community (an unmanicured garden is a symbol of antisocial attitude), and today this remains one of its strongest roles—as attested by the elaborate topiaries of many homes in the region.[8]

Following the Second World War and the advent of the welfare state, the government continued to promote homeownership and the further decentralization of urban living, making the entire rural territory of Belgium a de facto place for living. While in countries like the Netherlands and Sweden planning activities were centralized and administered by national institutions, in Belgium the government supported housing and the planning of amenities by subsidizing local authorities and private owners, thus devolving the reurbanization of the country to a myriad of actors.[9] As has been noted, the middle-class colonization of the countryside took place in a piecemeal manner without the framework of a spatial planning policy, and this process of urbanization was the result of a governmental initiative rather than of laissez-faire politics. Housing policy was thus an extension of the Fordist mode of production into the realm of domestic life. Despite their vernacular and pastoral appearance, Belgian houses were the product of a well-organized industrial process whose main goal was to make the house itself an item of consumption to instigate wealth production. Since the 1960s, the middle class has built or purchased single-family houses much as they would consumer goods, a trend that consequently set the pace for the whole building industry.

In the last few decades, the progressive decline of the welfare state has only reinforced what was previously done. The success of living in the countryside peaked in the 1980s and 1990s when a new wave of detached homes flooded the already saturated countryside.[10] This time the motivation was the possibility of owning a second home. Moreover, many people from

neighboring countries such as Germany and the Netherlands relocated to rural areas in Flanders to own a larger home in a taxpayer-friendly country. This phenomenon, which occurred especially close to the national border, gave rise to "villa parks"—clusters of large villas with large gardens, detached from any existing rural centers.

An important aspect of the single-family home in Flanders is its resistance to change. This has led researchers to define the problem of housing in terms of *obduracy*.[11] What the political and economic process described above has left on the ground is very difficult to modify or alter. Not only are domestic habits extremely enduring and hard to change, since they give a sense of orientation especially within uncertain times, but also the house itself speaks to a system in which a specific spatial condition is linked with deep-seated social and juridical frameworks. It is hard, for example, to imagine that those who are accustomed to living in a detached home would allow the further subdivision of their property or the sharing of their garden, but the future of baby-boomer-built suburban housing raises many questions, especially considering recent social and economic changes. In Europe, there is a visible trend that sees the reduction of household size to an average of 2.5 persons per house, and a growing mismatch between the number of suburban houses and the newer generations' desire to live in cities.[12] After university, many people leave their parents' suburban houses. Another urgent issue is the rising elderly population, which finds itself increasingly isolated and lacking adequate care.[13] While the countryside offers some respite from the hectic life of cities, the increasing depopulation and lack of social services make their lives lonely and devoid of social interaction. This condition is not only detrimental for the elderly, but also for the social well-being of the suburban territory as a whole.

Indeed, today the large suburban home with its spacious garden is the antithesis of what seems to be the most desirable form of accommodation—namely a small house in the city—a condition that is even physically reflected in the area and program of these houses; a gap exists between their generous floor plans and the number of people who live in them. Moreover, many of the older suburban homes have a dated layout comprising many rooms, small corridors, and steep stairs. They also feature an overdesigned architecture—an external rustic façade and an abundance of differentiated spaces inside, each requiring a specific kind of furniture. This condition leaves little freedom to adapt the domestic space of the home to new functions such as a workspace. Finally, rigid zoning codes—introduced only after the chaotic spread of detached homes had already taken place—prevent the possibility of retrofitting existing properties and thus transforming the single-family house into a multifamily dwelling.

All these factors—relevant users, location, size, program, aesthetics, and flexibility of plan—have challenged the typology of the detached single-family home as the ideal house, and it is not difficult to predict that in less than twenty years, considering the changing demographics, part of the stock of suburban homes will become obsolete and lose part of its economic value. It is precisely this threat that can push for radical reform. Over the last decade, Flanders has timidly looked at alternatives to the single-family house, which address the possibility of densification and further subdivision of the existing allotments.[14] Although the juridical procedure for internal subdivision of the detached house can be complicated, new legislative measures have allowed the introduction of accessory dwelling units to existing family houses for care purposes. Yet possibilities such as this are still limited if we consider the magnitude of the problem. To effectively tackle the rapid obsolescence of suburban houses, one should consider another important factor in the radical change of these dispersed territories, namely the emergence of new forms of living in relation to changing conditions of work.

CHALLENGING DOMESTIC SPACE

With the rise of immaterial production, working activities have exceeded traditional spatial and temporal limits: work happens everywhere and at any time, and often within the home.[15] This condition is problematic because work tends to invade any aspect of life, but it becomes even more problematic when, for those who do not have a dedicated office, there is not sufficient room for more flexibly organizing work-related activities. For example, it is difficult (if not impossible) to host a workplace like a small office, a retail space, or a workshop within a detached home. Circulation and the pronounced functional identity of domestic rooms (i.e., living rooms versus bedrooms) are often an obstacle to working activities. This condition is made even more problematic by zoning codes and the juridical distinctions that make it impossible to use one's home as a workplace. And yet the only rising forms of production in these times of economic stagnation are small companies—of two to five people—that would otherwise fit well within a domestic space if the latter could only offer some flexibility.

The advantages of working at home are usually the sparing of commuting time and having a more flexible schedule. The disadvantages are working alone and a lack of social interaction. Communal living can increase the advantages and reduce the disadvantages of working at home by allowing people who do different work to share the same space. This situation is particularly convenient for artisans whose work requires bigger spaces and costly tools. In a shared workspace both square meters and working tools can be shared and thus have less impact on the budget of one individual company or person. Another advantage to working at home, or very close to it, is that it allows for the combination of domestic chores—in a generous communal area, for example, different families or workers can also organize a space for communal child care.

For these arrangements, suburban territories are both problematic and potentially beneficial. They are problematic because contemporary forms of work require a high degree of cooperation and social interaction, and these are the precise qualities that suburbia has traditionally been thought to lack. They have potential, however, because suburban places are today cheaper than city property and above all they are more generous in terms of space. What prevents a new scenario from blossoming is the lack of both services and flexibility beyond family living. Within this condition, a more cooperative way of living would challenge both the lack of flexibility of the single-family home and the introversion of domestic labor. Communal living implies a more rational use of space and resources and exposes domestic labor as work that is necessary and that can be shared among household members.[16] Spaces such as kitchens, living rooms, and gardens can be shared by different families. As mentioned before, today the average family is composed of two or three members, which means there is more possibility for families to share a greater number of domestic facilities, with the consequent reduction of domestic labor and energy consumption.

A PROJECT FOR LIMBURG: THREE STEPS FOR THE TRANSFORMATION OF A SUBURBAN TERRITORY

In 2016 we were asked by the environment authorities of Flanders to develop a planning strategy for a suburban area in Limburg, a region located in the eastern part of Belgium, at the border with the Netherlands and close to Germany and Luxemburg. Once a center of coal mining, then a pastoral retreat, several factors have led this suburban territory toward a condition of obsolescence, such as lack of economic development after the demise of its mining industry. Both its central geographical position within Europe and the establishment of the country's largest national park in 2006, the Hoge Kempen, are recognized as great resources and a fulcrum for reinterpreting this territory as a place that is desirable for both living and working. Our position toward the urban regeneration of this area was that, in order to be beneficial, the transformation of the Hoge Kempen area had to be gradually detached from the modus operandi of property within which every improvement of the urban condition inevitably results in its commodification. Against this possibility we proposed a scenario in which incentives for transformation and improvement could only be granted on the condition of common ownership of both land and housing and thus the withdrawal of both from the market.

Our proposal consists of three distinct and to some extent sequential steps. The first step is a short-term scenario, which proposes specific interventions primarily focused on public facilities. One of the most remarkable aspects of this territory is its lack of civic space besides commercial facilities and town centers. By civic space we mean space for purposes beyond commerce, housing, and circulation. The proposed facilities are at first positioned to reinforce and emphasize the edge of the national park with a path that makes the edge itself a public space. This path is defined by a sequence of civic centers that, like sentinels, guard the park and allow different communities to use their premises. These civic centers are the necessary first step to encourage communities to come together and organize themselves as a collective subject rather than as a mass of individual families. In such a way, the path along the national park can become the catalyst for other linear paths that define and reinforce the territorial features of this conurbation—the main road, the canal, and the river. A series of minimal interventions such as bus stops, benches, playgrounds, and platforms are the subsequent stepping-stones that highlight the paths as public "shorelines." Rather than simply functioning as the sum of autonomous settlements, this conurbation can become a more structured territory whose main reference points are public facilities that challenge the privacy of suburban life.

The second step proposes a planned partial demolition of existing houses to shrink the footprint of built space and to enhance open land for agricultural use. Most of the houses in this territory are detached family homes that are resistant to any alternative use, and many are either underused or vacant. Moreover, a number have been built outside concentrated settlements as self-standing structures along roads. Given the current demographic of this territory, which itself faces increasing depopulation, it is easy to imagine that in the next ten years most of these houses could become redundant. This then presents both a problem and a unique opportunity to put forward a scenario in which municipalities can financially support homeowners who decide to demolish their overdimensioned and underused homes and invest in more sustainable and collective forms of dwelling.

The third step resists the current situation—that of an increasingly depopulated suburb—and instead proposes that, given the evolution of the ways in which we live and work, suburban sites may become attractive once again. Yet this assumption is plausible only through a radical transformation of the economic and spatial rationales that have produced the suburban way of living in the last century. This step addresses the possibility of repopulating the suburbs, focusing on the retrofitting of existing settlements. This retrofitting is put forward through a series of housing types that question the standard of the detached single-family home by providing spaces that can easily adapt to different activities and forms of association. Because of the spacious gardens, each suburban plot can host another dwelling that can be organized to suit different kinds of households. For this reason, new buildings are conceived as incremental structures built in timber that can grow or shrink according to necessity without requiring too much labor or producing building waste. Their floor plan is made of equally sized rooms whose partitions are always structurally independent of the load-bearing structure. Rooms can be used in different ways and partitions can be easily installed or dismantled. A fundamental precondition for the flexibility of these housing types is a different model of ownership, which is no longer tuned to a parcel but rather to a system of facilities. Only a cooperative model of ownership that focuses on use value rather than exchange value can allow housing to remain agile vis-à-vis contingent use. Rather than putting forward a single vision, our project offers a range of possibilities that can be applied incrementally or independently of each other. Because the proposal can only be conceived as a gradual transformation—one that involves a myriad of actors, from the state to local municipalities to citizens—it is important to highlight all possible directions, as opposed to one defined way forward. Our proposals therefore should be understood as possible examples of what this transformation might entail, offering a glimpse of different living and working conditions we imagine for the near future.

1 See Dominique Vanneste, Isabelle Thomas, and Lieve Vanderstraeten, "The Spatial Structure(s) of the Belgian Housing Stock," *Journal of Housing and the Built Environment* 23, no. 3 (2008): 173–198.

2 Bruno De Meulder, Jan Schreurs, Annabel Cock, and Bruno Notteboom, "Patching Up the Belgian Urban Landscape," *Oase* 52 (1999): 78–113.

3 Greet de Block, "Designing the Nation: The Belgian Railway Project, 1830–1837," *Technology and Culture* 52, no. 4 (October 2011): 703–732.

4 Els Witte, Jan Craeybeckx, and Alan Meynen, *Political History of Belgium from 1830 Onwards* (Brussels: VUB University Press, 2000), 47–71.

5 Pascal De Decker, "Understanding Housing Sprawl: The Case of Flanders, Belgium, 2010," *Environment and Planning* 43, no. 7 (May 2011): 1634–1654.

6 See Erik Buyst, *An Economic History of Residential Building in Belgium between 1890 and 1961* (Leuven: Leuven University Press, 1992).

7 Sofie De Caigny, "Catholicism and the Domestic Sphere: Working-Class Women in Inter-war Flanders," *Home Cultures* 2, no. 1 (2005): 23–34.

8 Thomas Verbeek, Ann Pisman, Hans Leinfelder, and Georges Allaert, "For Every House a Garden...A Morphological Assessment of Residential Development in Flanders' Rural Areas," in *The Powerful Garden: Emerging Views on the Garden Complex*, ed. Valerie Dewaelheyns, Kirsten Bomans, and Hubert Gulinck (Antwerp: Maklu, 2011), 85–106.

9 See Wouter Bervoest and Marijn van de Weijer, "The Future of the Post-war Single-Family House: The Case of Flanders," in *Post-war Middle-Class Housing*, ed. Federico Zanfi and Gaia Caramellino (Brussels: Peter Lang, 2010), 23–35.

10 Xaveer De Geyter, *After Sprawl* (Rotterdam: NAI, 2002), 22.

11 Wouter Bervoest and Hilde Heynen, "The Obduracy of the Detached Single Family House in Flanders," *International Journal of Housing Policy* 13, no. 4 (2013): 358–380.

12 Maria Iacovou and Alexandra Skew, *Household Structure in the EU* (Colchester: Institute for Economic and Social Research, 2010).

13 Cecilia Tomassini et al., "Living Arrangements among Older People: An Overview of Trends in Europe and the USA," *Population Trends* 115 (2004): 24–34.

14 Mario Antoninetti, "The Difficult History of Ancillary Units: The Obstacles and Potential Opportunities to Increase the Heterogeneity of Neighbourhoods and the Flexibility of Households in the United States," *Journal of Housing for the Elderly* 22, no. 4 (2008): 373, 375.

15 Maurizio Lazzarato, "Immaterial Labor," in *Radical Thought in Italy: A Potential Politics*, ed. Paolo Virno and Michael Hardt (Minneapolis: University of Minnesota Press, 1996), 133–150.

16 See Dolores Hayden, "What Would a Non-sexist City Be Like? Speculations on Housing, Urban Design, and Human Work," *Signs* 5, no. 3, supplement "Women and the American City" (Spring 1980): 170–187.

North Western Metropolitan Area

Hoge Kempen National Park

University towns network

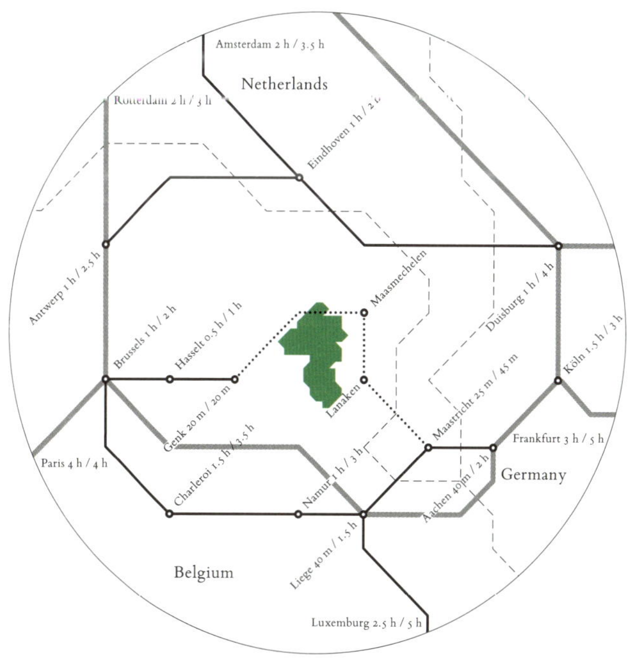

Time-distance projection by car/public transport

View of the conurbation stretching from Maasmechelen to Lanaken bordering Hoge Kempen National Park

2020

2030

2040

2050

Phasing of shrinking, 2020–2050

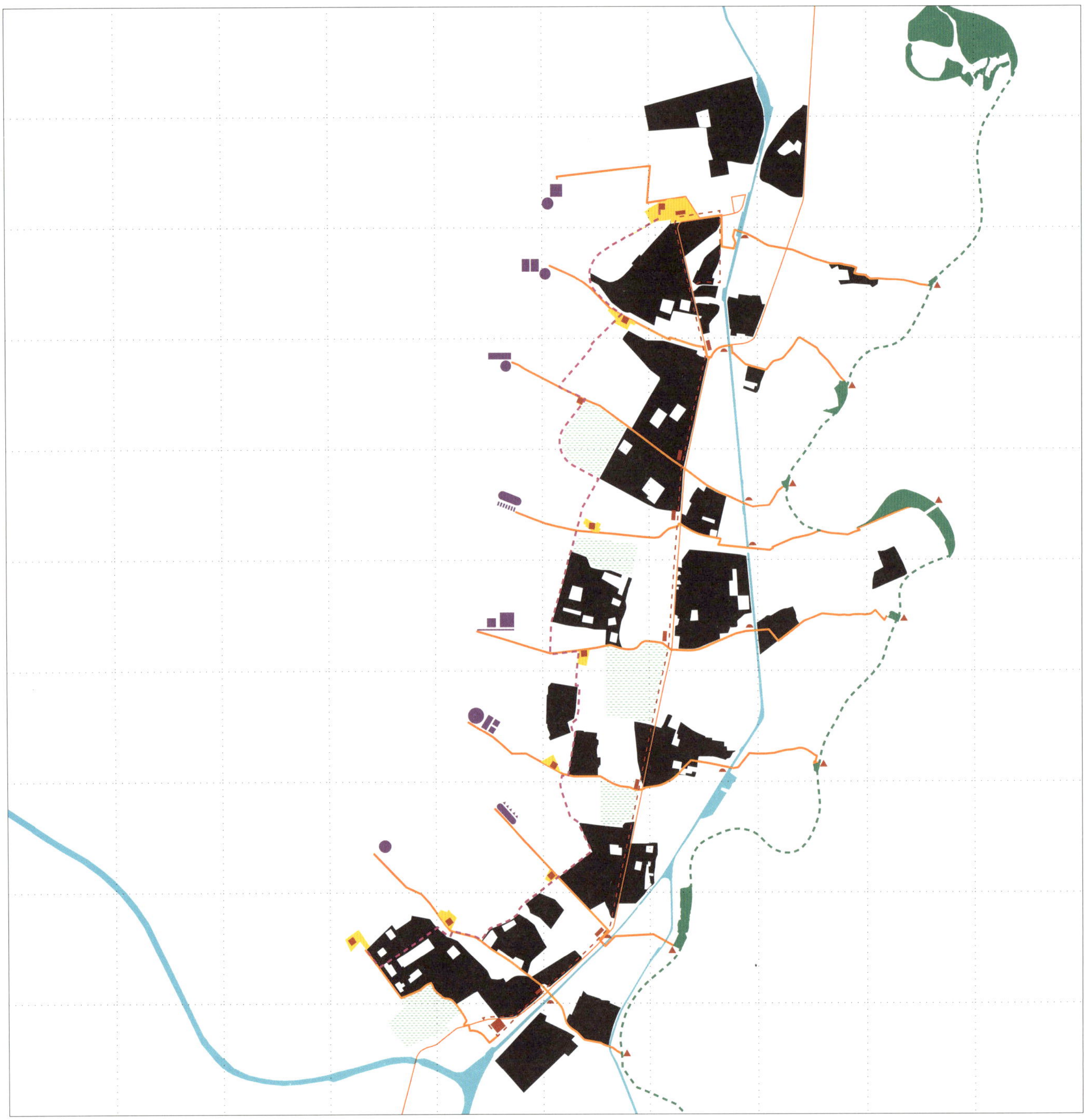

- Clearing
- Civic center
- Tram stop
- Canal pier
- River platform
- Activity areas along the river
- Agricultural field
- Urban area
- New tramline
- Transversal connection
- Linear pedestrian path and bikeway along the park
- Linear pedestrian path and bikeway along the Maas

Last stage of shrinking: settlements are self-contained and separated by reclaimed rural land

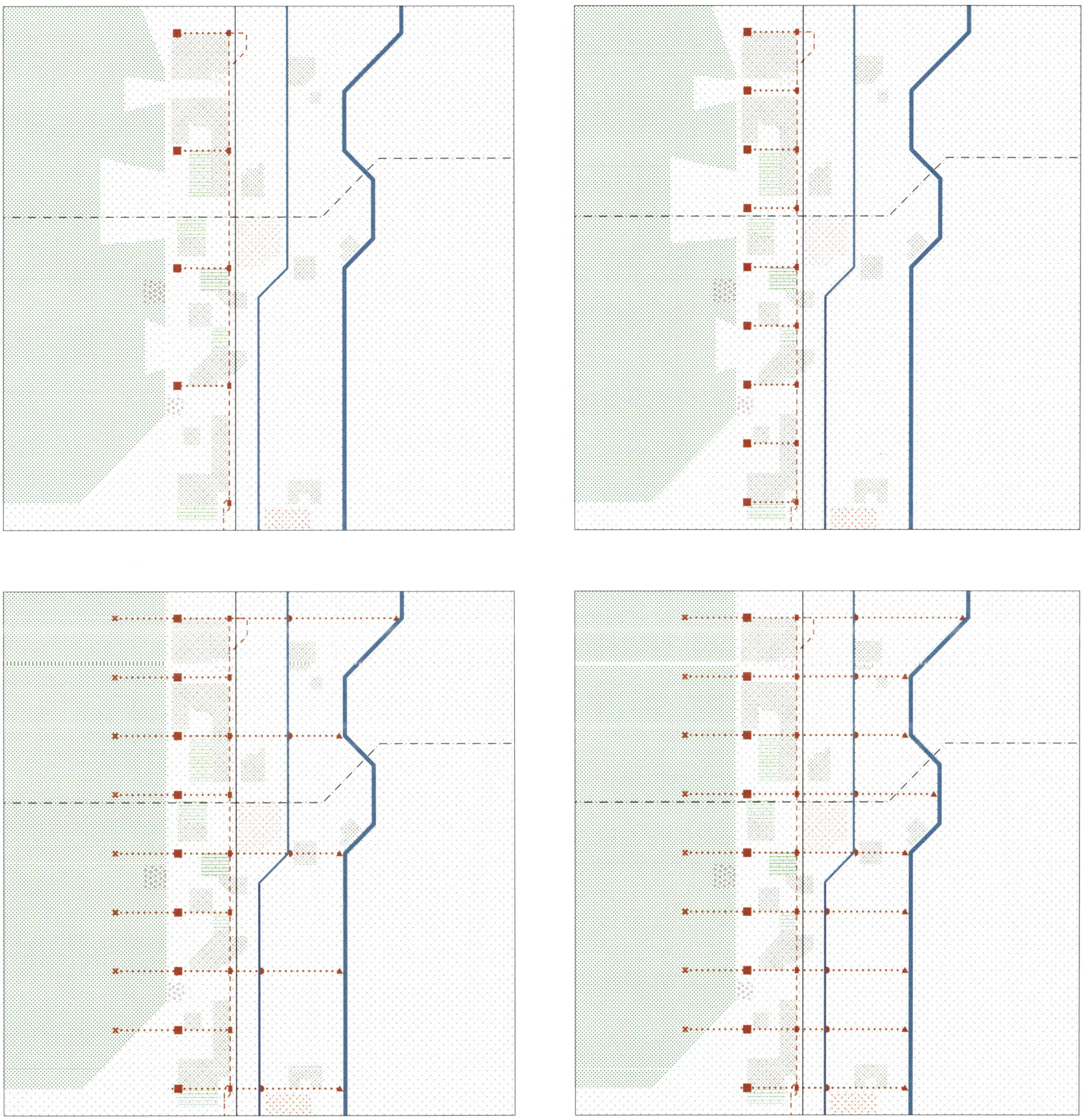

Phasing of strategic interventions. The proposed urban structure is based on the reading of the territory as a sequence of strips: from left to right, the forest, the main road that connects Maasmechelen to Lanaken, the canal, and the Meuse river. This sequence has the potential to become the backbone of an urban park that extends and defines the role of the national park. The dotted lines represent the system of paths, while the red dots show the public facilities, which range from civic centers, to bus stops, to floating platforms along the canal, to benches.

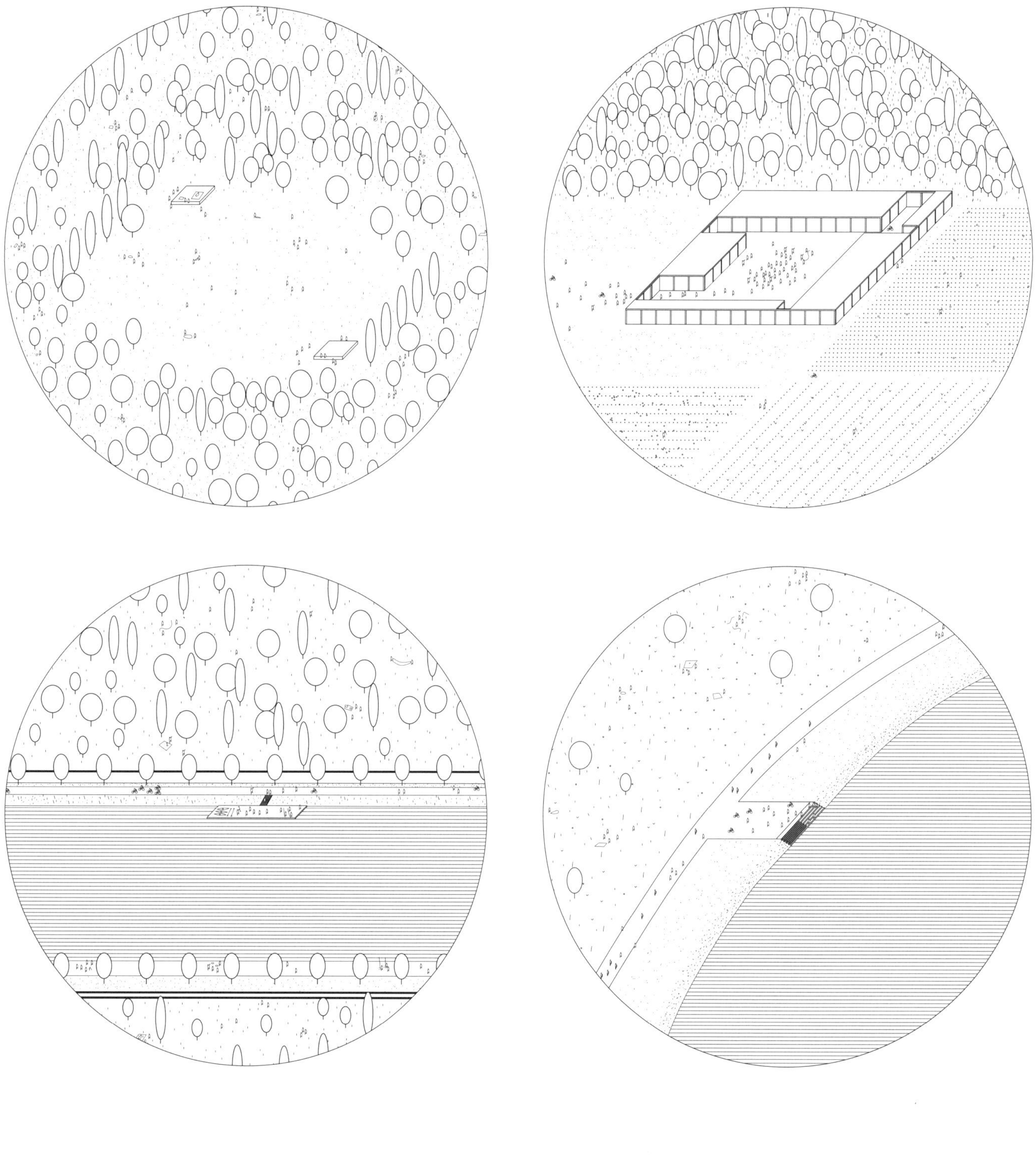

Clockwise: clearing, civic center, river platform, canal pier

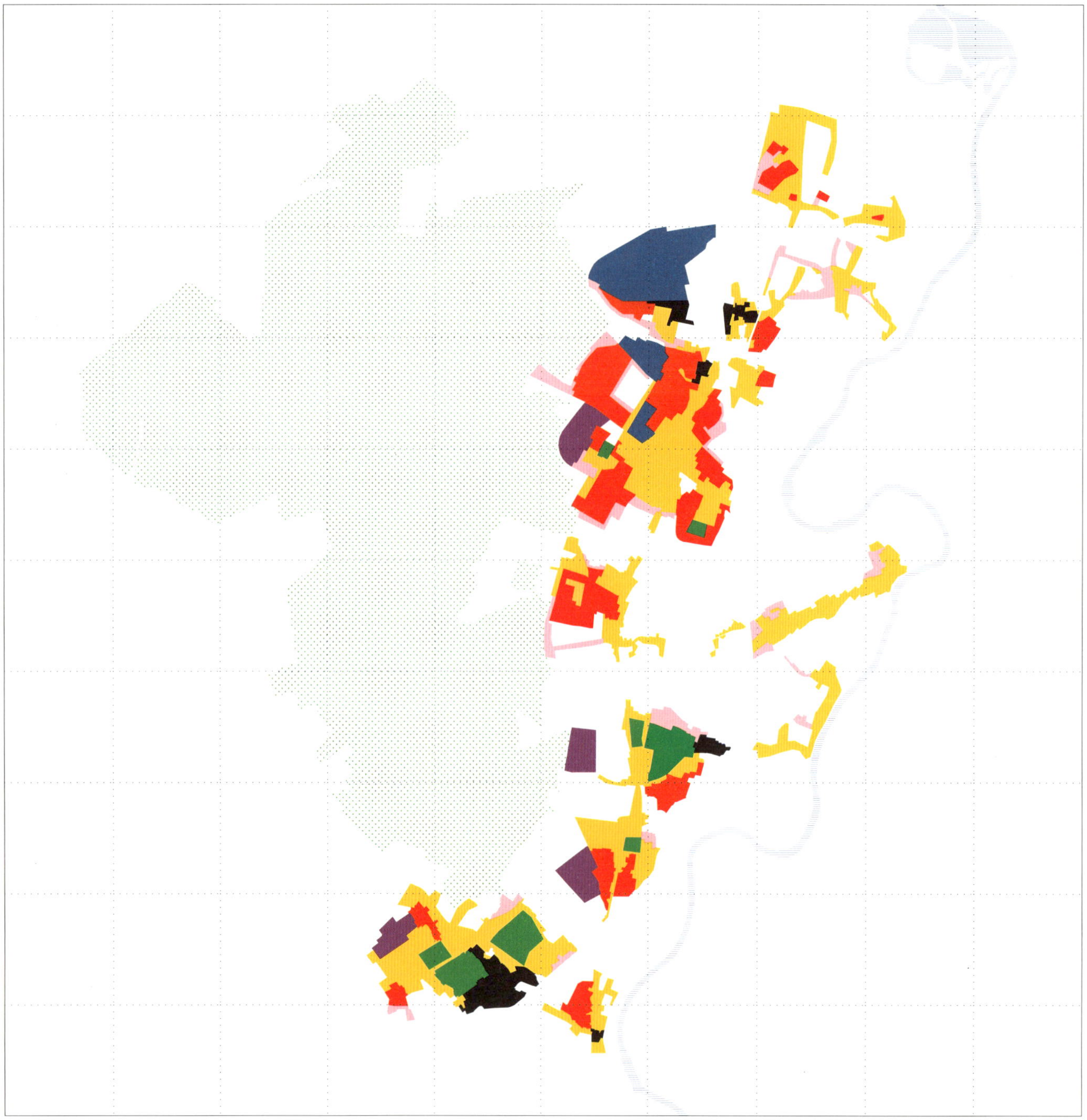

Settlement types

Settlement types selected for transformation (in blue)

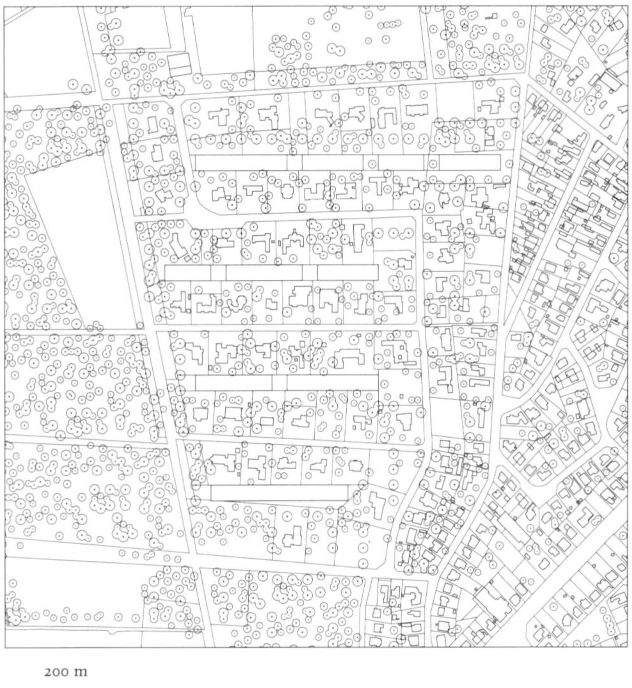

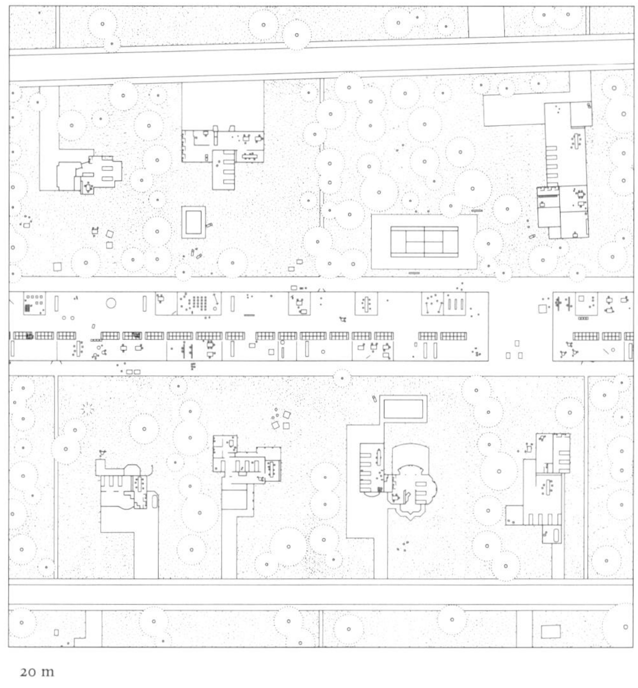

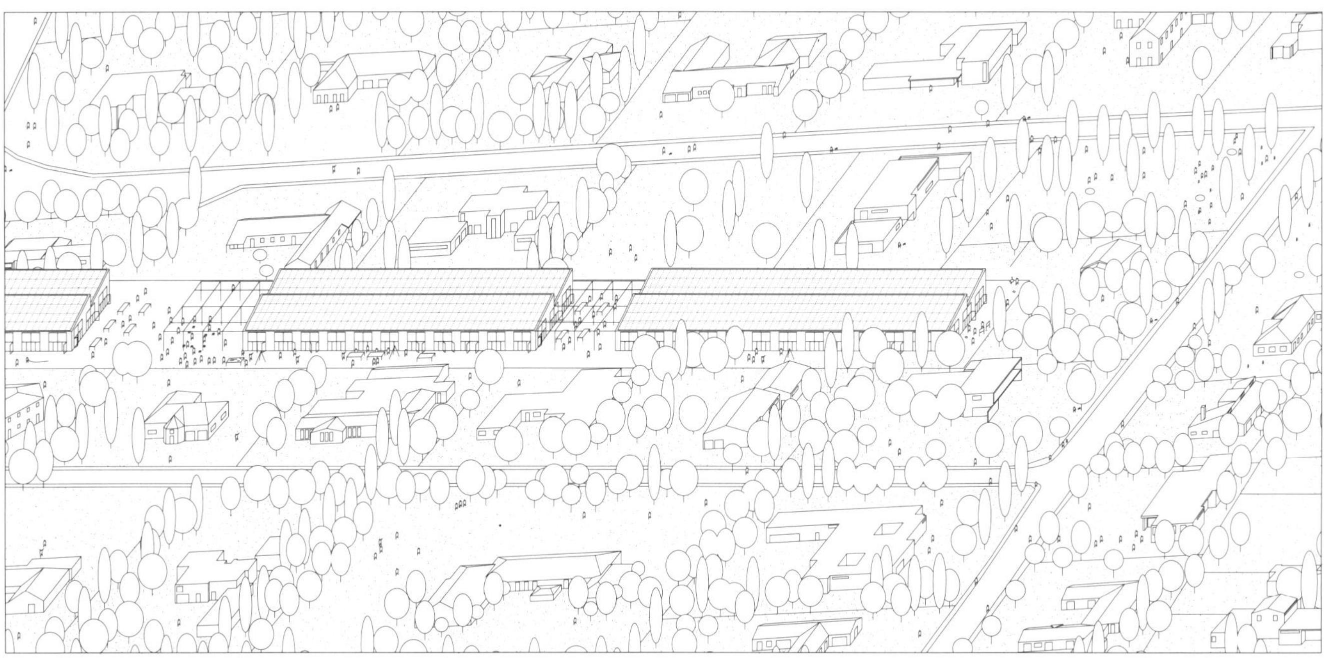

Densification of the villa park. Large villas are subdivided into smaller units to gradually become multifamily houses. A new structure is added to the back of the existing plots and consists of a simple shed for material and immaterial forms of production, with a central core containing basic facilities such as kitchens, bathrooms, and alcoves.

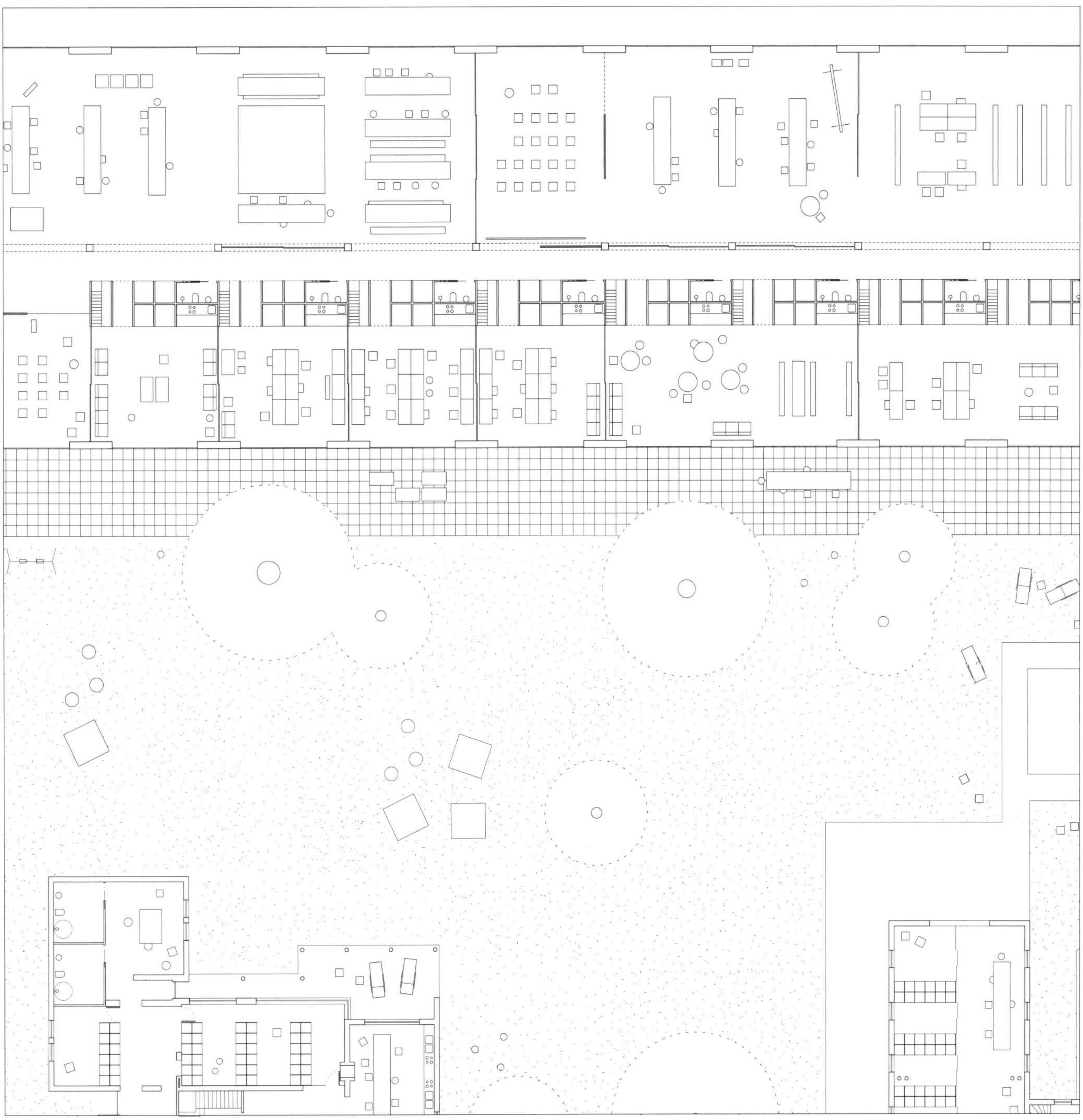

The cores define two areas: offices and meeting rooms on one side, and larger workshops on the other.

Detail of the ground-floor plan

5 m

Phases of densification of the villa park

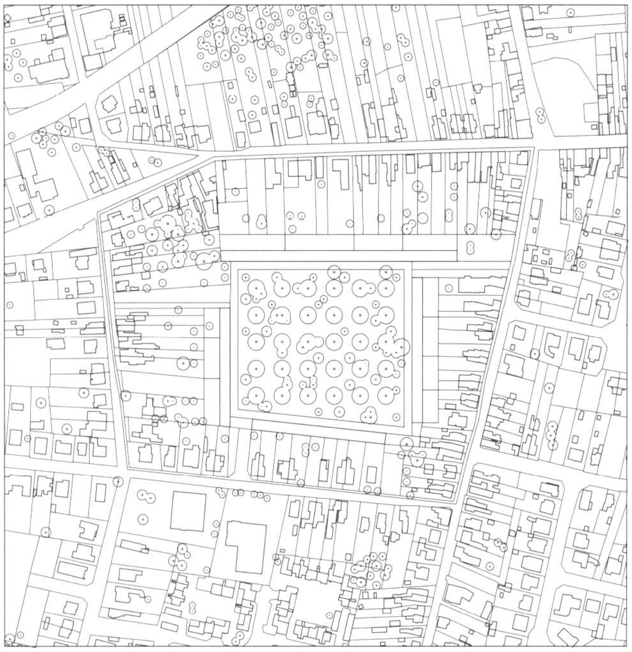

100 m

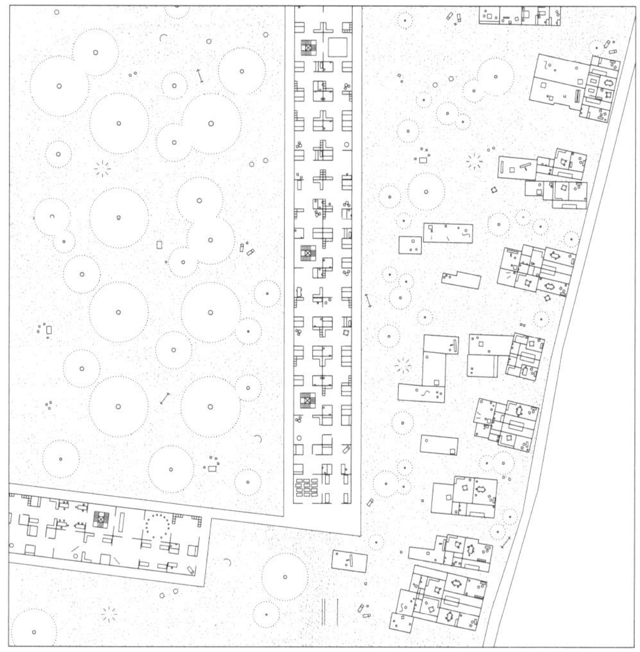

20 m

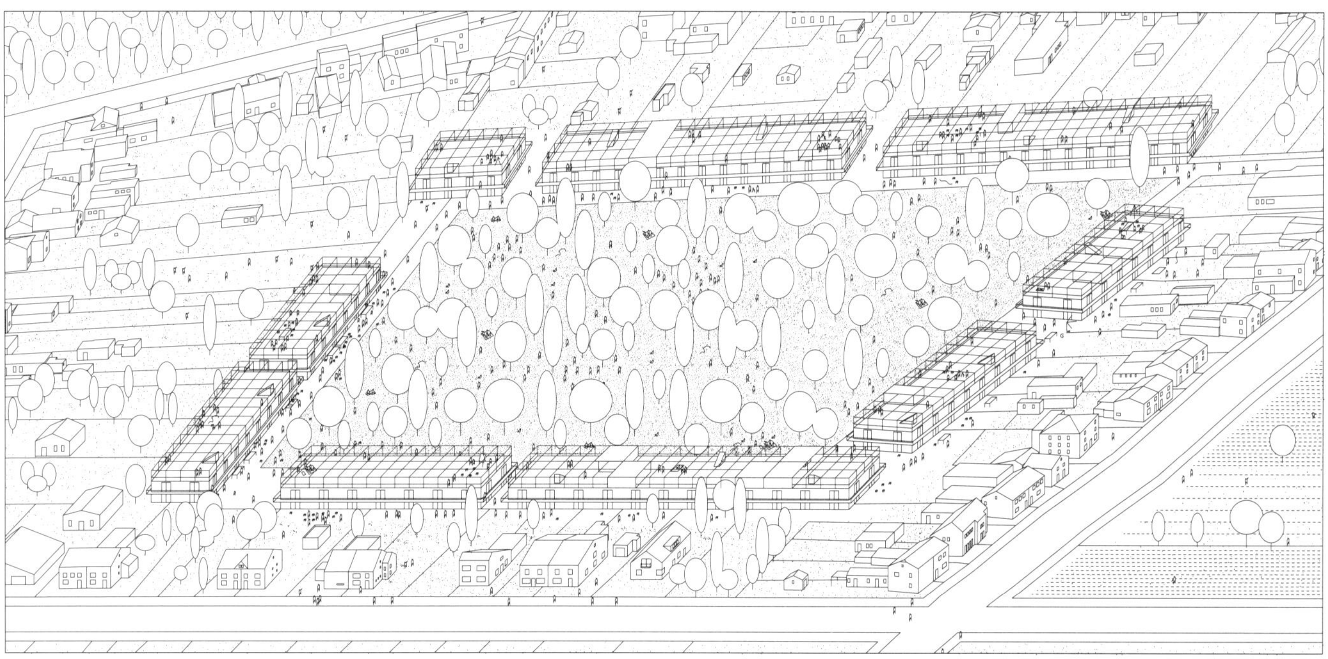

Densification of a block. The block is made of single detached homes aligned along the perimeter, with a large empty core made of unused properties. New houses are added inside the block at a certain distance from existing ones, so that the empty core of the block is now occupied. The new houses therefore frame the central void, making it the "common" of the block.

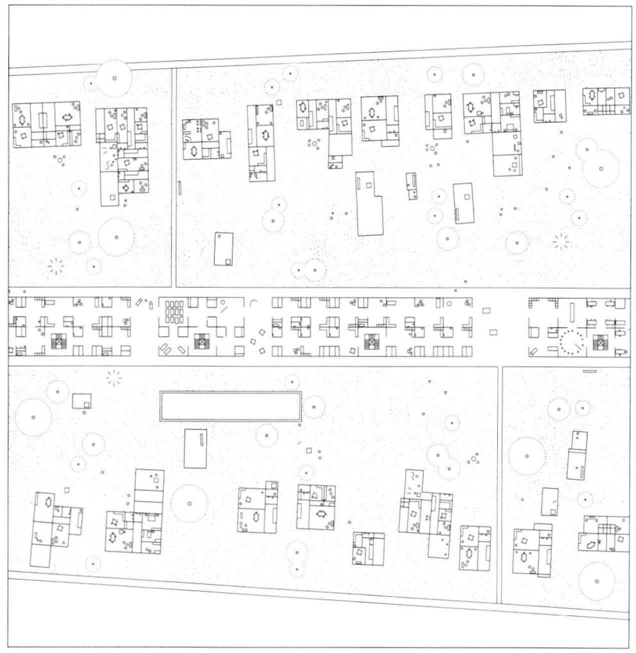

Densification of a block

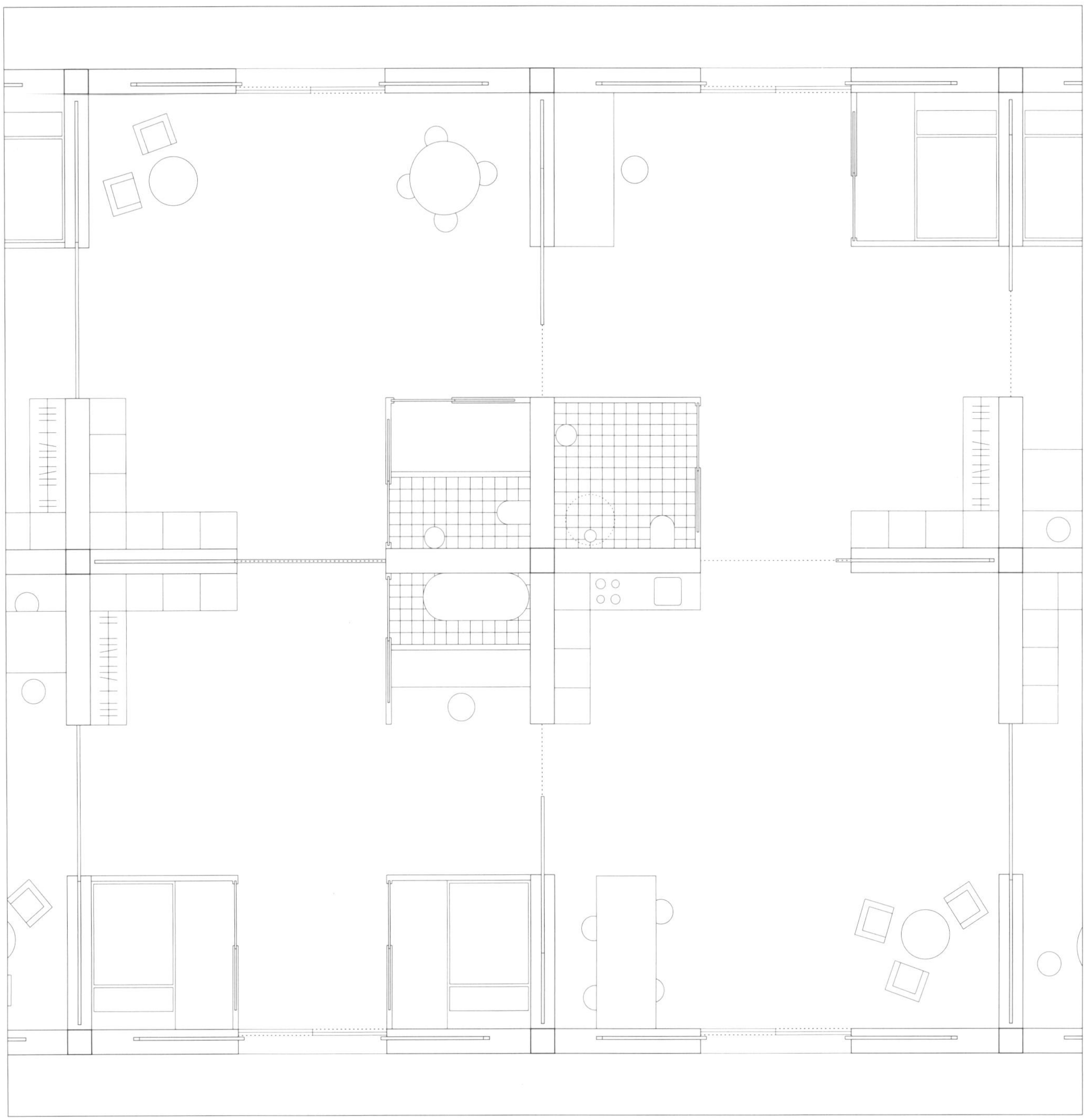

Plan of a new terraced house inserted into the inner part of the block. As the load-bearing structure is concentrated on the cruciform walls, it is possible to connect more units and organize different gradients of shared spaces and facilities. Different units can share a kitchen, a living room, or a workspace. The idea of home property as defined by conventional, unchangeable spaces is countered by a simple composition of rooms whose degree of connection evolves with the necessities of the dwellers.

2 m

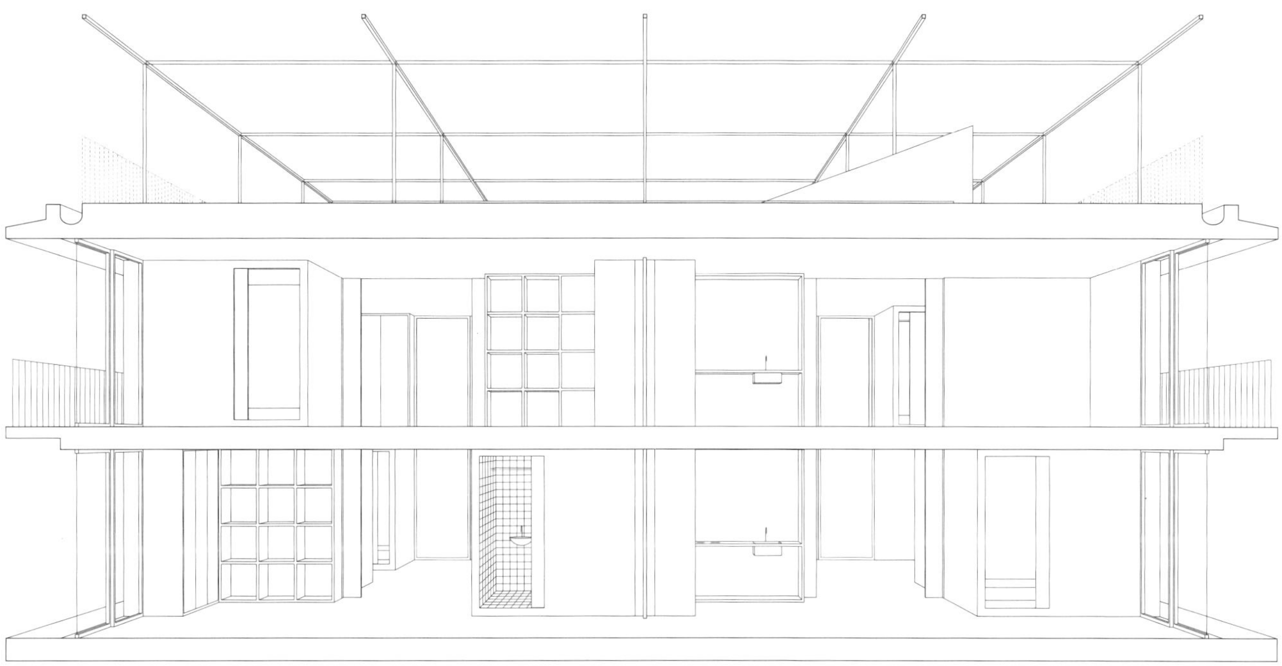

Section of a new terraced house inside the block

PARKLIFE

Densification of a garden city settlement. New houses are added to the plots of each existing house. Eventually the old house can be demolished, opening up the plot to alternative uses.

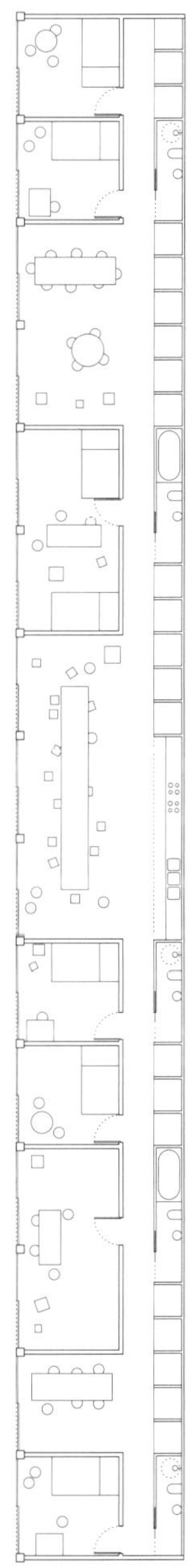

The house has a linear configuration, which allows its extension in time. This organization can accommodate multiple household formats, supporting networked families and living/working arrangements.

Plan of a new house added to a garden city plot

5 m

196

Phasing of the densification of a garden city settlement

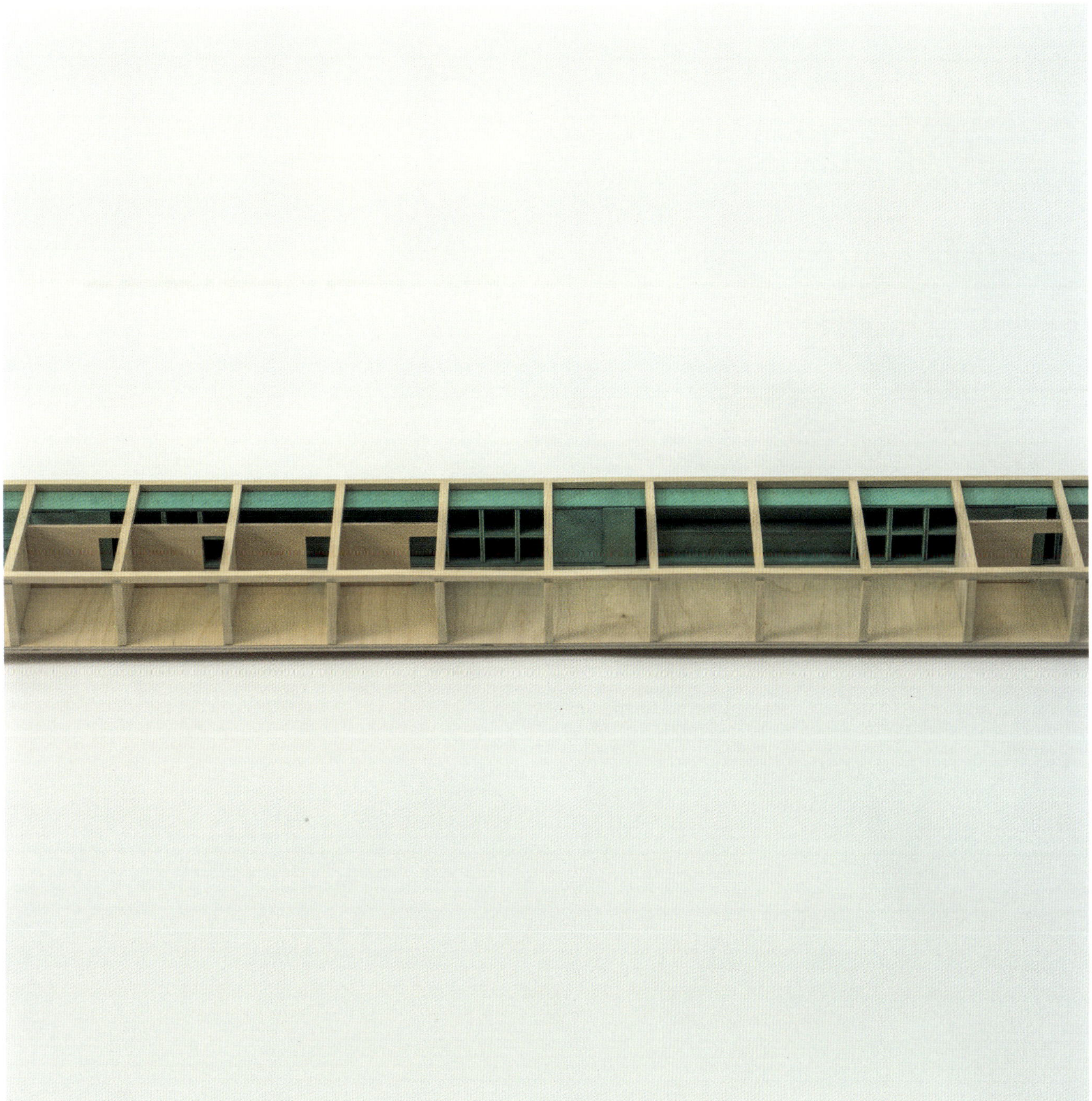

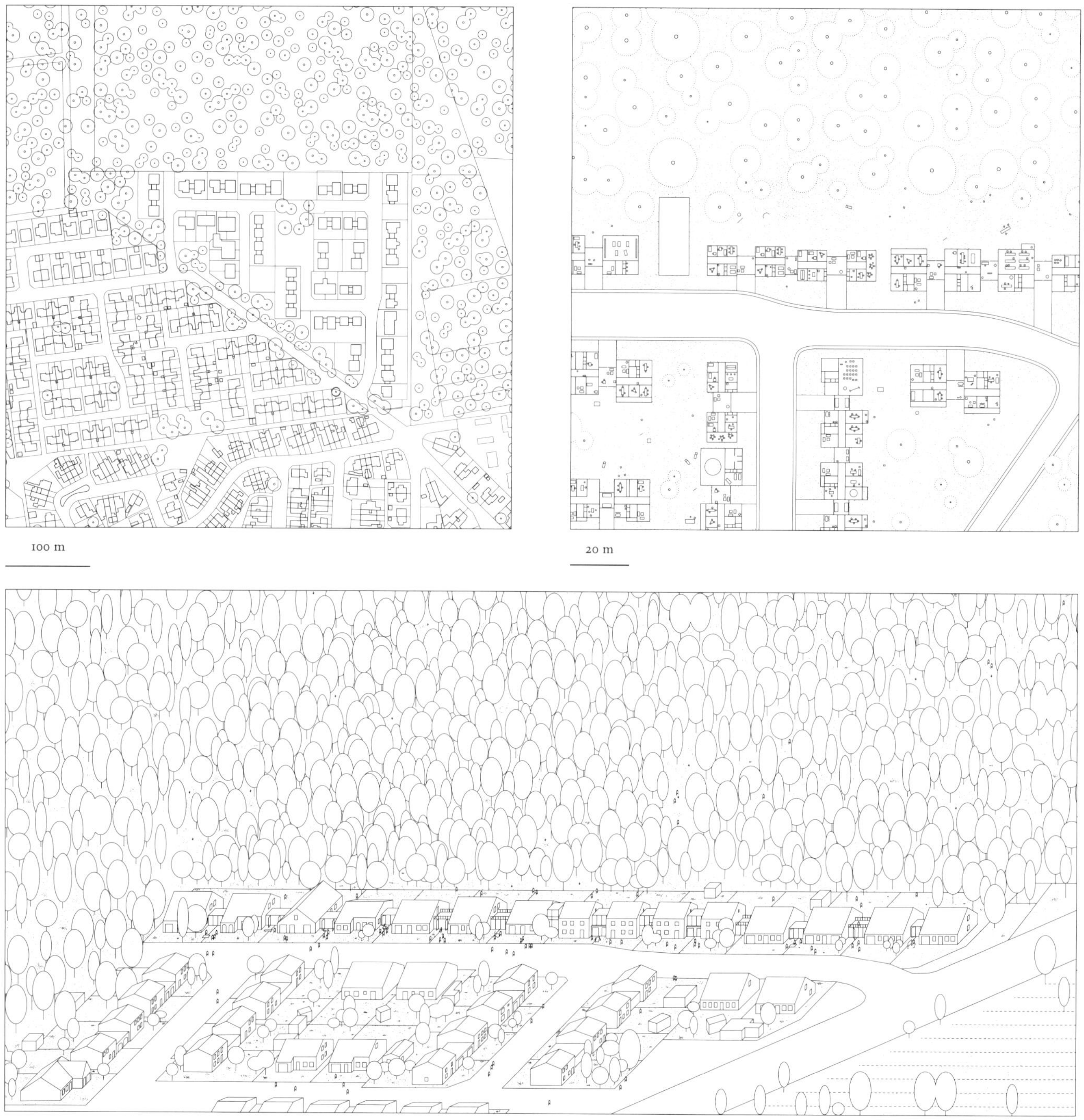

Retrofitting of a recent garden city settlement. The retrofitting links different properties to form larger units. The goal is to undermine the subdivision and unite the detached homes into larger entities.

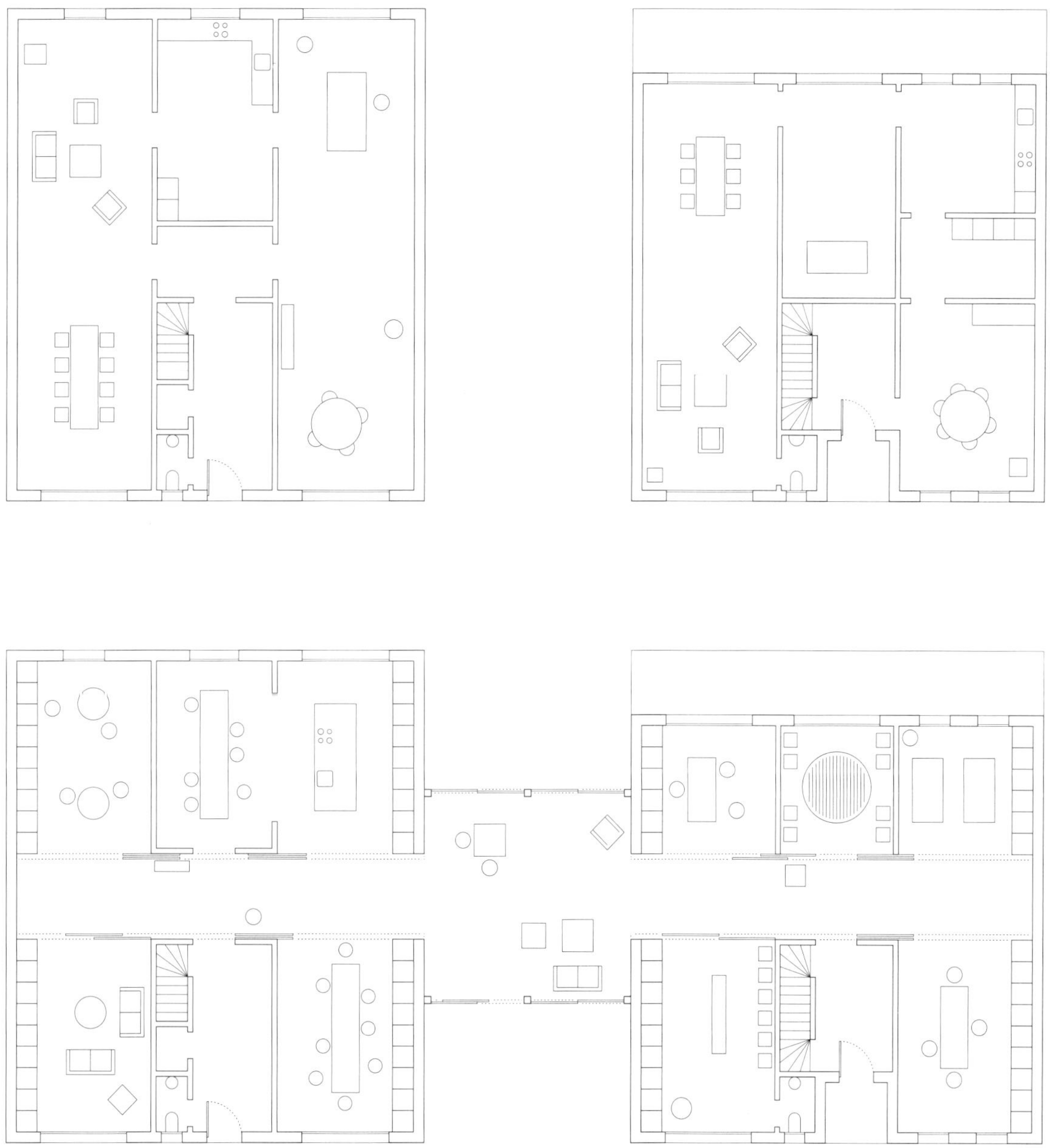

Once the pavilion is inserted, the original logic of the ground floor changes to allow for the sharing of facilities, such as kitchen and storage. Generous assisted rooms can be added, and all the bedrooms are located on the second floor.

Plan of an existing (above) and retrofitted (below) house in a recent garden city settlement

5 m

203

ONE-ROOM HOUSE (2017)

The project focuses on the simplest type of habitation: a one-room house. Domestic space is traditionally made of a composition of rooms, and each room is defined by a specific function (living room, bathroom, bedroom). Our project proposes one single space that can be used in many ways. As such the house revisits two canonical and yet peculiar projects for domestic space: Ludwig Mies van der Rohe's Farnsworth House in Plano, Illinois (1945–1951) and Philip Johnson's Glass House in New Canaan, Connecticut (1948–1949). In these houses, domestic space is reduced to one room within which the service core acts as separation that, without dividing the space, addresses different regions of it. In our proposal, the service core runs parallel to the house itself, thus making the latter a single room. In this sense, our proposal revisits also Johnson's less-known building in New Canaan, built simultaneously with the Glass House and located across the lawn from its entrance. This small rectangular building, known as the Guest House, is made of two main rooms flanked on one side by a service strip containing a small lobby, a storage space, and the bathroom. In our proposal, this service core is reduced to the minimum possible width and contains the kitchen appliances, the bathroom, wardrobes, sitting areas, generous storage spaces, and all installations. A system of sliding panels placed at regular distance allows the single room to be subdivided into an enfilade of rooms. Overall, the house is not constructed on the predetermined separation between living and working, but allows for a flexible use according to one's need. The house's structure corresponds to the structure of the pergola with its wooden beams and pillars. The house's walls are prefabricated wooden panels with preassembled insulation and external paneling. The concentration of the house's facilities and services along the eastern edge is meant to reduce to a minimum the organization of domestic installations and thus the cost of construction. Similarly to Johnson's Guest House, the openings toward the outside on the main elevation are of circular form. Yet, differently from Johnson's, they are larger and can be intended as both doors and windows, thus allowing for the maximum permeability between the inside and the outside space. The interior space of the house can be subdivided with sliding panels or temporary partitions, allowing for the free subdivision of the interior space into areas for living and for working according to the needs of the inhabitant.

The one-room house was initially developed as part of a residential subdivision near the Edersee in the district of Waldeck-Frankeberg (Germany). The form of the house was conceived not to occupy the meadow within which it was supposed to be built, but rather as the minimum infrastructure that could be placed on the site in order to make it inhabitable. This infrastructure was imagined as a simple timber pergola with a width of 4 meters that was to be covered with climbing or trailing plants and that becomes the support of the house itself. If built, the house would have framed the meadow by assuming the linear configuration of the pergola.

After completing the project, we understood its potential to become a housing prototype for a low-rise and dense cooperative settlement inspired by the principles of Ebenezer Howard's model for the Garden City. Expounded for the first time in his famous pamphlet *To-morrow, a Peaceful Path to Real Reform* (1898), Howard's garden city model popularized the garden suburb as one of the most ubiquitous forms of residential development in the twentieth century. Yet Howard's model was not meant to be a suburb but the opposite of it: as Lewis Mumford argued, the garden city had been conceived as an integrated foundation for effective urban life.[1] Howard's Garden City was proposed as a system of self-sufficient settlements based on cooperative principles: land was communally owned and houses shared gardens and domestic facilities like kitchens. Howard's model was inspired by his reading of *Looking Backward: 2000–1887* by the American author Edward Bellamy (1850–1898), which imagined a classless society devoid of poverty and property. An important aspect of Howard's garden city model was his proposal for a *cooperative quadrangle*, a housing type organized around a courtyard and based on shared domestic facilities and centralized housekeeping. Although several cooperative quadrangles were realized in the first applications of Howard's model, such as the garden suburb of Letchworth, the collective ethos of such a communal way of life became incompatible with the logic of garden suburbs based on single-family houses. Understood in the radical terms of cooperativism, Howard's seemingly suburban model is the opposite of suburbia and closer to a settlement based on the principles of commoning both land and living spaces.

Our project recuperates the original rationale of Howard's Garden City as cooperative settlement, by devising an open plan based on the repetition of the one-room-house prototype. The linearity and flexibility of the prototype allows not only the commoning of gardens and domestic facilities but also the combination of living and working. The modular structure of the house is deployed as a multitude of individual units that thanks to the linear structure of the pergola can expand or shrink according to the inhabitants' needs. Such a flexible system makes easily possible the retrofitting of individual households into communal houses and the installation of communal facilities to be shared across households. Such an evolving openness of the settlement is only possible with collective ownership of land, which is the prerequisite of this settlement's principles.

1 Lewis Mumford, "The Garden City Idea and Modern Planning," in Ebenezer Howard, *Garden Cities of To-morrow* (Abingdon-on-Thames: Routledge, 2006), 4

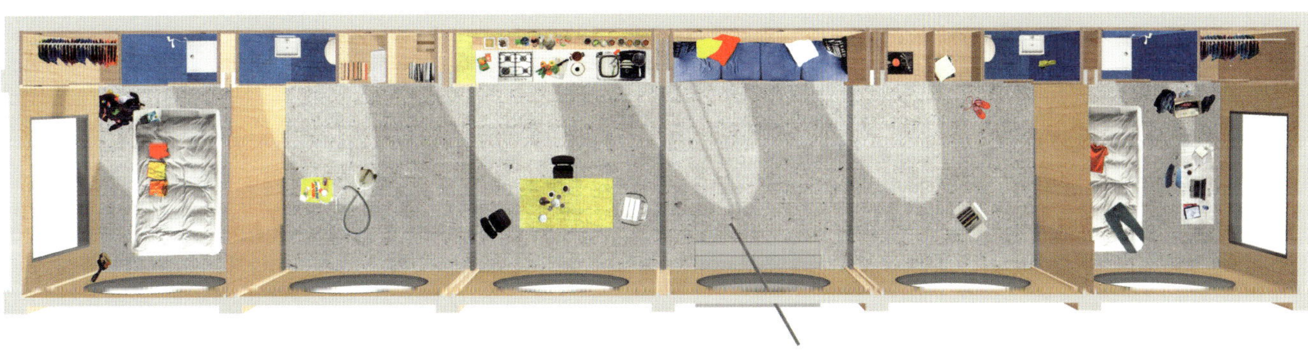

Settlement plan

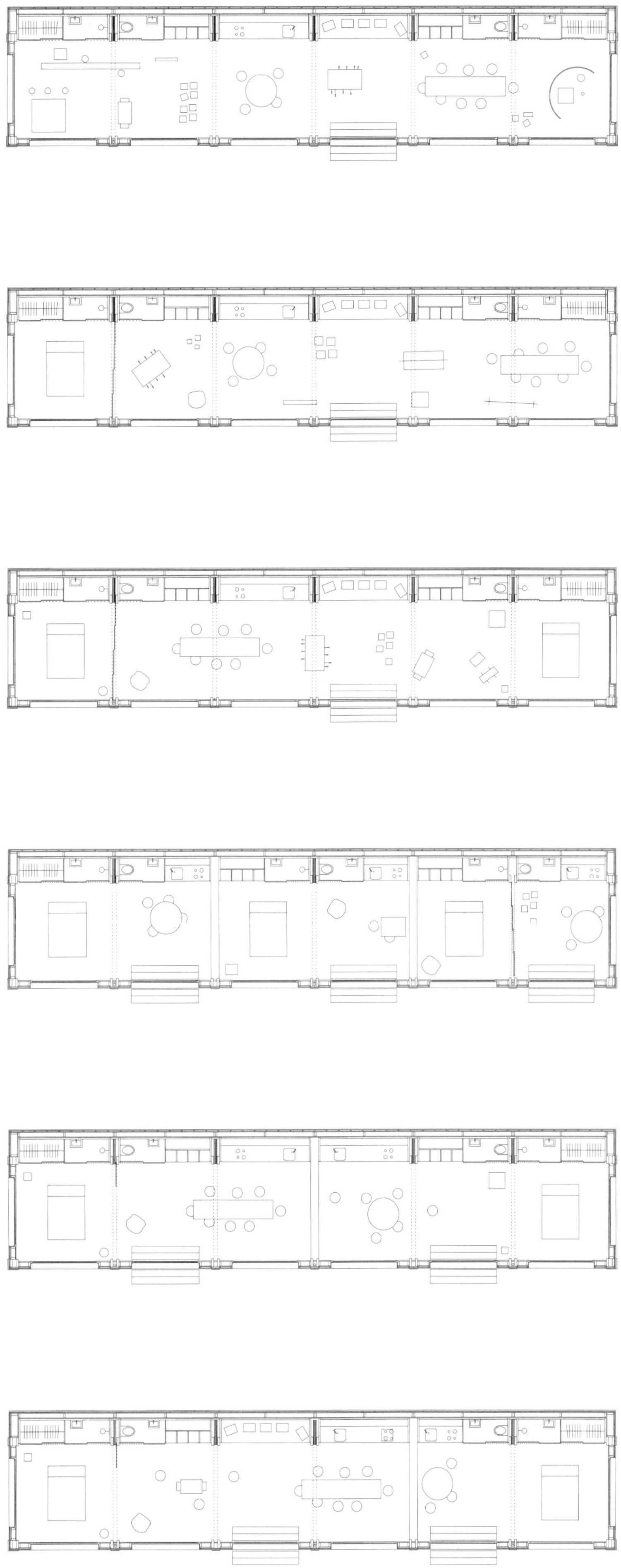

2 m

Possible transformation of a one-room house from one to multiple households

POSSIBILITIES (2017)

Linkeroever is a large modern neighborhood in the city of Antwerp, built from the 1960s on the left bank of the river Schelde. This vast area has been for decades the perfect battlefield of contrasting urban ideas, each trying to pragmatically tackle the changing conditions of the city. After a first urban competition for the planning of the area was organized in 1911, a subsequent call was launched in 1932–1933 with the ambition of bringing to Antwerp the ideas of modern urban planning. Among the several entries, projects by Le Corbusier and Paul Otlet attracted much attention although neither won the first prize. Notwithstanding recurrent attempts to find land for the city's expansion, the area has only been subject to real urbanization processes starting in the second half of the twentieth century. Built as a large urban expansion according to functionalist planning tenets, the current neighborhood is characterized by residential towers, large housing slabs, and a fragmented carpet of low-rise housing blocks hovering over a green strip. Its process of realization has changed through time; although initially conceived as a singular grand-scale project, it was eventually developed by many different stakeholders who took charge of smaller portions of the area. The fragmentation of the planning and construction process is visible in the array of different urban conditions, open spaces, and urban types. Separated from the historical city by the river but in direct relationship to it through a few tunnels, Linkeroever is also—like many satellite settlements built during the second half of the twentieth century—a largely monofunctional area. Nowadays, the area provides a large part of the social housing units of the city, most of which are owned by a few social housing companies.

Our project was developed as an entry to a recent competition launched by the city architect that called for the possibility of rethinking Linkeroever as a place where urban and natural environments could coexist and where a process of densification would allow the construction of affordable dwellings. The proposal we put forward is based on an understanding of the neighborhood as unfinished modern project that needs to be partially corrected and completed. The starting point of our approach is to offer a clear form to the area by reinforcing its boundaries. The design thus defines a main strip of four quadrants inside which densification happens, while the rest of the area is preserved from any new construction. The riverbank, at present privatized and fenced off, is imagined as a public linear park. Along the riverbank, a series of piers extend the park toward the water and function as *vaporetto* stops for a new boat service connecting Linkeroever to the rest of Antwerp. Each of the four quadrants is retrofitted by inserting new building types that respond to the existing condition and that offer new spaces of living and working in which the dichotomous relationship between the two is constantly questioned and reinvented. These interventions profit from the large amount of open space existing in between the residential blocks. Yet, rather than simply privatizing land, our proposal envisions the collective management of this resource and its future use to support both existing and future inhabitants with affordable houses and care and production facilities. This means that an important assumption of our proposal is that the social housing agencies who own the land do not sell it to private developers but develop it themselves for affordable housing projects. In terms of housing, rather than devising specialized spaces, the proposed types are almost nontypological in the sense that they reject an overconstraining individuation of spaces while offering open and unobstructed space.

Starting from the north, the first quadrant is characterized by terraced houses. The spatial structure of this type is defined by two simple elements: partition walls and a central core. By being placed at the center, the core creates two equal spaces without dividing them. The result is a domestic interior in which front and back are equal and can be organized in different ways. The second quadrant features a system of workshops and row housing inserted in the open spaces in between existing urban blocks and at the feet of existing slabs. Workshops are large factory-like spaces that allow the coexistence of multiple and different working activities, while the row houses are made of a sequence of rooms served by galleries. The third quadrant is characterized by patio houses. This typology fills the space in between the existing high-rise housing slabs. The fourth and last quadrant is characterized by towers. Placed within the open space of the gardens of row house blocks, the towers contain apartments served by a central core offering metropolitan ways of living through accommodations such as boardinghouses, residential hotels, and short-term residences.

After the competition, we were asked to refine our initial scheme and to focus on the central part characterized by the presence of social housing high-rise slabs. Our second proposal, rather than occupying the entire open space in between the slabs, concentrates the new built volume in limited areas around the existing structures, while it imagines the remaining open spaces as a forest. The new built volume around the residential slabs is conceived as a dense system of three-story townhouses, with flexible working space at the ground level and communal galleries. In more central parts within each of the proposed "islands," the ground floor is designed as a collective level with public facilities and larger spaces for production. In this case, the ground level is topped with two-story townhouses. The difference between each of the developed types, rather than in terms of functions and dimensions, has to do with basic spatial properties such as open versus closed, low-rise versus high-rise, linear versus clustered. The goal of the proposal is therefore to offer a set of possibilities through which to revisit the legacy of this large-scale postwar housing estate.

200 m

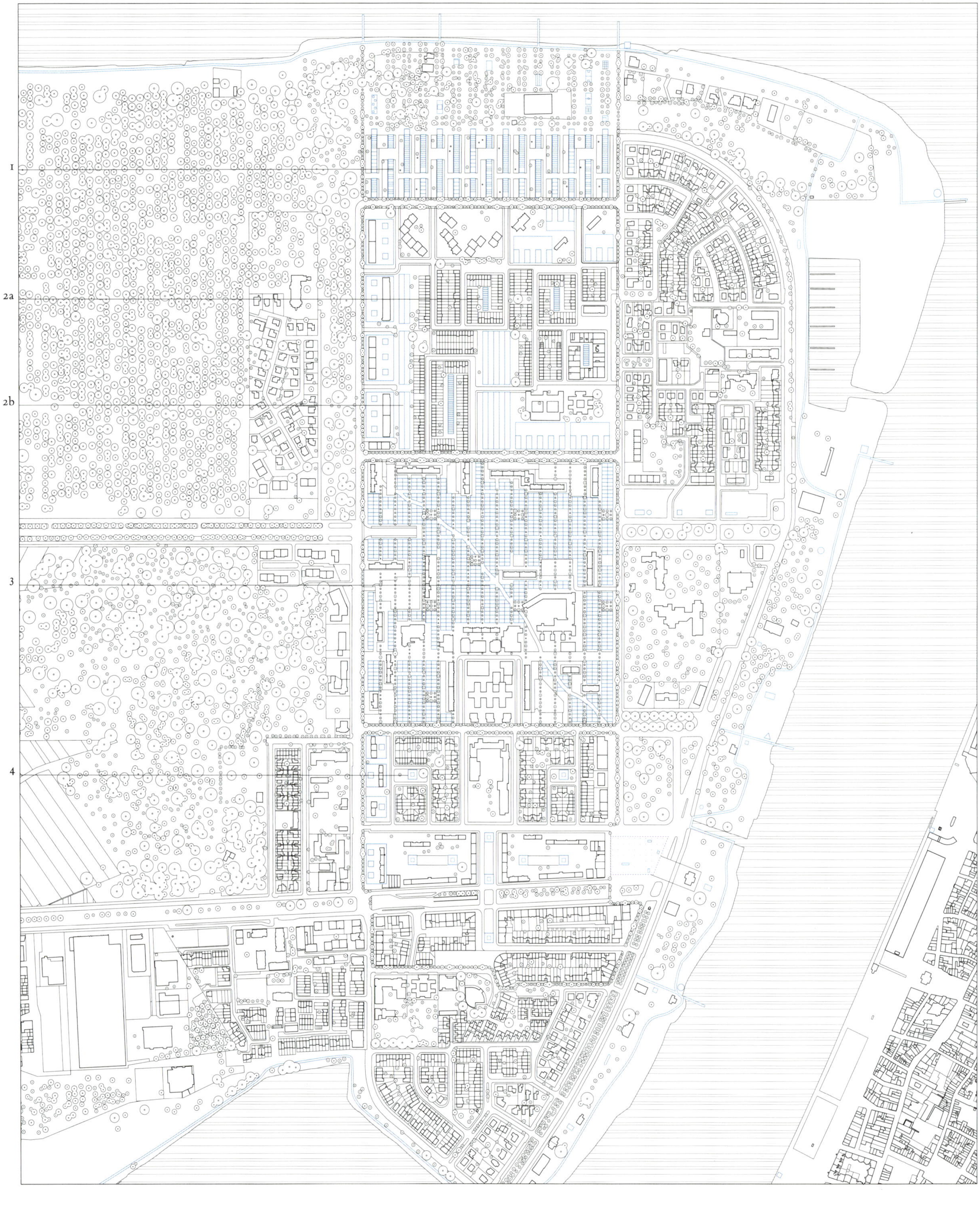

General plan for the transformation of the Linkeroever (first proposal)

1

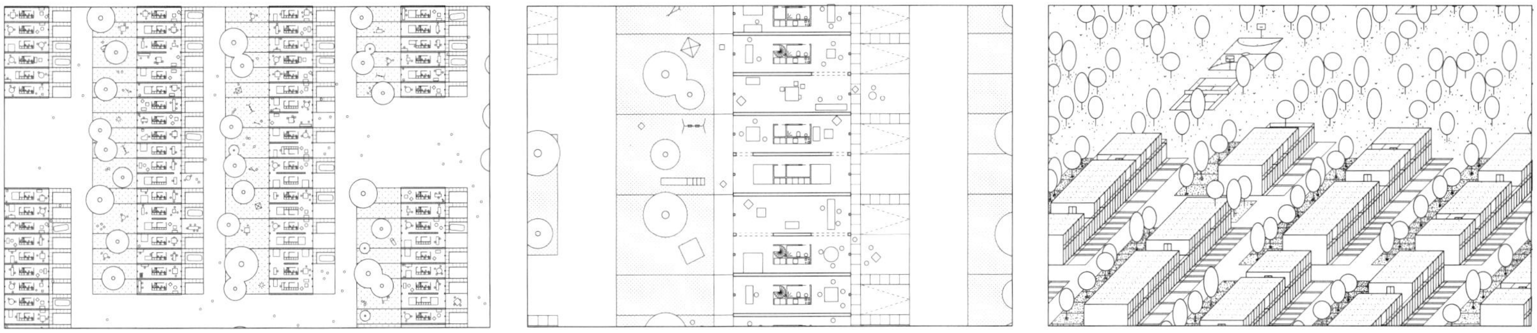

Terraced houses

2a

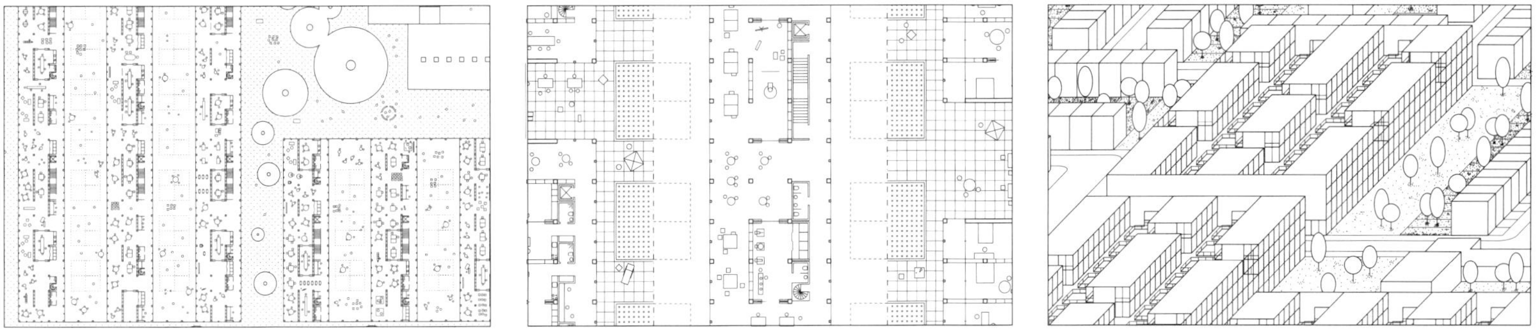

Workshops and row houses (in between blocks)

2b

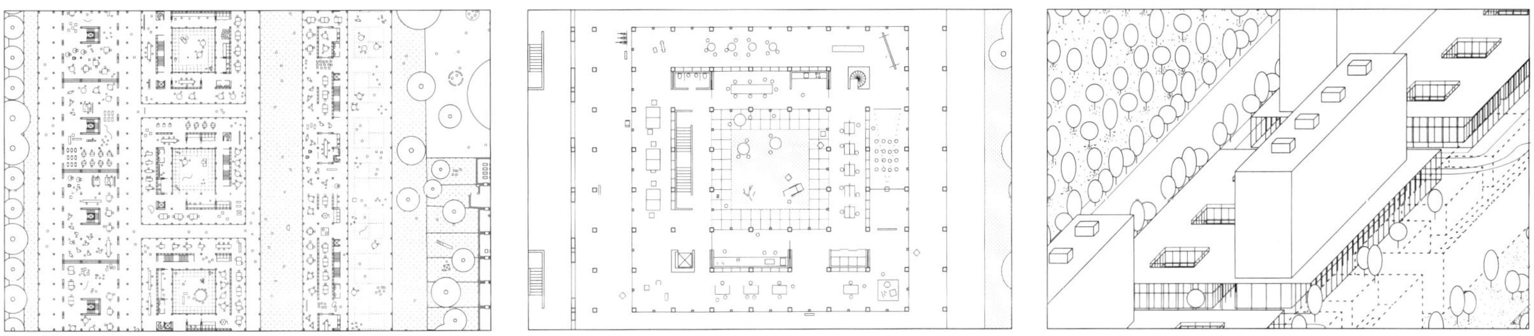

Workshops (at the feet of existing slabs)

3

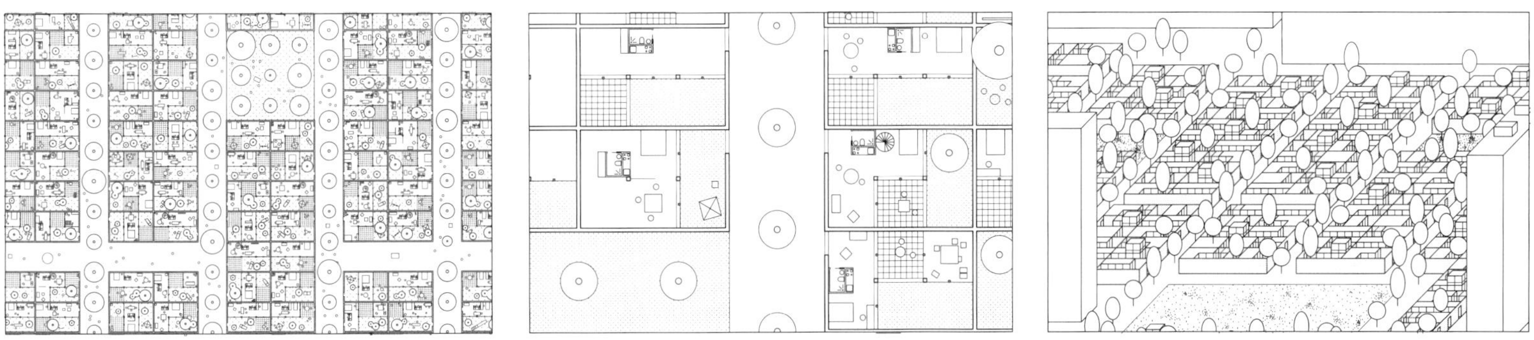

Patio houses

4

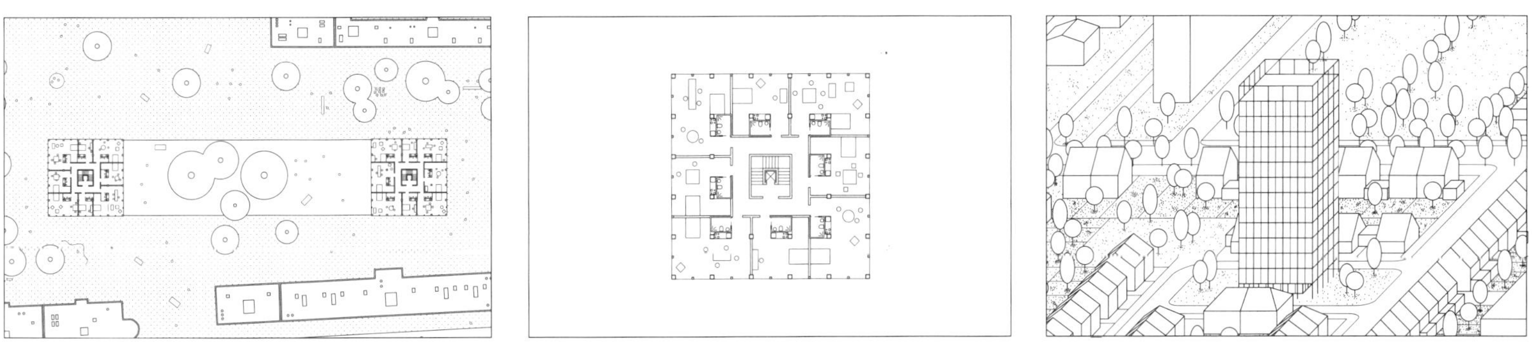

Towers

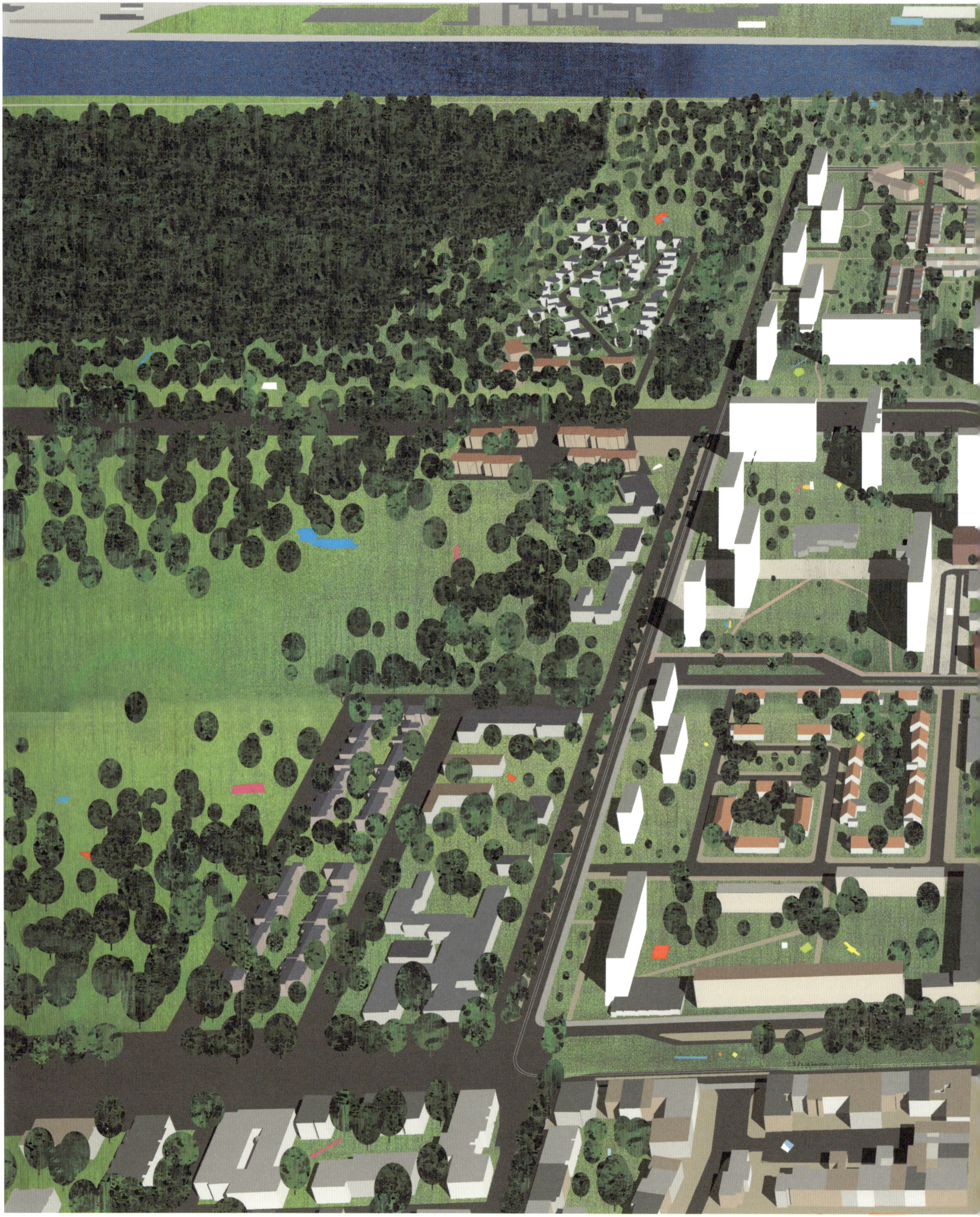

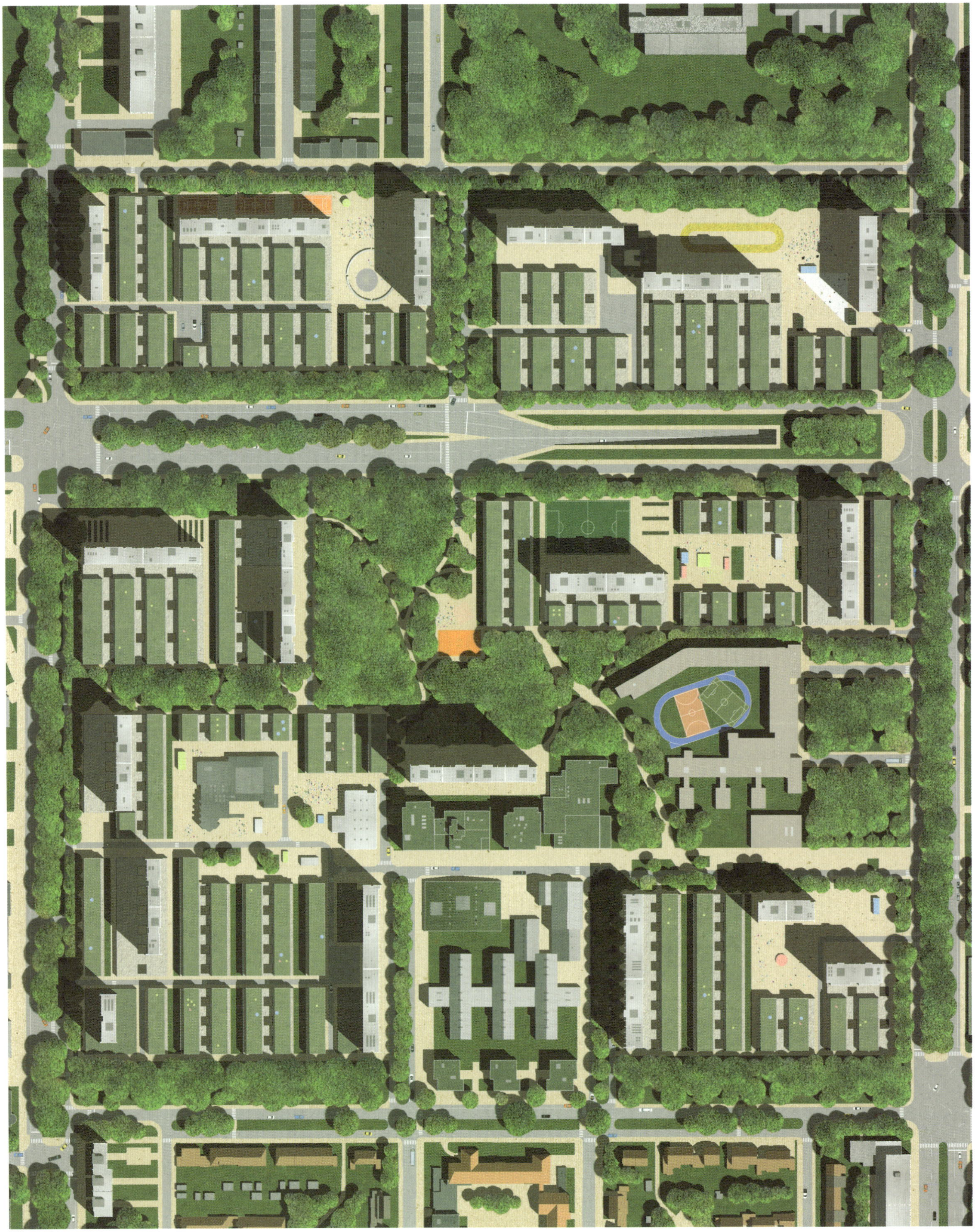

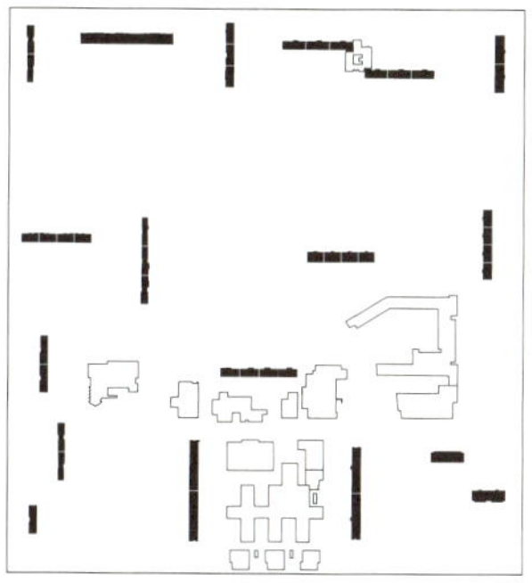

- Existing low-rise building
- Existing high-rise building

Islands of densification

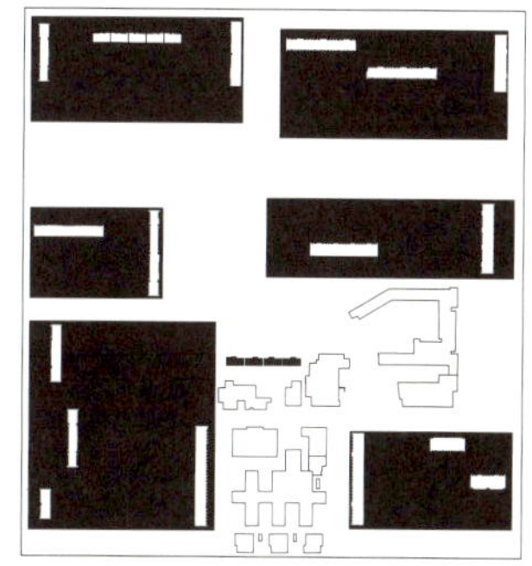

Existing buildings within the islands

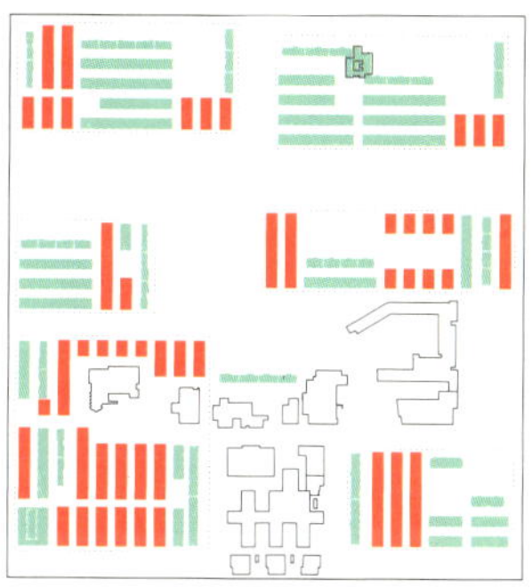

Ground floor

- Individual workspace
- Shared facilities and workspace

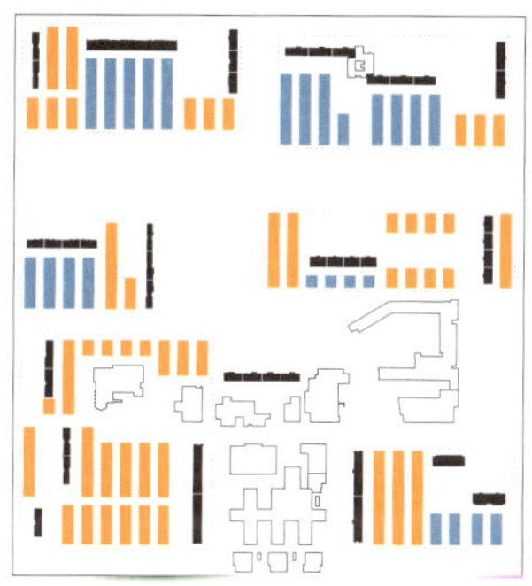

Upper floor

- Three-story townhouse
- Two-story townhouse
- Existing high-rise building

Forest

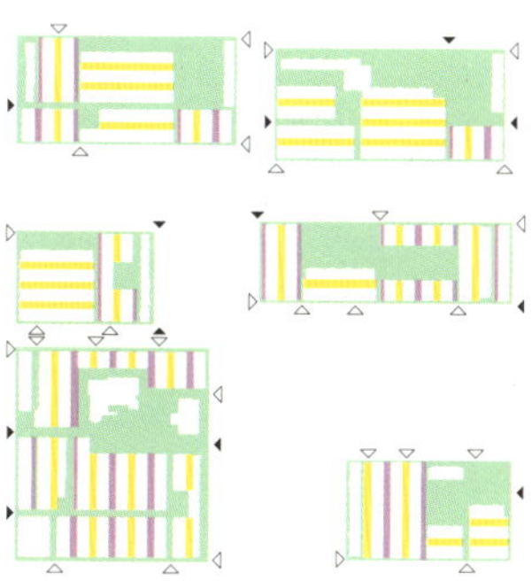

Circulation

- Pedestrian area
- Pedestrian access
- Car access
- Garden
- Gallery

Mobility network

- Parking
- Underground parking
- Public transport stop

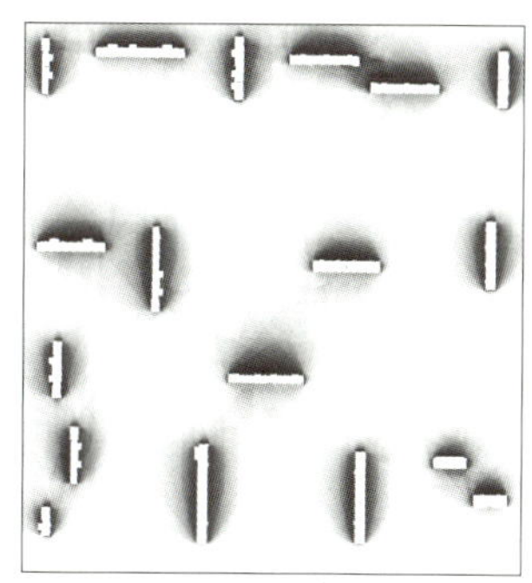

Shadows of existing high-rise buildings

General plan for the transformation of the central part of Linkeroever (second proposal)

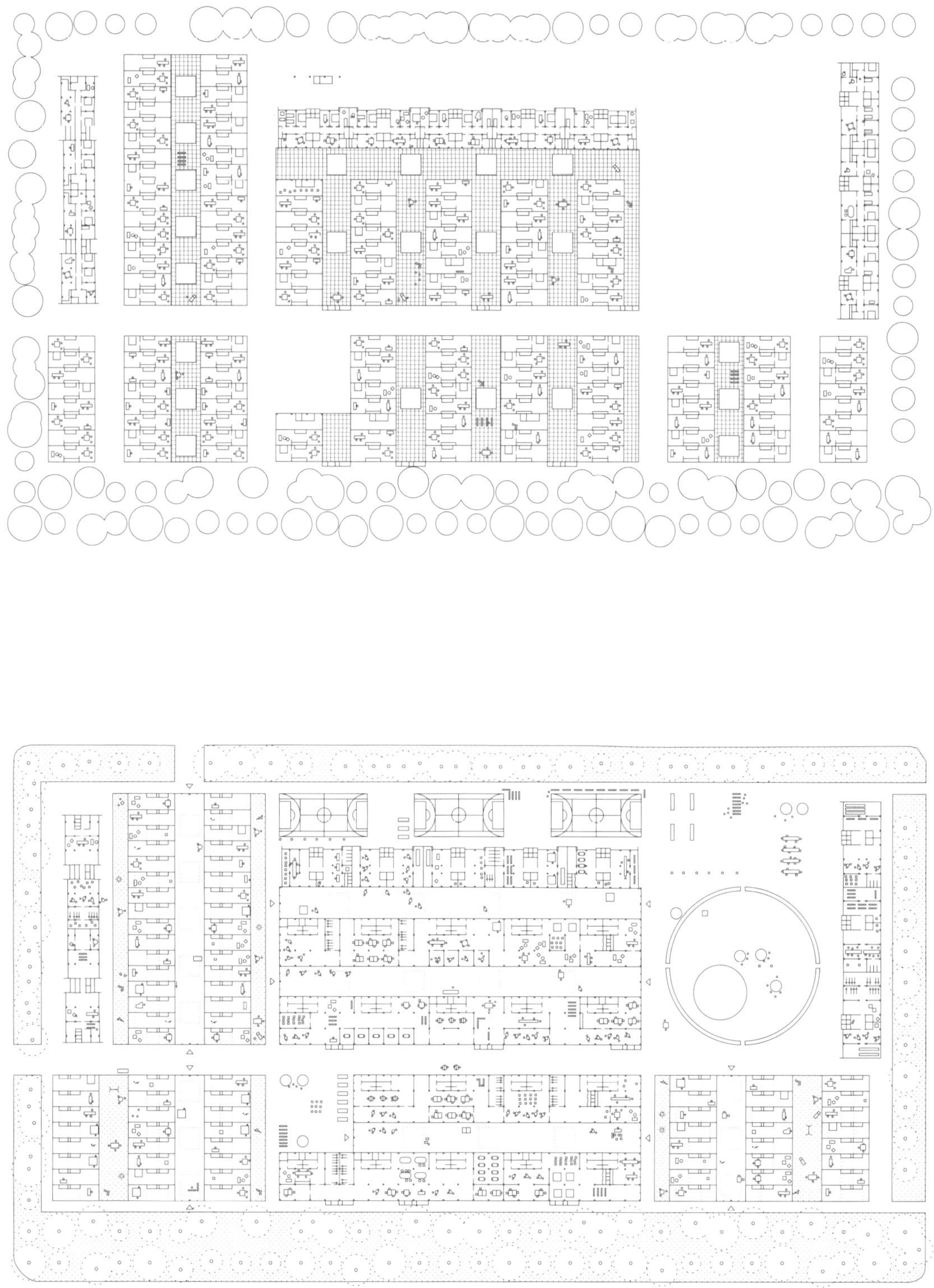

Ground-floor plan (below) and first-floor plan (above) of an island of densification (second proposal)

20 m

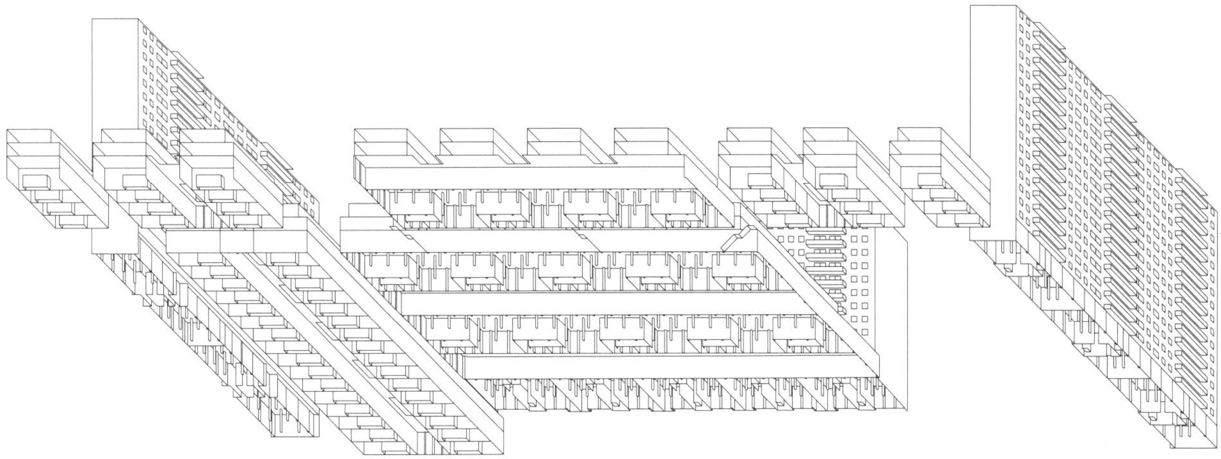

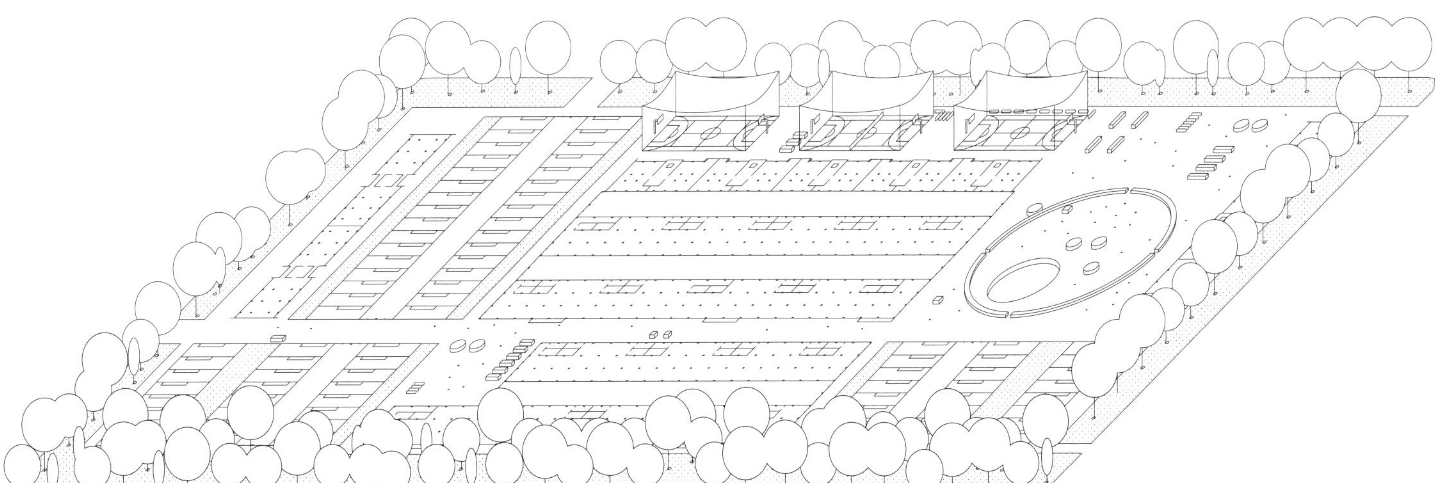

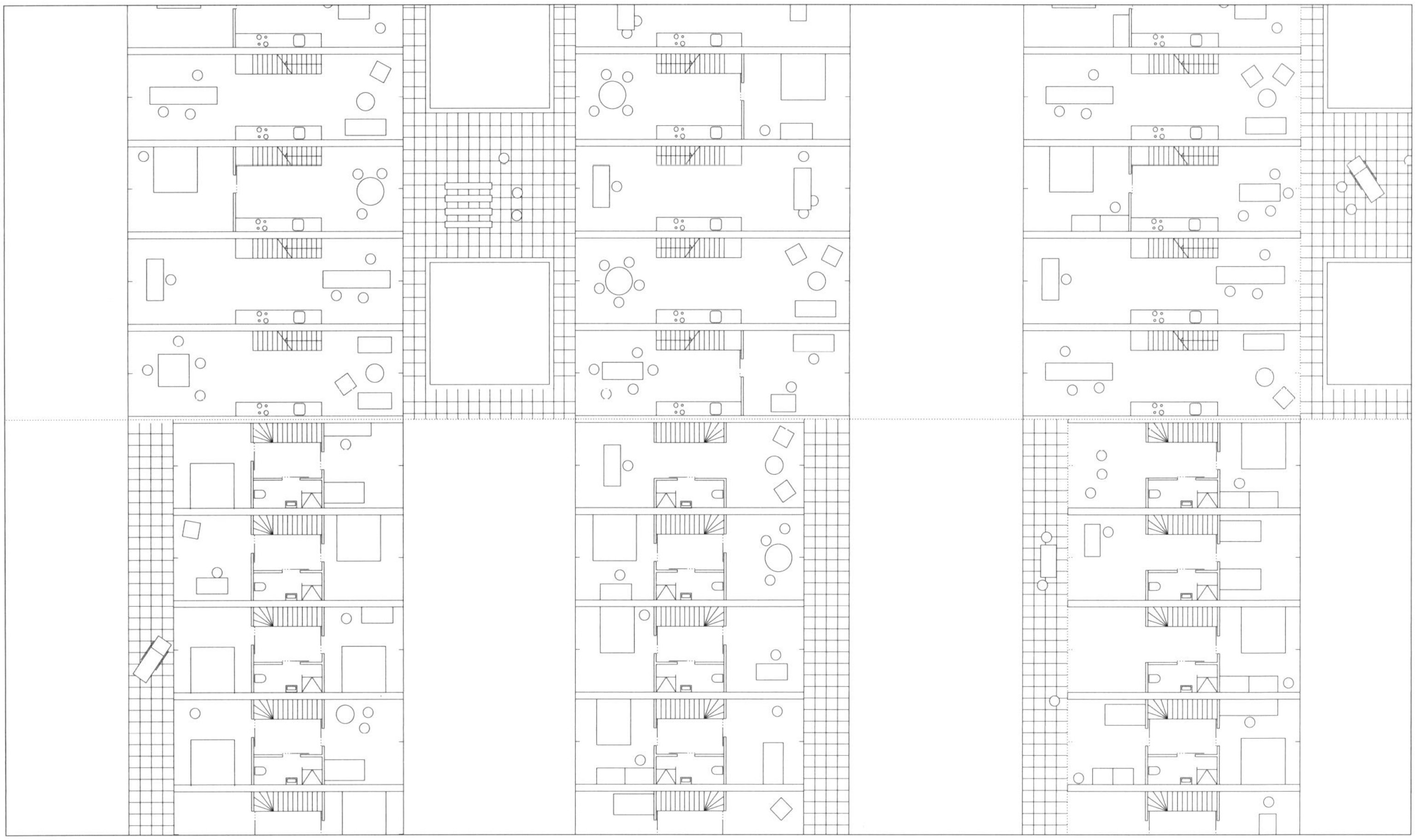

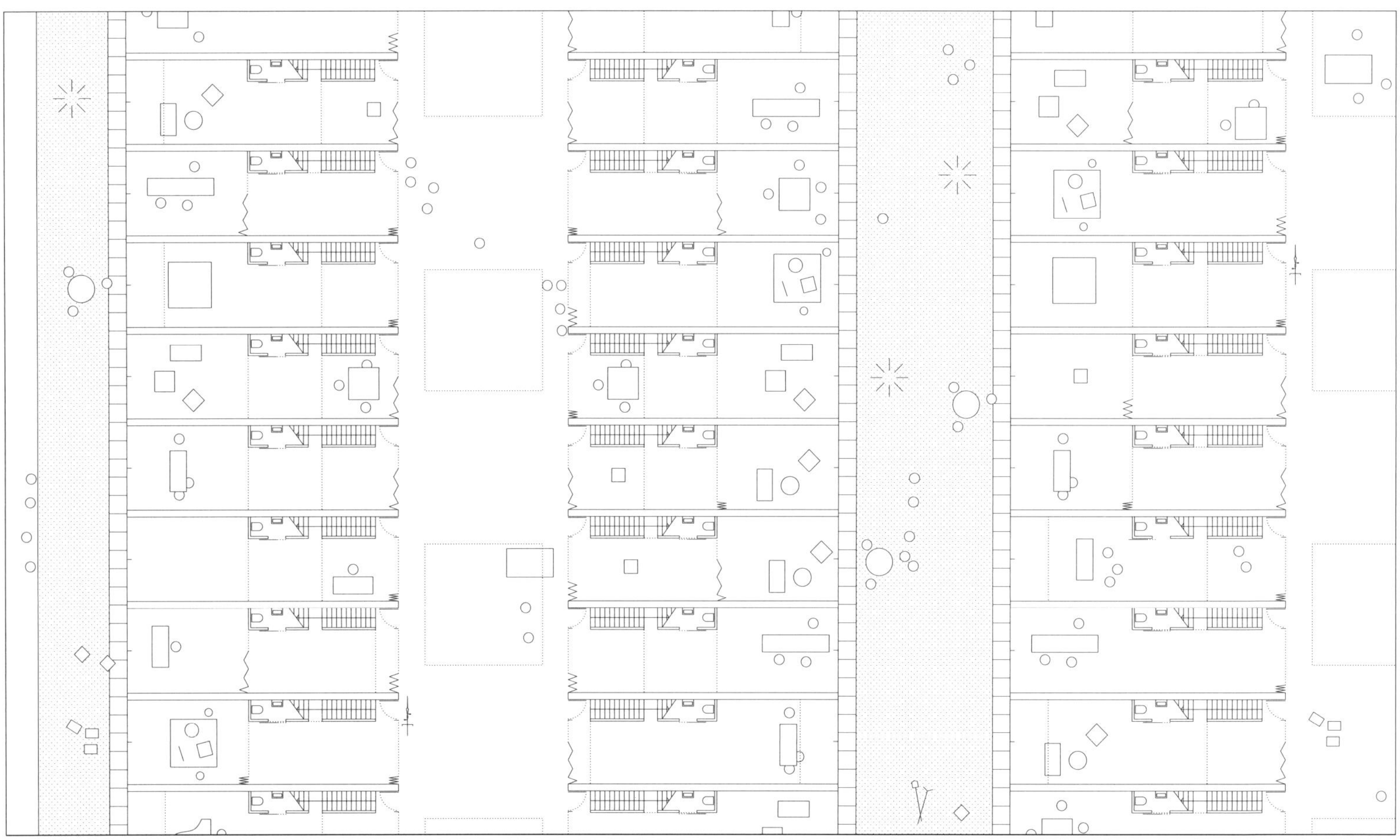

5 m

First- and second-floor plan of the three-story townhouses (second proposal)
Ground-floor plan of three-story townhouses (second proposal)

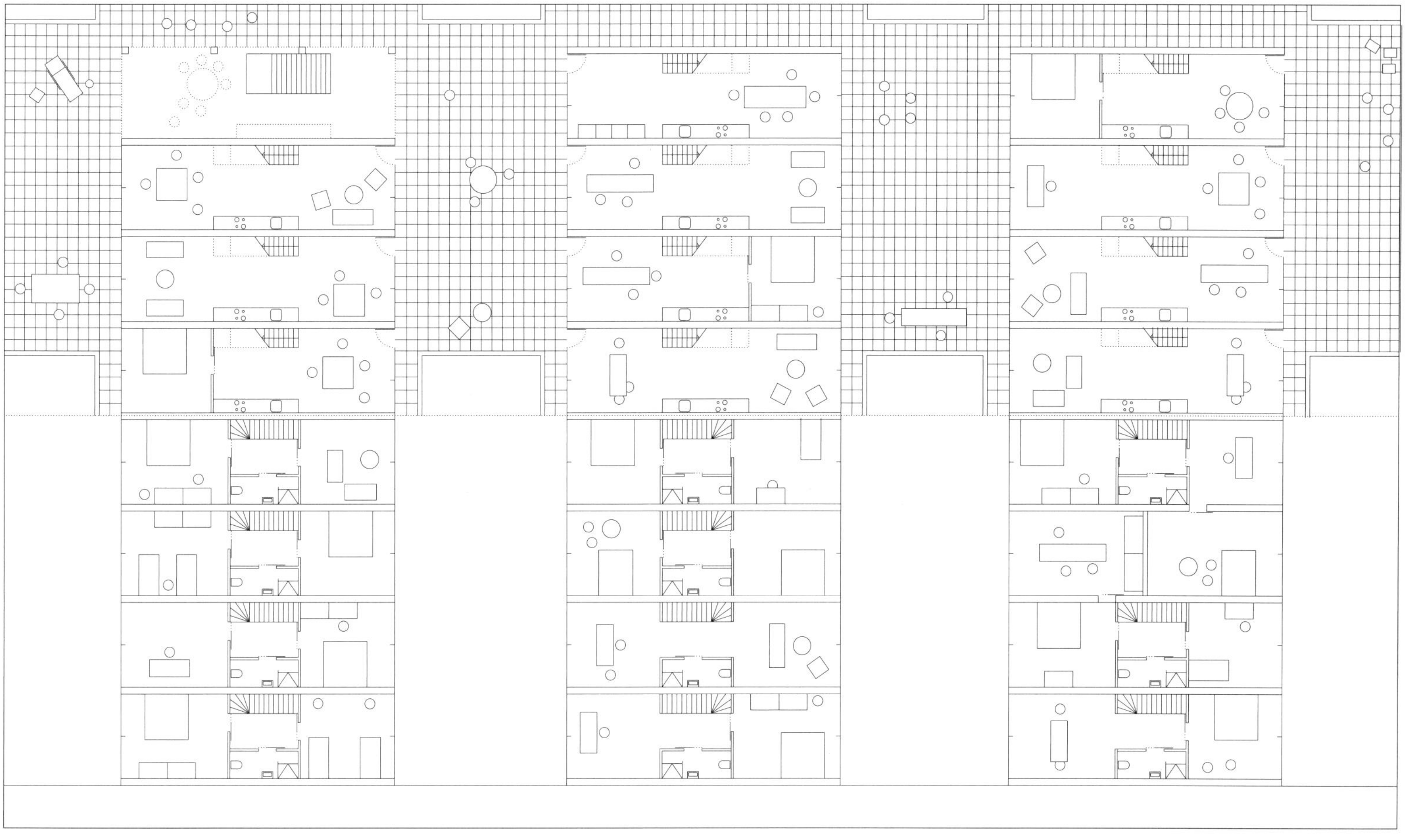

First- and second-floor plan of the two-story townhouses above the shared plinth (second proposal)
Ground-floor plan of shared facilities and workspaces (second proposal)

GARDENING AT NIGHT (2017)

This proposal is a study for a social housing block for 1 200 residents. It includes housing of different sizes and a plethora of communal facilities, most of them located on the ground floor. This model aims to challenge some of the characteristics of traditional social housing interventions, generally understood as large-scale residential blocks based on tenancy, where domestic labor is internalized inside each familiar unit, where working happens somewhere else, where units are typologically strictly defined by regulations, and where the agency of residents over the appropriation and transformation of their living space is limited.

Our proposal is based on an urban form framed around the simplest architectural qualities: built and unbuilt. In plan, the block is a square subdivided into 25 parts. This subdivision becomes a matrix that allows for an even distribution of buildings and open spaces, in a checkerboard manner. As such, the block becomes a field of possibilities, a gradient of public, communal, and private spaces. The block is a system of interconnected "rooms," each suggesting (but not prescribing) potential different uses: from coworking to child care, from sport to gardening. The buildings are organized as different types: urban villa, gallery block, and residential hotel. The urban villa is a freestanding block, the gallery block is made of two mirrored slabs with circulation in between, and the residential hotel is made of a tower on a plinth. Despite their typological diversity, from outside the buildings are all the same: they have uniform fenestration and they are enveloped by continuous balconies that can be used also as extensions of the living units. In contrast to the uniformity of the buildings, each open space is always different, each containing communal facilities for the whole compound.

The project revisits an archetypal form of social housing estates: the tower in the park, where freestanding buildings are surrounded by green areas. This model began to emerge in Europe after the Second War World and was greatly inspired by Le Corbusier's housing models such as the proposal for Îlot Insalubre no. 6 (1935–1936), the plan for the reconstruction of Saint-Dié (1945), and the Unité d'Habitation (1945–1952). These projects became the reference for the two most paradigmatic forms of social (and affordable) housing estates in Europe built since the 1950s: the English council housing estate and the French *grand ensemble*. Although the generous provision of green space brought by the tower-in-the-park typology was a great asset, its vastness made maintenance and appropriation by the inhabitants difficult. This condition was often exacerbated by the nature of the ground floor of the residential buildings, which, rather than becoming a public floor equipped with collective facilities, was occupied with garages, storage, and technical spaces. Another shortcoming of this model of housing was its typological rigidity. Although both the English and French models occasionally contained apartments for singles and couples, the majority were intended for the nuclear family. This underlines a crucial social factor that characterized social and affordable housing from its inception as philanthropic housing estates, that is, the fact that this type of housing was and still is granted only to families. Although social housing is based on tenancy, from its beginning the tacit goal was to introduce lower classes to the virtue of ownership by providing strictly privatized apartments. It is not by chance that the fate of many of these housings estates has been their privatization.

Our proposal reacts to these aspects by rethinking both the urban form of the block and the typology of the houses. While we maintain the typology of the tower in the park, the use of the checkerboard grid makes the spaces in between more defined. Whereas the green space in postwar social housing interventions was generally understood from a quantitative perspective, as the needed square meters of green space in relation to a certain number of inhabitants, in our proposal we imagine the open space as a series of open-air rooms, defined on each side by buildings and thus establishing a direct relationship with their ground floors and the collective facilities there contained. As for the housing types, rather than providing a limited catalogue of living units, we propose a structural system that allows infinite adaptations that can support all sorts of household associations and living combinations, ranging from traditional family units to living-and-working spaces, from cohousing to the residential hotel.

To maintain this typological openness, we have conceived a structural system in which prefabricated "wet cores" group together bathroom and kitchen. These cores, developed in the factory, are brought to the construction site and stacked on top of each other with the help of a crane once the concrete skeleton and slabs are completed. By being evenly distributed within the plan, the cores allow different subdivisions of each floor. When redundant, cores can be used as storage, cloak room, and laundry, yet at any moment they can always be converted into bathrooms and kitchens and thus allow further subdivision of the apartment into smaller units. Such a system can support easy conversions of houses into workspaces and vice versa, further subdivision of the house to obtain an extra room for assisted living, and negotiation of extra rooms among neighboring households. This flexibility of housing units can be achieved only thanks to the transformation of traditional tenancy and ownership regimes and the introduction of alternative forms of collective tenure so that housing ownership or tenancy are not based on the property or rent of one single unit but on participation in the system, whose criterion is the negotiation of space according to inhabitants' needs.

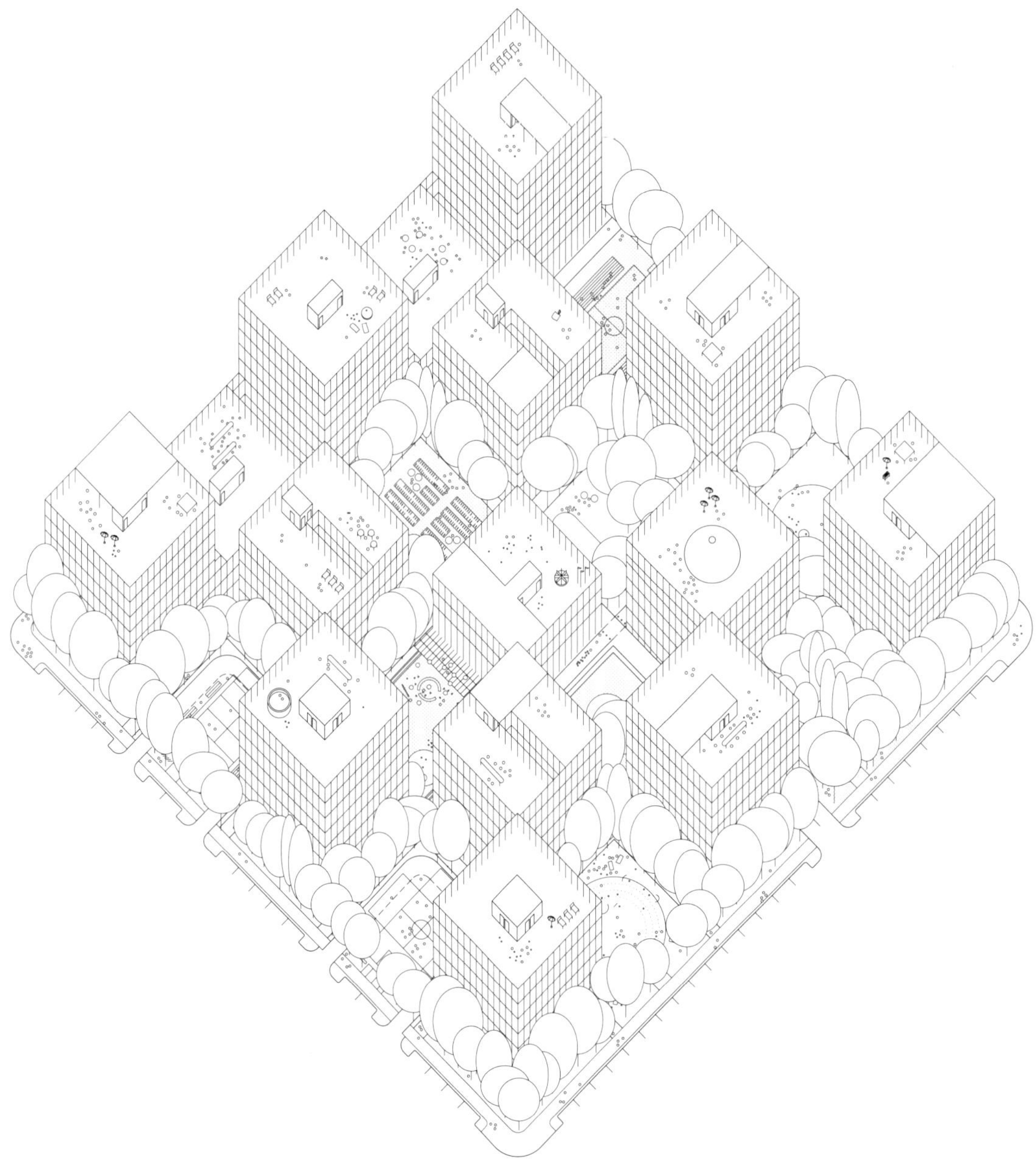

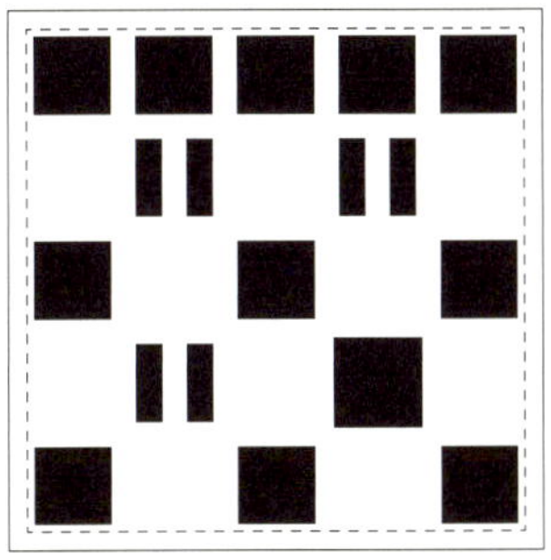

Built space

Unbuilt space

Public/private relationship

Public
Common
Semipublic
Private

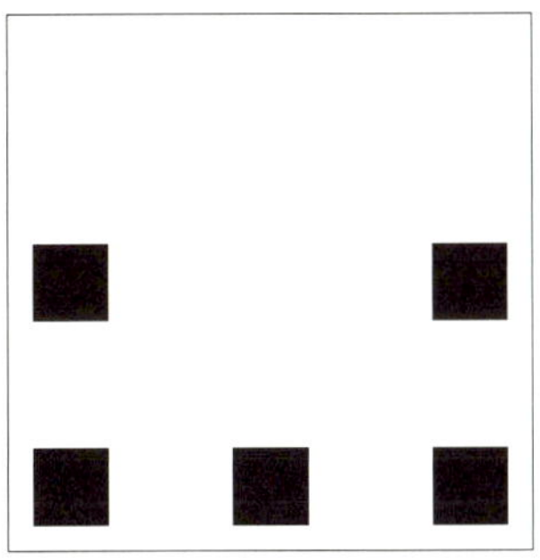

Typology A: urban villa

Typology B: gallery block

Typology C: residential hotel

Soft mobility

····· Pedestrian
- - Bicycle

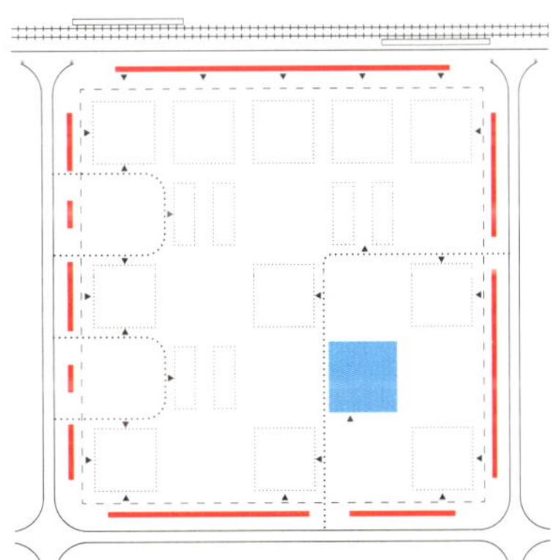

Car access and parking

Surface parking
Parking structure

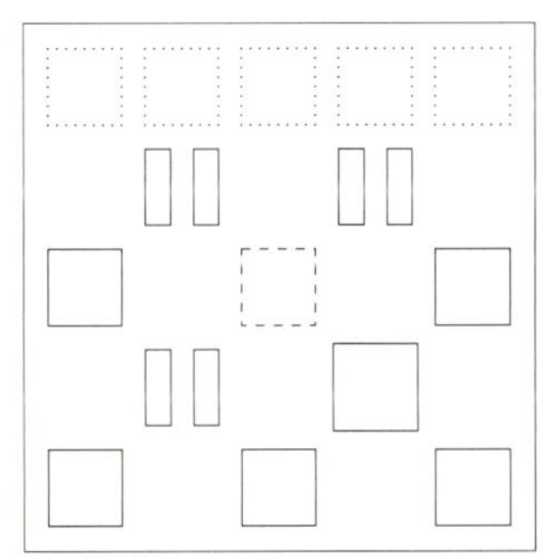

Ground floor

Working space/commercial
Workshop
Kindergarten

Surfaces

Rubber
Paved
Meadow
Gravel
Water

Gardens

Kitchen garden
Forest
Playground
Sport
School playground

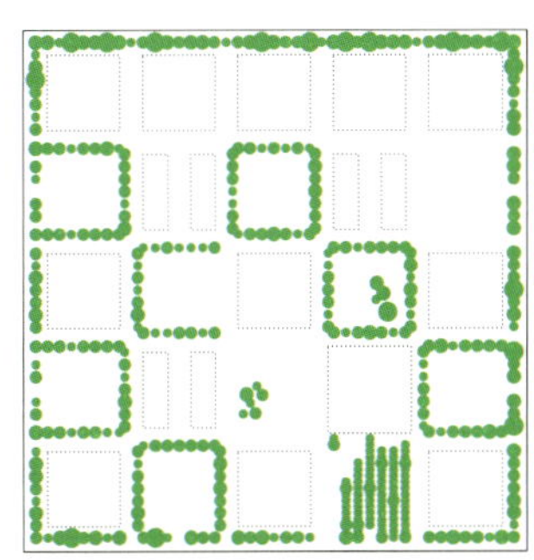

Vegetation

Tree

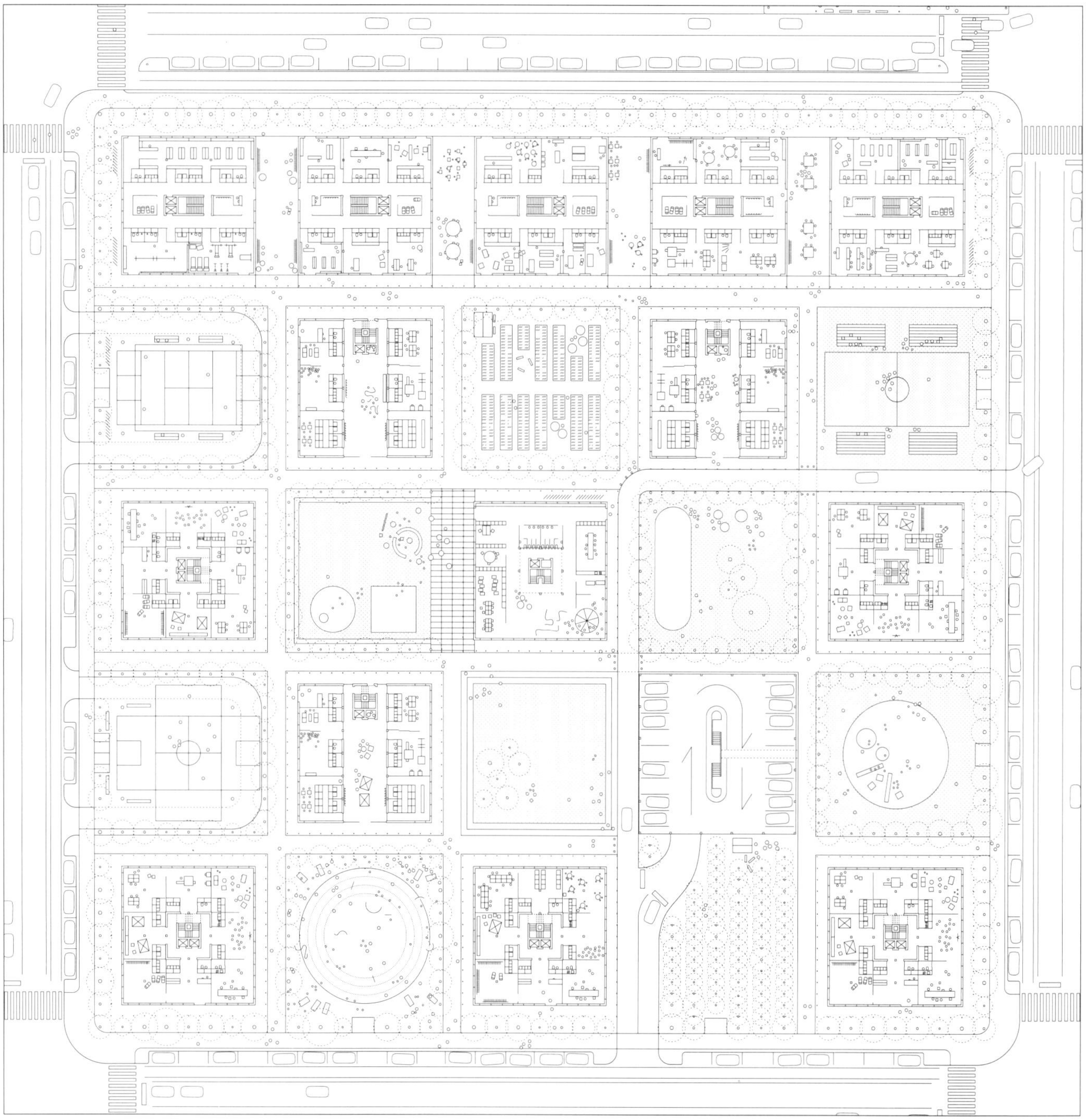

Ground-floor plan

20 m

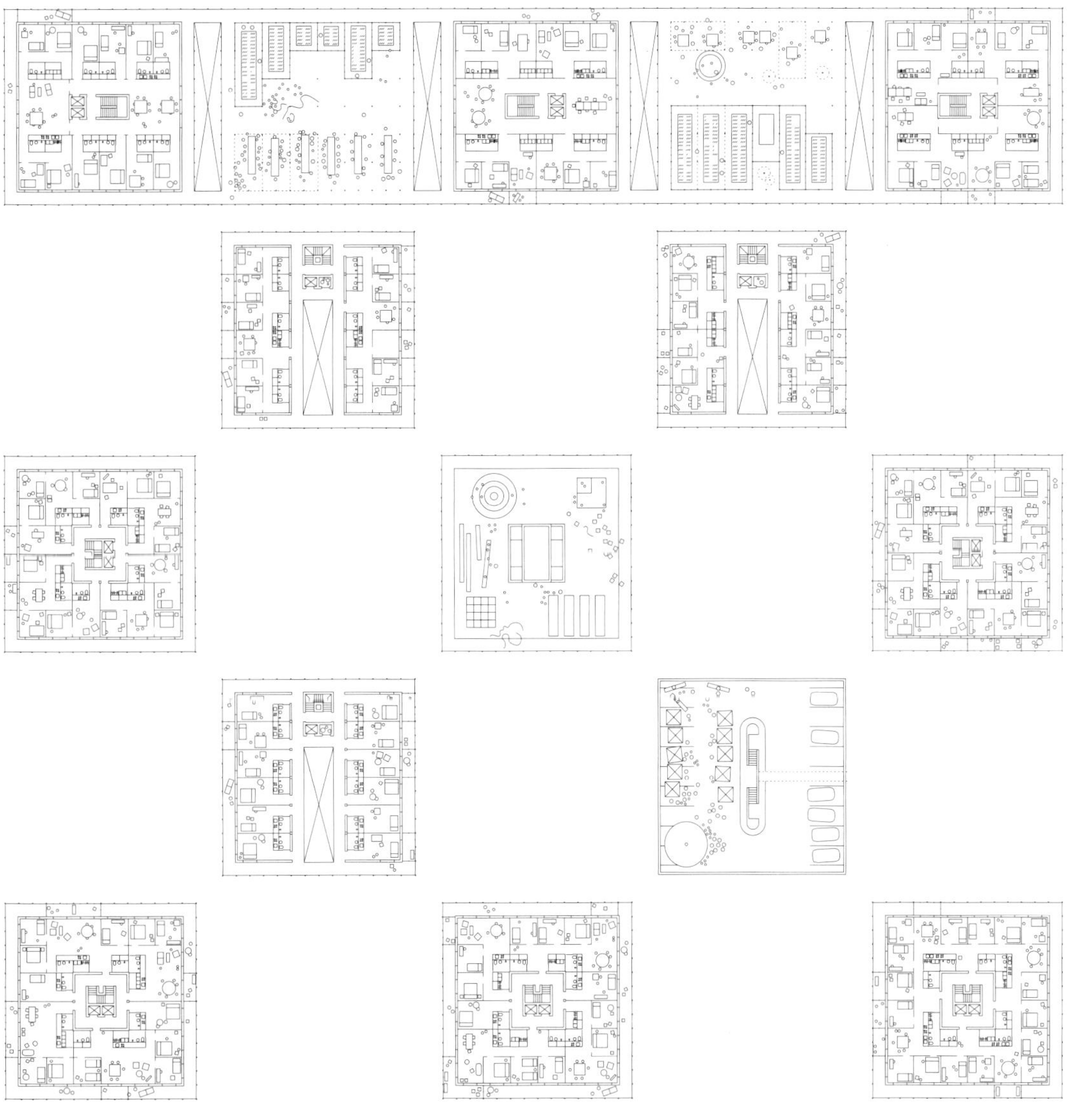

Typical plan

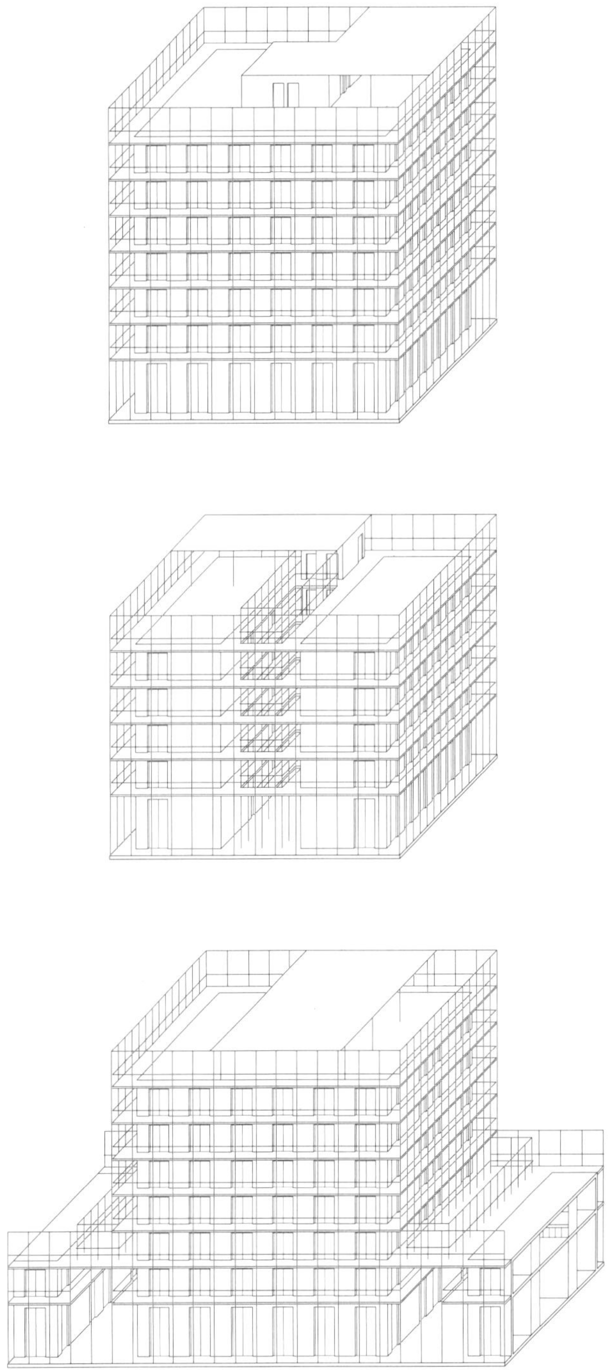

Typology A: urban villa (above), Typology B: gallery block (middle), and Typology C: residential hotel (below)

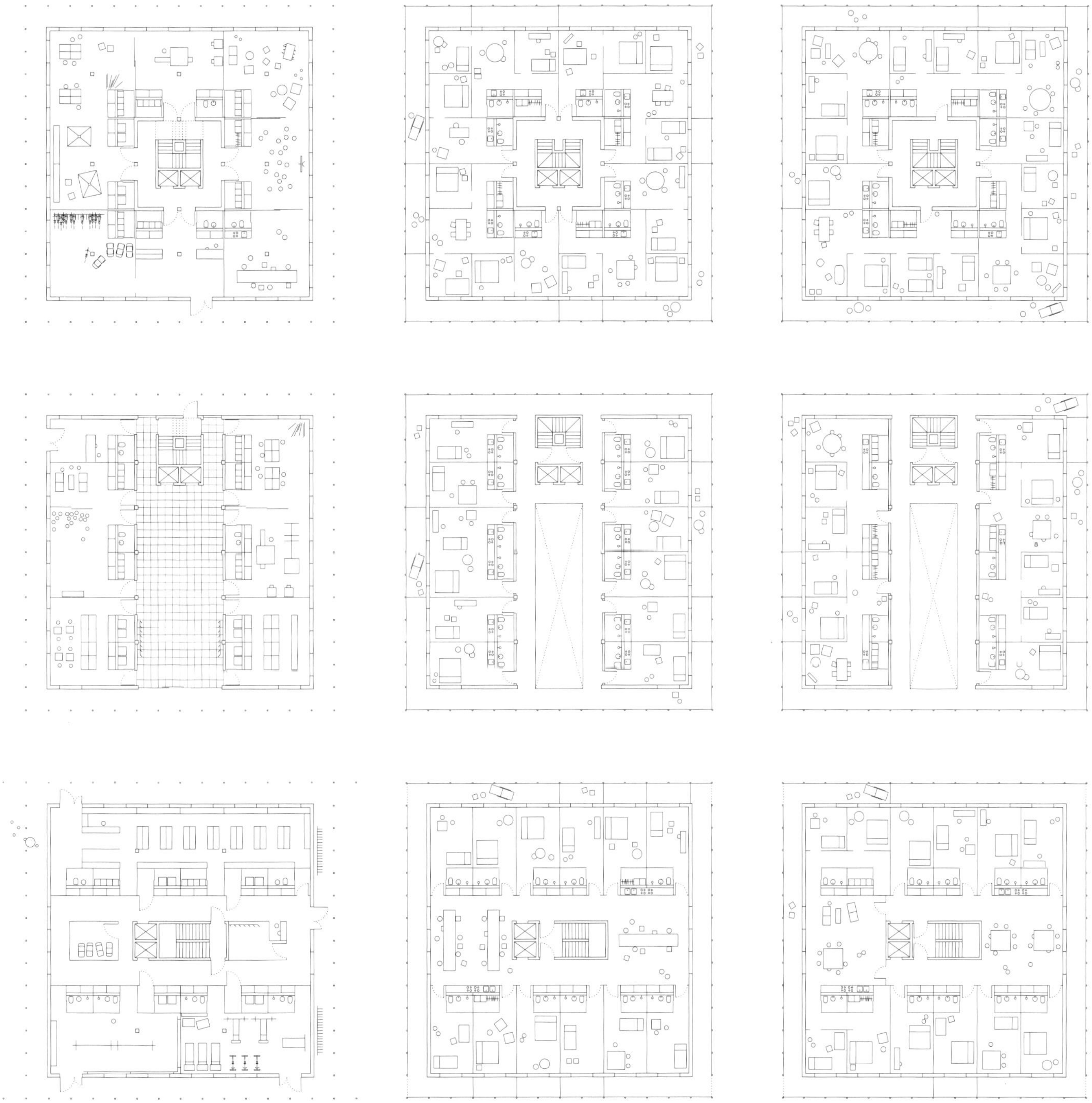

Ground-floor and typical plans of urban villa (above), gallery block (middle), and residential hotel (below)

10 m

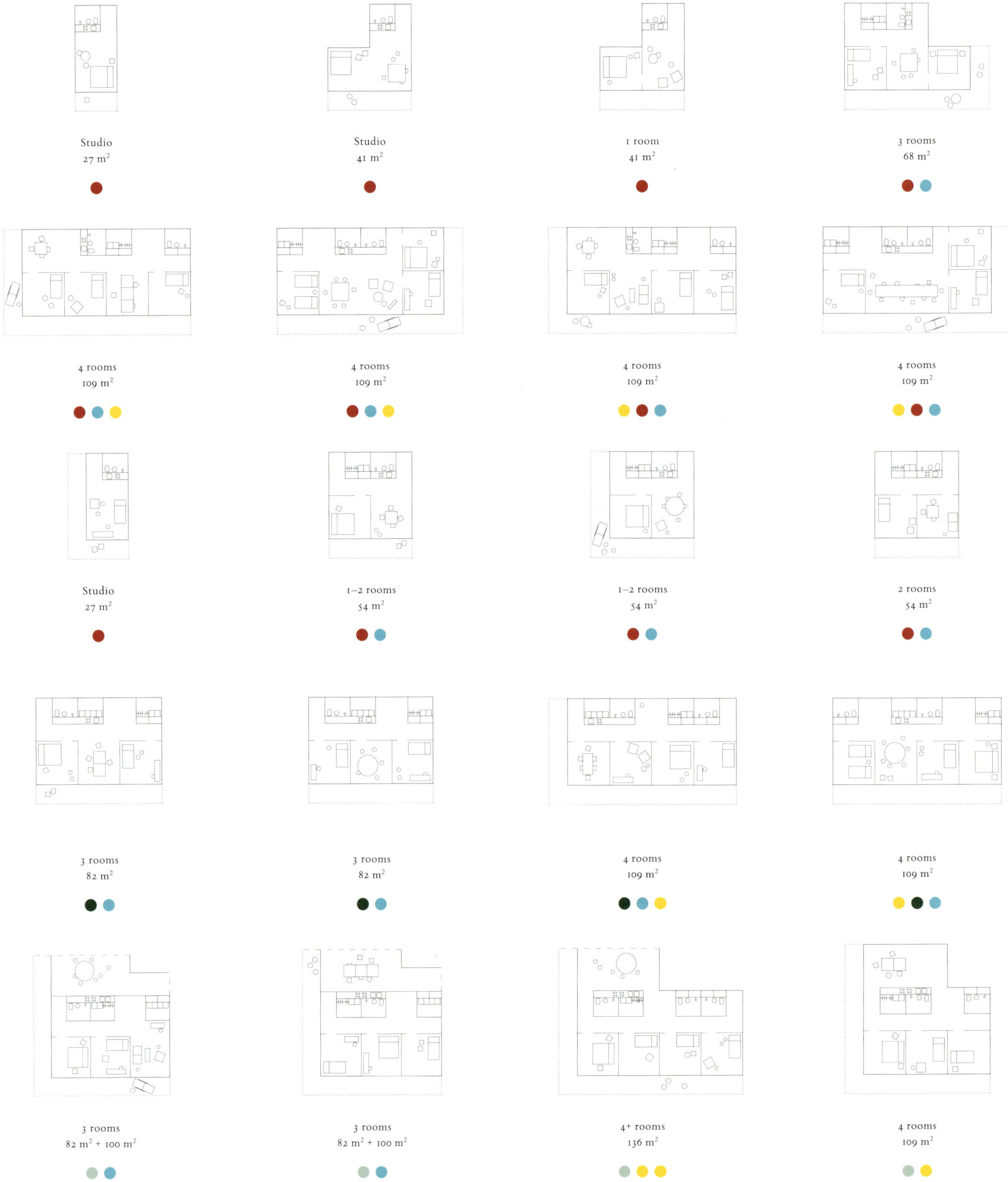

Unit variations and wet cores

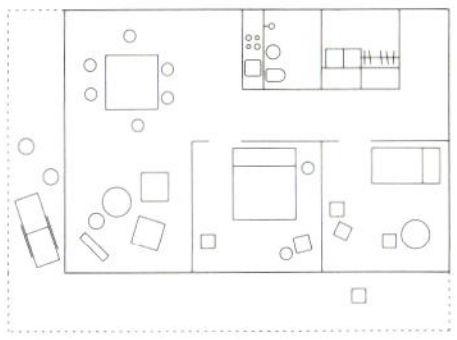

3 rooms
82 m^2

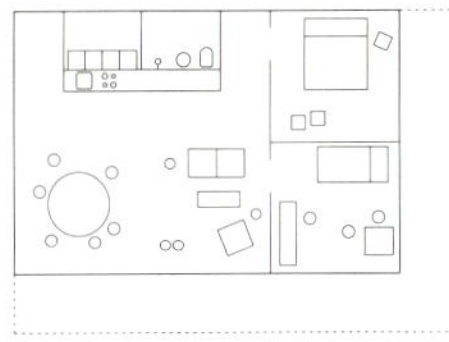

3 rooms
82 m^2

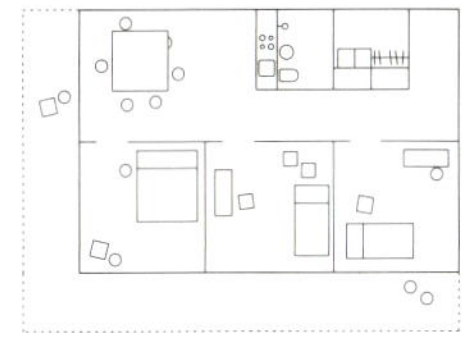

4 rooms
82 m^2

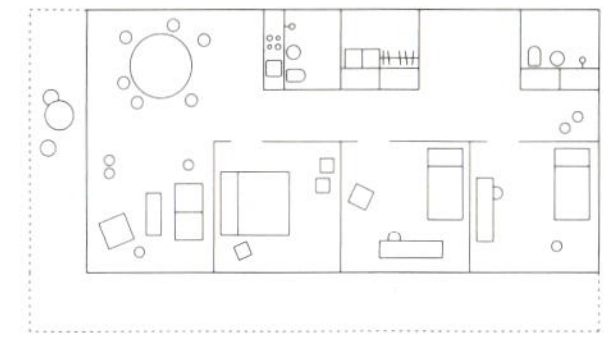

4 rooms
109 m^2

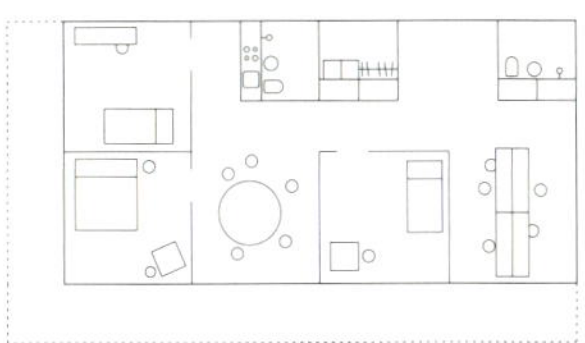

4 rooms
109 m^2

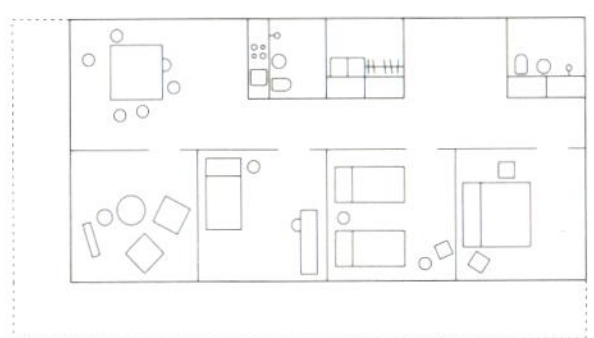

4+ rooms
109 m^2

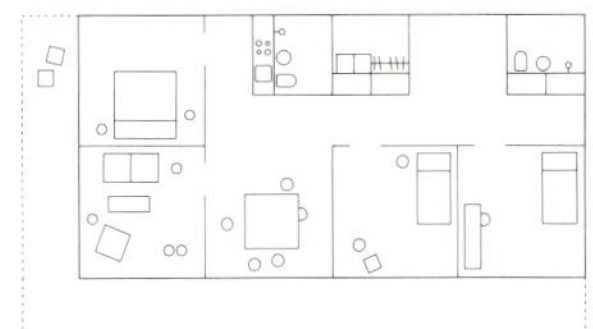

4+ rooms
109 m^2

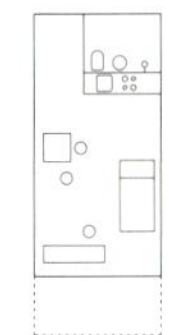

Studio
27 m^2

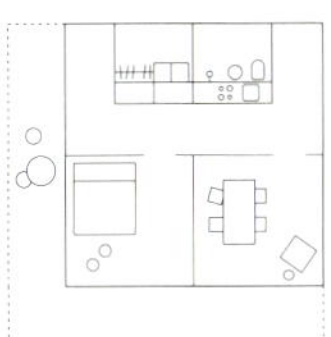

2 rooms
54 m^2

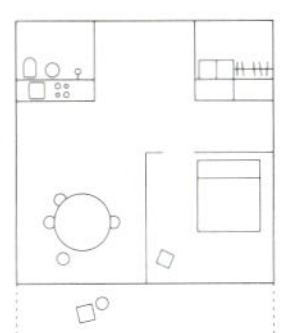

1–2 rooms
54 m^2

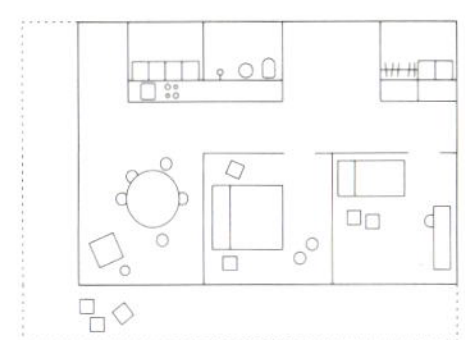

3 rooms
82 m^2

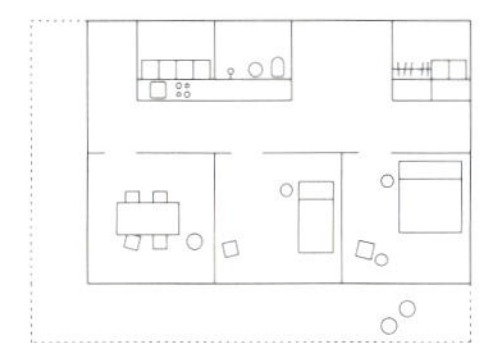

3 rooms
82 m^2

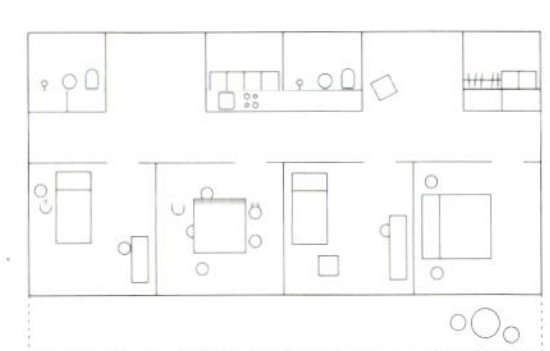

4 rooms
109 m^2

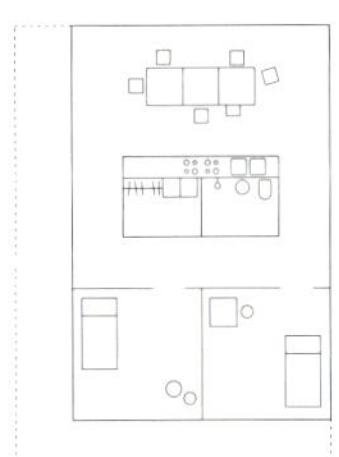

3 rooms
82 m^2

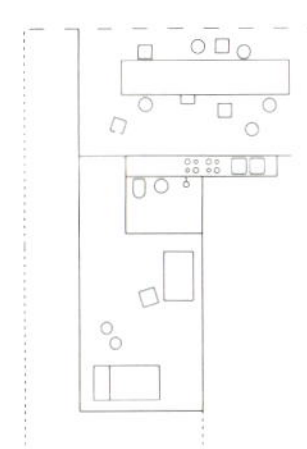

Studio
27 m^2 + 100 m^2

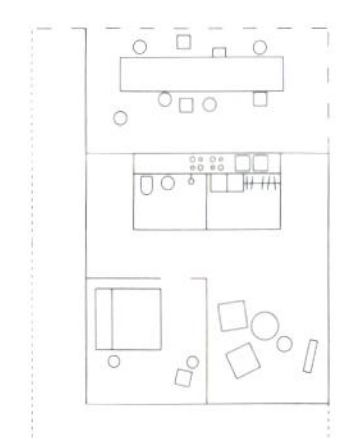

2 rooms
54 m^2 + 100 m^2

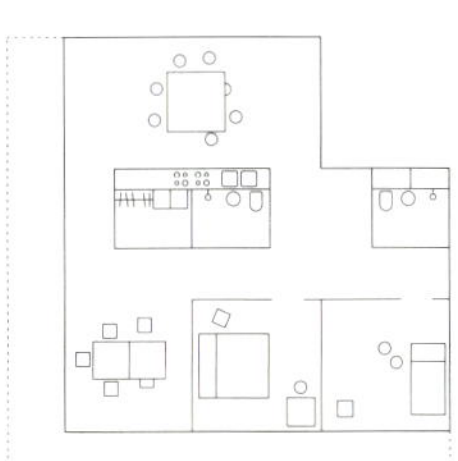

3 rooms
109 m^2

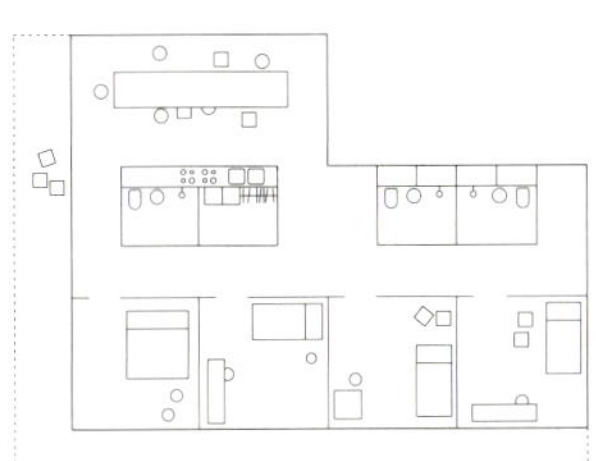

4+ rooms
136 m^2

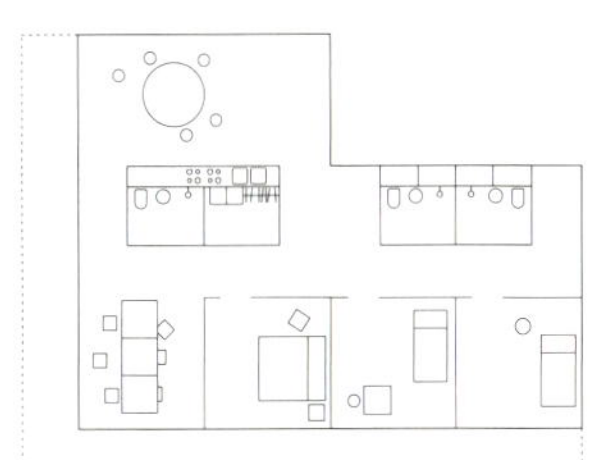

4 rooms
136 m^2

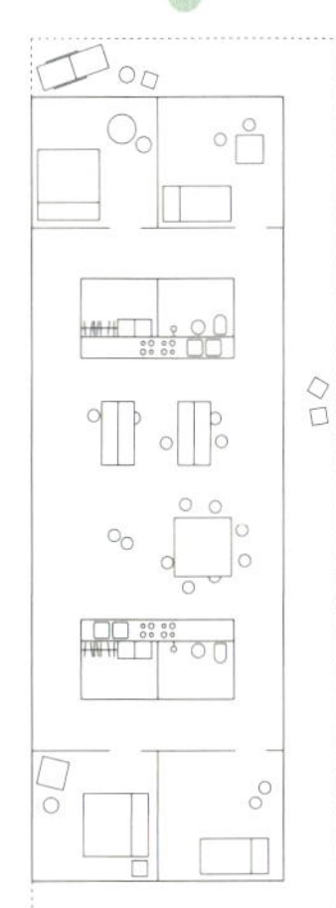

4+ rooms
164 m^2

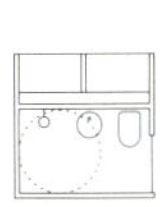

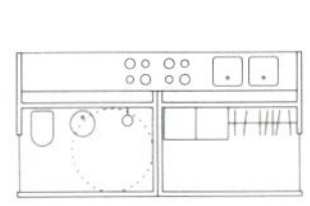

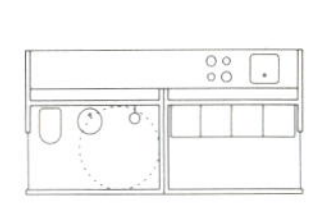

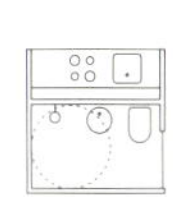

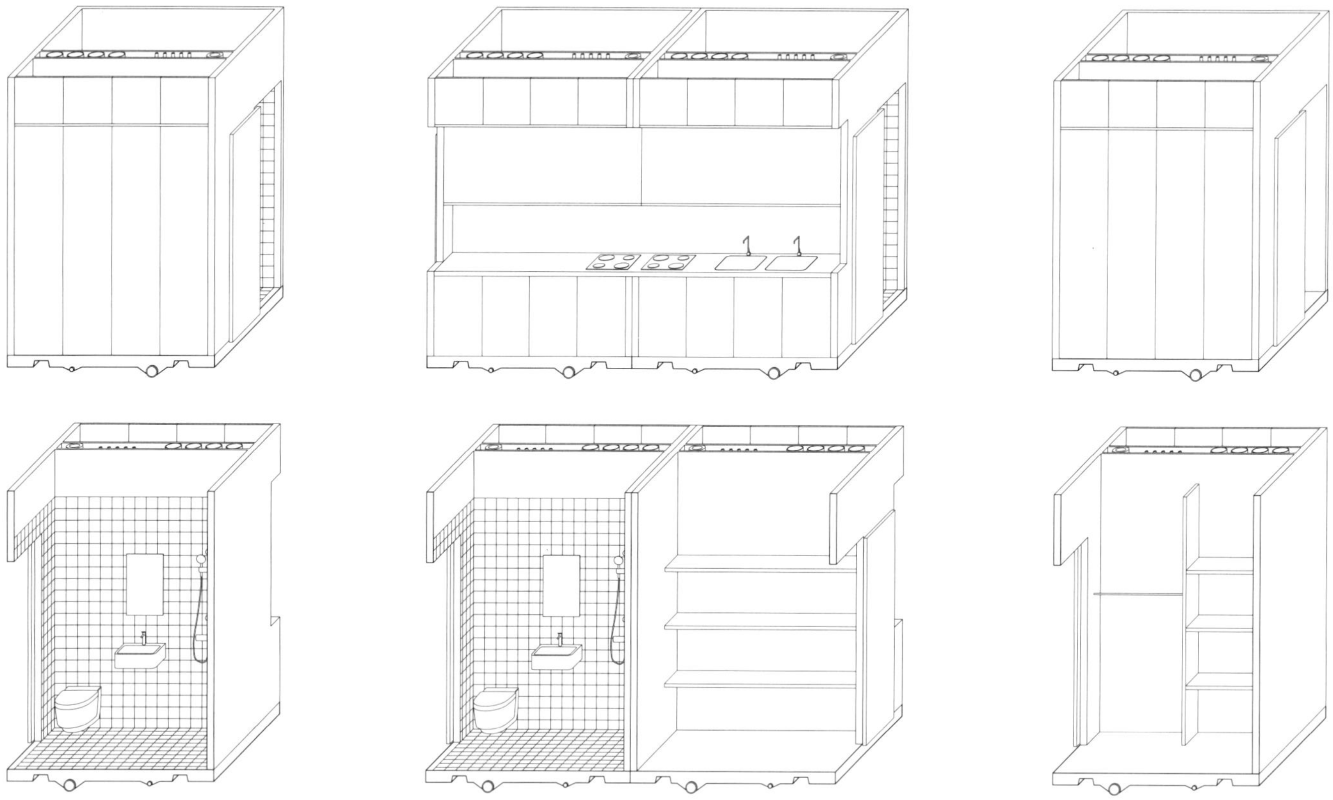

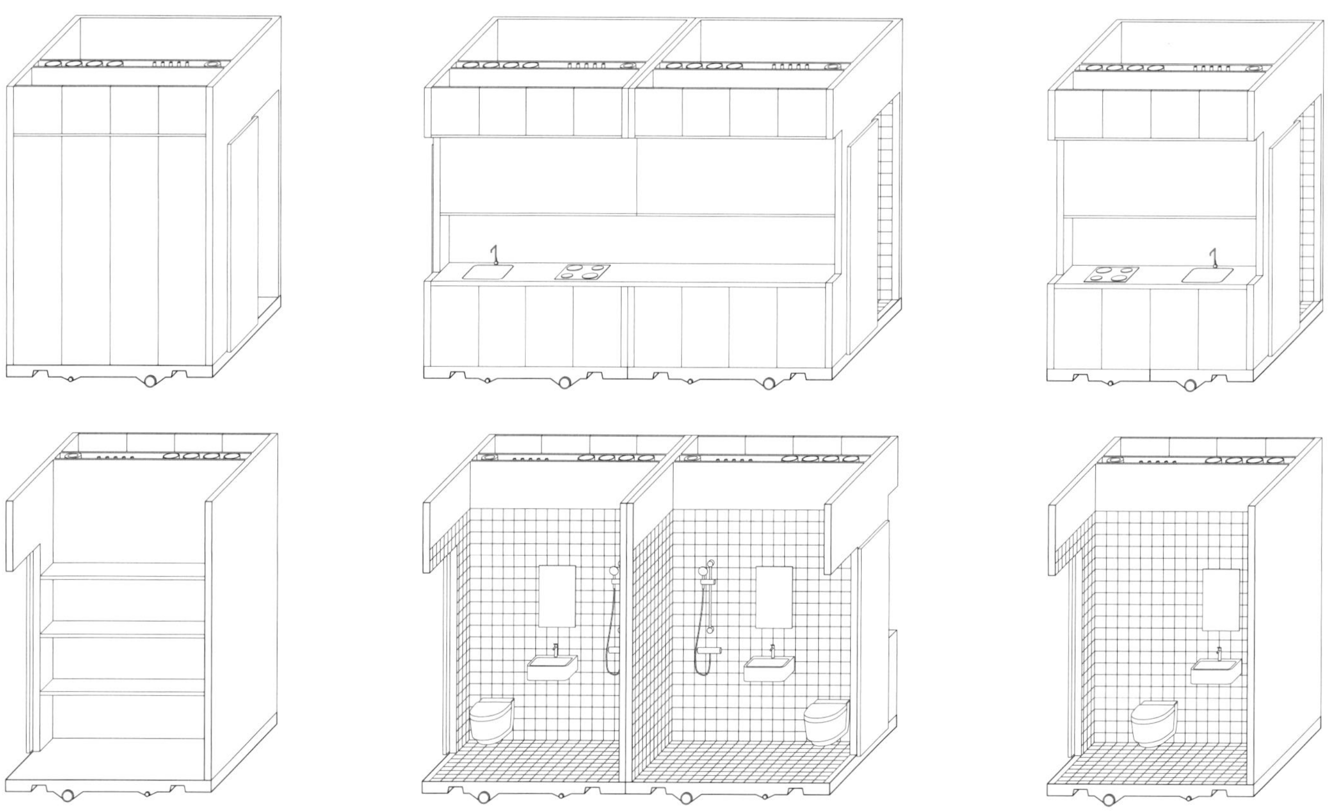

Catalogue of prefabricated wet cores

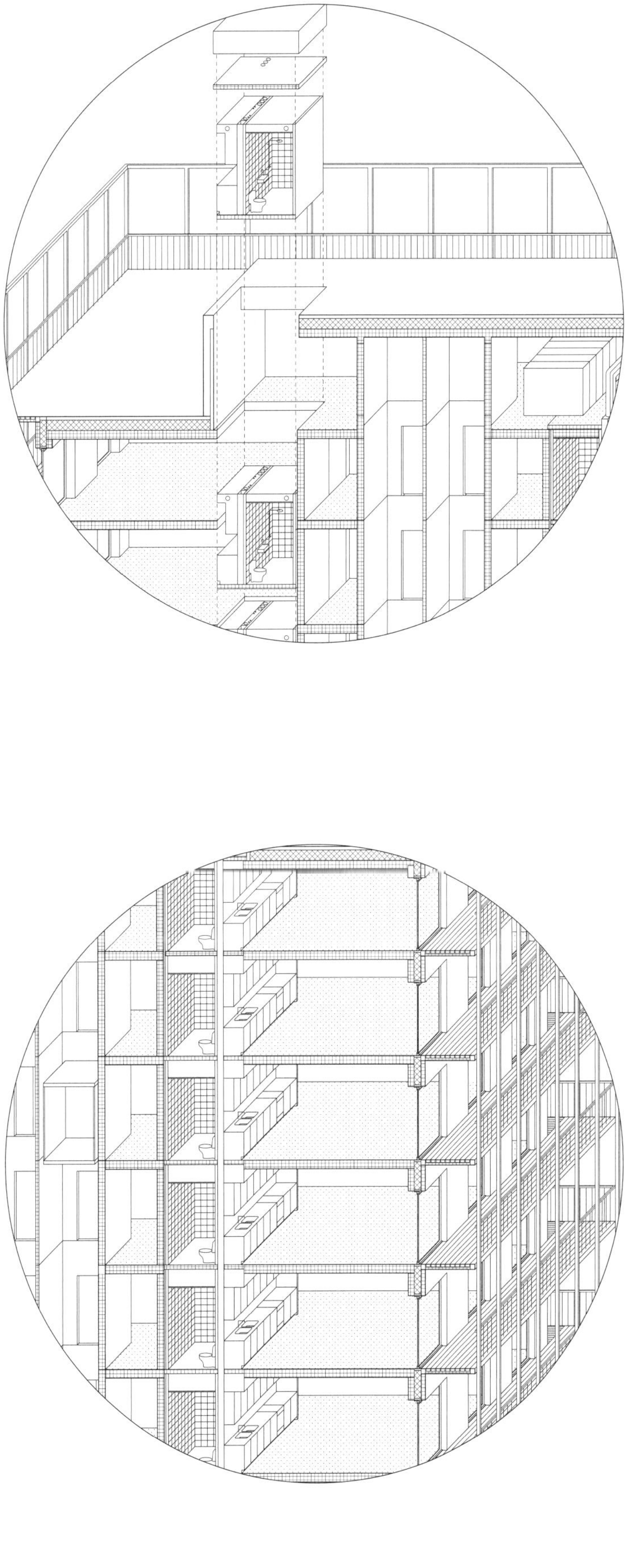

Insertion of prefabricated wet cores

DO YOU HEAR ME WHEN YOU SLEEP? (2019)

The project proposes a prototype for cooperative housing in London. The prototype evolves from a collaboration with Sun Co-op, an organization formed in 2017 with the goal of searching for alternative housing solutions related to its members' own way of living and working. Initially the project focused on Sun Co-op's housing building for approximately forty people, and later it evolved as a model applicable to different households that can go from small-scale to large-scale housing structures.

The project aims to deconstruct the "affordable housing complex" by translating the cooperative ownership structure into a communal house where typological experimentation and construction methods offer its residents the opportunity to modulate sharing and privacy, living and working, according to the needs and aspirations of future inhabitants.

Given the current economic situation, buying a house in London has become unaffordable to many, while rental conditions are often disadvantageous as the residents don't have control over their living space and are often forced into a condition of permanent nomadism. In response to this predicament, groups of individuals and families are coming together in small associations, grassroots initiatives, and cooperatives thanks also to the support provided by the municipality and the local boroughs to small developers, housing associations, community-led housing organizations, and self-builders. While many of these associations are formed primarily with the goal of entering the housing market, others wish to take the opportunity of collective ownership to test a more communal way of living based on the implementation of a cooperative contract amongst inhabitants.

The project started by looking at the online database of all public land in the city, and at the same time understanding the characteristics of those sites that are gradually made available for community-led housing organizations—allotments often designated as unused or misused zones and located next to railway lines, parking lots, and vacant spaces. Among the many areas, we selected a series of potential sites where public ownership status, geographic position, and surface conditions made it possible to imagine the development of a cooperative housing project. The selected terrains, often located in central London, although generally neglected represent a viable alternative to suburban sprawl, and could serve as the ideal background for experimentation. Based on the understanding of the conditions of these sites, many of which have an elongated form, we developed a prototype for a communal house where every inhabitant is equipped with a private room (which can be double or triple occupancy according to necessity) with shared kitchens, living rooms, and terraces. These rooms can be grouped together in different ways, giving form to a multiplicity of households, ranging from the one-bedroom apartment to two large apartments sharing a kitchen. The modular configuration allows for these households to evolve through time and to expand or shrink according to the changing demographic. This is possible due to the cooperative ownership system, in which every member of the co-op owns a share of the whole building rather than a specific portion of it. The building includes spaces for work, providing the residents with office spaces, workshops, and meeting rooms that can also be open to the local community and can be used for leisure activities. The co-op becomes its own governmental organ, scaling up administration and decision-making processes, daily expenses, and duties from the individual to the community, while providing a more independent financial and administrative setting. Operating with self-organizing principles, the prototype can be implemented autogenously, which in this context grants inhabitants control over the building processes. The use of timber for the structure and the main building components is motivated by the wish of the members to participate in the construction process and therefore favors the acquisition of those administrative and technical skills that can reduce the need of external developers and contractors.

The prototype is conceived as a repeatable structure of a maximum of three floors that can be implemented on different sites and adapted to different urban conditions, thus resulting in different configurations. By looking at the most recurring characteristics of the identified plots, we have developed three main potential configurations. In the case of long and very narrow plots, the structure acquires a linear configuration, and communal facilities, given the limited section, are concentrated at a few points along the narrow building. In the case of long but wider plots, the structure acquires a linear configuration yet defined by two parallel and adjacent strips, the first dedicated to private rooms and the second to the communal facilities; while the first faces the street, the second faces the back of the plot and eventually an internal garden. In the case of more regular rectangular plots, the communal space is placed at the center while the private rooms define the edge of the plots. Although these configurations are very different, the guiding principle remains the same throughout the various possible applications, namely the subdivision of the building based on individual rooms that can be brought together and give forms to different living spaces. These different configurations allow us to imagine how this project, rather than remaining confined to the ad hoc architecture of small sites and community-led initiatives, could trigger the development of a wider urban strategy aimed at reclaiming the many neglected sites in the city, a strategy that may be directly embraced by public authorities and more forcibly advance a solution to the current housing crisis.

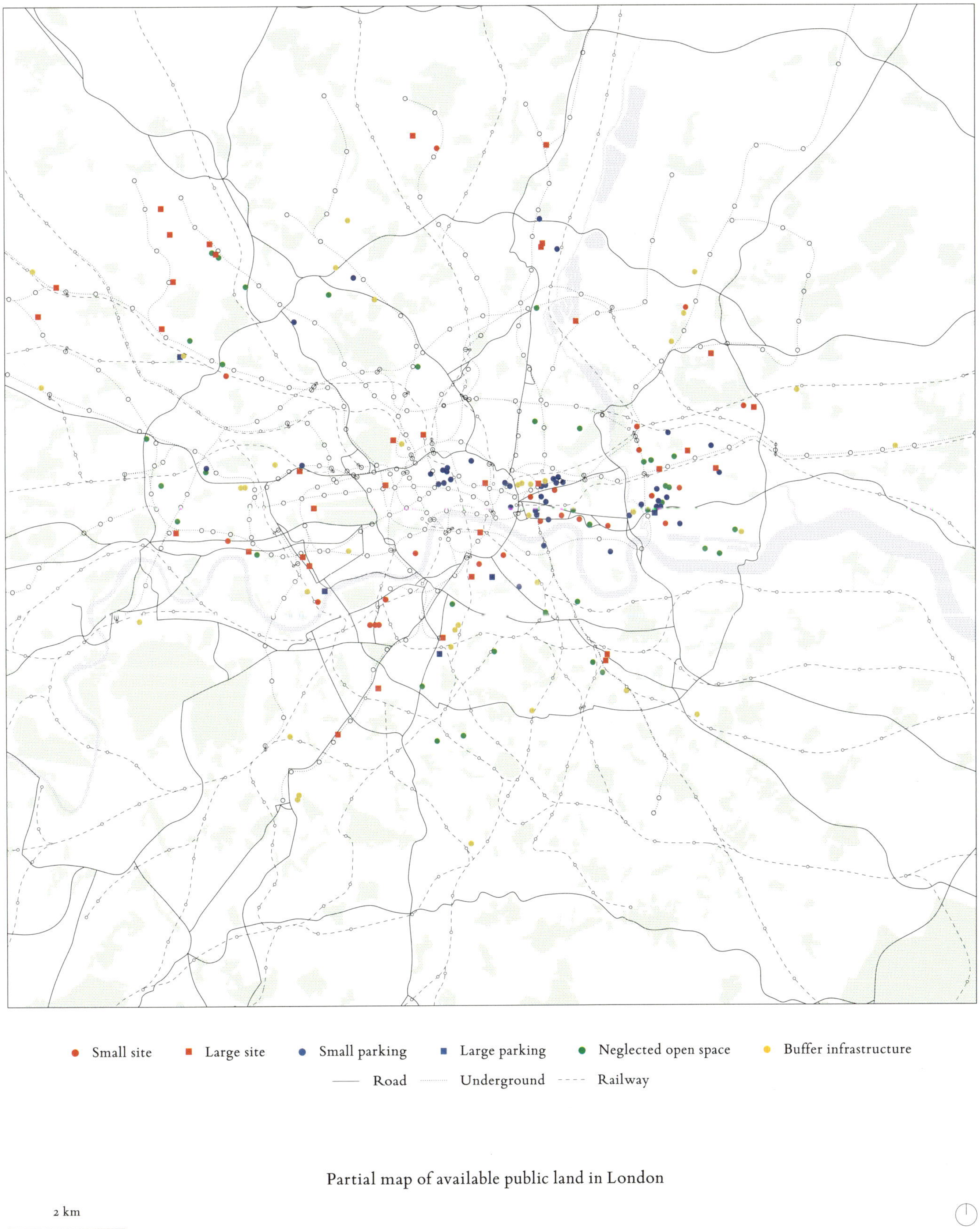

Partial map of available public land in London

Single bedroom — 19 m²

Two single bedrooms with shared bathroom — 38 m²

Single bedroom with parlor — 38 m²

Double bedroom — 38 m²

Duplex room — 52 m²

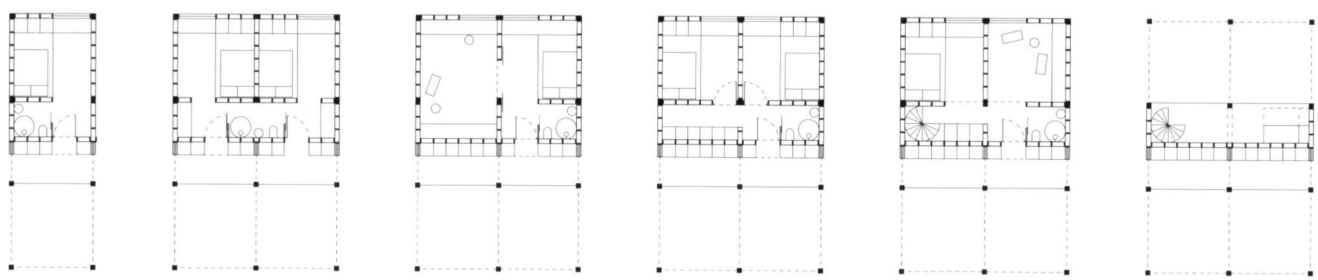

One-bedroom apartment — 26 m²

Two-bedroom apartment — 52 m²

Three-bedroom apartment — 77 m²

Two apartments with shared kitchen — 155 m²

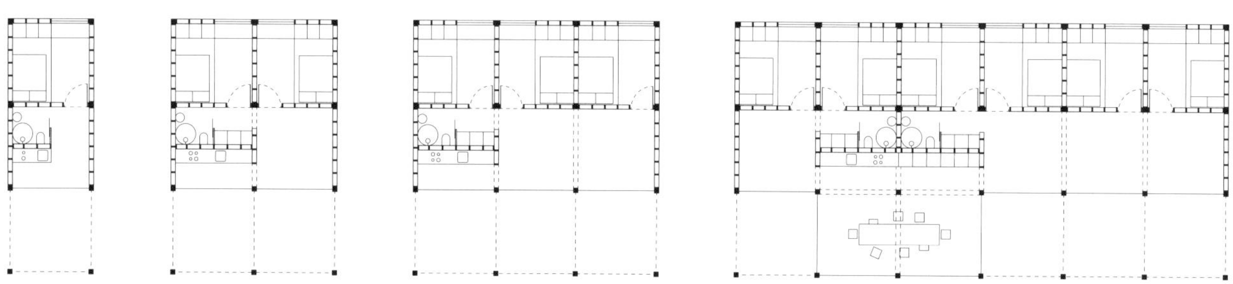

Composition of rooms, from studio to larger housing units

2 m

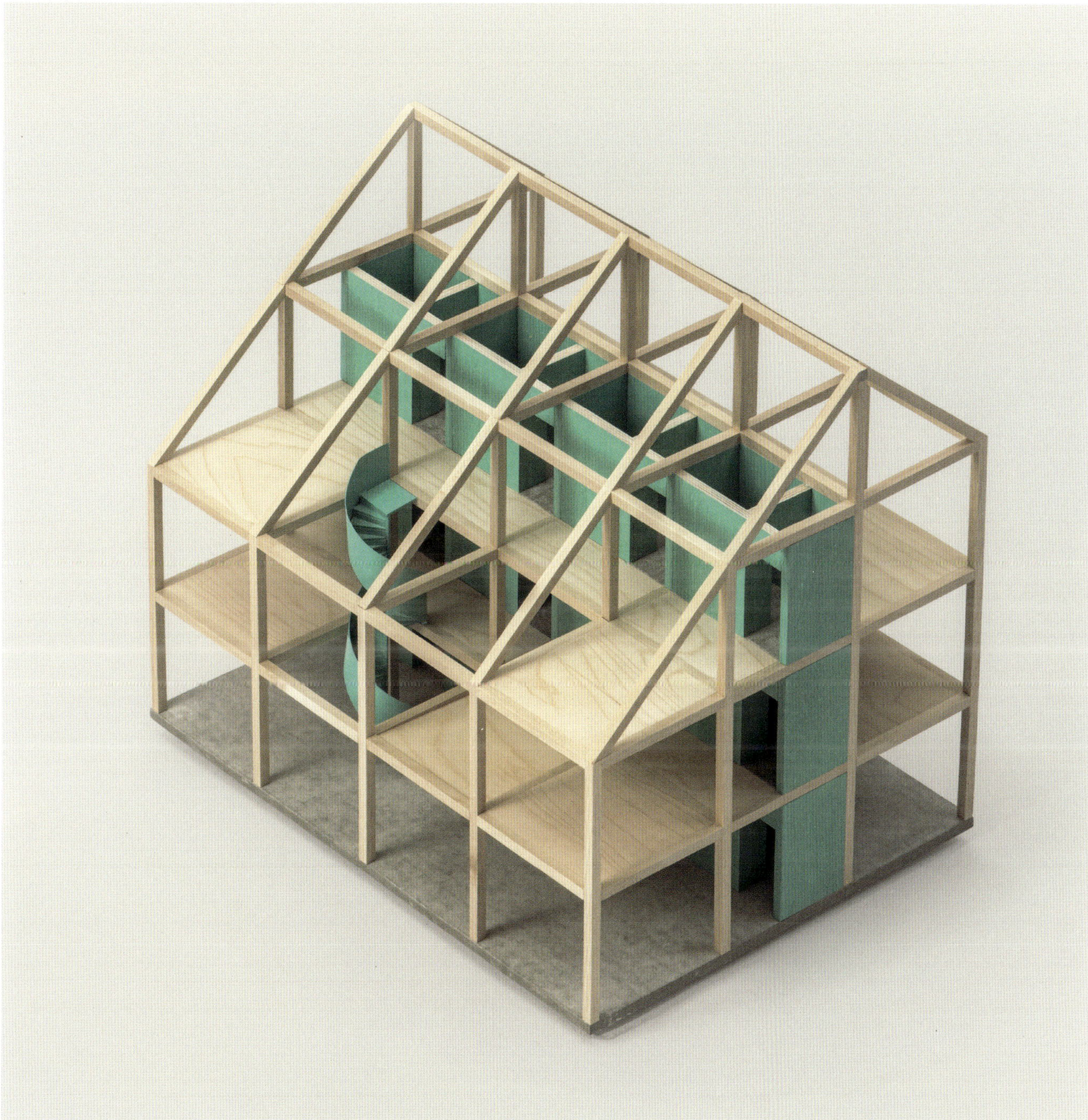

249

Studio
One-bedroom apartment

Two-bedroom apartment
Three-bedroom apartment

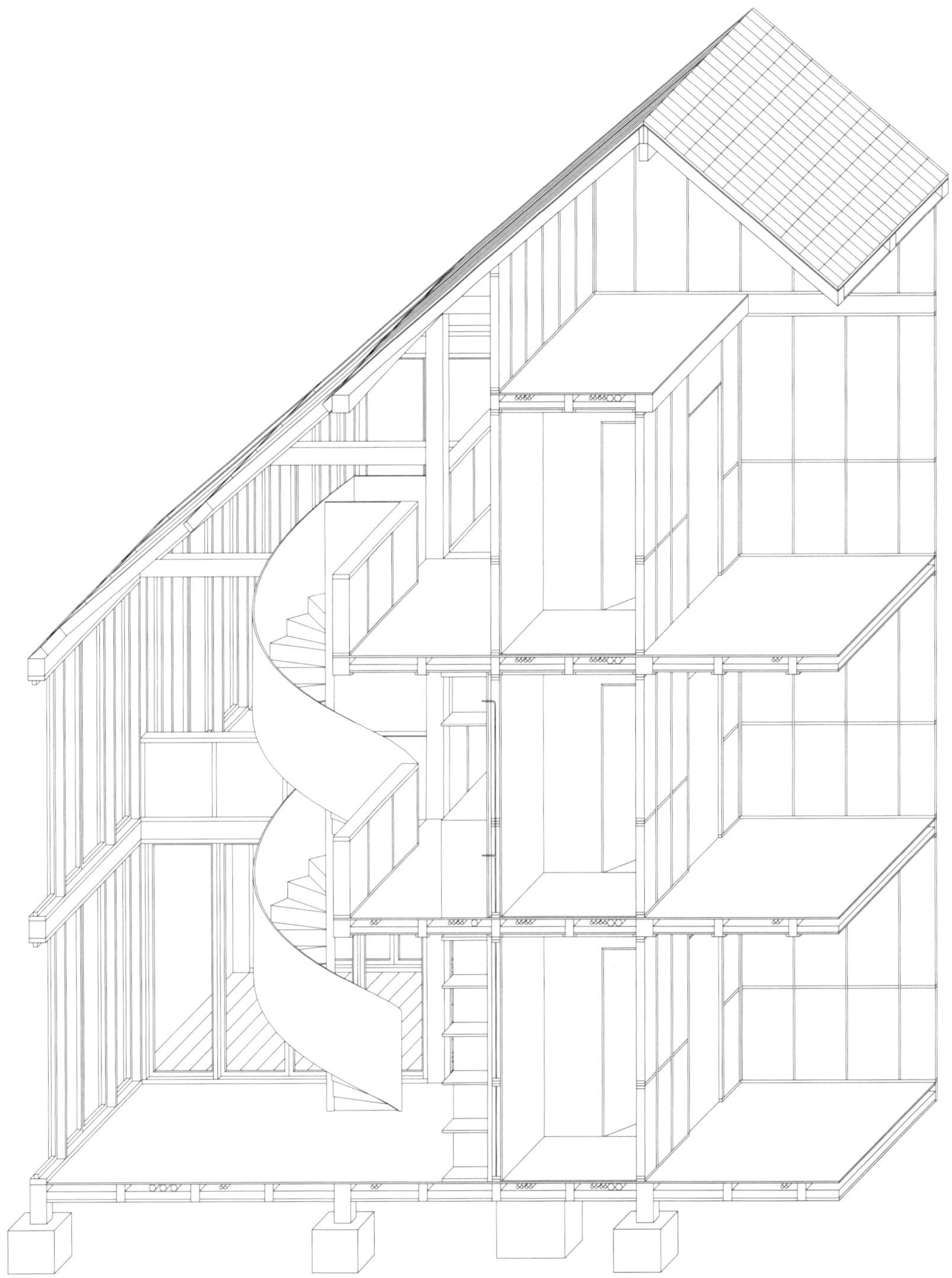

Technical section

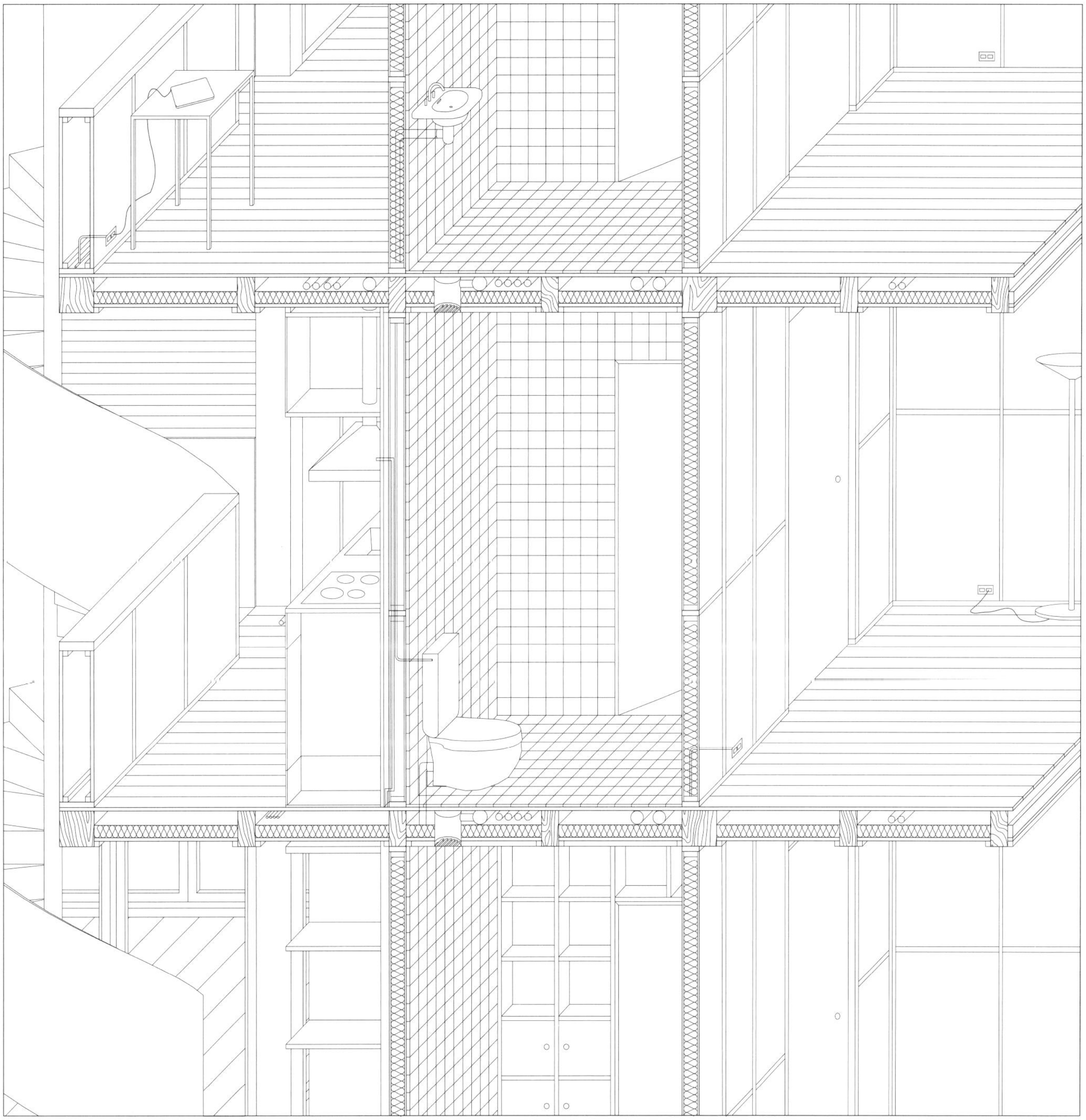

Technical section (detail)

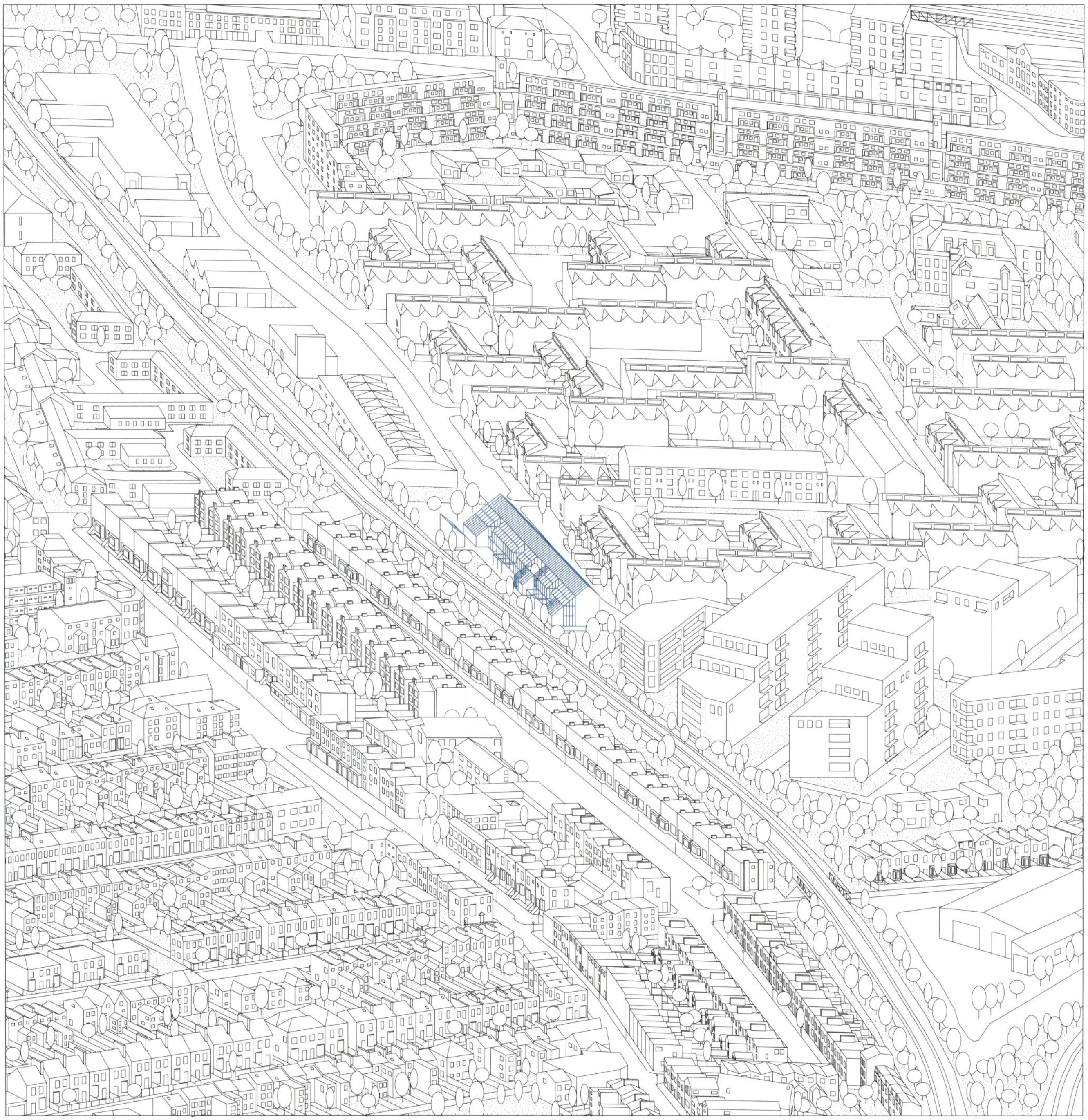

Brixton, London

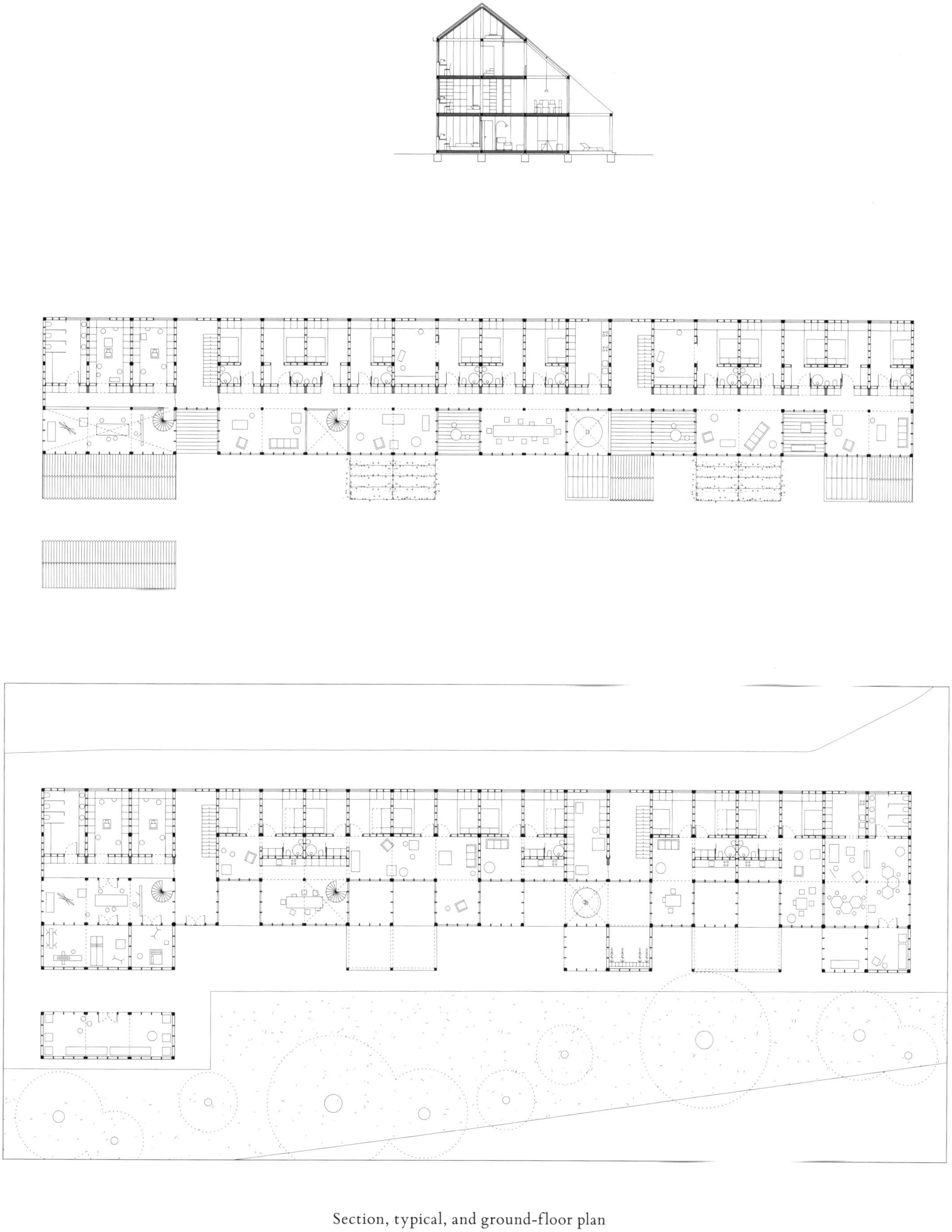

Section, typical, and ground-floor plan

10 m

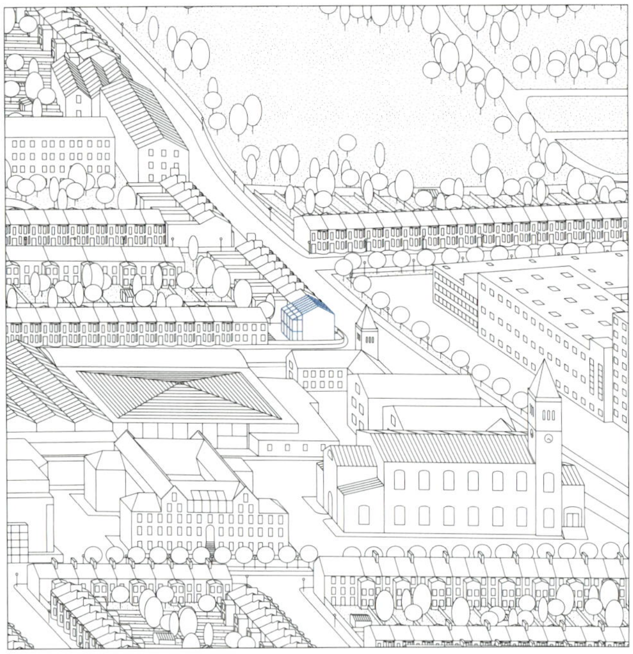

Newham, London

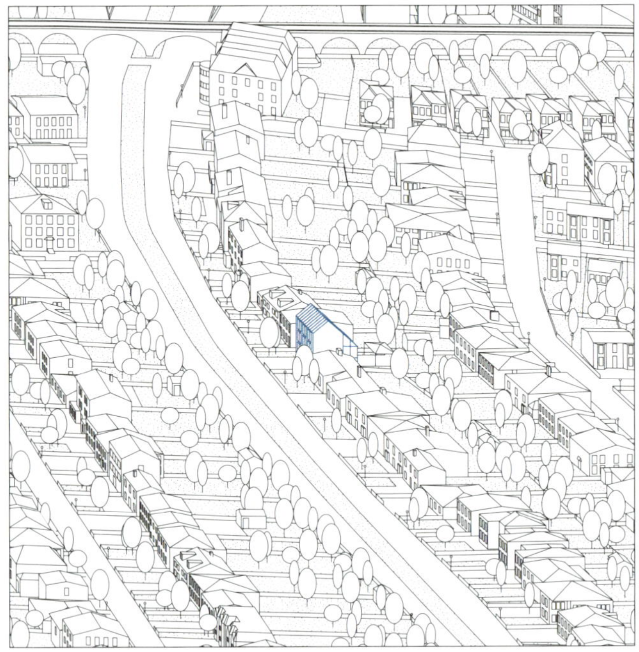

Barnet, London

Croydon, London

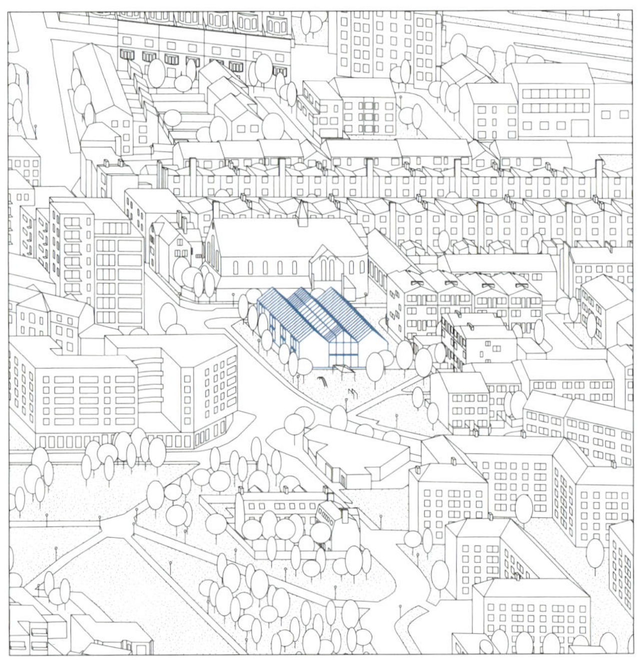

Southwark, London

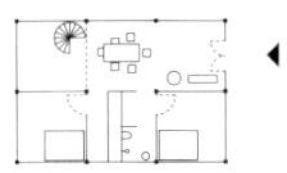

Newham, London

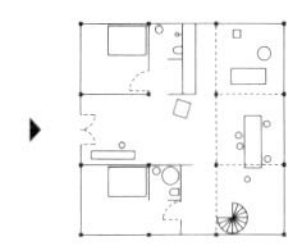

Barnet, London

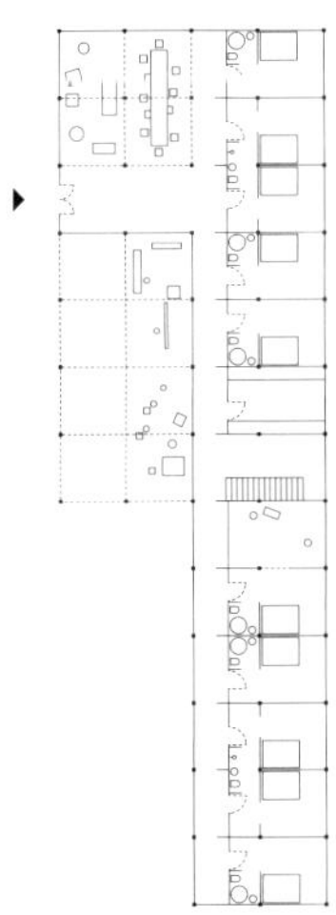

Croydon, London

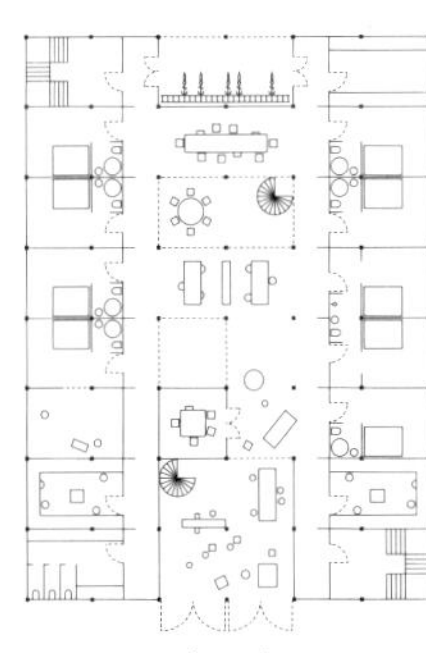

Southwark, London

Ground-floor plans

10 m

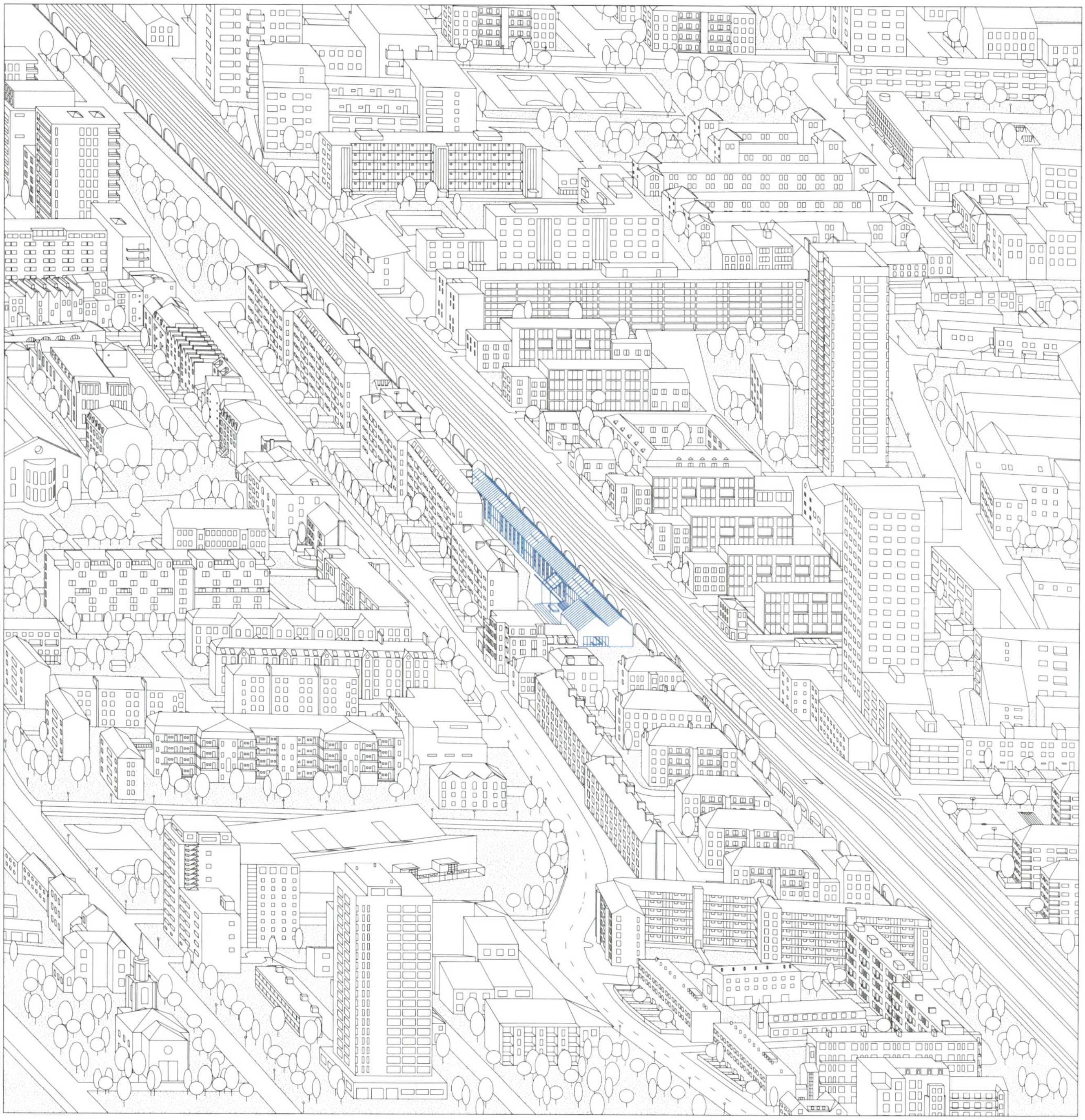

Shadwell, London

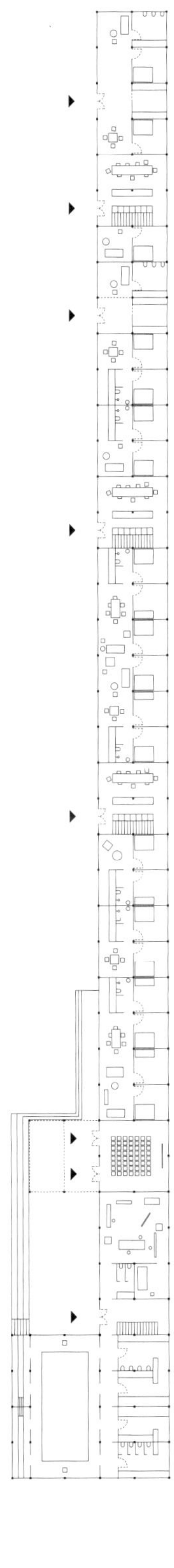

Ground-floor plan

10 m

260

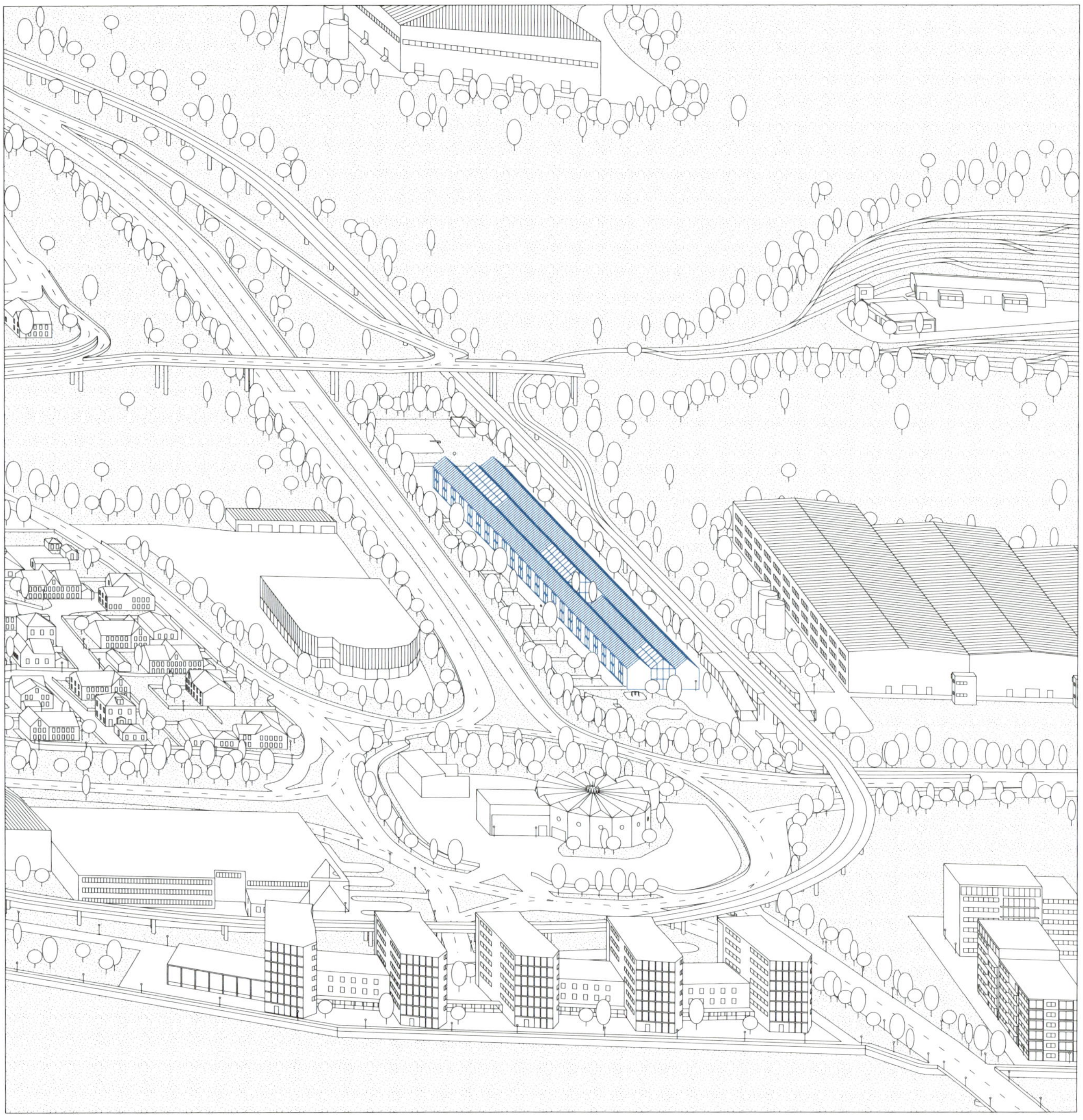

Newham, London

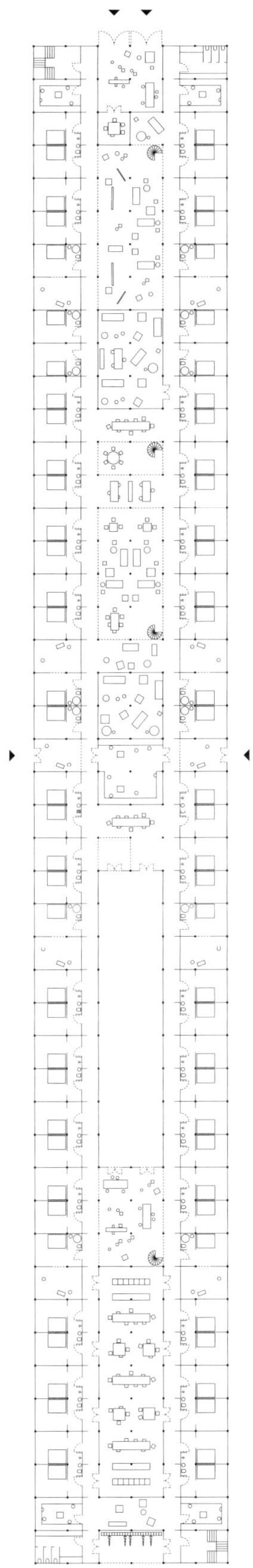

Ground-floor plan

10 m

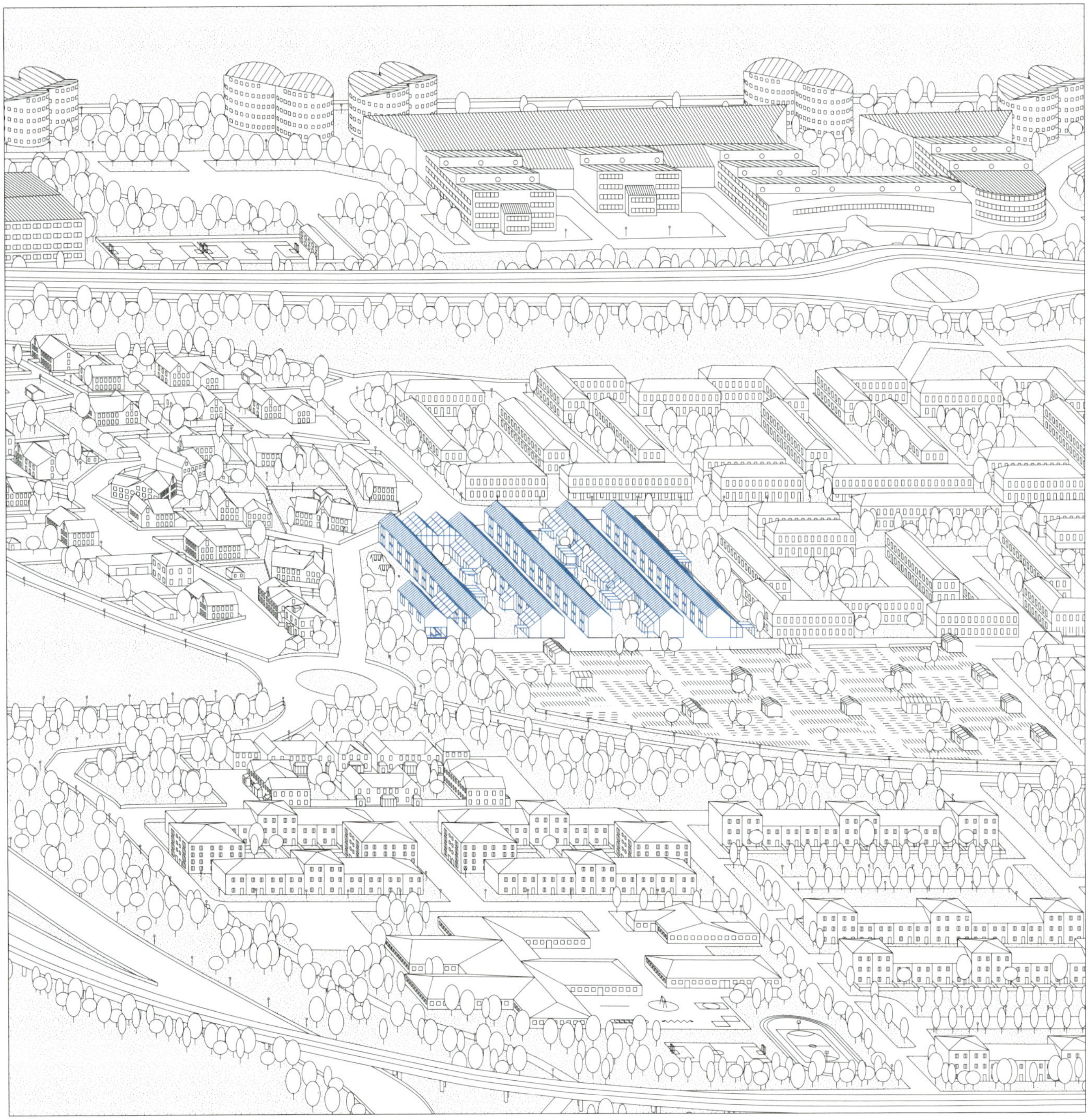

Newham, London

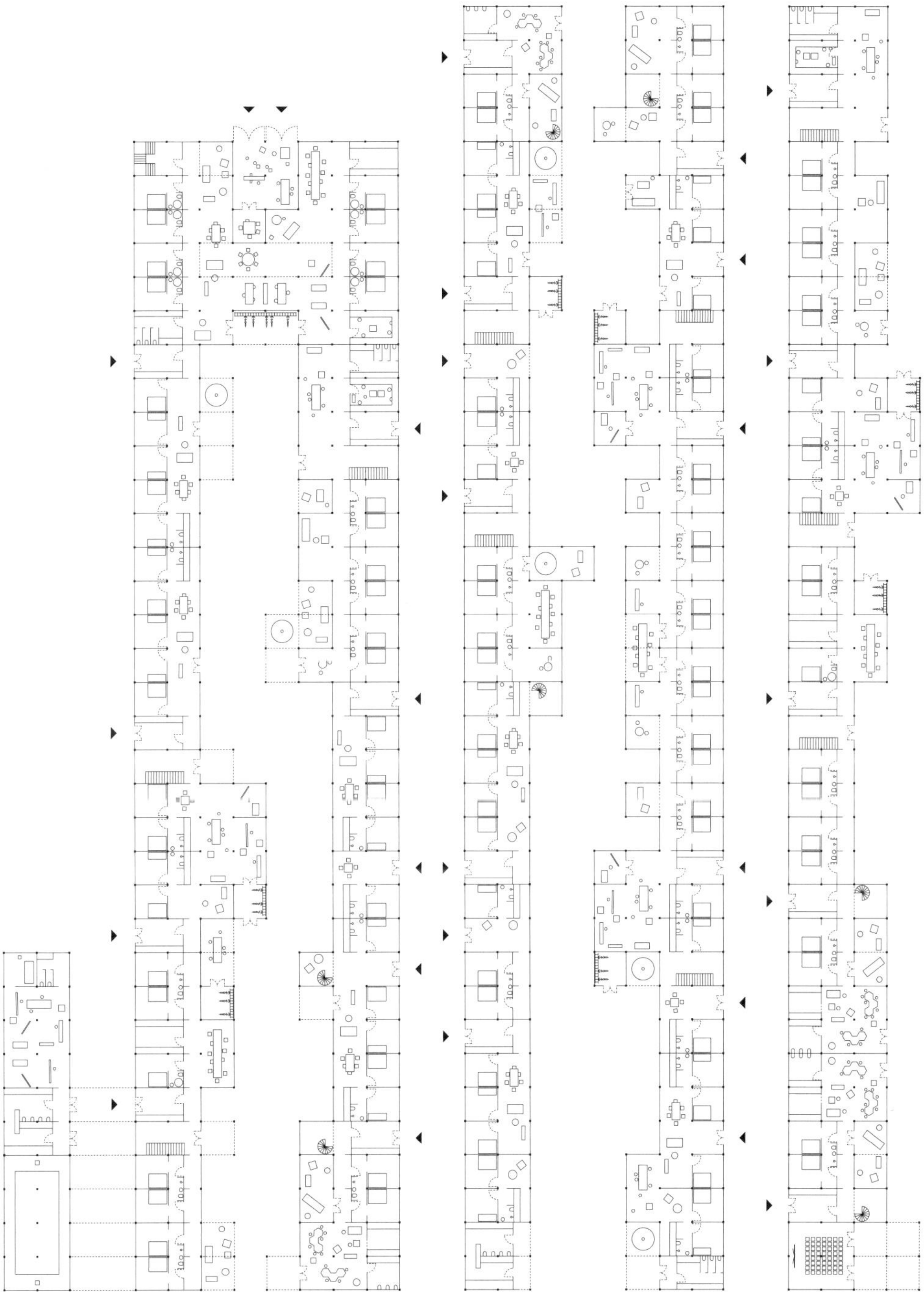

Ground-floor plan

10 m

266

THE OPPOSITE SHORE (2021)

Suburbs are arguably among the most controversial legacies of the twentieth century. They embodied a way of life driven by the pastoral dream to live away from the city. Yet the bottom line of the suburbs was the idea of private property as the fundamental social datum of liberal democracy. Suburbs in Europe are today in decline as both a social and an environmental construct. Yet the suburbs are there and will be there for a long time to come. Taking this decline as an opportunity, *The Opposite Shore* suggests the gradual yet radical structural transformation of suburbs, involving the remaking of both their settlement form and their social contract toward a cooperative way of living. This transformation includes retrofitting of existing houses, even distribution of public facilities, reduction of impermeable surfaces such as redundant roads and parking, demolition and then reconstruction of new typologies that can accommodate living and working spaces in close proximity with each other, and the transformation of private properties such as individual gardens into collective open spaces.

Our proposal focuses on the territory of the valley of the river Dender (Belgium) that runs in a north-south direction a few kilometers west of Brussels. This territory, characterized by economic stagnation and diffuse urbanization, allows a critical look back at the historical formation of the suburbs as a political project and economic policy. The proposal is based on the idea that a desirable and sustainable way of living together would be based on a new social contract that supports decommodified forms of land tenure, cooperation, and care. We believe that such a social contract would lead to a radical transformation of both housing typologies and settlements forms. Because of their low density, the suburbs can make room for building more homes for those in need, and retrofitting of existing ones to accommodate a generous share of communal facilities. In this way, the necessary transformation of suburban settlements becomes an opportunity to radically rethink them as laboratories for new forms of cooperation, care, and civic solidarity.

Following the careful analysis of this suburban territory, three different settlement types have been selected as case studies: the "block," the "garden city," and the "meandering block." The block is a recurring settlement resulting from the incremental construction along its edges of row houses. The inner open space at the center of the block, beside the strip of private gardens at the back of each house, often contains a few remaining agricultural fields, often of considerable dimensions. Our strategy concerns the subdivision into smaller units of the existing row houses and the gradual filling in of all available vacancies along the edges of the block; at the back, we imagine the start of a gradual process of "commoning" of the gardens through the removal of all those fences that strongly characterized this open space. In this way, households get the opportunity to jointly develop a new building at the back of their gardens, with shared facilities and extra living spaces. With more units participating in the transformation, the new inner building becomes the frame of a large collective garden inside the block.

The garden city, unlike the block, is the result of a coherent urban project. This character is reflected by the architecture of the houses, which are generally similar to each other in terms of type, materials, and style. As in the block, our strategy concerns the retrofitting of the existing houses through their internal subdivision so that each house can host multiple households. Proposed interventions concern the transformation of the ground floor by adding verandas on the front or side of each house—in the space today generally used for parking—and the retrofitting of existing garages as a series of additional rooms that can be used for both living and working. At the back of the houses, the strategy comprises the gradual demolition of the garden fences and the construction across the common garden of a "longhouse," a linear shed that contains shared facilities that can be used by all inhabitants of the block such as laundries, workshops, collective kitchens, and meeting rooms.

The meandering block is a large settlement found in the outskirts of Aalst, one of the main urban centers in the Dender valley. Unlike the previous settlement types, the meandering block is not immediately legible, since it is geometrically more articulated and of overall larger dimensions. Although seen from the street this settlement is characterized by the typical landscape of row houses, seen from the top it reveals the presence of large open spaces. Our strategy concerns the possibility of densification through the construction of new buildings placed perpendicular to the existing streets/row houses and penetrating deep into the block, thus taking advantage of the open space at its center. These fields are transformed into common gardens to be used by the entire community. The new building contains facilities and services at the ground level, while it can host both living and working spaces at the upper levels.

This project of densification and commoning is based on the principle of indivisibility of land as put forward by the urbanist Hans Bernoulli in his seminal pamphlet *Die Stadt und ihr Boden* (1946). Bernoulli argued that the only way to rationally plan the city for the people's benefit was to prevent the individual property of land. He advocated that communities should never sell land and instead should buy it whenever possible. Moreover, he argues that once a community is able to own indivisible land it should grant rights of use to individuals on the basis of their compatibility to the common good. Following these principles, our proposal is based on the possibility for settlement-scale communities to manage land collectively so that new affordable housing can be built while revenue from the selling or renting of housing units is directly invested in the building and maintenance of collective facilities. This project of retrofitting which includes both demolition and reconstruction of large quantities of housing is regulated by the public sector through specific guidelines applicable to the entire Dender Valley.

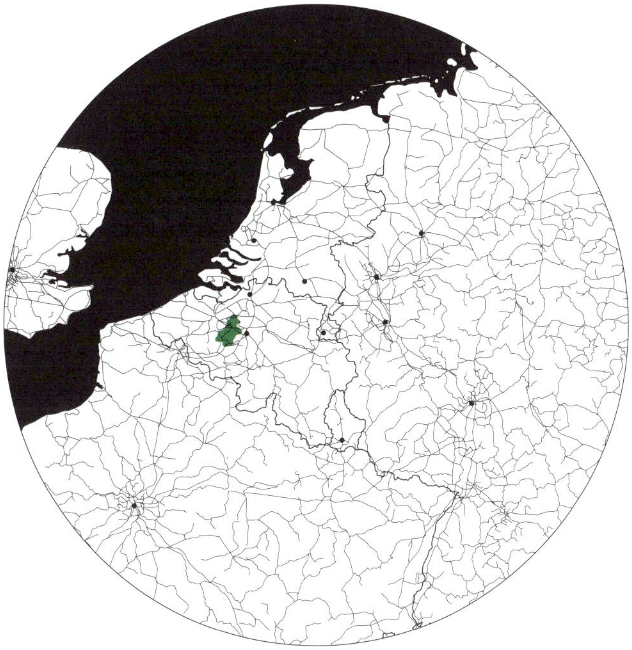

North Western Metropolitan Area

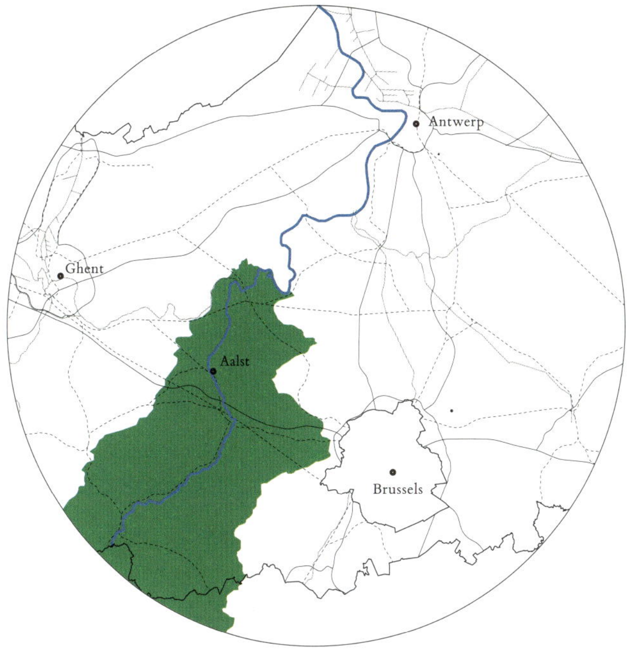

Dender valley

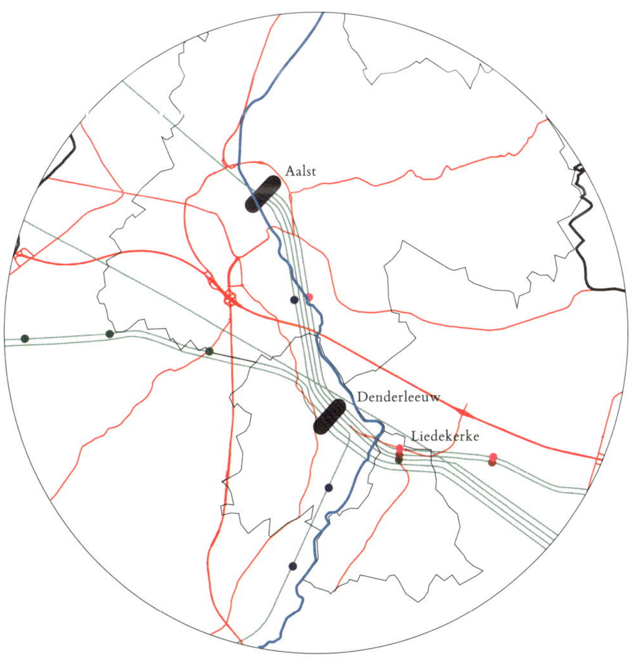

Transport network
railway line (green)
motorway (red)

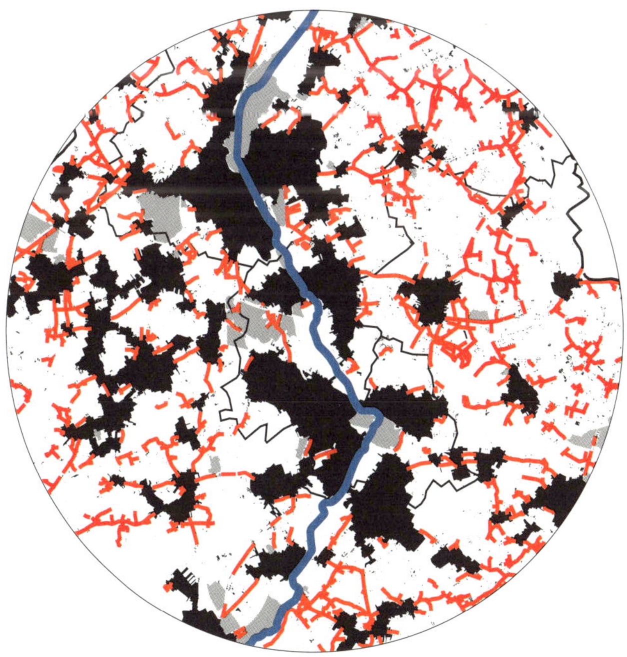

Built fabric
dense settlement (black)
ribbon development (red)

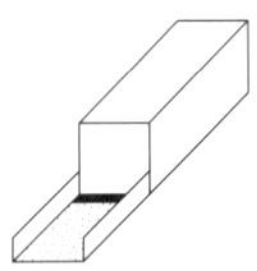

Under-occupied building

60% built surfacc
60% sealed surface

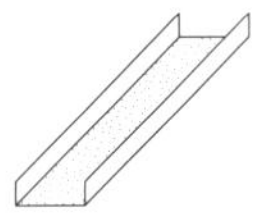

Green permeable area

0% built surfacc
0% sealed surface

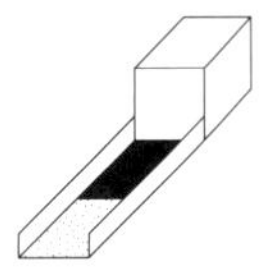

Built-up area with unnecessary sealed surface

30 % built surfacc
60% sealed surface

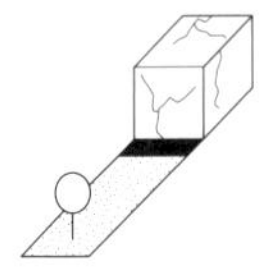

Derelict/abandoned building

30 % built surfacc
30% sealed surface

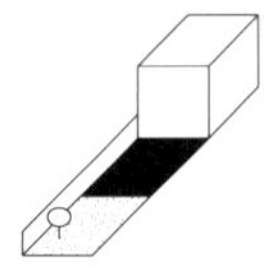

Built-up area with unnecessary sealed surface

30 % built surfacc
60% sealed surface

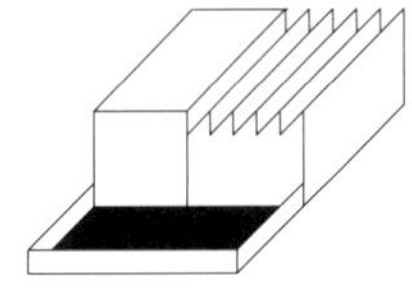

Ex industrial plant

60 % built surface
100% sealed surface

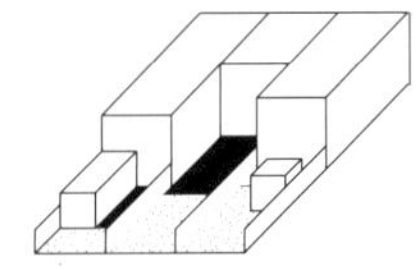

Individual properties with unnecessary paved surfaces and additional buildings

55 % built surface
70% sealed surface

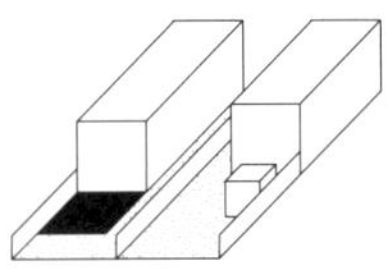

Individual properties with unnecessary paved surfaces and additional buildings

40 % built surface
70% sealed surface

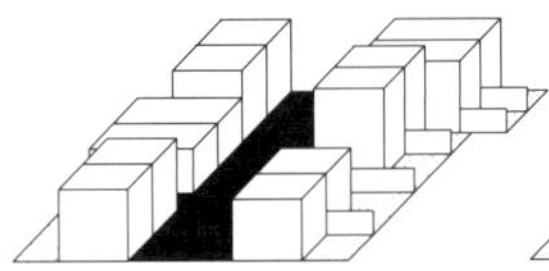

Individual properties along secondary roads–ribbon settlements

40 % built surface
70% sealed surface

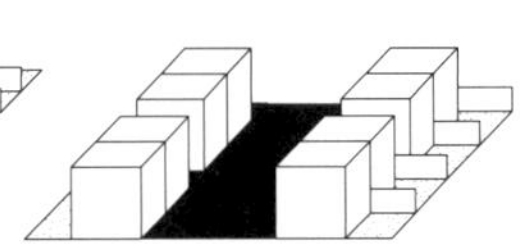

Settlements with over-dimensioned roads paved with asphalt

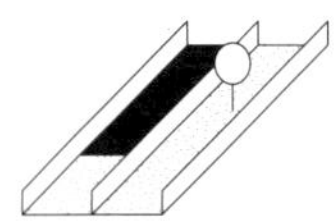

Unnecessary sealed area in a rural context

0% built surface
60% sealed surface

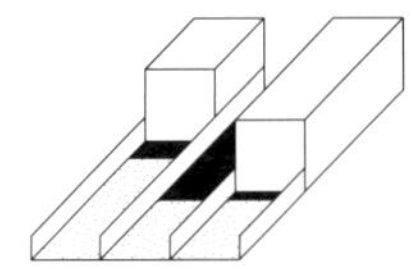

Unnecessary sealed area in an urban context

0% built surface
60% sealed surface

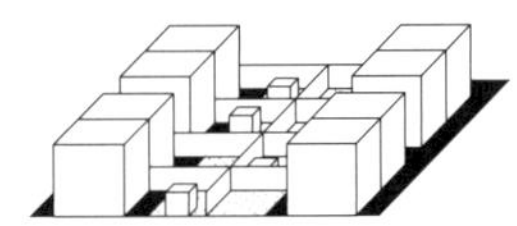

Single-family houses with individual private gardens

50% built surface
80 % sealed surface

Analysis of current condition

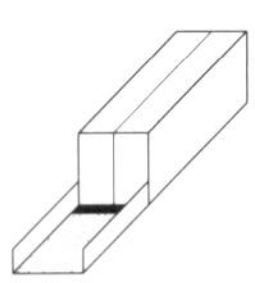

Densification of under-occupied houses

60% built surface
60% sealed surface

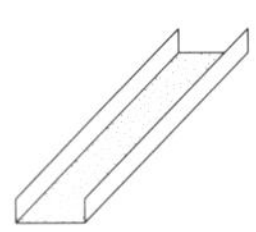

Prenventing the conversion of green areas

0% built surface
0% sealed surface

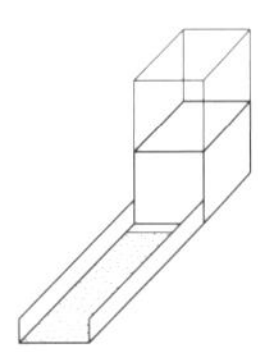

Densification of already built-up areas + removal of unnecessary sealed surfaces

30% built surface x2
30 % sealed surface

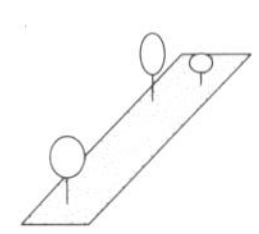

Removing derelict buildings and restoring the soil

0% built surface
0% sealed surface

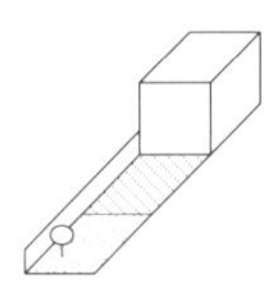

Replacement of unnecessary sealed surfaces with permeable materials

30% built surface
30 % sealed surface

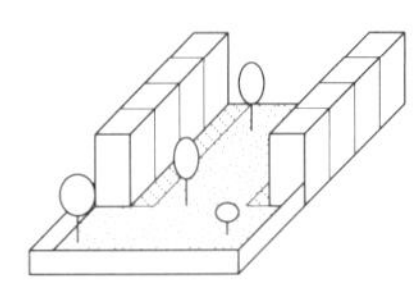

Re-using brownfield areas for new developments

30% built surface
30 % ssealed surface

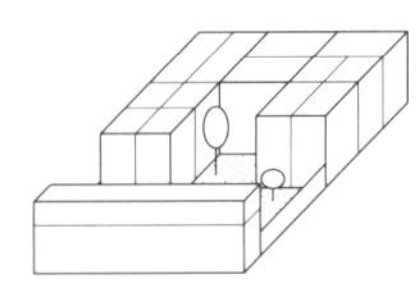

Densification of the existing dwellings + creation of new collective houses

55% built surface
50 % sealed surface

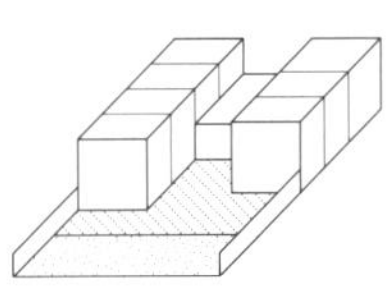

Densification of the existing dwellings through the addition of domestic spaces

50% built surface
50 % sealed surface

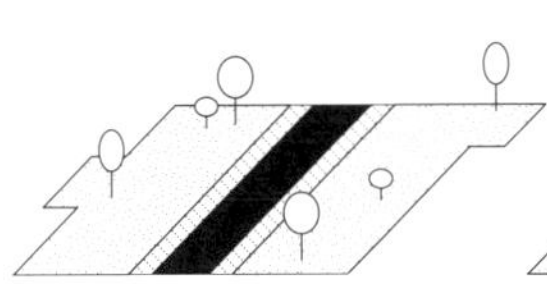

Demolition of ribbon settlemens

50% built surface
50 % sealed surface

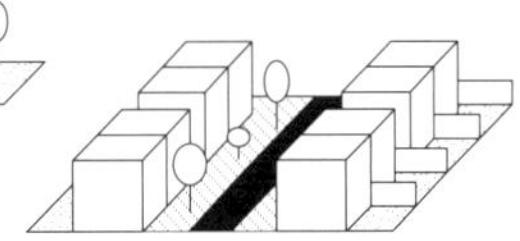

Replacement of traditional asphalt with permeable materials and reduction of the roads' footprint

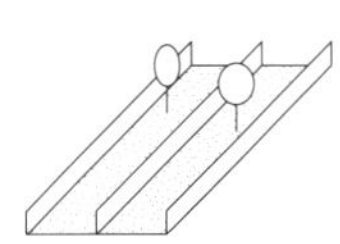

Conversion of the sealed area into green field through soil recovery

0% built surface
0% sealed surface

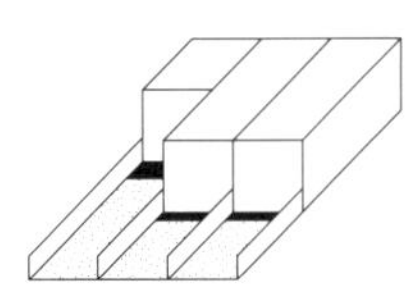

Exploitation of already sealed surface and densification through infill

60% built surface
60% sealed surface

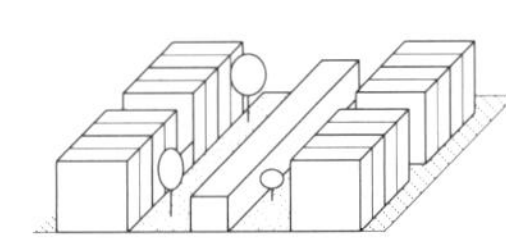

Elimination of property limits and densification through the creation of communal spaces outside the houses

50% built surface
50% sealed surface

Retrofitting strategy

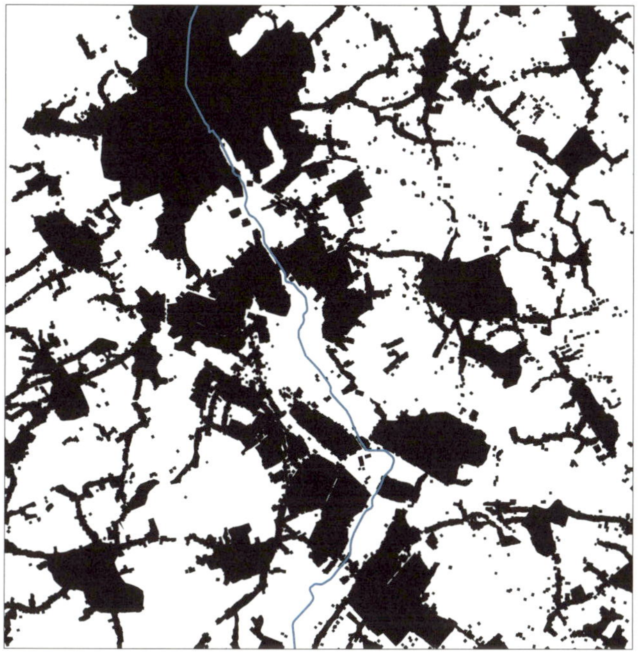

2020

2040

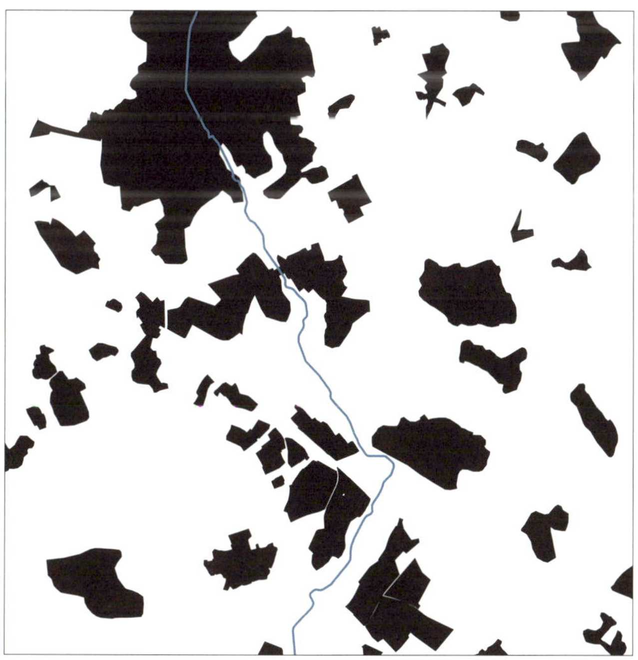

2060

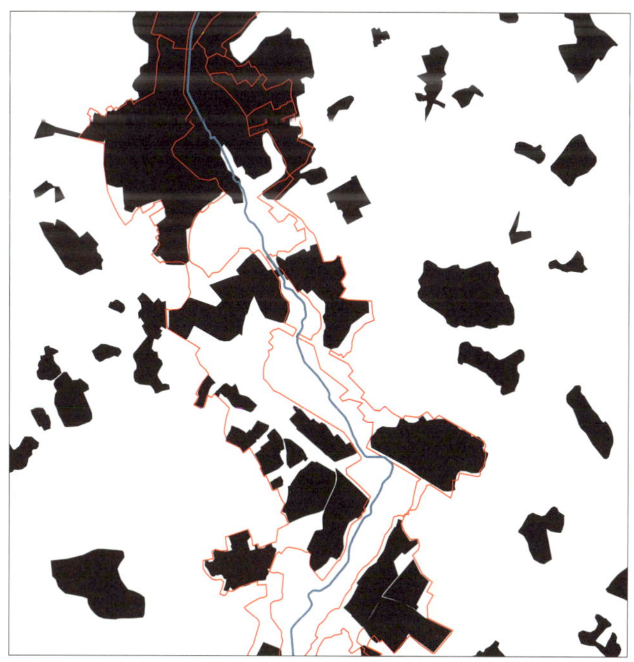

New pedestrian paths

2 km

Phasing of shrinking, 2020–2060

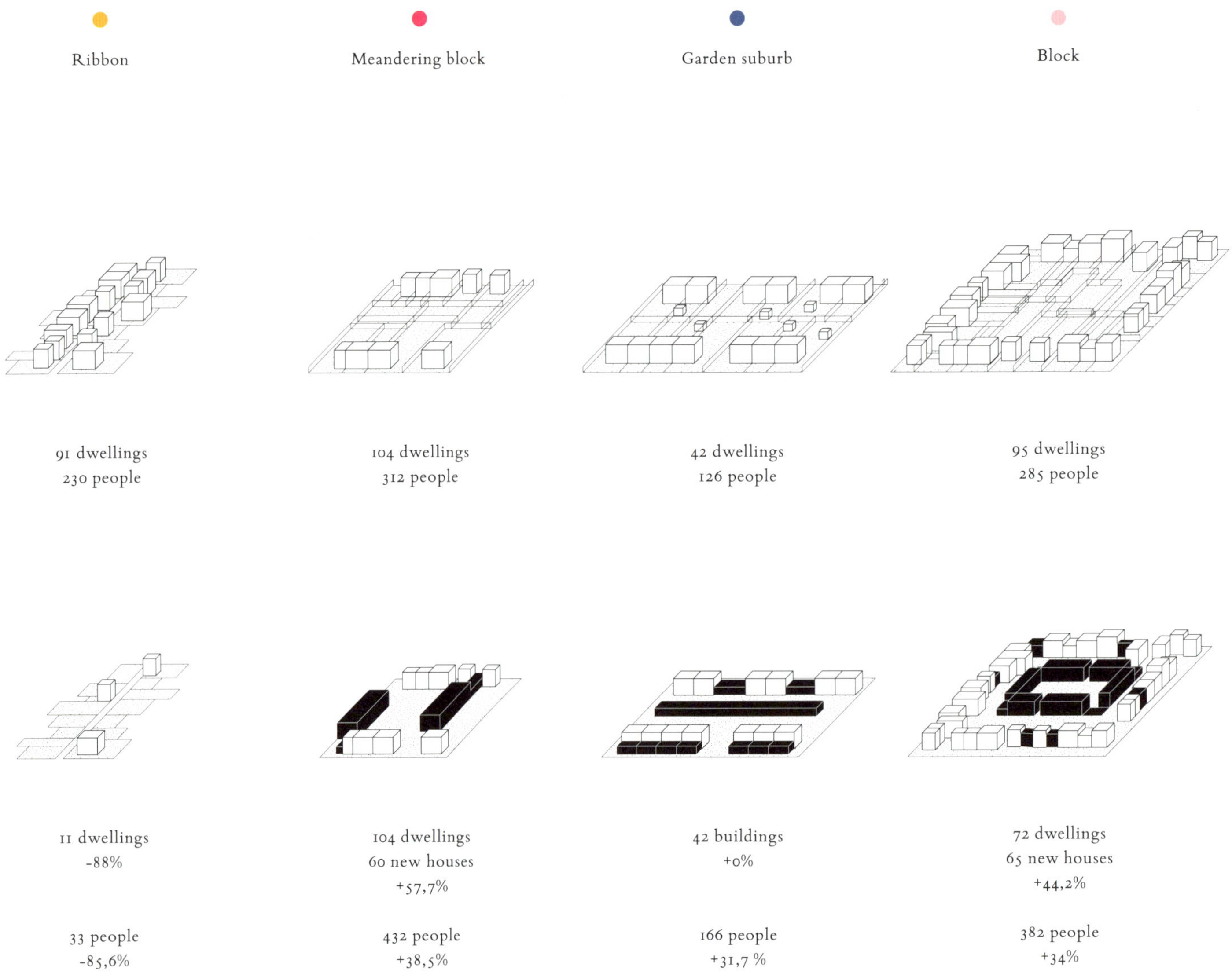

Settlement, analysis of current condition (above) and retrofitting strategy (below)

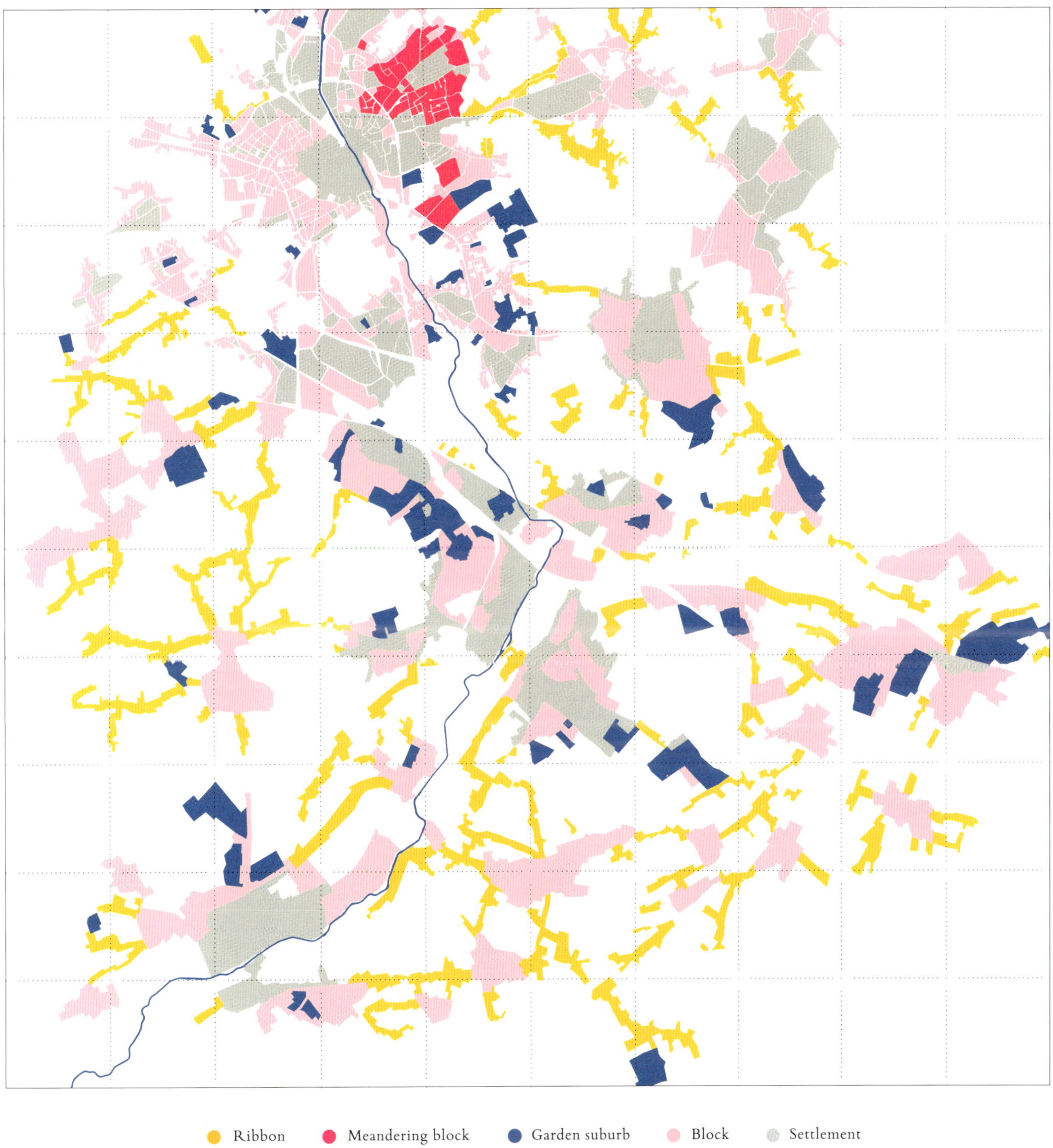

Settlement types

274

Retrofitting of block settlements

By "commoning" their plots, households get the opportunity to jointly develop a new living and working building at the back of their gardens, where shared facilities and extra living spaces can be accommodated. Following this initial step, existing houses along the block's perimeter road are subdivided into smaller units. With more units participating in the transformation, the new inner building becomes the frame of a collective garden inside the block.

Phasing of block retrofitting

10 m

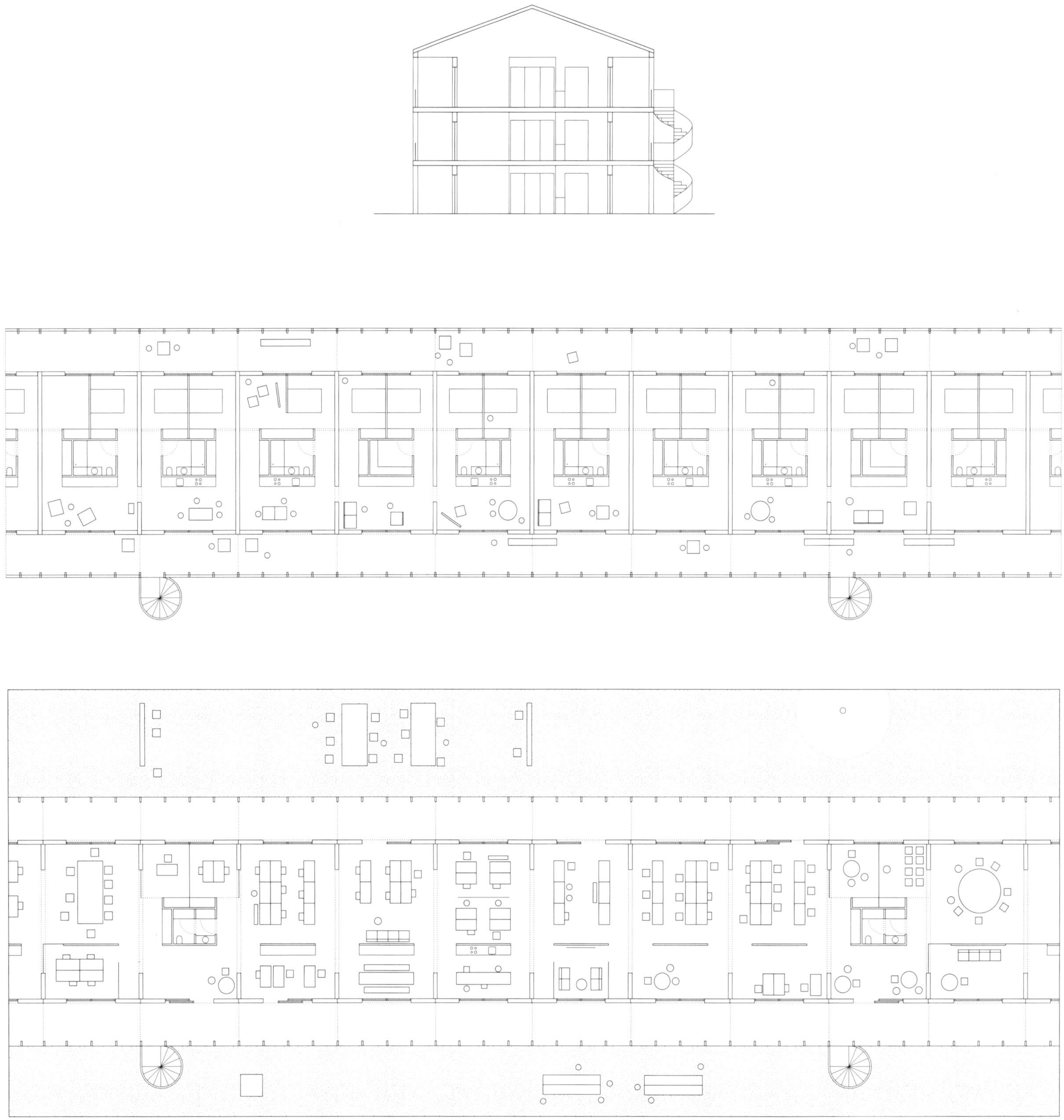

Section, typical floor plan, and ground-floor plan of the new living and working building. The basic apartment accommodates two or three inhabitants, but it can expand depending on the needs of the household, either by opening an interior door or through the veranda. The ground floor is divided into a larger bay devoted to workspace, and a narrower bay that includes shared domestic facilities.

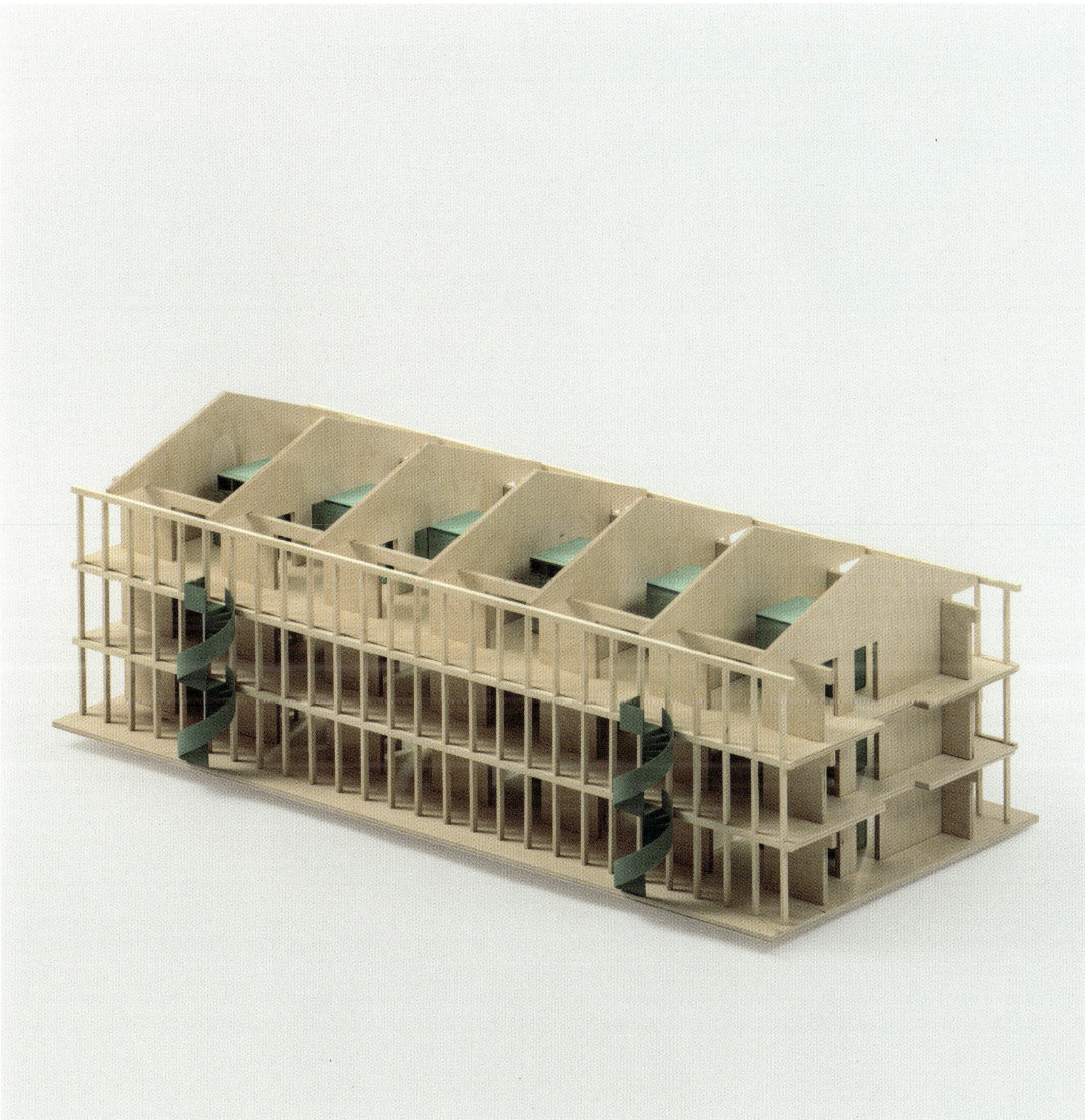

282

Retrofitting of a garden suburb settlement

283

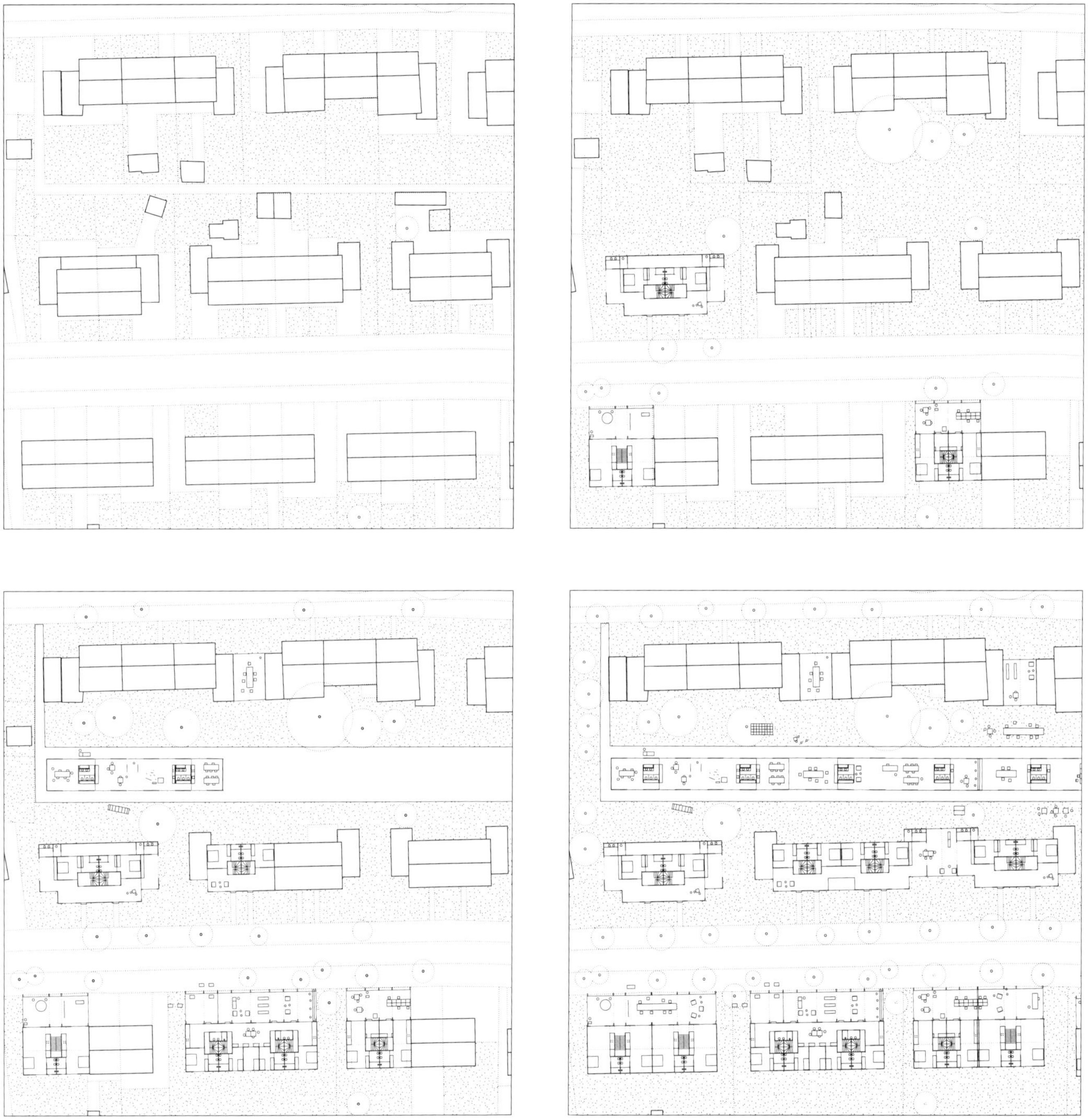

Phasing of the retrofitting of a garden suburb in Denderleeuw. The strategy comprises the gradual demolition of the garden fences and the construction of a longhouse where shared facilities are contained. In the meantime, existing houses are subdivided into smaller units and retrofitted through the transformation of their ground floor with the addition of verandas for both living and working.

Phasing of garden suburb retrofitting

10 m

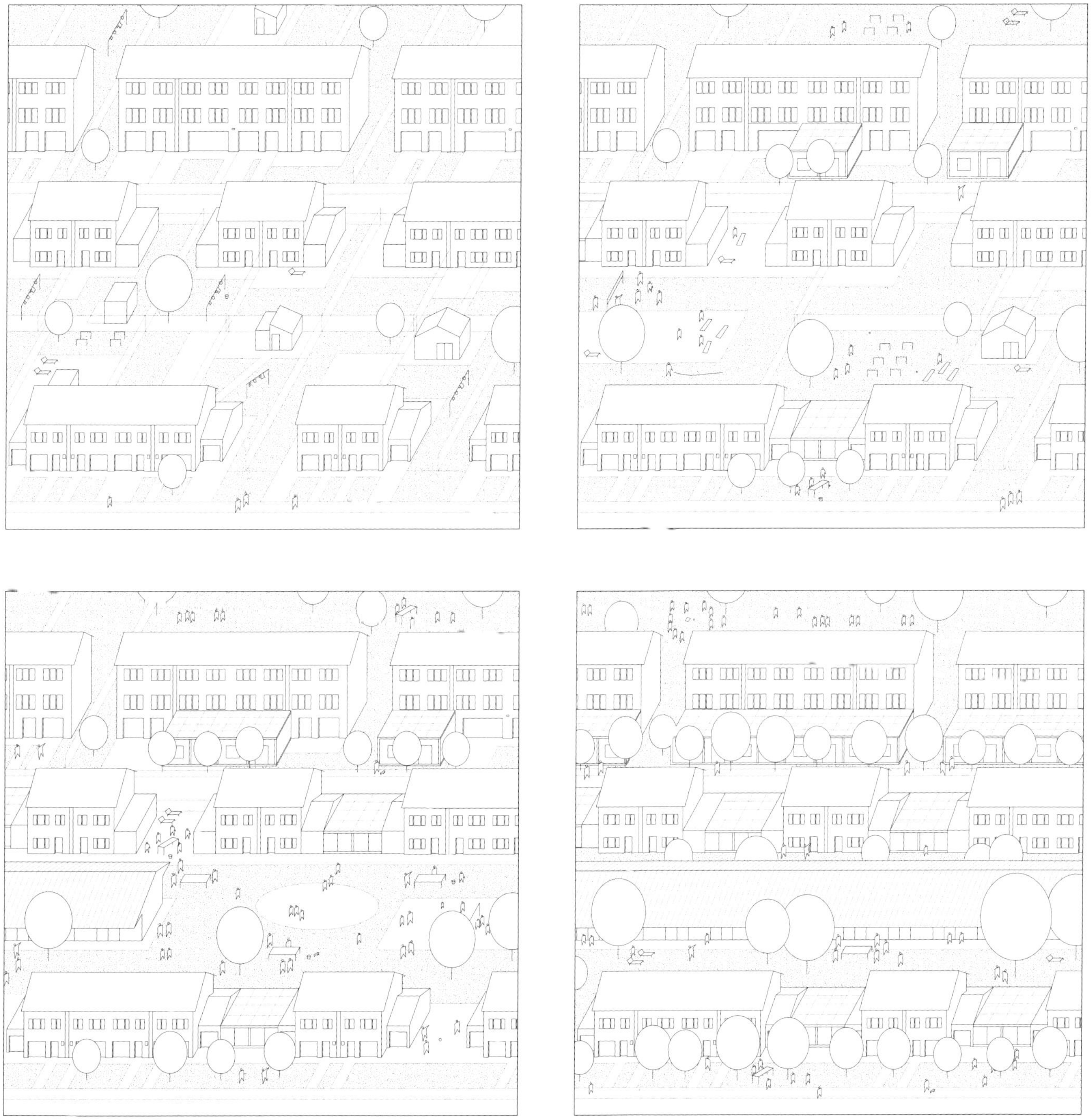

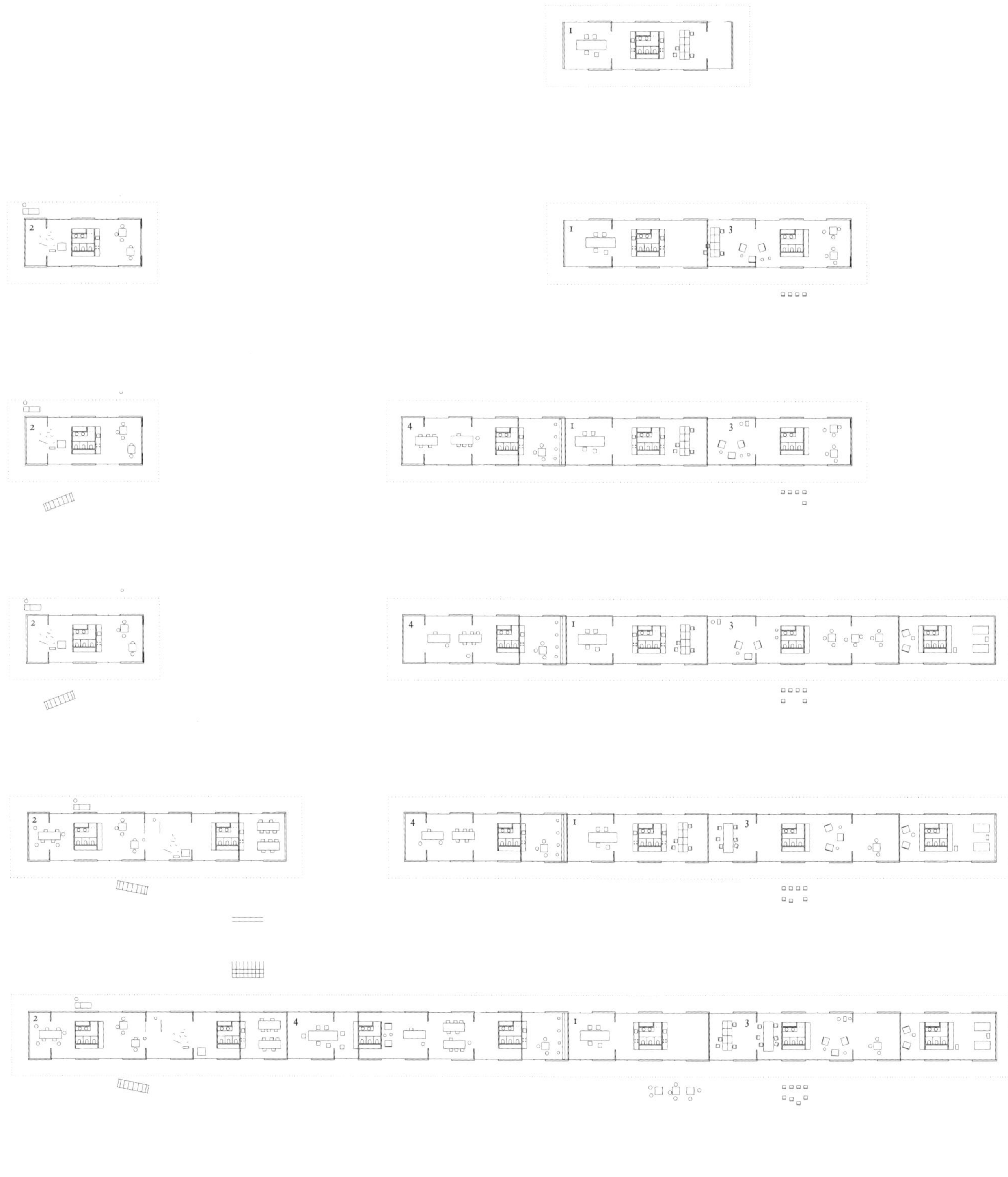

Plan of incremental longhouse

(1) communal kitchen, (2) child care, (3) workspace, (4) elderly care

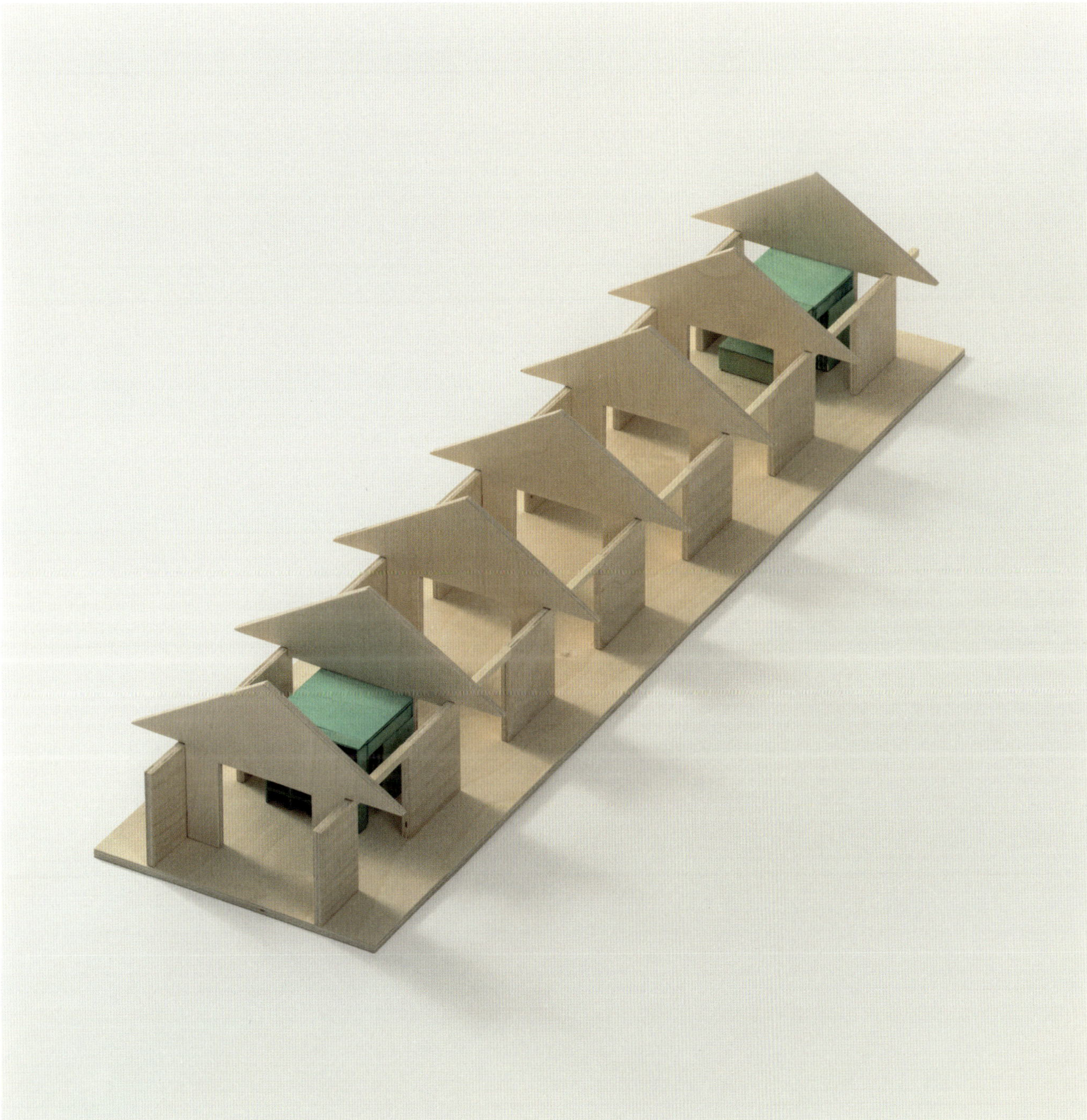

Existing condition

Demolition of vertical circulation core and paved surfaces

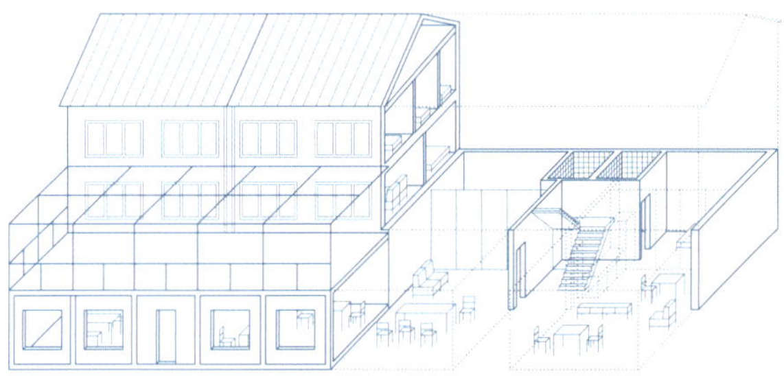

Construction of front veranda and new vertical circulation

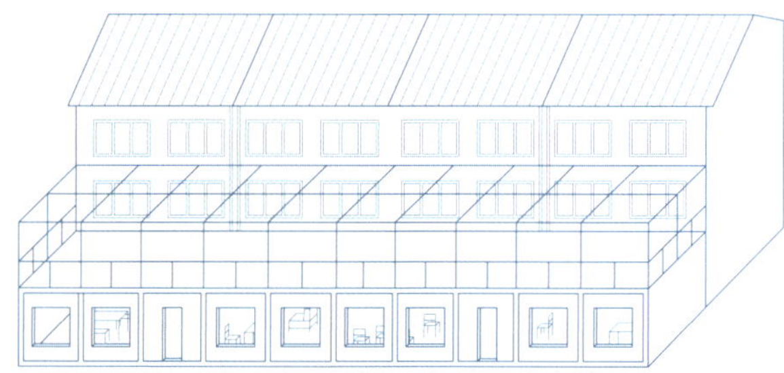

Final stage of construction

Retrofitting strategies with front veranda

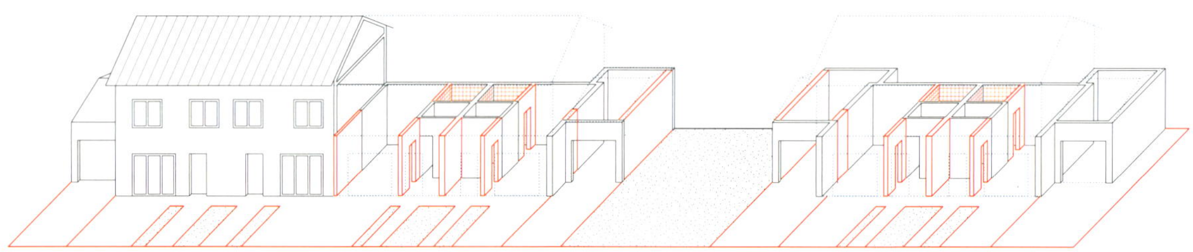

Demolition of internal partitions and paved surfaces at ground level

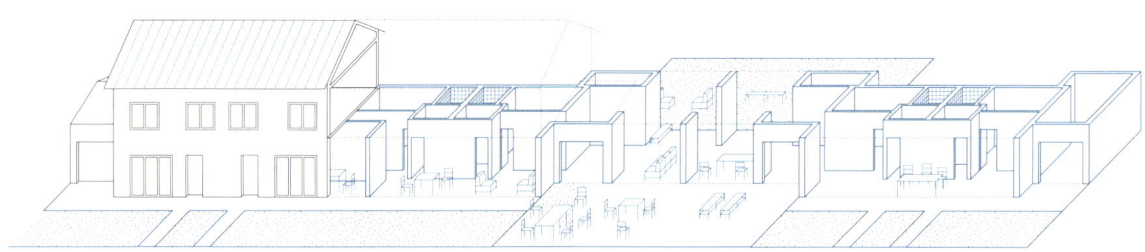

Construction of lateral veranda and internal partitions at ground level

Final stage of construction

Retrofitting strategies with lateral veranda in between garages

Second floor

First floor

Ground floor

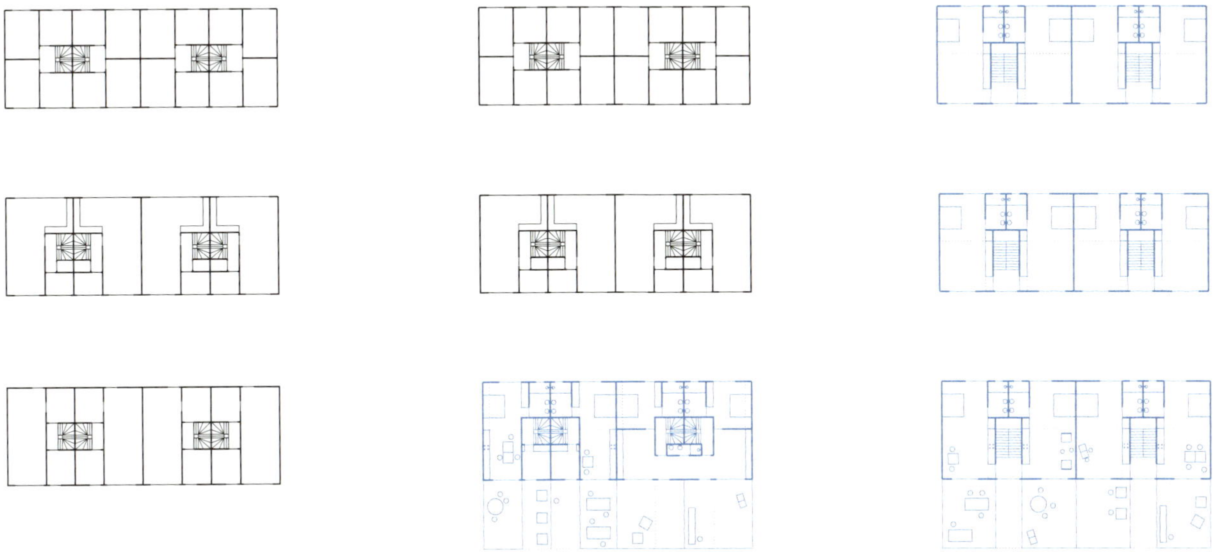

Existing condition with four independents units

Retrofitting of the ground floor with two studios and one two-bedrooms unit, and four independent units on the upper floors

Retrofitting of the entire building with 12 studios

Second floor

First floor

Ground floor

Retrofitting of the entire building with four one-bedroom units and two large communal units

Retrofitting of the entire building into a large communal unit (21 bedrooms)

Retrofitting of the entire building into a large communal unit (23 bedrooms)

First floor

Ground floor

Existing condition

Retrofitting of the entire building into one large communal unit (18 bedrooms)

290

292

Retrofitting of a meandering block settlement

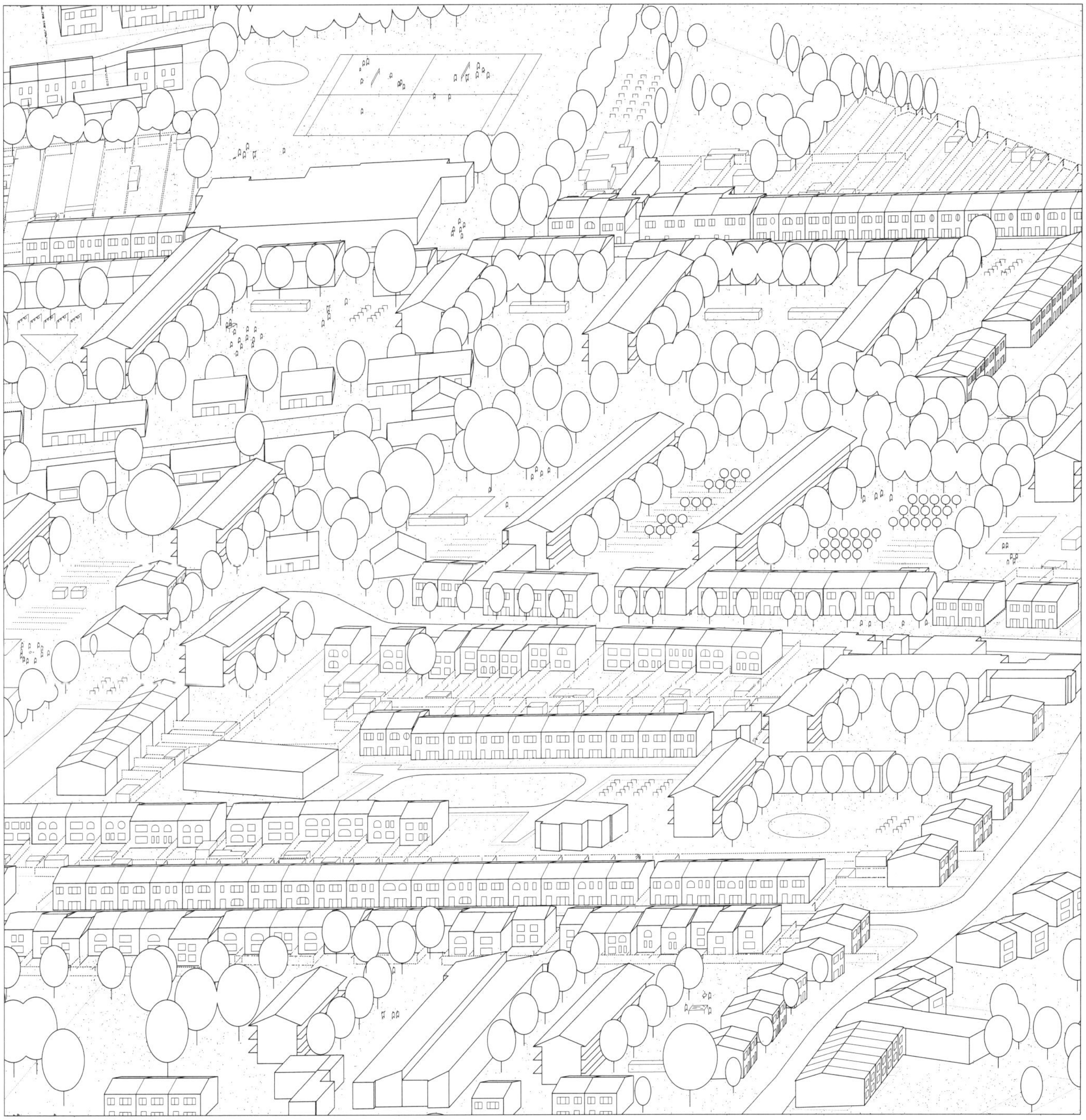

The strategy is based on the demolition of the garden fences and the gradual construction of new linear living and working buildings, perpendicular to existing row houses and located on empty plots in the inner part of the settlement.

Phasing of the retrofitting of a meandering block

10 m

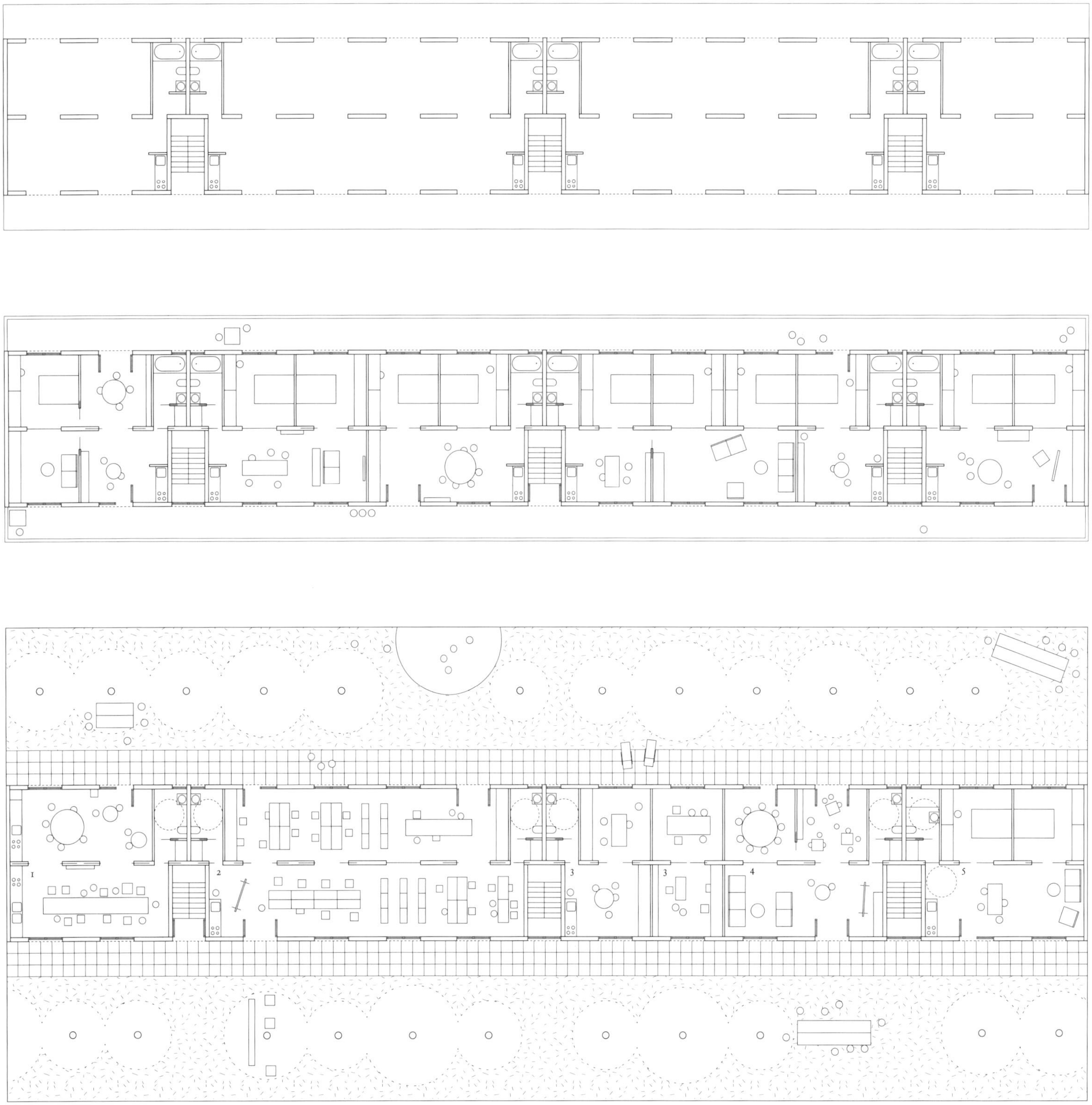

Structural, typical, and ground-floor plan of the new living and working building. In the apartments on the upper levels, kitchens are kept small since the units rely on the communal kitchen on the ground floor.

(1) ground floor hosting large communal kitchen, (2) open workshop, (3) meeting room,
(4) child and elderly care facility, (5) apartments for persons with reduced mobility

5 m

Technical section: the structure is made of identical CLT panels

LONGHOUSE (2021)

This project proposes a prototype for municipal workshops to be built in the extreme periphery of Rome, a territory also known as the *agro romano*. It envisions workshops built by the municipality and run by associations of local inhabitants as community centers. Besides hosting social and care facilities, municipal workshops offer workplaces to the nearby community. Municipal workshops are thus a response to the urgent need for spaces for "near-working," that is, working remotely but not from home.

The prototype is tested in the settlements of Rome's Municipio XI, an area that includes a large number of suburban settlements, most of them built illegally in the last forty years. These are the so-called "O Zones": a bureaucratic term that identifies illegal settlements that were legalized after the fact with the payment of a fine. It was precisely the practice of after-the-fact regularization that encouraged landowners and settlers to build without formal permits. Such settlements are referred to as *toponimi* (literally "place names"): illegal settlements awaiting official recognition—and an official name—from the municipality. Once these settlements are legalized, the municipality provides them with only a bare minimum of infrastructure such as roads and basic services. Today, the *agro romano*, especially in its eastern portions corresponding to the Ager Tusculanus, can be considered an archipelago of settlements deprived of any form of social welfare. These settlements are the bare embodiment of the logic of private property as the only "right" left to people, after the state and the city refuse to guarantee any other form of social protection or welfare. The project's municipal workshops represent the attempt to provide these settlements with a noncommercial social space that supports both productive and reproductive activities by combining them into one civic structure.

The daily life imposed by the lockdown during the coronavirus pandemic has made the need for nearby workplaces even more urgent, as many people were left with the only option of improvising their workstations in their homes, which are often unsuitable for combining living and working. Yet the coronavirus emergency has made evident a long-standing problem of many contemporary cities, which is a chronic crisis of care. This crisis is motivated by decades of privatization of public assets and economic austerity that resulted in budget cuts for everything that concerns the welfare of citizens. The ubiquity of freelance work has worsened this situation, leaving many people without any possibility of social security. Many workers are not only deprived of a proper workplace but also and especially of those social links and rights that came from collective workplaces, such as mutual support and unions. This condition has produced not only work precarity but also domestic precarity: young working families, elderly and disabled residents are left to organize their care autonomously, with dire existential (and financial) consequences.

Confronting this situation, a group of researchers, urbanists, and policymakers active in Rome has proposed to build municipal workshops in the Roman suburbs.[1] They propose the municipal workshop as a free-of-charge and safe space with a robust internet connection and reachable by foot or bike from the surrounding houses. Municipal workshops condense into one structure workplaces and care services. In this way, by offering convertible workspace, municipal workshops can act as an active platform for the social and political organizing of freelance workers and all those dependent workers who have been forced or have chosen to work from home. Besides offering space for immaterial and material workers, each municipal workshop offers a suite of spaces dedicated to care activities (child care, elderly case, communal kitchen, medical assistance) and social services (library, meeting hall, info point for work-related issues). Moreover, municipal workshops offer emergency homes for homeless persons or for those who for various reasons cannot live in their home, due for example to domestic violence. By combining workstations and reproductive facilities, the municipal workshop can manifest the interdependence of waged work with all those unwaged or professionalized domestic activities that are the inevitable flip side of what we consider "work."

In terms of buildings, municipal workshops are meant to be distributed across the city as "units" in order to cater to a pool of users that is neither too small nor too big, so that the workshops can be sustained over a long term by an active community of nearby inhabitants. While construction and repairs are the responsibility of the municipality, the daily functioning and maintenance are provided by the residents, who sustain these duties with voluntary work. In this way, municipal workshops counter the public-private partnership model that has dominated many "public" initiatives in the last decades, by introducing a public-commoning alliance between the city administration and associations of residents.

Our proposal formalizes the municipal workshop as a two-story rectilinear structure whose length can be adapted to local conditions. In plan the structure is organized as a two-bay system defined by a long supporting wall in which one bay is left unobstructed and acts as multifunctional space while the other bay is subdivided into rooms which host both workstations and specific programs. This organization is meant to counter the trend of open space, typical of many co-working spaces, offering instead a scenario defined by a gradient of spaces from small to large, from intimate to collective. The form of the municipal workshop is reminiscent of the longhouse, a type of inhabitation that appeared in many parts of the world at different times and whose communal organization upset the traditional coincidence of household and family. As such, municipal workshops are meant to go beyond the public/private dichotomy and become communal domestic spaces that expand domesticity outside the private home as a collective infrastructure of mutual support.

1 See Carmelo Caravella, Piero de Chiara, and Giulio de Petra, "Officine municipali: un luogo per la nuova forma comune del lavoro," in *Ricerca su Roma*, https://www.ricercaroma.it/officine-municipali-un-luogo-per-la-nuova-forma-comune-del-lavoro/.

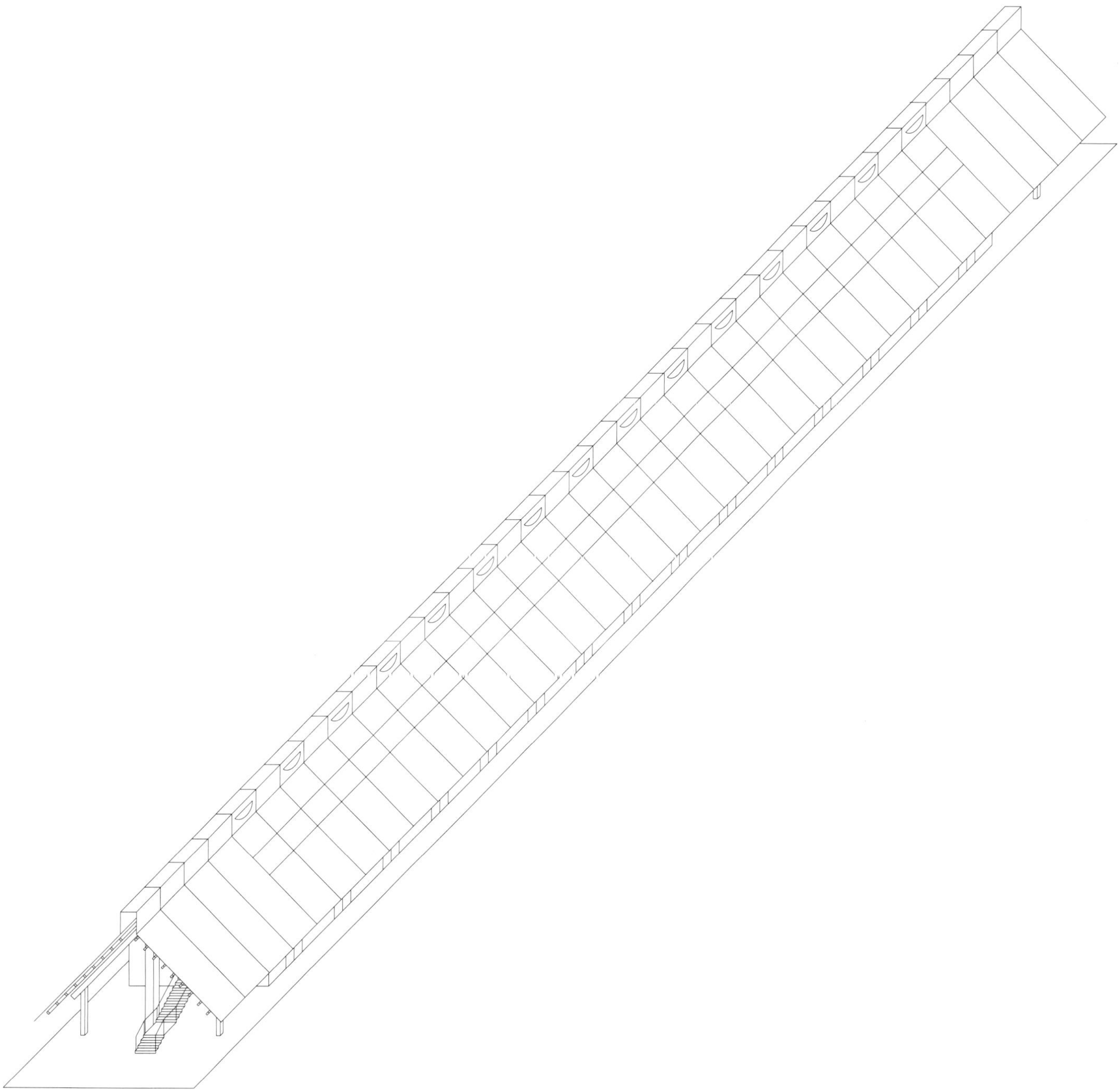

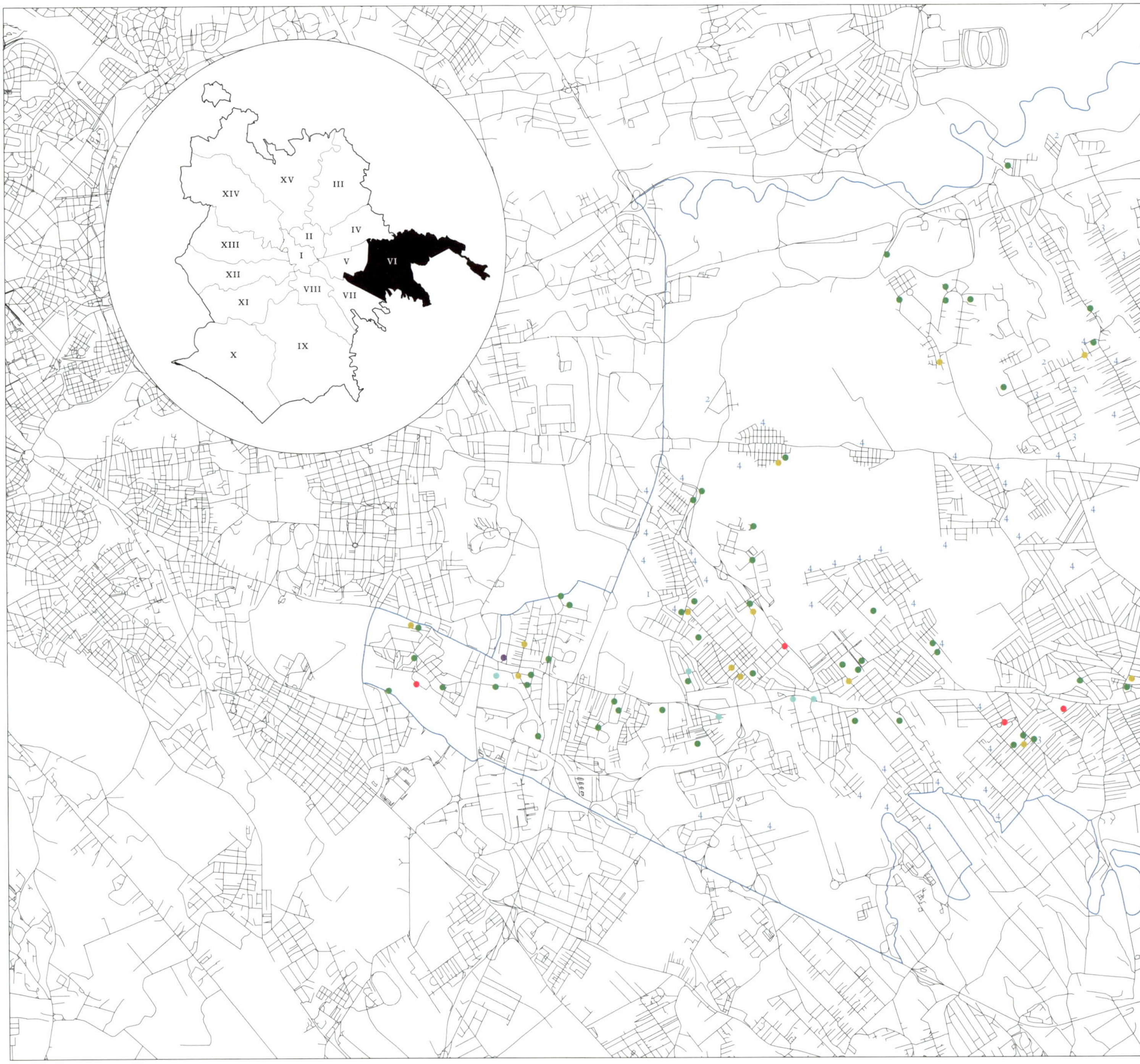

1 Longhouse for 50 users 2 Longhouse for 75 users 3 Longhouse for 100 users 4 Longhouse for 150 users

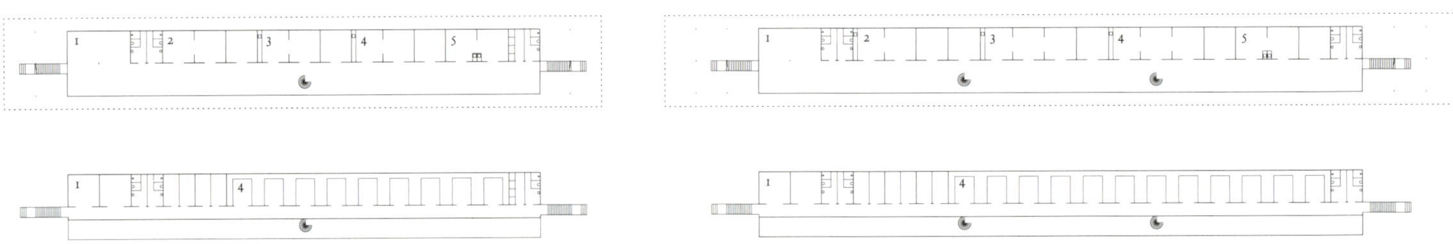

Plans of longhouses for 50, 75, and 150 users

(1) multifunctional space, (2) elderly care, (3) child care, (4) working station, (5) workshop hardware

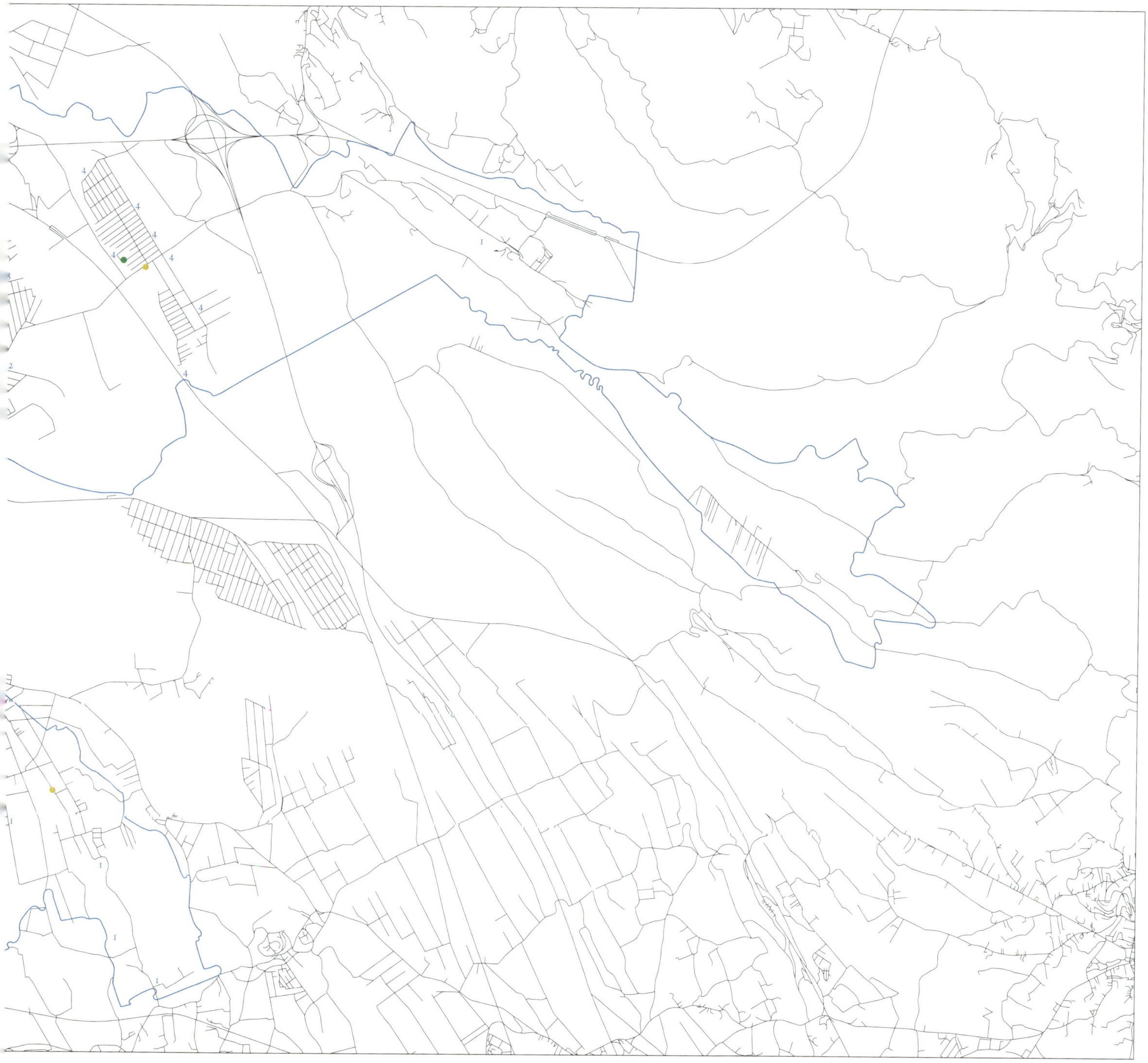

Existing facilities : ● Hospital ● Kindergarten ● Bookshop ● Cultural venue ● Private school ● Primary school

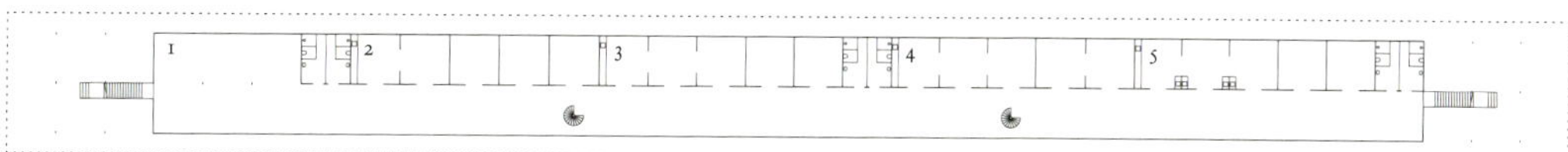

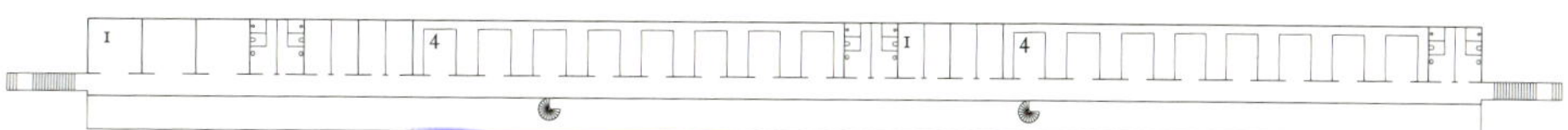

Monfortani

952 inhabitants
0,12 km²
7 933 inh./km²
142 users

Colle della Valentina

341 inhabitants
0,16 km²
2 162 inh./km²
51 users

Fosso dell'Osa

770 inhabitants
0,22 km²
3 886 inh./km²
115 users

Castiglione

234 inhabitants
0,23 km²
1 015 inh./km²
35 users

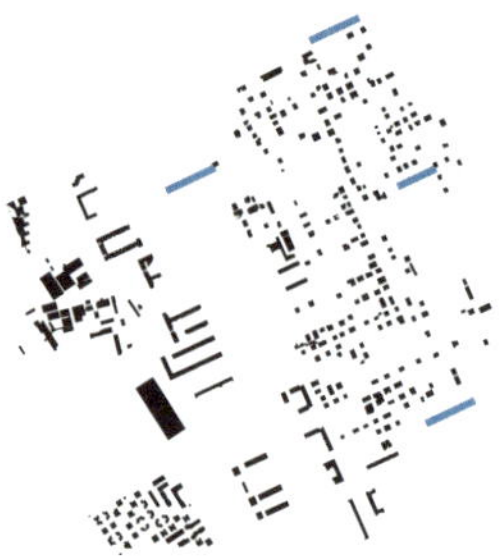

Ponte di Nona

6 332 inhabitants
1,82 km²
3 488 inh./km²
949 users

Prato Fiorito

7 093 inhabitants
1,02 km²
6 953 inh./km²
1063 users

Villa Verde

5 853 inhabitants
0,62 km²
9 394 inh/km²
877 users

Torre Angela

19 777 inhabitants
1,43 km²
13 830 inh./km²
2 966 users

Corcolle

5 788 inhabitants
Corcolle Est – 0,48 km²
Giardini di Corcolle – 0,87 km²
Corcolle Est – 11 993,37 inh./km²
Giardini di Corcolle – 10 387,36 inh./km²
868 users

Villaggio Prenestino

7 026 inhabitants
2,28 km²
3 080 inh./km²
1 053 users

Castelverde

12 427 inhabitants
4,12 km²
3 018 inh./km²
1 864 users

Placement strategy and distribution of Longhouses according to number of inahbitants

Colle Prenestino

7 500 inhabitants
3,20 km²
2 344 inh./km²
1125 users

San Vittorino

479 inhabitants
0,21 km²
2 228 inh./km²
71 users

Fosso San Giuliano

973 inhabitants
0,64 km²
3 373,87 inh./km²
145 users

Rocca Cencia

3 505 inhabitants
0,64 km²
5 435 inh./km²
525 users

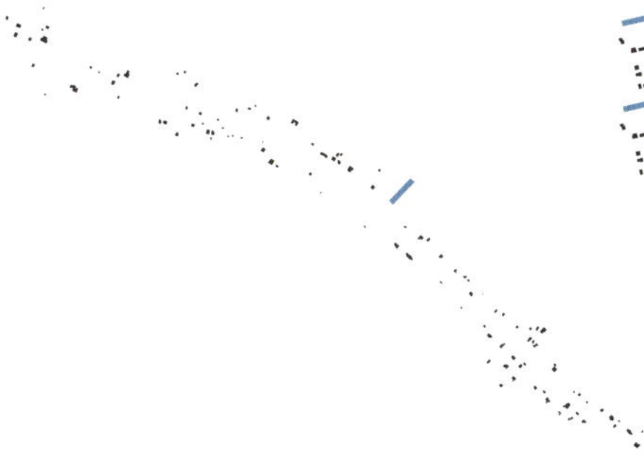

Gallicano

180 inhabitants
0,73 km²
246,81 inh./km²
27 users

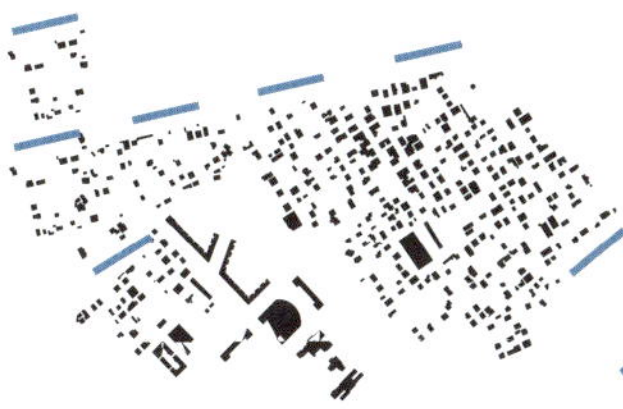

Valle Fiorita

12 696 inhabitants
1,17 km²
10 839 inh./km²
1 904 users

Colle del Sole

3 805 inhabitants
0,80 km²
4 752,69 inh./km²
570 users

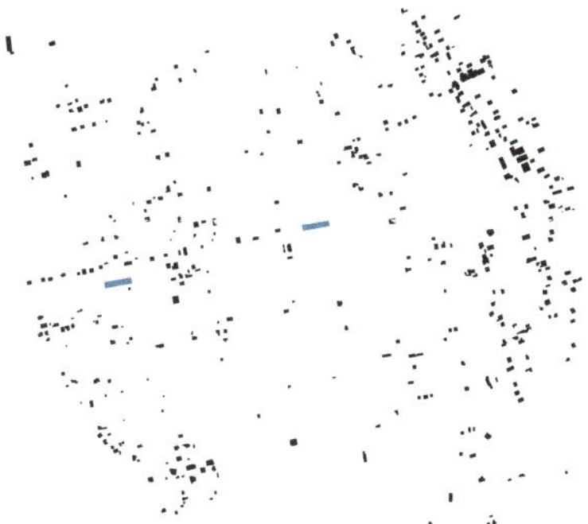

Fontana Candida

1 855 inhabitants
3,43 km²
540 inh./km²
278 users

Torre Nova

24 929 inhabitants
2,34 km²
10 636 inh./km²
3 739 users

Borghesiana

11 360 inhabitants
2,66 km²
4 278 inh./km²
1 704 users

Finocchio

22 482 inhabitants
4,78 km²
4 702 inh/km²
3 372 users

Edge   Spine

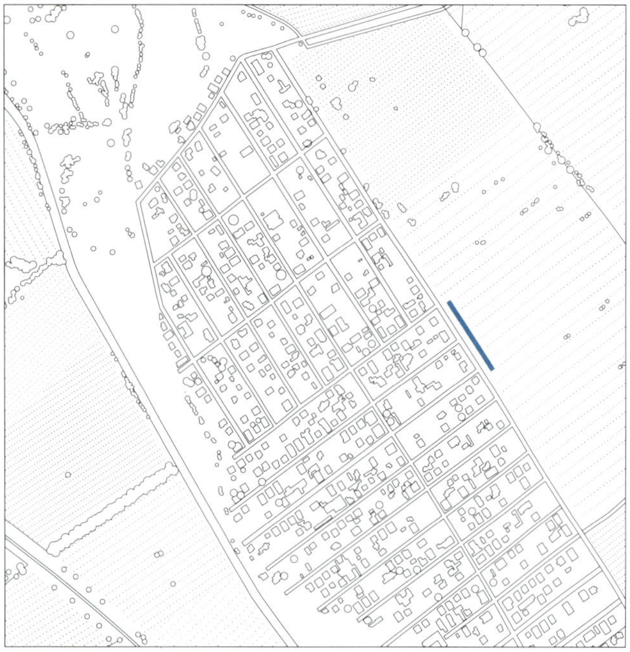

Giardini di Corcolle

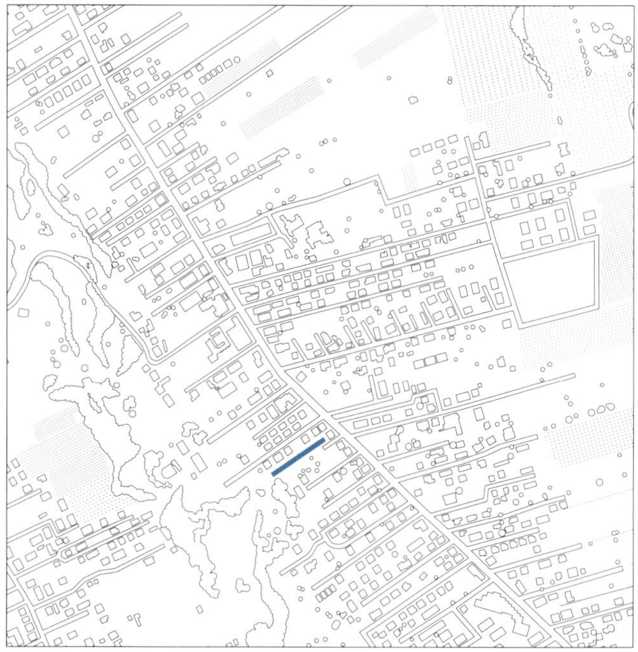

Castelverde

San Vittorino

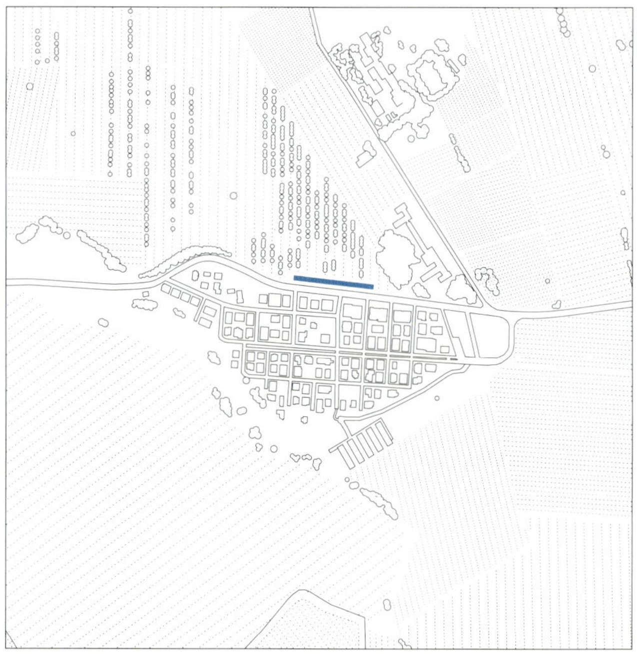

Monfortani

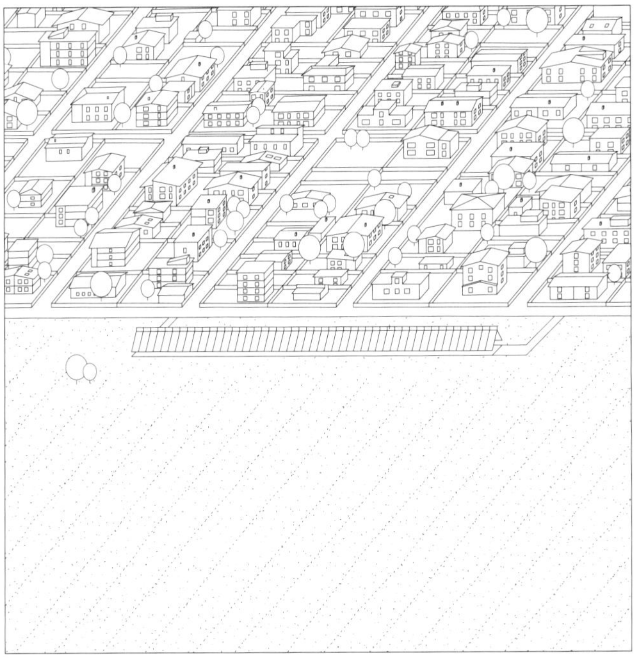

Giardini di Corcolle

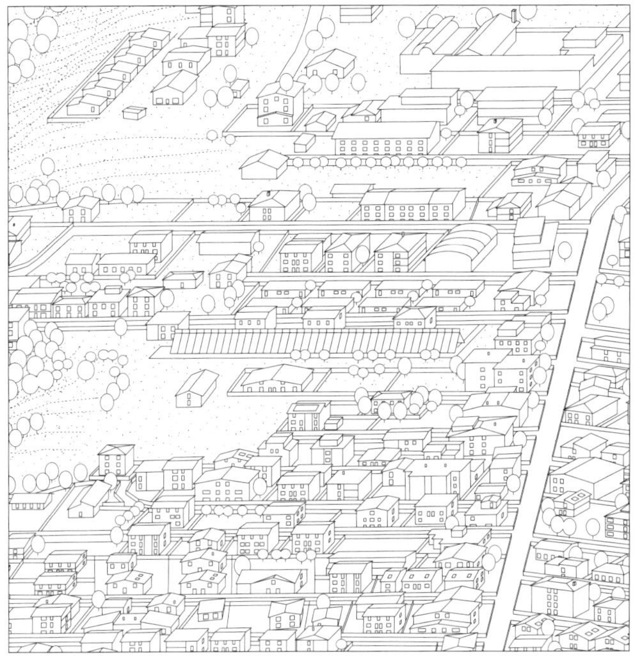

Castelverde

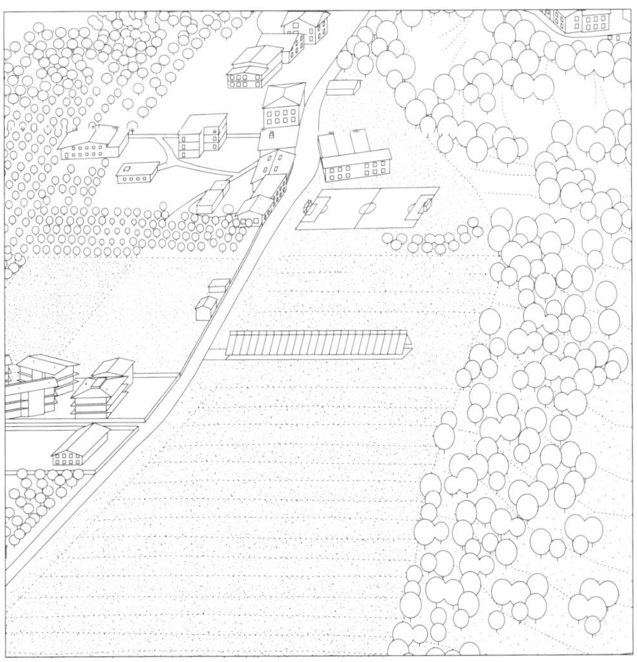

San Vittorino

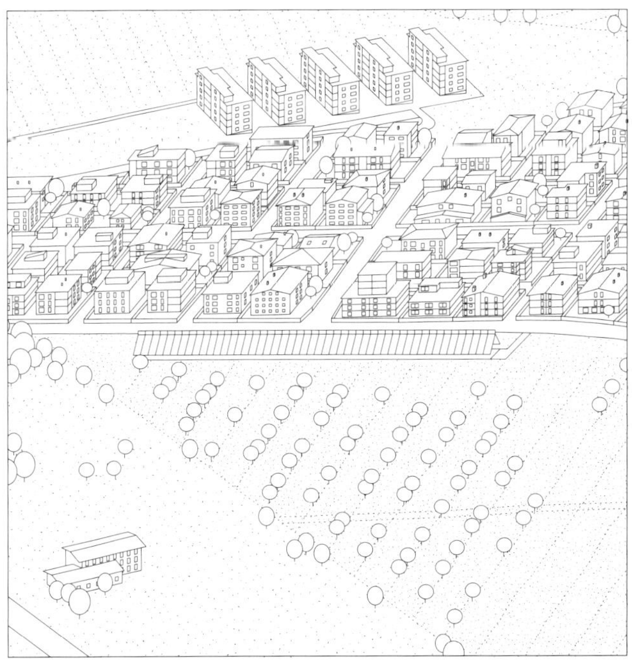

Monfortani

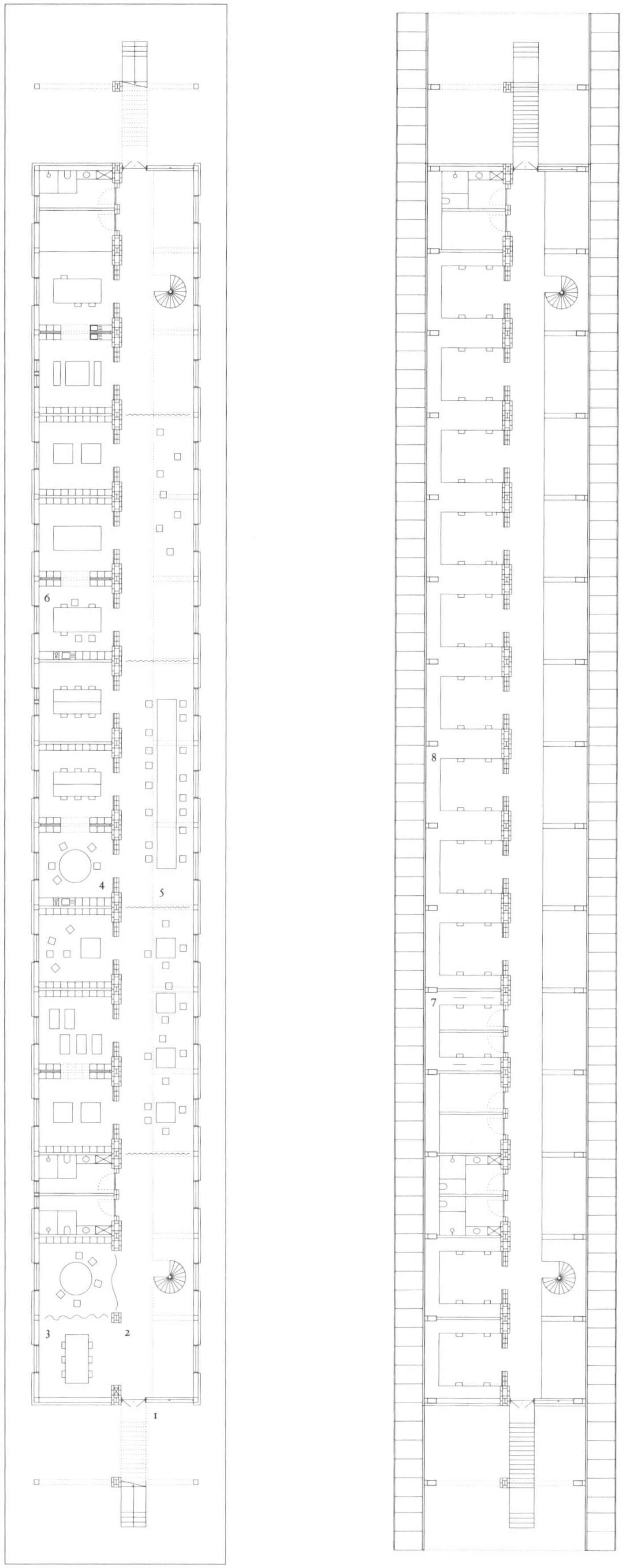

Ground-floor and first-floor plan of the longhouse for 75 users

(1) entrance, (2) lobby, (3) multifunctional rooms, (4) kitchen, (5) gallery space, (6) meeting room, (7) quiet room, (8) desk aisle

The structure of the building is in timber with the exception of the central supporting longitudinal wall, built in concrete blocks. Thanks to its mass and internal ventilation system, the long wall performs as a cooling and warming device during the hot and cold seasons. Hit in winter by the rays of the sun through the long skylight window placed on the southern pitch of the roof, the wall warms up, releasing heat in the different parts of the building. Thanks to this solution, mechanical heating is limited to the northern half of the building.

Technical section

310

AFTERWORD: THE REAL WORLD[1]

Tuomas Toivonen

The first image in this book is the plan of a hunter-gatherer campsite. An open constellation of crescent wind shelters, each large enough to fit an extended family or kinship group.

Here, architecture debuts at its peak: simple, sophisticated structures that express and mediate the social relations of people on the move. As the origin point of architecture, instead of Laugier's solitary hut, for Dogma this origin plan shows the emergence of architecture as a technique for coexisting and living together.

In *Living and Working*, the plan is cast as the "ultimate protagonist of space"—as a precise instrument for organizing and regulating life and work; solitude, togetherness, and relationships.

Despite their compositional qualities—and in this case, their "dogmatic" noncompositionality—when examined carefully, plans are where the intentions of architecture are carried and revealed. Plans are notations for the social fiction of architecture—they always describe scenarios in the way they orchestrate space, mediate private and public realms, connect and isolate. What is also implied, here, is that architecture as a practice must also be about social organization, and involves the management of the individual and collective.

Living and Working represents a new phase of work that collects a volume of research and writing and a constellation of case studies from 2013 to 2021. While Pier Vittorio Aureli and Martino Tattara are established and influential figures in architecture discourse and academia, their office Dogma has been the laboratory for developing their discursive positions and research into the form of architectural projects and proposals. For Aureli and Tattara, the central themes of their earlier work—history, politics, domesticity, labor, typology, and the city—are still present, but their treatment here is a departure from the work in their first monograph *11 Projects* (2013). *Living and Working* plots a new a trajectory for Dogma as an architectural practice, perhaps also describing some of the dilemmas Aureli and Tattara are facing as distinguished thinkers who are intent on practice.

Compared to Dogma's earlier work, these new projects immediately appear very different in scale and scope. Their early projects, such as A Simple Heart, Stop City, and City Walls, belong to a rich tradition of polemical, speculative paper architecture, and are open about their references—Cedric Price and Andrea Branzi. The early works carry the DNA of the Capital Cities program—a series of studios Aureli and Tattara taught in the mid-2000s at the Berlage Institute, resonating with the influence of Elia Zenghelis, whom they studied and taught with: the architecture of mass housing delivering a political substance at the scale of infrastructural interventions in the flesh of the city.

Perhaps this trait ends with Live Forever: The Return of the Factory (2013), included in this book. This project could also be regarded as the first project of the new phase, as it begins a string of research and projects focused on living and working. Live Forever: The Return of the Factory also represents a kind of hinge or inflection point in Dogma's trajectory and coincides with the beginning of our collaborations.

In successive works the confrontational quality and scale of the urban volumes dissipate, although the formal aspects and geometry of these new projects continue in the same orthopraxy—decisive, articulate, and precise. Their compositional logic begins (or ends) with figures that are less often square—even though other "dogmatic" devices are used. Dogma's signature square form, which projects the autonomy of the architectural object and establishes a strong "center" within itself, has given way to the here-dominant even-bay system that is systematically used in the division of plans into equal rooms.

These recent case studies express a carefulness toward their contexts—often blending in, mimicking, editing, and sometimes hiding in their settings, which are often suburban,

1 "This is the true story of seven strangers picked to live in a loft and have their lives taped to find out what happens when people stop being polite (can you get the phone?) and start getting real." Airing on Music Television in 1992, *The Real World* was a genre-defining early reality-television show that captured (and choreographed) the collective life of young creatives living together in a New York loft.

fitting into infrastructural interstices and leftover spaces, filling in gaps, connecting and completing existing patterns and structures. Notably, the projects in this book feel as if they are also taking shape in a more plausible space, offering fewer reasons why any of these projects couldn't be built. The radicality of the proposals is often embedded in the social organization and patterns of life and work that are expressed in the plans, and only hinted at in the views. Dogma takes a clear stance on prioritizing use value over commodity form, and this is expressed in many of the typologies—with their commoning spaces and blurring of boundaries of property—making the buildings less fungible as assets. The plans balance distributions of equal rooms, individual cells, and shared spaces that superimpose and contain all categories of Arendtian work: reproductive labor, productive work, and action in the form of communal relations are all present within the perimeters of the plan. In comparison to Dogma's earlier oeuvre, they paint a softer, more suggestive—and perhaps more convivial—picture, a tableau from another genre of social fiction than before. Here, architecture makes progressive maneuvers less "against" and more "within" the contemporary condition of the city and society.

One of the reasons for this may be that many of these case studies result from direct engagements with various stakeholders and their specific concerns—municipalities, artist associations, cooperatives, student housing bodies, community land trusts, and cultural organizations—protagonists that are very much aligned with Dogma. Following the timeline of projects, we can see how Dogma's historical and theoretical research, and each encounter with stakeholders, investigates and introduces new themes—such as ownership and management models (Communal Villa, Berlin), technical and structural elaboration (Gardening at Night, Moscow), cooperative management and land trusts (Do You See Me When We Pass, Brussels), and self-build construction methods (Do You Hear Me When You Sleep, London)—that have since acquired a central position in their repertoire and work. We can also see implied a series of learning curves that bring into the works an increasing level of detail, precision, and a kind of drift toward "the real." This increasing drift is manifested in many ways—in how technical aspects such as plumbing or dimensioning of structures are represented in elaborated detail, or how fundamental legal and financial conditions and arrangements are introduced and developed.

This shift is perhaps reflected in the demographics—the projects no longer preoccupied primarily with the precarity of the "young worker" class, as Aureli and Tattara are not so young anymore themselves. The convivial domestic life and work of the projects open a broader, more nuanced, inclusive sphere that includes further consideration of class, labor, gender, and family, but also of articulated property relations, economies, and future flexibility.

The shift in position that *Living and Working* follows also leads Dogma to become another type of practice—one that requires professionalism, managerial skill, and a permanent workforce to tackle large projects for public clients.

Perhaps one culmination of this shift into "the real" is Promised Land, a joint project between Dogma and New Academy.[2] It was conceived as a manual for decommodified housing, combining analysis with a conceptual toolkit and illustrated with several case studies (including Do You Hear Me When You Sleep) developed with NGO stakeholders in different cities. In this project we challenged each other's positions to develop a set of precise countermoves, expanding the scope of architecture so as to tackle each obstacle with readings of the terrain, and exploring tactics to maneuver beyond them: The history of land ownership begins with primitive accumulation, but how to choreograph projects against its current asset form, swimming the streams of global finance? What strategies have been used to consolidate housing into forms of ownership that safeguard their use value, not commodity status? How could construction labor cooperatives become a platform for building an alternative stock of social housing? How to combine new patterns of living and working with cooperative forms, commoning of spaces and

2 Pier Vittorio Aureli, Leonard Ma, Mariapaola Michelotto, Martino Tattara, and Tuomas Toivonen, "Promised Land: Housing from Commodification to Cooperation," https://www.e-flux.com/architecture/collectivity/304772/promised land-housing-from -commodification-to -cooperation/.

typologies? How to build decommodified housing with a core agenda of social organization within our current conditions?

We first met in 2013, after I saw Pier Vittorio present Live Forever: The Return of the Factory at the Kosmos theater during the Tallinn Biennale. The project explicitly addresses the reality of "young workers," who are absorbed in immaterial labor, without long-term prospects, and for whom distinctions between work and free time have dissolved (if they ever existed). Juggling uncertain incomes from a mosaic of gigs and project-based work, while balancing student debt and escalating costs of living, has become a normal exercise for generations born after the late 1970s, restricting access to credit or the accumulation of capital assets. In their predicament, the idea of homeownership, family life, or having children seems often unrealistic. The project functions as an "embodiment of this condition [of precariousness of life], and at the same time [as] the frame holding it. The aim of the project is not to eliminate the ethos of the social factory, but to make it explicit."[3] The proposal reimagines social housing as a collective factory for these workers, and casts architecture as a form of welfare that supports a dignified daily life, while giving this emergent new working class a legible, physical presence in the city.

3 Pier Vittorio Aureli and Martino Tattara, "A Simple Heart: Architecture on the Ruins of the Post-Fordist City," *Architectural Design* 81, no. 1 (2011): 119.

Despite its scale, its at times brutal adherence to the "dogma of Dogma," I could recognize in Live Forever a project that spoke to my own experience. I had been such a young worker, and recently witnessed the capacity of coordinating architecture, labor, and collective action to manipulate this condition. After fifteen years of working freelance, as part of collectives, social initiatives, and cooperatives, and running a small practice, I had just completed an intense process which had begun with my decision to close my office, spend a hands-on year on our own construction site, and finally, after completion, start our new work as bath operators of a public sauna that I had designed and built together with Nene Tsuboi, my partner. For us, this transition to a new mode of life and labor took the shape of a building—its form, its use, its tenure.

Later, when we invited Pier Vittorio and Martino to Helsinki, they would stay at the *kabinetti*, in the south wing of Kulttuurisauna, where a work desk and a couple of mattresses were set up for our visiting lecturers. During the hottest week of summer, it felt like a monastic Etoile de Mer on the Baltic: an isolated cabanon/cell, turned away from the common atrium garden, the salon, saunas, and other facilities where our bathers and students would congregate and we would all gather for meals.

Around the same time we had found out about a general plan to heavily redevelop the Hakaniemi waterfront in our neighborhood in Helsinki, and our discussions led to the idea that we should preemptively engage with the city by making an alternative proposal, before plans were consolidated. Dogma developed a case study, Tower and Plinth (2014) on the future site, and it was published as a project cahier, "Living/Working: How to Live Together in Merihaka," coinciding with an event organized together with the city's urban planning department. The day after, we met and had a discussion with the local chief of planning in his office. As planning presupposes profit-oriented projects on public land, what kinds of initiatives would it take to open the door for alternative scenarios? The chief explains that no project can be given special status, and planners cannot account for any agenda or intention in their work. In most cases the city will cede development rights to the highest bidder, he continued: and as architects and planners, our hands are tied—we have no power to choose or steer (which of course is only half-true).

As public land was out of reach, we still tried another scenario in Merihaka as infill on private land, pairing together a developer with the local student housing association. With this infill project and the developer-plus-student-housing combination, the planners gave us an initial green light for launching the planning process. Amid the old, melancholic, bare-faced concrete towers, Dogma had politely positioned new towers; the area's planner clearly liked the project: "it almost looks like it has been there always."

However, seeing the design, the landowner's eyes opened to the development potential of their property, and they decided not to sell. They thought they could probably pump more building rights with less restrictions out of their site if they could drop the student housing, build more parking, expand the elegant volumes, and kick out the difficult architects who tried to stay in control of the equation and end result. No towers, no plinth—but since Dogma had made accurate drawings of the neighborhood for their project, and I was then in charge of redoing the district's signage, a trace remains… the large, square enamel-plate axonometries that are scattered around Merihaka are all drawn by Dogma.

Perhaps this anecdote can reveal something about the nature of architectural practice and its limits. *Living and Working* frames architecture as an instrument to regulate and shape both the built environment as well as the relations within the society that inhabits it. Dogma's projects insist that text and image cannot be separated—and that the nonfigurative composition of form and its social/political intention are both essential. For this reason, Dogma's architecture has so far been mostly confined to paper, where both of these aspects remain under control. However, the trajectory of the projects in this book anticipates Dogma's architecture leaving the page and entering the city—but under what terms?

For any project to exist in the terrain of the city, its formal and social program must navigate the demands and constraints imposed by the realpolitik of policy, planning, land use, and market mechanisms, even if it's positioned to oppose them. In other words, any counterproposal must perform better on the criteria of the proposal it is competing against, while also delivering its agonistic, alternative agenda. How would such a practice operate, if it aligns the design, ownership, funding, and management of the architecture it produces?

In Tallinn, at the Kosmos theater event's roundtable after Pier Vittorio's presentation, I had made a suggestion:[4] "While the theme of this Biennale is Recycling Socialism—in your project, socialism is represented as the use of the building as social housing, but the exact same architecture could be built as an attractive free market loft development." I don't remember what Pier Vittorio's answer was, and neither does he. We recently discussed this, and he still sees the project as an attempt to revisit the possibility of building social housing, but focused on this new subject. Le Corbusier's Unité was chosen as reference to revisit, but as it focused on the family as the only type of household, Dogma's project set out to propose a framework where different kinds of households were possible. The project supposes that the state would build the social housing—but in the form of a project that promotes a different social mold than what social housing has always been based on heretofore.

4 This question is mentioned in Krivý's article, and then requoted in van Gerrewey's text. Maroš Krivý, "Participation, Housing and the Question of 'Good Architecture,'" *Footprint* 13 (Autumn 2013): 170; Christophe van Gerrewey, "How Soon Is Now? Ten Problems and Paradoxes in the Work of Dogma," *Log* 35 (2015): 27–47.

In the projects collected in this book, architecture appears less a normalizing apparatus and more a set of devices for framing and mediating the life and work of its inhabitants, and their myriad relations. The plans suggest superimpositions of different kinds of households, striped and dotted with patterns of varying privacy. The most private element has crystallized into the form of a technical core as an individual "sophisticated hut." The aggregation of equal rooms creates a gradient of intimacy from the private bed to the generosities of interior and exterior commons, held within limits. Appearing simultaneously casual and ritualized, daily life and work fills these orthogonal intervals. The geometric clarity of architecture evokes a set of oppositional, radical priorities: form and type are freed from the burden of profit, liberated from norms, becoming a device for emancipation and political visibility. Architecture, in its most potent disposition, dissolves the boundaries between the public and private spheres, capable of absorbing both polis and oikos into its form, anticipating the society that will inhabit it.

The new phase of work that *Living and Working* opens sees Dogma venture out of their square castrum, now camped somewhere on the wild edge of the land, observing, investigating, and cultivating a broader field.

PROJECT CREDITS

LIVE FOREVER: THE RETURN OF THE FACTORY

Proposal for Social Housing in Tallinn (Estonia), 2013. Developed within the framework of the Tallinn Architecture Biennale 2013. Team: Pier Vittorio Aureli and Martino Tattara with Luciano Aletta, Valentina Rigoni, Radu Remus Macovei.

AFTER HILBERSEIMER

Proposal for the retrofitting of Ludwig Hilberseimer's settlement unit, Chicago (USA), 2014. Developed within the framework of the exhibition *Chicagoism* at The Art Institute of Chicago, 2014. Team: Pier Vittorio Aureli and Martino Tattara with Luciano Aletta, Hubert Holewik, Mauro Forlini.

PRETTY VACANT

Proposal for the transformation of Quartier Léopold in Brussels (Belgium), 2014. Study. Team: Pier Vittorio Aureli and Martino Tattara with Lorenz Alarik Adriaens, Hubert Holewik, Mauro Forlini.

TOWER AND PLINTH

Proposal for affordable housing in the Merihaka district, Helsinki (Finland), 2014. Commissioned study. Team: Pier Vittorio Aureli and Martino Tattara with Ezio Melchiorre, Hubert Holewik, Luciano Aletta.

EVERYDAY IS LIKE SUNDAY

Proposal for the transformation of office parks into living and working spaces (Belgium), 2015. Developed within the framework of the BWMSTR Label 006 program, 2015. Team: Pier Vittorio Aureli and Martino Tattara with Luciano Aletta, Ezio Melchiorre, Ophélie Dozat, Hubert Holewik, Giovanna Pittalis.

COMMUNAL VILLA

Proposal for a living and working space. Project and installation developed within the framework of the exhibition *Wohnungsfrage* at Haus der Kulturen der Welt, Berlin (Germany), 2015. With Realism Working Group. Team: Pier Vittorio Aureli and Martino Tattara with Luciano Aletta, Ezio Melchiorre, Ophélie Dozat, Giovanna Pittalis.

LIKE A ROLLING STONE

Proposal for boardinghouses in London (UK), 2016. Project and installation developed within the framework of the Venice Architectural Biennale 2016, British Pavilion. With Black Square. Team: Pier Vittorio Aureli and Martino Tattara with Luciano Aletta, Ezio Melchiorre, Andrea Migotto, Stéphanie Savio.

PARK CITY

Proposal for urban transformation and new housing typology in Limburg (Belgium), 2016. Commissioned study by the Departement Omgeving, Flanders. Team: Pier Vittorio Aureli and Martino Tattara with Andrea Migotto, Elena Calafati, Ezio Melchiorre, Tommaso Mola Meregalli, Matteo Novarino, Antonio Paolillo.

ONE-ROOM HOUSE

Proposal for a house prototype at the Edersee (Germany), 2017. Commissioned project developed within the framework of the exhibition *Ways of Life*, Kassel, 2017. Team: Pier Vittorio Aureli and Martino Tattara with Matteo Novarino, Maria Paola Michelotto.

POSSIBILITIES

Proposal for the transformation of the Linkeroever area, Antwerp (Belgium), 2017 (first phase) and 2021 (second phase). Developed within the framework of the international competition *Linkeroever*, 2017—First prize. Team: Pier Vittorio Aureli and Martino Tattara with Tommaso Mola Meregalli, Matteo Novarino, Dag von der Decken.

GARDENING AT NIGHT

Proposal for a mid-rise housing block in Russia, 2017. Developed within the framework of the *Open International Competition for Standard Housing and Residential Development Concept Design*, Russia, 2017. With NOW for Architecture and Urbanism. Team: Pier Vittorio Aureli and Martino Tattara with Ezio Melchiorre, Luciano Aletta, Antonio Paolillo, Yi Ming Wu.

DO YOU HEAR ME WHEN YOU SLEEP?

Proposal for a cooperative living and working space in London (UK), 2019. Commissioned project developed in collaboration with Sun Co-op, London. Team: Pier Vittorio Aureli and Martino Tattara with Antonio Paolillo, Barbara Mazza, Marie Oudon, Mariapaola Michelotto.

THE OPPOSITE SHORE

Proposal for urban transformation and new housing typology in the Dender valley (Belgium). Commissioned study by the Departement Omgeving, Flanders and developed within the framework of the Venice Architecture Biennale 2021. Team: Pier Vittorio Aureli and Martino Tattara with Celeste Tellarini, Mariapaola Michelotto, Anna Panourgia, Antonio Paolillo, Yi Ming Wu, Daniele Ceragno.

LONGHOUSE

Proposal for Municipal Workshop in Rome, 2020. Study. Team: Pier Vittorio Aureli and Martino Tattara with Mariapaola Michelotto, Celeste Tellarini, Frederik Dahlqvist.

The MIT Press would like to thank the anonymous peer reviewers who provided comments on drafts of this book. The generous work of academic experts is essential for establishing the authority and quality of our publications. We acknowledge with gratitude the contributions of these otherwise uncredited readers.

publication supported by a grant from
The Community Foundation for Greater New Haven
as part of the **Urban Haven Project**

Designed by Nene Tsuboi
Printed and bound in China.

Photos of models on pages 187, 199, 249, 279, 287
by Frans Parthesius

Library of Congress Cataloging-in-Publication Data

Names: Aureli, Pier Vittorio, 1973- author.|
Tattara, Martino, 1976- author.
Title: Living and working / Pier Vittorio
Aureli and Martino Tattara.
Description: Cambridge, Massachusetts:
The MIT Press, 2022
Includes bibliographical references.
Identifiers: LCCN 2021018195 |
ISBN 9780262543514 (paperback)
Subjects: LCSH: Dogma (Architectural office) |
Domestic space. | Work environment.
Classification: LCC NA1173.D64 A4 2022 | DDC 728--dc23
LC record available at https://lccn.loc.gov/202101819

10 9 8 7 6 5 4 3 2